CONFLICT, CRISIS, AND WAR IN WORLD POLITICS

CONFLICT, CRISIS, AND WAR IN WORLD POLITICS

AN INTRODUCTION

PATRICK JAMES

Dana and David Dornsife Dean's Professor Emeritus of International Relations, Department of Political Science and International Relations, University of Southern California, USA

JAMES M. SCOTT

University Professor and Chair, Department of Politics and Government, Illinois State University, USA

Cheltenham, UK • Northampton, MA, USA

© Patrick James and James M. Scott 2025

All rights reserved. No part of this publication may be reproduced, stored in a retrieval system or transmitted in any form or by any means, electronic, mechanical or photocopying, recording, or otherwise without the prior permission of the publisher.

Published by
Edward Elgar Publishing Limited
The Lypiatts
15 Lansdown Road
Cheltenham
Glos GL50 2JA
UK

Edward Elgar Publishing, Inc.
William Pratt House
9 Dewey Court
Northampton
Massachusetts 01060
USA

A catalogue record for this book
is available from the British Library

Library of Congress Control Number: 2024948205

Printed on elemental chlorine free (ECF) recycled paper containing 30% Post-Consumer Waste

ISBN 978 1 0353 1159 0 (cased)
ISBN 978 1 0353 1161 3 (paperback)
ISBN 978 1 0353 1160 6 (eBook)

Printed and bound in the USA

CONTENTS

List of figures ix
List of maps xi
List of tables xii
Acknowledgements xiii
Supplementary materials xiv

1 Understanding the challenges of conflict, crisis, and war **1**
   Prologue 1
   Overview 2
   "That's just theory" 3
   Scientific realism 6
   Analytic eclecticism 8
   Systemism 10
   Summing up and moving forward 15

PART I   UNDERSTANDING THE PROBLEM

2 Conflict, crisis, and war in world politics **18**
   Prologue 18
   Overview 18
   International conflict 19
   International crisis (and near crisis) 22
   International war 26
   Conflict, crisis, and war 41
   Summing up and moving forward 43

3 The evolution of conflict, crisis, and war **44**
   Prologue 44
   Overview 44
   A world of war 46
   Trends and patterns in conflict 47
   Crisis 55
   War 57
   Summing up and moving forward 65

4 The issues **66**
   Prologue 66
   Overview 66

Issues in general	67
Territory	71
Religion	74
The intersection of territory and religion	77
Summing up and moving forward	89

PART II EXPLAINING THE PROBLEM

5 System-level explanations — 92
Prologue	92
Overview	92
Systems, realism, and conflict	94
Power transition theory	99
The East Asian system	102
Summing up and moving forward	113

6 State-level explanations — 116
Prologue	116
Overview	116
States and conflict	117
The democratic peace	126
Visualizing conflict, the democratic peace and regime type	133
Summing up and moving forward	135

7 Individual-level explanations — 137
Prologue	137
Overview	137
Major approaches to individual-level explanations	138
Human nature	138
Human experiences and psychology	142
Psychological factors and our understanding of conflict, crisis, and war	147
Summing up and moving forward	153

8 Understanding crises — 156
Prologue	156
Overview	156
The nature of international crises and project-based research	157
Origins	160
Processes	162
Outcomes and legacies	166

An international crisis in profile: the Soleimani assassination – 2019	170
Summing up and moving forward	182

9 Understanding civil wars — 183

Prologue	183
Overview	184
The meaning and an approach toward analysis of civil war	185
Origins of civil war	188
A systemist graphic analysis of civil war onset	192
Summing up and moving forward	200

10 Multilevel explanations — 205

Prologue	205
Overview	205
A comprehensive sense of cause and effect	207
Civil war in the United States	211
A systemist causal analysis of the civil war in the United States	217
Lessons for today	230
The American civil war and results from aggregate data analysis	231
Summing up and moving forward	233

PART III COPING WITH THE PROBLEM

11 Taking matters into their own hands: state-based approaches to managing conflict, crisis, and war — 236

Prologue	236
Overview	236
Diplomacy and negotiation: definition and context	238
Diplomacy and negotiation: uses, effects, and consequences	240
Economic coercion: definition and context	243
Economic coercion: uses, effects, and consequences	245
Defense, deterrence, and alliances	247
Using force: definition and context	260
Uses of force and conflict, crisis, and war	261
Arms control and disarmament: definition and context	263
Arms/control/disarmament and conflict, crisis, and war	269
Summing up and moving forward	270

12	**Working with and through others: IGOs, NGOs, and conflict, crisis, and war**	**272**
	Prologue	272
	Overview	273
	International law: definition and context	274
	International law and compliance: the empirical record	278
	International governmental organizations: definition and context	279
	International governmental organizations: the empirical record	291
	Non-governmental organization: definition and context	294
	NGOs in action	298
	Summing up and moving forward	300
13	**What do we know about conflict, crisis, and war?**	**303**
	Prologue	303
	Overview	304
	A systemist graphic review	304
	Revisiting the central argument	314
	Future research and final thoughts	318
14	**References**	**319**
	Index	347

FIGURES

1.1	A systemist perspective on functional relations in a social system	11
1.2	Systemist notation	15
2.1	Russian war against Ukraine	29
2.2	The ladder of escalation	42
3.1	Global deaths in conflicts, 1400-2013	48
3.2	Death from conflict and war, 1989-2021	49
3.3	MID dyads by year and dataset	50
3.4	Global, state-based conflict trends, 1946-2021	53
3.5	Non-state conflicts, 1989-2021	54
3.6	Armed conflict by region, 1946-2021	55
3.7	International crises, 1918-2017	56
3.8	Death rates in state-based conflict, 1946-2021	58
3.9	The frequency of great power war, 1500-2015	59
3.10	State-based conflict locations, 2021	60
3.11	The geography of non-state conflicts	61
3.12	Political marginalization, climate change, and conflict in African Sahel states	63
4.1	War on sacred grounds	78
4.2	Defending the faith	79
5.1	Power transition theory and East Asia	103
5A.1	Regions of war and peace	115
6.1	Regime type, foreign policy, and international relations	127
7.1	Prospect theory and foreign policy analysis	152
7.A1	The operational codes of Donald Trump and Hillary Clinton	155
8.1	International crisis: Solemani Assassination - 2019	172

9.1	Civil war onset	193
10.1	Events leading up to the civil war	221
11.1	The structure of negotiation (adapted from Lauren et al. 2007)	239
11.2	Top ten countries in military spending, 2022	248
11.3	The great delusion: liberal dreams and international relations	258
12.1a	The institutions of the European Union	286
12.1b	The institutions of the European Union	287
12.2	The structure and institutions of the United Nations	290
12.3	The Boomerang Model of NGO activity	298
12.4	The impact of human rights international non-governmental organizations (INGO) shaming on humanitarian intervention	301
13.1	Conflict, crisis, and war	305

MAPS

2.1	The politics of water in the Horn of Africa	21
3.1	Here be dragons	46
5.1	Hainan Island	93
10.1	Fort Sumter and the American Civil War	206
11.1	Nuclear weapons states, 2020	254

TABLES

1.1	Examples of linkage types	13
1.2	Systemist notation	15
4.1	Issues in near crises	71
8.1	Research findings about the onset of international crises	161
8.2	Research findings about the processes of international crises	163
8.3	Research findings about the outcomes and legacies of international crises	167
8.4	Profile of an international crisis: Soleimani Assassination – 2019	173
9.1	Definitions of civil war	186
9.2	Research findings about the onset of civil wars	188
9.A1	Research findings about the processes of civil wars	202
9.A2	Research findings about the outcomes and legacies of civil wars	203
10.1	Events leading to the civil war: an inventory of causes	218
10.2	The Civil War and results from aggregate data analysis	232
11.1	Types of third-party diplomacy	240
11.2	Top ten countries in military spending, 2022	248
11.3	Major arms control treaties since World War I	266
11.4	Participants, purposes, and types of arms control	268
12.1	UN Security Council vetoes by P5 members, 1946–2022	282
12.2	A typology of international organizations	282

ACKNOWLEDGEMENTS

We are grateful to Sarah Gansen for extraordinary work on the systemist diagrams that appear in this book.

SUPPLEMENTARY MATERIALS

Supplementary materials for this book can be found online at: https://www.e-elgar.com/textbooks/james/

1
Understanding the challenges of conflict, crisis, and war

PROLOGUE

After a long buildup, Russia launched an invasion of Ukraine in February 2022, seeking to replace its Western-leaning regime and annex much of its territory. Initially, expectations for Ukrainian resistance were low, and many predicted a speedy Russian victory. However, a determined Ukrainian opposition denied Russia the quick-strike victory it sought. Aid, American in particular and Western in general, poured into Ukraine. These resources helped an unwavering Ukrainian resistance to first blunt the initial wave of Russian attacks in the south, east and north of Ukraine. Increased assistance, including extensive intelligence sharing and other support led by the US, helped the Ukrainian regime to turn Russia away from Kiev in spring 2022, and then turn the tables with counterattacks in the northeast (around Kharkiv) and south (around Kherson) that liberated much of the territory seized by the initial Russian attacks. Over the next six months, successful Ukrainian military counterattacks in the north and south reversed much of the initial Russian gains.

As the war ground on into its second year, Russia engaged in deadly bombing attacks with missiles and drones, tried to shore up the defenses of the territory it still held, and worked to marshal its forces for new attacks. Russian leader Vladimir Putin issued various threats and warnings about escalation, including nuclear attacks. In Ukraine, President Volodymyr Zelenskyy led his country's efforts to strengthen its military, defend its territory, engage in operations to regain areas seized by Russia, and sustain and expand support to Ukraine from NATO and other countries. In the summer of 2023, Ukraine began a counteroffensive seeking to break Russian lines of defense in the south and east and regain Ukrainian territory under Russian occupation, but progress was slow and not much territory has changed hands since then. In the spring of 2024, the situation on the battlefield can be described as a stalemate. In the West, the US and NATO have worked to support Ukraine in the short term and also to shepherd the successful entry of both Finland and Sweden into NATO to further isolate Russia in the long term. At the same time, the US led efforts to carefully manage relations with China, seeking to prevent its outright alignment with Russia.

As these recent events suggest, the problems of conflict, crisis, and war are persistent in world politics, and escalation from one to the next deserves attention. Indeed, collectively speaking, conflict, crisis, and war have long been regarded as the central problem of international relations. This recent chapter of world events suggests that grappling with strife and its many forms – even large-scale, state-to-state war thought by many to be obsolete – continues to challenge the players in world politics. Conflict in all its forms continues to have dramatic implications for the world community, and its potential consequences for the survival of states and its enormous costs in lives and treasure have combined to keep it at the center of attention for policymakers and for International Relations (IR) scholars seeking to understand and explain it, as well as to prepare for it and prevent it.

OVERVIEW

This text focuses on understanding conflict, crisis, and war as central challenges in the international security arena. We focus on coverage of the nature, dynamics, and trends of conflict, crisis, and war, the major approaches to explaining them, and key central avenues for managing them. To do so, we incorporate and engage with major scholarly work and policy practices while implementing conceptual and organizational coherence and cohesion. Our approach encourages comprehension of major concepts, theories, and practices, critical thinking, and opportunities to think and work through puzzles and problems toward explanations and solutions, including those that involve real-world applications. The central argument of the pages that follow is that explanation and understanding of conflict, crisis, and war and avenues for coping with and managing their challenges requires an integrated approach that not only addresses multiple levels of analysis, but also connects them to each other for more thorough and nuanced understanding.

Additionally, insights from educational psychology argue in favor of a greater balance between verbal and visual means of communication. Thus, our textbook implements graphics throughout, with a special emphasis on conveying arguments about cause and effect in a way that maximizes understanding and retention among students. Among other things, a core element of our approach applies an innovative graphing technique pioneered by co-author Patrick James and the Visual International Relations Project (VIRP), which provides visual tools to increase and improve communication throughout the discipline of IR beyond what can be achieved through the exchange of words alone (see https://ww.visualinternationalrelationsproject.com and https://www.imageandpeace.com/2022/02/16/introducing-virp-at-usc/). Applying the systemist graphic technique to the analysis and explanation of conflict, crisis, and war represents a major integrative contribution to our understanding and application of arguments about cause and effect in a way that maximizes understanding and retention. In addition, boxes of three kinds in the text highlight various issues with a range of purposes. First, we include "For Example" boxes to present historical or contemporary events to illustrate a concept or idea. Second, we incorporate "In Focus" boxes to zero in on a point of explanation in greater depth. Third, and finally, all chapters end with a "Consider This" box that calls for reflection on a puzzle or problem that emerges from the preceding material.

We thus hope that our audience finds this text an essential contribution and tool for those seeking to understand conflict, crisis, and war. It blends review of existing scholarly work and evidence with original analysis and explanation and unique visual tools for integration and synthesis. We believe its pages contain a unique combination of words and images that provide sufficient coverage in terms of (a) scope and depth; (b) conceptual coherence and cohesion; and (c) accessibility to teaching and learning. Our analysis of conflict, crisis, and war draws on both words and images, notably the application of a graphic technique for communication that we introduce in this chapter. Thus, the book is a work that seeks to look at its subject matter from multiple points of view. In other words, it is understood that both depth of understanding and breadth of explanation have value – contributions, respectively, associated with the humanities and social sciences.[1]

Core foundations of this volume include *scientific realism*, *analytic eclecticism*, and multi-level and integrated *systemism*, which we summarize in the following sections. Before we do so, we briefly describe our orientation to theory and its nature, role, and uses in the study of world politics generally, and conflict, crisis, and war in particular.

This chapter unfolds in five additional sections. Section two establishes the meaning and importance of theory. The third section introduces scientific realism as the foundation of our quest for knowledge. Scientific realism holds that unobservable factors – as well as those we can see – can and do play a vital role in explaining the world. Section four introduces analytic eclecticism as a way of putting together explanations for conflict, crisis, and war that are not restricted to ideas taken from a single theoretical frame of reference. The fifth section conveys systemism as a graphic method that conveys arguments in a way that promotes logical consistency and comprehensiveness. Section six sums up the accomplishments of this chapter and sets the stage for the next one.

"THAT'S JUST THEORY"

At some time or another, virtually every potential reader of this text has heard someone say something like "that's just theory", usually to describe something as opinion, disparage some argument or explanation, or dismiss an assertion as speculative and unrelated to the empirical world. Of course, this popular view of theory misunderstands its nature and role in science generally, and in social sciences such as Political Science and the study of IR. In terms of world politics, a theory is simply a way to explain the world around us and is essential to making sense of "facts". Theory, an explanation of how events and actions fit together, is essential to understanding and explaining issues in world politics such as conflict, crisis, and war.

Theory is necessary to try to understand the patterns and practices of world politics: why international actors behave the way they do, why and how the events and actions that make up world politics occur, and what they mean. It is a set of analytical tools for understanding the cause-and-effect relationships between and among phenomena. We rely on theory to make sense of relevant facts, explain the behavior of states and other organizations, and understand the choices of policymakers and the consequences of policies they enact.

Theories are strategic simplifications of the world to bring important features into clearer focus. Think of theories as lenses, such as those you might find in a good pair of sunglasses.

---

[1] For a classic exploration of understanding and explanation, see Hollis and Smith (1992).

A theory simplifies reality to reduce the "glare of the sun" and to sharpen the clarity of key factors. Indeed, empirical theory aims at explaining causal relationships and patterns among the phenomena being studied and it is indispensable for cause-and-effect explanation of real or observable phenomena in the world that addresses "why" and "how" questions.

Theory rests on three fundamental requirements to increase our confidence of causality in a specified relationship and it has four dimensions or components. In terms of the fundamental requirements, think in terms of two factors, X (cause) and Y (effect):

- Causal theory requires X and Y to *covary* – they must change together, or you cannot claim that one causes change in another.
- Causal theory requires proper *temporal order* – X must come before Y in time because causes must come before effects, or they cannot be causes.
- Causal theory requires *nonspuriousness* – other plausible or likely causes of Y (say, A, B, and C) must be eliminated or accounted for as best as possible in order to isolate the true effect of X on Y.[2]

Consider the needs of causal theory, as just enumerated, in the context of one of the worst things that can and does happen: genocidal warfare. In a comprehensive study of genocide throughout history, Jones (2017) identifies a sense of humiliation among perpetrators as arguably the single most important cause of such horrendous events. Through reference to any number of familiar and obscure cases, Jones (2017) establishes that a high level of perceived humiliation (X) and genocidal actions (Y) covary with each other.

Perhaps the most notorious example is that of the National Socialist Party in Germany, led by the demagogue Adolf Hitler, which carried out the Holocaust. Hitler exploited humiliation over harsh terms imposed by the Versailles Treaty to stimulate intense violence against Jews, who he blamed falsely for betraying Germany and causing its defeat in World War I. With regard to temporal order, note that humiliation (X) comes before genocidal actions (Y). Meticulous research by Jones (2017), citing studies from literally thousands of other scholars, provides overwhelming evidence that humiliation is nonspurious as well. While other factors are obviously also relevant, and individual instances can be expected to contain unique features, rage among perpetrators fueled by perceived humiliation is a thread running through many cases of genocide.

Resting on the preceding requirements for a causal argument, theory involves four central dimensions of components: description, explanation, prediction, and a basis for prescription (which is effectively a by-product of the first three).

- Description: Theory directs attention to particular aspects of the world that are most important to the phenomenon in question and offers clear and logical description – nominally (in words) and operationally (in terms of empirical indicators, evidence, and measures). This is rarely an "all or nothing" process and description can be improved over time. Consider the key concept of democracy, for which the Varieties of Democracy

---

[2] Chapter 10 focuses on multilevel causation in search of a full explanation for conflict, crisis, and war. We introduce and apply a typology of causes from Kurki (2002) in that chapter.

(V-Dem) Project (Coppedge et al. 2020) stands as the state of the art. The V-Dem Project has identified six basic dimensions of democracy – electoral and participatory are two examples – and its work greatly enhances theorizing about conflict, crisis, and war whenever regime type is something to consider.

- Explanation: Theory provides cause-and-effect explanations of the linkages between those aspects of the world on which it focuses, laying out causal effects (relationships between two or more phenomena) and causal processes (mechanisms connect cause to effect). To continue with the example of democracy, a vast program of research has revealed a sustained association with conflict. For *pairs* of states, democracy and peace covary, and increasingly sophisticated debates concern temporal order and nonspuriousness.
- Prediction: Theory provides a basis for anticipating future events and developments based on its empirical description and explanation. Take, for instance, escalation. An improved ability to forecast locations at risk of escalation could help leading states and international organizations to allocate attention and resources more effectively to conflict prevention and management.
- A Basis for Prescription: Theory may also provide a basis for prescribing behavior or policy – that is, it may lead to normative conclusions about what should be or not be done. The tragic failure of the UN in general and US in particular to take decisive action facilitated genocide in Rwanda (McDoom 2020) and, in turn, produced spillover effects that led to what some have called the Asian Third World War (Jones 2017).

With these requirements and dimensions in mind, we further note three additional elements of theory. First, contrary to what is implied in the "that's just theory" mantra, theory must/should be tested against empirical evidence to gauge its accuracy and utility. "Truth claims must be tested", as it is said. Second, there is some value in the principle of parsimony as well, which holds that simpler explanations should be preferred over more complicated ones, all other things being equal. Detail and complexity for their own sake are of no advantage to explanation unless they really offer better explanations of how, when, and why something happens.

Finally, as is reflected in our organization of Part II and the discussions of theories of conflict, crisis, and war, theorizing can take place at many different levels of analysis, including those at the international system, state, individual/small group, and multiple levels. The broadest of these levels is the system or international system level, where emphasis is placed on the impact of the structural characteristics of the international system itself – including anarchy, the distribution of power, interdependence, globalization, and others – on those interactions. At the state or national level, attention is directed to the states – or units – themselves, and emphasis is placed on the attributes of countries and nations, such as the type and processes of government and its institutions or the economy, culture, or other national attributes, and how these factors shape policy goals and behavior and the interactions among the players. At the individual level, attention is directed to people – policymakers, business CEOs, and other influential persons. This level of analysis emphasizes the personalities, perceptions, and preferences of individual decision-makers and their effects on policy and interactions. As we emphasize as we proceed, theory will tend to be most convincing when factors from multiple levels of analysis are combined in a logically consistent way. In sum, it is helpful to remember that theories are tools to be used and one theoretical approach or another may be useful in some situations but not others.

One qualification to add at this point concerns the approach toward levels of analysis. In principle, social systems exist all the way up from the household to the global community. It therefore would be possible to carry out analysis with aggregations at levels other than the three featured in this volume. Take, for example, the dyadic level, which tends to focus on the experiences of interstate pairs within conflict processes. Much has been learned in this way and the results of research based on dyads composed of states are reported in the pages of this volume. In an overall sense, however, the text is organized across the three levels of analysis that became conventional with the advent of Waltz (1959).

IN FOCUS: THE SYSTEM LEVEL OF ANALYSIS AND WAR

In later work, Waltz (1979) focused on properties of the international system, notably the distribution of capabilities among great powers, in accounting for the recurrence of war. Along the way, he identifies and refutes a rival explanation at the system level. Waltz (1979) finds fault with the theory of imperialism, which focuses on the expansion of capitalism as a basic explanation for war. The critique from Waltz (1979) returns to a key element of cause and effect, namely, temporal order. Imperialism and war occurred for centuries *before* the development of capitalism in Great Britain in the 18th century and subsequently around the world. This particular economic system, according to Waltz (1979), thus cannot serve as a full explanation for imperialist warfare.

Could a theory be developed within which imperialism plays some role in explaining conflict? If so, how might that be accomplished?

SCIENTIFIC REALISM

This study adopts *scientific realism* as its foundation in the quest for knowledge about conflict, crisis, and war. Scientific realism is committed to the idea that theories provide knowledge of the world and, at any given time, some elements are unobservable (Chakravartty 2011: 1; Wight 2007: 381, 2016: 37). Unobservables are things that cannot be detected with unaided senses but nevertheless taken to be real. Some unobservables become detectable when appropriate instruments of measurement are developed, while others remain at least partially or even fully unseen (Chakravartty 2007: 4). Radio waves, for example, are unseen but clearly exist through sounds that people can hear via any number of devices.

Perhaps the most obvious example of the above-noted process in the domain of IR is government declassification of material, which in turn increases the possibilities for observation. In some instances, information may come to light long after events, and the story of what happened evolves as a result. In the case of the Cuban Missile Crisis, for example, several of those involved in the decision-making on the US side wrote purportedly "tell all" books soon after the events took place. Given the sheer volume of classified material, however, these books fell short of conveying all that went on in what the media at the time portrayed as a one-sided victory for the US in a well-managed crisis. Information that came out later caused at least two important changes in interpretation. One is that the world came much closer to nuclear war than it even seemed at the time due to the role of accident and misunderstanding that aggravated an already difficult situation. The other shift in meaning concerned the outcome; the US removed its missiles stationed in Turkey in exchange for the USSR doing the same thing in Cuba. While the case still stands as a "win" for the US, it should not be regarded as some kind of rollover.

Scientific realism stands in opposition to the "mystification of residuals" – a belief that some things lie beyond the realm of explanation and thus are not worth studying (Babbie 2001). From a scientific realist point of view, unobservables create priorities for empirical research in the quest for knowledge. Thus explanation, rather than mystification, is the mind-set concerning that which is not yet grounded in the empirical world.

Consider scientific realism in the context of IR. A concept such as democracy, which plays an important role in many models of domestic politics and foreign policy, began as an abstraction. It had philosophical origins in Plato and elsewhere in the ancient world. After thousands of years and countless publications, democracy has come to be measured rigorously through comprehensive time series datasets such as V-Dem.

Instead of being the product of coincidence, accumulating evidence is an outcome anticipated from consistent application of scientific principles. A detailed treatment of scientific principles is beyond the scope of this study, but a few basic traits are easy to convey. The process of scientific investigation, understood in general terms, commences with a research question that may arise from either inductive or deductive thinking.

Inductive reasoning refers to making inferences from specifics to generalities. For example, noticing that states involved in war tend to be near each other could lead to the inference that proximity is a condition enabling conflict. Deductive reasoning refers to making inferences from generalities to specifics. One example would be a hypothesis that democratic leaders are likely to be more judicious about the interstate conflicts within which they become involved, because of a greater likelihood of overthrow if defeated. Later chapters reveal support from previous research for each of the preceding inferences, even though they are derived in different ways. The main lesson is that ideas can come about in varying ways, but what matters most is whether or not a proposition turns out to be supported by evidence.

In a general sense, the process unfolds as follows. Scholars review previous research on a given question, to the extent it exists, to identify priorities for work to get underway. They then formulate a hypothesis of the form "If X, then Y is more likely than otherwise" to guide further efforts to answer the question. (The proposition may take a compound form, with a set of variables rather than a single "X" being put forward as the explanation for "Y".) Specific orderings of events and mechanisms are identified as processes (Grzymala-Busse 2011: 1268). Data gathering then takes place to evaluate the hypothesis, about which confidence either increases or decreases as results are obtained from analysis. The process then goes through a new cycle. Confidence in a theory, which consists of a logically interconnected set of hypotheses derived from an axiomatic basis, is enhanced or diminished on the basis of empirical research.

Take, for example, the evolution of answers to the following research question: "Does internal conflict lead to external conflict for a state?". Intuition favored the idea, but initial data analysis refuted it. In a major breakthrough, Wilkenfeld (1968) used regime type as an intervening variable and found connections between various types of internal and external conflict. Research eventually converged on the special properties of regime type in the context of interstate pairs – famously summed up as the "democratic peace" noted above. Put simply, pairs of states made up as democracies are less likely to be in conflict with each other, most notably, staying out of war as compared to the propensities of other dyads. The answer to the research question about connection of internal with external conflict now is "yes", as per intuition from long ago, but with important nuances involving intervening variables and a range of processes corresponding to cause and effect.

> **FOR EXAMPLE: RUSSIA, UKRAINE, AND CHANGES IN REGIME TYPE**
>
> While it had been moving in the direction of democracy after the fall of the USSR, the Russian successor state experienced backsliding. The Russia of today, under the full control of President Vladimir Putin, no longer remembers a democracy. Its trend toward aggression directed at neighboring states is clear to see as a correlate, at least, of the shift toward dictatorship. Events in the Crimea, Georgia, and most dramatically Ukraine support that assertion. Note also that Ukraine experienced a Russian invasion as its political system shifted away from corruption and toward the rule of law in recent years. For such reasons, *change* in political systems may be just as important to monitor as the type. Russia and Ukraine have moved in opposite directions with regard to regime type and the presence of a Western-style democracy, possibly even aligned with NATO, can serve as part of an explanation for why Putin initiated the war and persists in fighting even after running into a costly stalemate.

ANALYTIC ECLECTICISM

Even as research moves forward, some limitations can be expected to persist. Scientific progress therefore is understood in pragmatic terms – the quest for knowledge is an ongoing process. To achieve the best possible results, we adopt *analytic eclecticism* as the approach to research that follows on from a scientific realist perspective. Sil (2009: 649) provides a summary statement of analytic eclecticism (see also Sil 2000; Katzenstein and Sil 2008; Sil and Katzenstein 2010: 415, 417): "Analytic eclecticism is a problem-driven approach featuring the extraction, adaptation, and integration (but *not* synthesis) of discrete concepts, mechanisms, logical principles, and interpretive moves normally embedded in emergent research traditions, each identified with distinct styles of research reflecting distinct combinations of ontological and epistemological principles."

Analytic eclecticism is gaining traction within the field of IR because of disappointment with results from what have come to be known as "paradigm wars". Adherents of realism, liberalism, and other paradigms fight what seem like endless battles on behalf of their paradigm against others. By contrast, analytic eclecticism seeks to combine together the most promising ideas and methods, regardless of their point of origin. In a word, analytic eclecticism is pragmatic (Cornut 2015: 3).

Sil and Katzenstein (2010) identify three markers of eclectic scholarship: (1) an open-ended approach to problem formulation; (2) middle-range causal arguments; and (3) an emphasis on practical application. Analytic eclecticism is pragmatic, as manifested in its search for middle-range theoretical arguments with potential relevance to issues of policy and practice. In addition, analytic eclecticism addresses problems of wide expanse that incorporate more of the complexity that characterizes real-world situations (Sil and Katzenstein 2010). Causal accounts that include interactions among different types of causal mechanisms normally taken in isolation from each other within separate research traditions thereby emerge (Sil and Katzenstein 2010: 412). For all of the preceding reasons, analytic eclecticism represents a major departure from paradigm-driven research.

IN FOCUS: PARADIGMS AND COALITIONS

A basic component of the realist paradigm is the idea that coalitions form and break up because of efforts toward balancing. The power-oriented realist point of view, however, might seem unable to offer a complete explanation in all cases of coalitional change. The evolving position of Israel in the Middle East is interesting to ponder in connection with a paradigm such as realism as compared with analytic eclecticism. At one time, Israel had only enemies in the Middle East, but peace agreements with various states, such as Egypt, and the comprehensive Abraham Accords, dramatically altered the position of Israel. On the one hand, such changes might have followed on from realist-style power politics. On the other hand, it is possible that factors beyond the distribution of capabilities have played a role in shifting coalitions within the Middle East, which would be the expectation based on an analytic eclecticist point of view.

With that point of difference in mind, what do you see as potentially important in accounting for the ways in which coalitions persist and change?

Theorizing, as noted earlier, seeks to describe, explain, predict, and even prescribe. Analytic eclecticism is adopted to obtain the best results possible across that set of objectives. With its inclusive search for causal factors – beyond paradigms, as per the title of the book from Sil and Katzenstein (2010) – analytic eclecticism is not subject to blinders imposed by allegiance to a given school of thought which, in turn, could result in leaving out something important. This positive trait of inclusiveness does entail a risk, however, regarding explanation in particular – what if would-be causal factors accumulate and end up creating a maze of contradictory statements? This question leads naturally into systemism, a method that lends itself to the inclusion of interactions among different types of causal mechanisms at different levels of analysis, which can credibly claim to deal with tendencies toward logical inconsistency.

SYSTEMISM

Systemism is a graphic approach toward representation of arguments – in the present context, those about IR. The systemist philosophy of Bunge (1996) emphasized theoretical completeness – moving beyond a focus either on units or wholes – agents and structures as sometimes labeled in IR. While Bunge (1996) included a visual approach toward putting forward ideas, over the course of two decades James (2002, 2022) developed the notation for diagrams that are implemented in this book to represent both theoretical arguments and series of events.

Systemism requires a commitment to "understanding a system in terms of a comprehensive set of functional relationships" (James 2002: 131). Figure 1.1 depicts functional relations in a social system from a systemist point of view in the context of the international system and any designated region within it. Variables operate at macro (X, Y) and micro (x, y) levels.[3] (The specific shapes and colors that appear for respective variables are explained at a later point.) Conventional in IR, as included in the figure, are designation of processes in a region as macro and the state as micro (Singer 1961).[4] So, for example, the "System" might be Asia. Outside of the system is the environment – the greater international system – within which variable "E" resides. To continue with the example of Asia, the environment would be everything outside of that region. The environment can be expected to provide inputs into, and experience outputs from, the system. A system in IR, put simply, is a region, with the world beyond its boundaries as the environment. The role of the individual is not ignored within this frame of reference, but instead classified by location. An individual might even act at a global level, beyond the region, but this is likely to be quite rare.

Within a regional system as depicted by Figure 1.1, four basic types of linkages are possible: macro-macro (X → Y), macro-micro (X → x), micro-macro (y → Y), and micro-micro (x → y). In addition, effects may go back and forth with the environment, such as E → X, E → x, Y → E, and y → E. In this generic figure, upper- and lowercase characters correspond to macro- and micro-level variables, respectively. It is difficult to specify in advance how causal connections operate within and beyond a system, so all possible types are displayed. The nature of cause and effect depends on specification of mechanisms, which are identified by scholars addressing particular systems – global or regional. Note also that the figure depicts a set of ideal types – exactly one linkage of each variety. Systemist figures that describe real cases will have more of some connection types than others. Along those lines, one valuable feature of the systemist graphic approach is that it can identify which types of connection are missing altogether and thus especially in need of incorporation within a model.

---

[3] We use the term 'variable' throughout as a form of shorthand in reference to the components of systemist diagrams. The systemist approach can represent arguments that are outside of the empirical world as well (e.g., normative analysis), so the term 'component' might be a more inclusive one to keep in mind for future applications.

[4] Other possibilities for designation of a system include the state or another political unit in a diagram with a geographic structure. In addition, an academic discipline such as International Relations can serve as the system, with the world beyond as its environment.

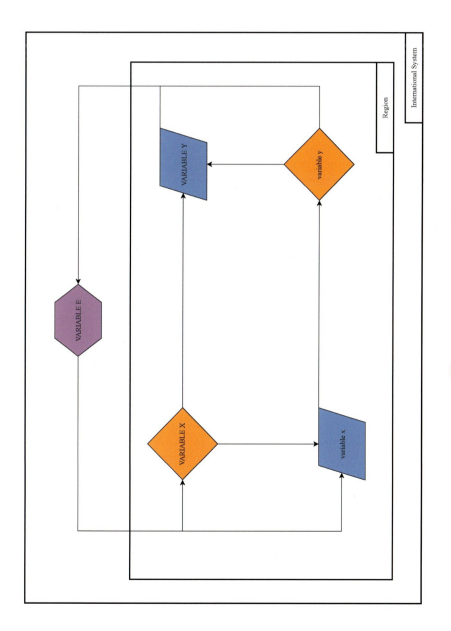

Figure 1.1 A systemist perspective on functional relations in a social system

Adoption of systemism entails specificity for causal mechanisms. How are any two variables connected to each other? Assessment of "Y" as a function of "X", by intuition, begins with an incremental or linear relationship. More complex specifications are added as necessary. For example, some linkages may be incremental, such as water cooling down or heating up by degrees, and then step-level, with temperatures of 0 and 100 Celsius resulting in freezing and boiling, respectively. Functional form also is important in strengthening the falsifiability of a theory by increasing the specificity of its causal mechanisms.

Table 1.1 conveys an example for each type of linkage portrayed in Figure 1.1. The system and environment vary from one instance to the next. As it turns out, one pair of connections does fit together. We introduce these illustrations further in turn.

For "TIGHTNESS AND DISCRETENESS OF ALLIANCE SYSTEMS → WORLD WAR I", a Macro-Macro connection, a wide range of evidence comes to mind. The authoritative study of Albertini (1952) tells the history of the Triple Alliance versus the Triple Entente in the lead-up to the Great War, now known as World War I. As each alliance became more cohesive, it also pulled away from contact with the other. In a pathbreaking work, Holsti (1972) used statistical analysis to show how that process occurred; ultimately, the two sides communicated on the battlefield as a result of their inability to negotiate a peace.

With regard to "mass migration via Mexico to US" → "internal hyperpartisanship for US and tensions with Mexico", a micro-micro linkage, events in real time offer a great deal of confirmation. While many in the public hold moderate views on the subject of migration, research reveals that extreme and opposing opinions dominate the media (Citrin, Levy, and Wright 2023). Advocates of open versus closed borders drown out middle-ground positions in the US and relations with Mexico steadily worsen in the absence of comprehensive immigration reform.

Consider "CHINESE QUASI-HEGEMONY IN EAST ASIA" → "anxiety in Taiwan", a Macro-micro connection. The rapid rise of China changed the power structure of East Asia, with the US less obviously inclined to respond to increasingly assertive policies. This, in turn, stimulates concern in Taiwan, which has evolved into a democracy that features a hybrid rather than purely Sinic identity (Gartner, Huang, Li, and James 2023). Since the People's Republic of China (PRC) sees Taiwan as historically within its sovereignty, anxiety rises about a potential takeover and even an invasion in light of enhanced capabilities on the mainland.

For "Cuban revolution brings communist regime to power" → "RIVALRY IN LATIN AMERICA BETWEEN CUBA AND US", a micro-Macro linkage, decades of evidence are available for review. Early on in the existence of the Castro regime, the US backed an ill-fated attempt by Cuban exiles to overthrow it (Janis 1982). Rivalry has been the norm ever since, with prominent instances being the violent conflicts in Nicaragua and El Salvador. The US and Cuba continue to back different factions throughout Latin America.

Consider two connections together, from (i) the System (Macro) to the Environment: "RIVALRIES IN EUROPE" → "SCRAMBLE FOR AFRICA" and (ii) the Environment to the System (Macro): "COLONIALISM" → "INCOHERENT BORDERS IN AFRICA". Competition in Europe extended outward during what became known as the "scramble for Africa" in the 19th century. With their more advanced military technology, European states imposed colonial regimes on territories that did not correspond with traditional boundaries

Table 1.1 Examples of linkage types

Type of Linkage	Example
Macro → Macro	TIGHTNESS AND DISCRETENESS OF ALLIANCE SYSTEMS → WORLD WAR I
micro → micro	mass migration via Mexico to US → internal hyperpartisanship for US and tensions with Mexico
Macro → micro	CHINESE QUASI-HEGEMONY IN EAST ASIA → anxiety in Taiwan
micro → Macro	Cuban revolution brings communist regime to power → RIVALRY IN LATIN AMERICA BETWEEN CUBA AND US
Environment → System (Macro)	COLONIALISM → INCOHERENT BORDERS IN AFRICA
Environment → System (micro)	PANDEMIC → government mandates and attendant political controversies
System (Macro) → Environment	RIVALRIES IN EUROPE → SCRAMBLE FOR AFRICA
System (micro) → Environment	decadence of Imperial Rome → DECLINE AND FALL OF ROMAN EMPIRE

related to ethnolinguistic identity. Incoherent borders persist in the postcolonial era of independent African states and impact significantly upon politics and policy on that continent (Moyo and Nshimbi 2019).

Next comes a linkage from the Environment to the System (micro): "PANDEMIC" → "government mandates and attendant political controversies". The COVID-19 pandemic spread throughout the globe and brought about a wide range of policy responses (Brock and Hale 2023). Government mandates included lockdowns, the wearing of masks, and vaccinations. To say that those policies continue to be controversial, even after repeal, is an understatement. Even in the most peaceful of the advanced democracies, protesters took to the streets; for example, the "Freedom Convoy" disrupted movement in the Canadian capital of Ottawa and stimulated a very intense response from the prime minister (Alden 2022).

Finally, consider a connection from the System (micro) to the Environment: "decadence of Imperial Rome" → "DECLINE AND FALL OF ROMAN EMPIRE". The memorable six-volume study from Gibbon (1776–1789) offers great detail about how Rome fell into ruin, eventually hiring mercenaries to fight its battles and ultimately collapsing after being sacked on multiple occasions by increasingly successful invaders.

IN FOCUS

Since its beginning on October 7, 2023, as we write, the Gaza War continues to exact a heavy price in terms of human life and material destruction. Intuition is enough to be aware that no single factor could offer a convincing account for such a complex and devastating conflict.

With a focus on the types of connection conveyed in Table 1.1, how might a compelling account of the Gaza War be put together?

Table 1.2 summarizes the notation that appears in systemist graphics. Shapes and colors are used to distinguish the roles played by respective components within a diagram. A few correspond to familiar traffic lights – green, orange, and red, respectively, mean go, pause, and stop. A blue parallelogram is used to identify a point of convergence, while a purple hexagon indicates a node at which pathways converge and diverge. Before any connections are introduced in a diagram, the starting point is the designation of a diagram's system, recognizable visually as its "inner box", and the corresponding environment, the diagram's "outer box", in which the system is embedded. For example, the region of "Europe" can serve as the system, with the "International System" as its environment. Within "Europe", the macro level (the upper part of the system with variables in all uppercase characters) would be the region as a whole, while the micro level (with variables in all lowercase characters found in the lower part of the system) consists of the activities of individual actors within Europe.

Table 1.2 Systemist notation

Initial Variable	(green ellipse)	The starting point of a series of relationships.
Generic Variable	(rectangle)	A step in the process being depicted.
Divergent Variable	(orange diamond)	Multiple pathways are created from a single linkage.
Convergent Variable	(blue parallelogram)	A single pathway is created from multiple linkages.
Nodal Variable	(purple hexagon)	Multiple pathways are created from multiple linkages.
Co-constitutive Variable	(double rectangle)	Two variables that are mutually contingent upon each other.
Terminal Variable	(red octagon)	The end point of a series of relationships.
Connection Stated in Study	→	A linkage explicitly made by the author.
Connection Crossing Over	—⋀→	Two separate linkages that do not interact.
Connection Inferred from Study	┈┈>	A linkage inferred by the reader but is not made explicit by the author.
Interaction Effect	←——→	Two variables that depend upon the effect of each other.

SUMMING UP AND MOVING FORWARD

The remainder of this text focuses on coverage of the nature, dynamics, and trends of conflict, crisis, and war, the major approaches to explaining them, and the central avenues for managing them. We proceed in three major parts, followed by a concluding chapter discussing the future of conflict, crisis, and war. Part I, which consists of chapters 2–4, addresses the problem descriptively, laying out our understanding of key concepts, beginning with conflict, and moving on to crisis and near crisis, international (interstate) war, and civil (intrastate) war (Chapter 2); the patterns and trends of these forms of conflict over time (Chapter 3); and the issues and challenges of strife in modern times (Chapter 4). Part II examines explanations of conflict, crisis, and war, first focusing on system-level (Chapter 5), state-level (Chapter 6), individual/small group-level (Chapter 7) efforts. Chapters on crises (Chapter 8) and civil war (Chapter 9) follow, in each instance applying explanations based on the system-, state-, and individual/small group-levels. Chapter 10 then focuses on efforts to integrate the informative yet incomplete explanations of arguments at these separate levels in multilevel approaches, with the American Civil War as the illustrative case. Part III explores approaches to prevent, manage, and resolve conflict, crisis, and war, including state-based (Chapter 11), and IGO-based/NGO-based approaches (Chapter 12). Chapter 13 offers summation and conclusions about conflict, crisis, and war.

Throughout, we include a regular series of core feature boxes that encourage and assist comprehension of major concepts, theories, and practices, critical thinking, and opportunities to think and work through puzzles and problems toward explanations and solutions, including those that involve real-world applications (In Focus boxes, For Example boxes, and Consider This boxes). We hope the pages that follow help readers to make sense of the challenging and complicated events and interactions of conflict, crisis, and war in world politics.

> **CONSIDER THIS: THEORY AND THE PROBLEM OF CONFLICT, CRISIS, AND WAR**
>
> Although many dismiss theory as something speculative and unrelated to the empirical world, often with a disparaging "oh that's just theory" comment, theory is explanation of how events and actions fit together and is essential to understanding and explaining issues in world politics such as conflict, crisis, and war. Thinking about the nature of theory:
>
> *What does theory bring to the study of conflict, crisis, and war?*

PART I
UNDERSTANDING THE PROBLEM

2
Conflict, crisis, and war in world politics

PROLOGUE

World events can be intense at times, but they also provide the occasional comic relief. Perhaps that is the way, at least for now, to look at the almost surreal events surrounding a huge balloon from China that crossed US airspace starting on January 28, 2023.[1] Comparable in size to the Statue of Liberty, the solar-powered balloon had high-tech equipment that could collect communications signals and other data. Officials from the US government maintained that the Chinese sent the balloon for intelligence purposes. On February 4, a US fighter jet shot the balloon down off the coast of South Carolina. Fortunately, no escalation – from conflict, through crisis, to war – took place as a result of this bizarre episode involving the two leading powers of the 21st century. However, as the current chapter makes obvious, danger is never far away in a world where billions of people, thousands of nations, and about 200 states are trying to coexist in what feels like an ever-shrinking space.

OVERVIEW

Conflict, crisis, and war are the major concepts that guide our study of world politics. These events may be thought of as rungs on the ladder of escalation. The ladder in this instance is one that must be identified through research rather than assumed to have the normal properties of even spacing for its rungs and clear visibility along the way. It might even be easier to think of the problem facing world leaders in conflict as one of climbing *down* safely, rather than falling and ending up in full-scale war. After entry into conflict occurs, the goal from the standpoint of our security as human beings is to stay up on the roof, figuratively speaking, rather than descending. One misstep along the way could cause a leader to tumble downward into conflict, crisis, and ultimately even war.

To the relatively familiar steps on the imaginary ladder of escalation above, we add one more: near crisis. This type of event indeed is what it sounds like on the basis of intuition. A near crisis is a conflict that has reached a certain level of intensity but falls short of crisis

---

[1] The details that follow are based on reporting from CBS (2023).

conditions. Such events are especially well suited for comparison to crises – differences that emerge, as will become apparent later in the volume, are especially helpful in accounting for escalation.

This chapter unfolds in five additional sections. The second through fourth sections define and give examples of international conflict, crisis, and war. Section five brings the basic concepts into engagement with each other. The sixth and final section sums up what we have learned about conflict, crisis, and war and sets the stage for Chapter 3.

INTERNATIONAL CONFLICT

International conflict is defined as "any interaction delimited in time and space, involving two or more international entities (whether states or transnational actors) which possess non-identical preference orderings over two or more sets of alternative choices" (James 1988: 5). Advantages of that definition, as James (1988: 5–6) observes, include an encompassing approach toward recognition of actors, along with a plausible sense of mixed-motive interactions and allowing for strife that does not necessarily include violence. The definition is a bit "wordy" because of its inclusive character, so it is appropriate to unpack the contents in sequence.

First, the definition identifies international conflict as an event rather than a situation. Tensions over the American border with Mexico represent an ongoing situation, with specific events designated as conflicts. Consider, for example, the North American Leaders Summit of January 2023 – often referred to as the meeting of the "Three Amigos". At that event, the leaders of the US, Mexico, and Canada negotiated any number of issues, with the Mexican border as one of the most obvious points of contention.

Second, an international conflict can be interstate or more inclusive in terms of the actors involved. An example of interstate conflict would be the clash over Hans Island, an obscure location in the Arctic that both Denmark and Canada claimed as exclusive territory. The events in this conflict consisted of episodic visits to the very small and remote island, in turn, by Danish and Canadian expeditions that left flags and a few other items identified with their respective countries. After years of these ritualistic expeditions, Denmark and Canada agreed on June 14, 2022 to an approximately equal division of Hans Island. The underlying issue that produced the low-level conflict between two erstwhile NATO allies involved Arctic sovereignty – rising in salience in tandem with climate change that is pointing toward the Arctic as a viable shipping lane in the future. Some international conflicts, however, are not purely interstate. Non-state actors are important – perhaps increasingly so – in the way that many international events play out. In the above-noted border tensions between Mexico and the US, for example, Amnesty International regularly challenges the policies of both governments in connection with the rights of migrants.

FOR EXAMPLE: CONFLICT OVER THE GRAND ETHIOPIAN RENAISSANCE DAM

The Nile River has served as the backdrop for numerous major historical water events. The historical dispute over Nile River allocation issues between Egypt (downstream) and Ethiopia and Sudan (upstream) has been intense and prolonged. The current Nile River conflict is the result of Ethiopia's construction of the Grand Ethiopian Renaissance Dam (GERD), the building of which began in 2011 and was nearing completion at the time of this writing. From the start, while Ethiopia has framed the matter as one of necessity, Egypt has maintained that the dam threatens its water security, and overall regional security as well. According to Ayferam (2023), the conflict is also one of ontological security, threatening national identity: for Egypt, the identity centered on the place of the Nile River in its history, culture, and civilization; for Ethiopia, the role of the dam as a "sovereignty project" symbolizing unity and responses to national poverty.

The stakes and intensity of the conflict made military options a real possibility. For example, in 2010, Egypt and Sudan plotted to take military action against Ethiopia to protect their interests in the Nile (Abebe 2014: 33). In 2019, Ethiopia warned that the issue might lead to war with Egypt, and two years later, Egypt and Sudan engaged in joint military operations as a signal of the salience of the ongoing conflict over the dam (Elasfar 2023).

At the very heart of the matter is the complicated issue of how to share the water resources of the Nile River. As Waal (2015) put it, "Running low is Egypt's nightmare, and more than 80 percent of the Nile's water comes from rain that falls on the Ethiopian highlands and is then carried north by the fast-flowing Blue Nile." Despite multiple efforts at negotiations and a 2015 agreement of principles signed by Egypt, Ethiopia, and Sudan, the countries in conflict fundamentally disagree over the dam itself, as well as how to manage water flows (Madden 2019). Egyptian president Abdel Fattah Al-Sisi called for all the countries of the Nile Basin to work cooperatively toward basin-wide agreements at the 74th United Nations General Assembly in 2019 but warned that "the continued impasse in the negotiations on the dam will have negative repercussions on the stability as well as on development in the region in general, and in Egypt, in particular" (Terpstra 2019). Two years later, Sudan's prime minister Abdalla Hamdok called on the African Union, the United Nations, the European Union, and the United States to mediate the conflict over the Nile water being used to fill the GERD (Abdelaza 2021).

By the end of 2023, the GERD was virtually complete and multiple water fillings had occurred since mid-2020. While Ethiopia held a celebration marking the 12th anniversary of the start of the project, "Egypt's Minister of Water Resources and Irrigation Dr Hani Sewilam indicated that the continued uncooperative unilateral measures to operate the Grand Ethiopian Renaissance Dam could harm his country and cause immeasurable damage to the social and economic stability of Egypt" (Middle East Monitor 2023).

Source: https://www.istockphoto.com/vector/nile-river-map-gm868972840-144655183

Map 2.1   The politics of water in the Horn of Africa

Third, adversaries can have points of agreement even while in conflict – hence the reference in the definition to mixed motives. At the Three Amigos meeting noted above, efforts to negotiate points of difference took place against the backdrop of many areas of agreement. The Arctic visits for Canada and Denmark had been much the same – two members of NATO who agreed on many, but not all, things. By contrast, extreme cases of strife – where virtually no points of consensus exist – are referred to as "zero-sum games". This terminology, which has made it into everyday language, comes from the study of strategic interaction known as game theory. Zero sumness refers to each adversary seeing any gain for the other side as equated with a loss for itself. In that sense, it is easy to see why conflicts over territory turn out to be among the most likely to escalate.

Taken together, the preceding characteristics create an inclusive sense of international conflict. Clearly a wide range of events is available for study – a good thing in principle because a more exclusive definition could bias research in favor of one frame of reference or another. At the same time, many conflicts are limited in scope and potential for escalation. It can be difficult at the time of events – and the Chinese balloon floating over the US is an excellent example – to know whether strife will intensify or subside. Prediction, put simply, is a tricky business.

INTERNATIONAL CRISIS (AND NEAR CRISIS)

Crisis, as a word, conveys intensity and time pressure – even danger. Within the study of conflict processes, the International Crisis Behavior (ICB) Project has developed concepts and data that have become the "industry standard" over the years since its founding in 1975. The ICB Project defines an international crisis via two conditions: "(1) a change in type and/or an increase in intensity of *disruptive*, that is, hostile verbal or physical, *interactions* between two or more states, with a heightened probability of *military hostilities*; that, in turn, (2) destabilizes their relationship and *challenges* the *structure* of an international system – global, dominant, or subsystem" (Brecher and Wilkenfeld 1997: 4–5). This definition is comprehensive; it refers to how escalation of conflict may affect the ways in which actors relate to each other, as well as the structure of the system within which they reside. The ICB data include 487 international crises and 1,078 crisis actors from 1918 to 2017, with data collection still in progress (Brecher, Wilkenfeld, Beardsley, James and Quinn 2023). The cases span the globe and include a wide range of issues within the basic categories of military-security, political-diplomatic, economic-developmental, and cultural-status.

Each international crisis incorporates the experiences of one or more actors. What, then, is meant by a "crisis actor"? A foreign policy crisis for an individual state is

> a situation with three necessary and sufficient conditions deriving from a change in the state's internal or external environment. All three are perceptions held by the highest-level decision makers of the state actor concerned: a *threat to one or more basic values*, along with an awareness of *finite time for response* to the value threat, and a *heightened probability of involvement in military hostilities*" (emphasis in original, Brecher and Wilkenfeld 1997: 3)

The concept of a foreign policy crisis therefore recognizes the subjective element in world politics. The same sequence of events may be perceived as a crisis by the decision-makers of one or more states, while many others do not detect any threat from what is observed. The range in crisis actors in the ICB dataset is from one, in many cases, up to 21 for "Entry into World War II".

Individual foreign policy crises combine to tell the full story of an international crisis.[2] Consider, for example, the Cuban Missile Crisis in 1962 – perhaps the most famous international crisis of the 20th century. This ICB case began with US perception of a foreign policy crisis on October 16, 1962 when the CIA presented to President John F. Kennedy photographic evidence of Soviet missiles in Cuba. The US responded with a decision on October 20 to blockade all offensive military equipment en route to Cuba. This US announcement triggered a foreign policy crisis for both Cuba and the USSR on October 22. Events stayed at a high level of intensity until November 7, when the US and USSR reached agreement on the essential points of difference. The US would be allowed to intercept and inspect Soviet ships leaving Cuba and photograph the missiles. The following day the superpowers negotiated the removal of IL-28 bombers that Prime Minister Fidel Castro had claimed as Cuban property. Castro conveyed his agreement to the US on November 20, 1962, and that terminated the crisis for all three actors.

The Cuban Missile Crisis involved three foreign policy crisis actors: Cuba, the US, and the USSR. The high-level confrontation challenged the structure of the dominant system; in other words, it raised the question of whether the US would maintain its position as the leader or give way to the USSR. While there is some controversy to this day about who "won", at the time the US clearly emerged as the victor in the court of world opinion. With regard to disruption in processes, the case included only minor clashes – a relatively low level of violence – but is remembered as highly intense because of the risk of escalation to nuclear war.

Since it is very well known – even depicted in movies such as *Thirteen Days* – the Cuban Missile Crisis is suitable for the introduction of crisis-oriented concepts but perhaps less so for an in-depth review. While endlessly fascinating, the case is not representative of international crises because it often is cited as the most dangerous situation of all arising from superpower competition during the Cold War. Instead, the details of "East China Sea", an ICB case from 2016, show the events of a more typical international crisis.

FOR EXAMPLE: INTERNATIONAL CRISIS – THE EAST CHINA SEA

Located in the East China Sea, the Senkakus (Diaoyus in Chinese) comprise a small chain of five core islands. These islands are uninhabited and of questionable economic or strategic value, but in spite of that are simultaneously claimed by China, Taiwan, and Japan. The United States transferred control of the islands to Japan in 1972, which has administered them since then. Japan does not recognize foreign claims to the islands, nor has the United States taken a clear stance on the islands' sovereignty. However, the United States has committed to defending Japan should it come under attack in the process of

---

[2] Descriptions of ICB cases in this chapter are based primarily on Brecher, Wilkenfeld, Beardsley, James and Quinn (2023).

exercising administrative control.

Although the sovereignty of the Senkaku/Diaoyu islands has been disputed for decades, their significance in Sino-Japanese relations has increased sharply since 2010. On September 7, 2010, a Chinese fishing boat collided with a Japanese Coast Guard vessel in the waters surrounding the islands. Japan detained the boat and crew, and arrested its captain, which produced a major diplomatic row. In 2012, over Chinese objections, the Japanese government purchased the islands outright from a private owner. These two incidents drastically increased the prominence of the dispute; Chinese efforts to undermine the Japanese claim then increased. Since 2012, official Chinese Coast Guard ships routinely have conducted incursions into the territorial waters surrounding the islands, and official Chinese aircraft have regularly flown into their associated airspace. The US, for its part, expanded its rhetorical support for the Japanese position. As part of the official US policy to "deter conflict and coercion", Washington also increased diplomatic and security coordination with Tokyo.

During the very early hours of the morning of June 9, 2016, a Chinese military incursion in the disputed Senkaku/Diaoyu islands triggered a foreign policy crisis for Japan. With perception of the first foreign policy crisis, the international crisis known as East China Sea also began. At 12:50 a.m. a People's Liberation Army (PLA) military frigate entered the contiguous waters adjacent to the Senkaku islands' territorial waters. The contiguous zone stretches 12 nautical miles beyond the 12 miles of territorial waters, which hug the islands themselves. For roughly two hours before the Chinese ship entered the zone, a Japanese military destroyer attempted to contact the vessel and advised it to change direction. The Chinese ship, however, maintained its course straight toward the islands' territorial waters. Although their entry was not protested by the Japanese, three Russian warships passed through the contiguous zones from 10 p.m. on June 8 to 3 a.m. on June 9 and added to the tumult. Most notably, the ships sparked concern about potential Chinese and Russian coordination. While Russian military ships had entered the contiguous zone before, it marked the first time that a Chinese military vessel broached the region.

Japanese prime minister Shinzo Abe assembled a crisis management team to monitor the situation. Abe was notified of the ship's presence at around 1 a.m. on June 9. At around the same time, the Chinese ambassador was called in to the Japanese Foreign Ministry, where the Japanese Vice Minister of Foreign Affairs, Akitaka Saiki, demanded that Beijing remove the ship from the contiguous zone. The Chinese ambassador did not officially accede to the demand, but relayed that escalation was unwanted and that he would report back to his superiors. Vice Minister Saiki felt that there was legitimate concern among Japanese officials at the time that the incursion would lead to a serious military clash between Chinese and Japanese forces. Ultimately, this did not occur, as the Chinese ship left the contiguous zone at 3:10 a.m. and headed north.

While the departure of the Chinese frigate lessened immediate tensions, it did not terminate the crisis altogether. On June 9, Abe ordered the Japanese Navy and Coast Guard to be on alert. Yoshihide Suga, the chief cabinet official, noted at a press briefing that "China's actions unilaterally escalate tensions in the area, and we are seriously concerned". China, for its part, did not confirm that a military vessel had sailed around the islands, and publicly reaffirmed its belief that the Senkaku islands are Chinese territory. A Chinese Ministry of National Defense statement read as follows: "For China's military vessels to pass through waters under the country's own jurisdiction is reasonable and legitimate, and other countries have no right to make irresponsible comments."

The US acknowledged the incident but did not express judgment. On June 9 a State Department official said in a press briefing that the US had been in touch with the Japanese government, and that they were monitoring the situation closely, but referred reporters to the Japanese for further details about the incident.

The crisis terminated shortly after it began, on June 14, 2016; a joint military exercise among Japan, the United States, and India allayed Japanese concerns that China might attempt a land grab. Japan's crisis ended around the start of a previously planned annual military exercise between Japan, India, and the United States dubbed Exercise Malabar. The exercise consisted of two portions: a harbor phase followed by an at-sea phase. The harbor portion began on June 9 in Sasebo, a port city in southwestern Japan along the East China Sea, and the at-sea phase began on June 14 in the Philippine Sea. As the exercises began, Japan was awaiting any significant response from China regarding their protests toward the Chinese incursions near the Senkaku islands. The initiation of the at-sea phase served to assure Japan of the strength of US commitments to defend Japanese interests. Moreover, the lack of any significant Chinese response in the interim reassured Japan that the crisis would not escalate further.

Crises in world politics, as apparent from the preceding example, involve hostile interactions with the potential for escalation of conflict between adversarial states. While Japan, China, and the US all played significant roles, just one holds the status of a crisis actor. Only the leadership of Japan perceived a threat to basic values, finite time for response, and a greater likelihood of military hostilities. The leaders of China and the US did not perceive any particular threat to basic values. This serves as a reminder that, within an international crisis, the experiences of those involved can vary from one case to the next. An international crisis, in other words, can include many actors that perceive a foreign policy crisis or just one that does.

Near crisis is a concept related to crisis, with one key difference with regard to perceptions of its actors.[3] A near crisis actor perceives a threat to basic values and finite time for response, but not an increased likelihood of military hostilities. Like an international crisis, a near crisis represents a disruption in processes and challenge to system structure, but at a lower level of intensity.

FOR EXAMPLE: NEAR CRISIS - MH17 AIRPLANE CRASH

This near crisis took place in the aftermath of the Euromaidan movement and revolution that overthrew President Yanukovych and the Ukrainian government in February 2014. The revolution in Ukraine took place in the context of the discussion of whether Ukraine should strengthen its ties with Europe by signing the EU association treaty – or if it should remain oriented toward Russia. A Russophone portion of the population in Ukraine did not approve of the revolution and protested in favor of closer ties with Russia. In March

---

[3] For detailed development of the near crisis concept and associated data, see Iakhnis and James (2021).

2014, Russia annexed the Crimea region of Ukraine after a Russian military intervention. The protests that followed in the Donetsk and Luhansk regions escalated into an armed pro-Russian separatist insurgency. Armed conflict between the Ukrainian government and the pro-Russian separatists followed.

On July 17, 2014, commercial flight Malaysia Airlines Flight 17 (MH17) from Amsterdam to Kuala Lumpur was shot down by a BUK-missile, which had been transported from Russia to the separatist-controlled Eastern Ukraine. The crash killed all 283 passengers and 15 crew members, including 193 Dutch citizens, 43 Malaysians, 27 Australians, and citizens from several other countries. The shootdown of the airplane sent shockwaves through the international community, triggering a near crisis for Ukraine and, in turn, for Russia as accusations mounted against it. Ukraine's government stated it had evidence that the Russian military and its separatist allies brought down the flight, while Putin blamed Ukraine for the crash. The United States and United Kingdom responded by calling for an impartial and credible international investigation. The UK also requested an emergency meeting of the United Nations Security Council (UNSC).

On July 21, the UNSC adopted a resolution that demanded (i) safe access to the crash site; and (ii) those responsible for the disaster would be held accountable. In the following days, the Organization for Security and Co-operation in Europe (OSCE) worked with the separatists to gain access to the region and transport the bodies back to Amsterdam for further investigation. Several countries, including the Netherlands, Australia, Malaysia, and the United Kingdom, sent teams of investigators. On August 7, 2014, Australia, Belgium, the Netherlands, Ukraine, and Malaysia set up the Joint Investigation Team (JIT) to establish the facts of the case, determine responsibility, and gather criminal evidence for prosecution. The establishment of the JIT ended the near crisis for the parties involved since it would work toward justice and truth about the crash. In July 2020, the Netherlands announced that it would sue Russia for its alleged involvement in the accident. Russia continues to deny any involvement in the crash.

Near crisis, as the preceding example reveals, is adjacent to crisis. It facilitates comparison of similar, yet still significantly different, steps along the ladder of escalation. Near crisis involves a lower level of intensity and calls to mind an old saying: "an ounce of prevention is worth a pound of cure". If escalation upward to more dangerous levels of conflict can be prevented through the study of near crisis, notably in connection with crisis, it will be well worth the effort.

INTERNATIONAL WAR

Interstate War

Prevention of war between and among states motivated the foundation of International Relations as an academic discipline. This field of study came into being at the end of what those at the time called the "Great War" – now known as World War I. Most commonly referenced, as Quackenbush (2015: 32; see also Singer and Small 1972; Small and Singer 1982) observes, is the definition from the Correlates of War (COW) Project: "fighting between the regular military forces of two or more countries, directed and approved of by central authorities, where at least one thousand battle deaths occur". The COW definition is in line with implicit criteria from historians when asked independently to provide a list of wars (Singer and Small 1972; Small and Singer 1982). Note that the interstate focus of war as an event does not exclude other actors. The International Red Cross, for example, has been involved in protecting and saving lives under wartime conditions for many years. At the same time, the scope and scale of war ensures that states will be the principal combatants.

Data from the COW Project, in fact, have expanded to recognize the significant roles played by non-state actors.[4] An expanded typology contains the follow categories:

- Interstate wars
- Extra-state wars: colonial – conflict with a colony; and imperial – state versus non-state
- Intra-state wars: civil wars – for central control or over local issues; regional internal; and intercommunal
- Non-state wars: in non-state territory; and across state borders

Elaboration of the concept of war does not begin and end with the COW Project. Several other outstanding datasets on armed conflict, such as UCDP/PRIO (2023), are available and we make use of them as well as the pages of this book unfold.

IN FOCUS: EMPIRICAL DEFINITIONS OF WAR

Major concepts like war must be carefully defined in empirical terms. Consider two prominent efforts by political scientists.

CORRELATES OF WAR

In the Correlates of War data project, an empirical threshold of 1,000 battle deaths distinguishes war from other, smaller armed disputes. The Correlates of War data define a Militarized Interstate Dispute – or MID – as the threat, display, or use of military force short of war (less than 1,000 battle deaths) by one member state explicitly directed toward the government, official representatives, official forces, property, or territory of another state.

UPPSALA CONFLICT DATA PROGRAM

The Peace Research Institute of Oslo (PRIO) defines war empirically as an armed conflict reaching a cumulative total of 1,000 battle deaths, and then an annual total of 1,000 battle deaths each subsequent calendar year in its Uppsala Conflict Data Program (UCDP). PRIO also defines a major armed conflict as one in which a cumulative total of 1,000

---

[4] For more information about the COW Project and its datasets, see Sarkees and Wayman (2010).

> battle deaths has been reached, with at least 25 battle-related deaths occurring each subsequent calendar year. A minor armed conflict involves 25 battle-related deaths prior to reaching the 1,000 battle-death total.
>
> *Sources:* Correlates of War website, www.correlatesofwar.org; Uppsala Conflict Data Program website, www.pcr.uu.se/research/ucdp.

The Russian war against Ukraine continues at this time of writing. Figure 2.1 represents a systemist account of the war to date. We unpack this graphic via subfigures, a standard approach within systemism to facilitate understanding of the contents (James 2023).[5] The notation in the diagram corresponds to that of Table 1.1 from Chapter 1. Recall in particular that the macro and micro components, respectively, appear in upper- and lower-case characters.

Figure 2.1a is the first of the subfigures in which "Russia" serves as the system and the "International System" as its environment. The story might be told with a different structure for the diagram, but given that Russia initiated and sustained the war, the current choice makes the most sense. The macro and micro level of Russia as a system correspond, respectively, to government and society. There are two green ovals (i.e., initial variables), namely, "low standard of living among non-elite" and "Putin describes the collapse of the USSR as the biggest geopolitical catastrophe and intends to return to Russia's past glory". These initial variables mark the starting points of two separate chains of linkages. These variables are located at the micro level of the system because they describe processes that occur in society.

Figure 2.1b shows connections from both initial variables that start a causal process. While "low standard of living among non-elite" results in the generic variable "low levels of nationalism, small unmotivated military", the other one first generates the generic variable "anti-Ukrainian policies and rhetoric", also still located within Russia. In a second step, the latter generic variable connects to another generic variable, "subversive groups operating in Ukraine", and that one to the third one "heightened fear in Ukraine of Russian takeover". These are still micro level processes but are now placed in the "International System" as they occur at the societal level of Ukraine.

From there, the next subfigure, Figure 2.1c, introduces the first macro level variables. As a micro–macro level connection, the most recently mentioned generic variable connects to another generic variable, "UKRAINE SEEKS PROTECTION AGAINST RUSSIA FROM US AND NATO", which in turn leads into a second macro level generic variable, "US/NATO ADOPTS RHETORIC DESCRIBING PUTIN AS DANGEROUS AND A SERIOUS MILITARY THREAT", and then a third one "US/NATO ENACTS POLICIES TO SUPPORT UKRAINE AND (1) INTEGRATE UKRAINE INTO EU; (2) IMPLEMENT WESTERN DEMOCRACY; AND (3) ADD UKRAINE TO NATO". All of these are macro level variables in the International System as they capture processes outside of Russia that occur in the aggregate. From the last generic variable ensues a macro–macro level connection to the generic variable "UKRAINE JOINING NATO POSES EXISTENTIAL THREAT TO RUSSIA". It is placed in the system because it describes the impact of the developments for the Russian government.

---

[5] This figure builds upon figure 5 in Gansen and James (2022).

CONFLICT, CRISIS, AND WAR IN WORLD POLITICS

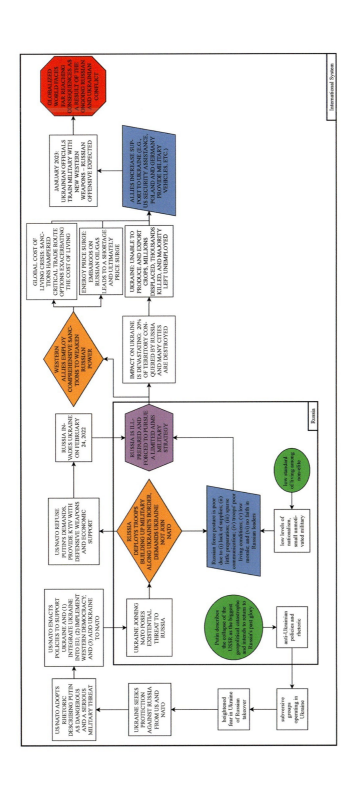

Figure 2.1 Russian war against Ukraine

CONFLICT, CRISIS, AND WAR IN WORLD POLITICS

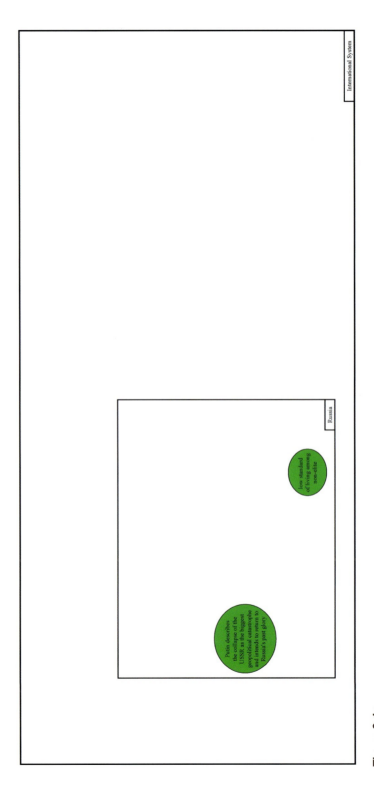

Figure 2.1a

CONFLICT, CRISIS, AND WAR IN WORLD POLITICS

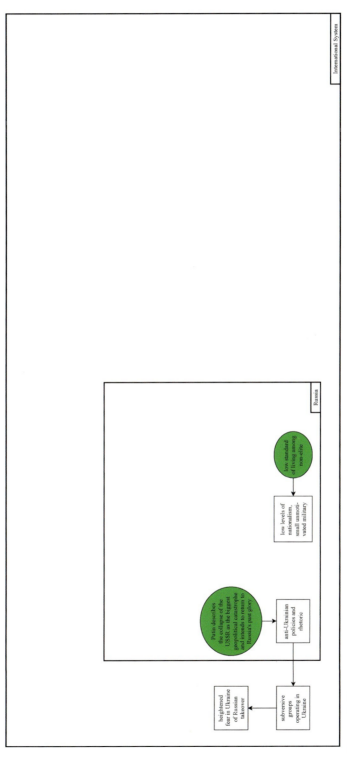

Figure 2.1b

CONFLICT, CRISIS, AND WAR IN WORLD POLITICS

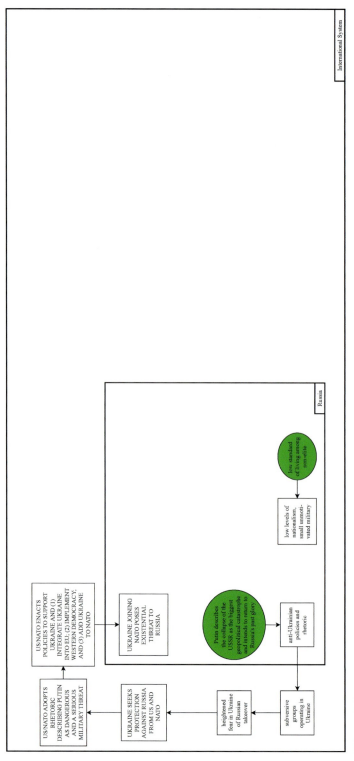

Figure 2.1c

CONFLICT, CRISIS, AND WAR IN WORLD POLITICS

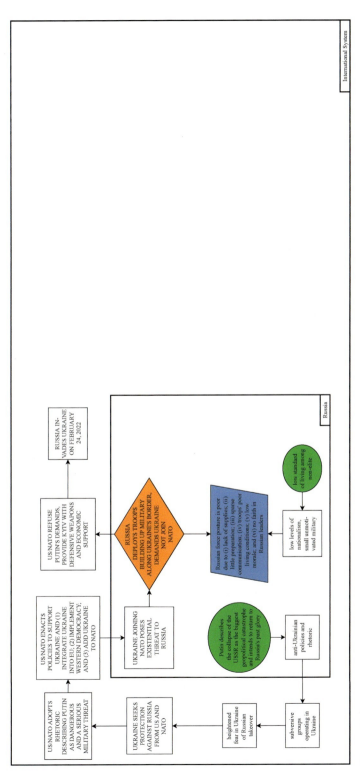

Figure 2.1d

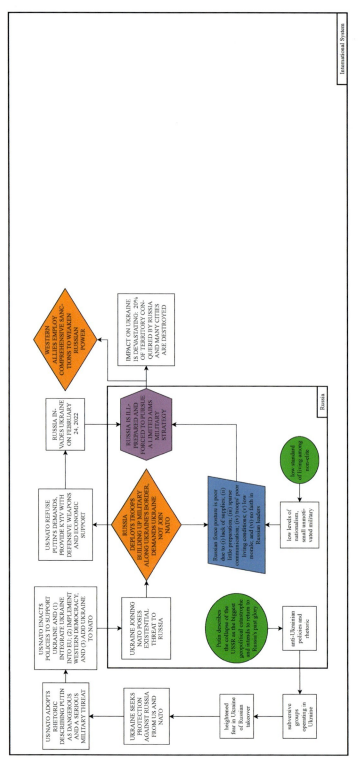

Figure 2.1e

CONFLICT, CRISIS, AND WAR IN WORLD POLITICS

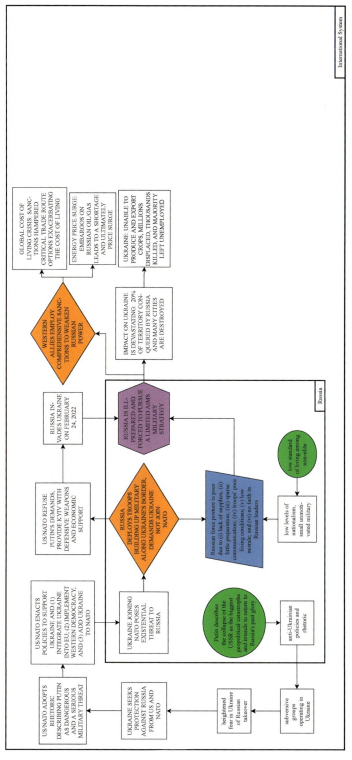

Figure 2.1f

CONFLICT, CRISIS, AND WAR IN WORLD POLITICS

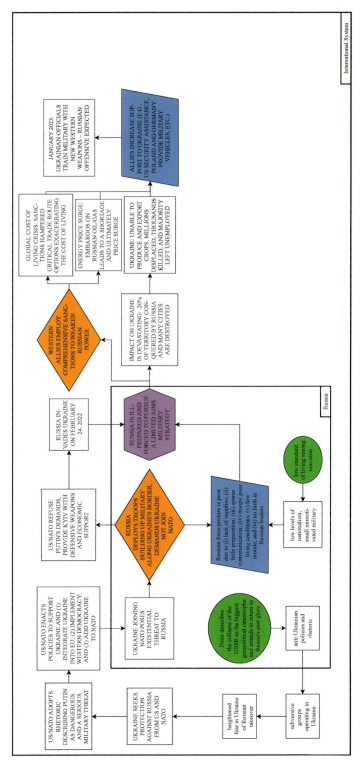

Figure 2.1g

CONFLICT, CRISIS, AND WAR IN WORLD POLITICS

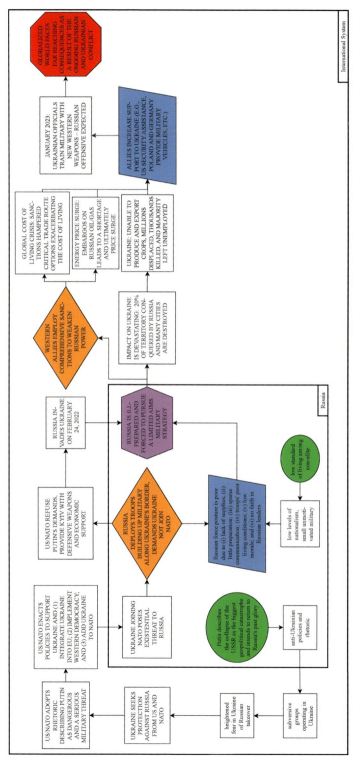

Figure 2.1h

From Figure 2.1d, it becomes obvious that the so-far linear development of the conflict has reached a new and much more elevated level of escalation. The previous generic variable, depicting a step in the process, connects to the first divergent variable of the diagram, "RUSSIA DEPLOYS TROOPS BUILDING UP MILITARY ALONG UKRAINE'S BORDER, DEMANDS UKRAINE NOT JOIN NATO". In its function as a divergent variable, this appears as an orange diamond and creates multiple pathways from a single linkage, visually illustrating the larger range of complications. The first one is another macro–macro connection up to the generic variable "US/NATO REFUSE PUTIN'S DEMANDS, PROVIDE KYIV WITH DEFENSIVE WEAPONS AND ECONOMIC SUPPORT" in the International System that then leads into another generic variable, "RUSSIA INVADES UKRAINE ON FEBRUARY 24, 2022". The second pathway created from the orange diamond is a macro–micro level one which, together with a connection from the generic variable "low levels of nationalism, small unmotivated military", merges into the convergent variable "Russian force posture is poor due to (i) lack of supplies; (ii) little preparation; (iii) sparse communication; (iv) troops' poor living conditions; (v) low morale; and (vi) no faith in Russian leaders".

As a blue parallelogram, only a single pathway ensues from the latter variable. Just like the single pathway from the most recently introduced generic variable, it leads into the nodal variable "RUSSIA IS ILL-PREPARED AND FORCED TO PURSUE A LIMITED AIMS MILITARY STRATEGY" in Figure 2.1e. This purple hexagon is placed at the macro level of the system as it describes an aggregate process that affects Russia as a state. Two pathways emerge from this variable, each of which leads into a variable at the macro level of the International System. The plain box "IMPACT ON UKRAINE IS DEVASTATING: 20% OF TERRITORY CONQUERED BY RUSSIA AND MANY CITIES ARE DESTROYED" and orange diamond "WESTERN ALLIES EMPLOY COMPREHENSIVE SANCTIONS TO WEAKEN RUSSIAN POWER" describe the consequences for, and events occurring in, the International System resulting from developments in Russia. One of the major continuing aims of Western retaliation is to cut Russia off from state-of-the-art technologies over the long term, particularly in the military and target markets such as the automobile industry.[6]

Figure 2.1f conveys macro level connections in the International System. The first one, from "WESTERN ALLIES EMPLOY COMPREHENSIVE SANCTIONS TO WEAKEN RUSSIAN POWER", produces two generic variables: "GLOBAL COST OF LIVING CRISIS: SANCTIONS HAMPERED CRITICAL TRADE ROUTE OPTIONS EXACERBATING THE COST OF LIVING" and "ENERGY PRICE SURGE: EMBARGOES ON RUSSIAN OIL/GAS LEADS TO A SHORTAGE AND ULTIMATELY PRICE SURGE". The second macro level connection is "IMPACT ON UKRAINE IS DEVASTATING: 20% OF TERRITORY CONQUERED BY RUSSIA AND MANY CITIES ARE DESTROYED" with "UKRAINE: UNABLE TO PRODUCE AND EXPORT CROPS, MILLIONS DISPLACED, THOUSANDS KILLED, AND MAJORITY LEFT UNEMPLOYED".

Each of the three generic variables introduced in Figure 2.1f leads into a blue parallelogram in Figure 2.1g: "ALLIES INCREASE SUPPORT TO UKRAINE (E.G., US SECURITY ASSISTANCE, POLAND AND GERMANY PROVIDE MILITARY VEHICLES, ETC.)". This

---

[6] For more details and in-depth analysis of the sanctions, see Bidder and Becker (2022).

point of convergence, in turn, connects with "JANUARY 2023: UKRAINIAN OFFICIALS TRAIN MILITARY WITH NEW WESTERN WEAPONS – RUSSIAN OFFENSIVE EXPECTED". This leads into the final variable in Figure 2.1h – the red octagon "GLOBALIZED WORLD FACES FAR REACHING CONSEQUENCES AS A RESULT OF THE ONGOING RUSSIAN AND UKRAINIAN CONFLICT".

Should the story just told in words, corresponding to a diagram, be taken as the final statement on the Russo-Ukrainian War? To do so would misunderstand the purpose of something like Figure 2.1. It is a starting, rather than finishing, point for analysis of an intense case of conflict – all the way up to interstate war. The diagram could be revised either to include possible important missing steps or delete things that might seem superfluous in the eyes of a critic. A new version of the figure also could include more steps taken before the initial, and after the terminal, variables. The key contribution of a systemist diagram such as Figure 2.1 is to complement the written word in a way that facilitates constructive dialogue about conflict, crisis, and war.

Figure 2.1 suggests other significant insights that bear mentioning before we proceed. The graphic includes various connections between internal and external processes. Foreign policy is influenced significantly by domestic factors and vice versa. At the same time, this book seeks to explain *international conflict*. Given that purpose, domestic factors naturally are included in the accounts provided, but occupy the role of independent or intervening, rather than dependent variables. All of that returns to the central purpose of the book as put forward in Chapter 1: an integrated approach to the study of conflict processes that brings together multiple levels of analysis.

IN FOCUS: THE SHIFTING FACE OF WAR

Conventional war is armed conflict in which the military forces of two or more states are used against each other, without the use of weapons of mass destruction, such as nuclear, biological, or chemical weapons.

Unconventional war involves armed conflict in which traditional battles between the organized militaries of the participants are less prominent (or avoided altogether). According to the US Department of Defense (2011: 490), it involves a range of military and paramilitary operations, normally of long duration, predominantly conducted through, with, or by indigenous or surrogate forces who are organized, trained, equipped, supported, and directed in varying degrees by an external source. It includes, but is not limited to, guerrilla warfare, subversion, sabotage, intelligence activities, and unconventional assisted recovery.

Asymmetric war pits two or more groups of very different military size or power against each other. To overcome the disadvantages stemming from this imbalance of power and technological superiority, the smaller or weaker participant often resorts to unconventional tactics rather than engage in traditional battlefield warfare.

Intrastate or Civil War

Civil war typically involves armed conflict between competing factions within a country or between an existing government and a competing group within that country over control of territory, resources, and/or the government. According to the Uppsala Data Program, civil wars that pit an existing government against a competing group are part of state-based war/conflicts, while those involving competing non-state factions or groups are part of non-state war/conflicts. Such wars come in various sizes and shapes, from expansive general wars, like the American Civil War of the 1860s, to more limited or unconventional conflicts, like those in Syria after 2011. As we discuss in the next chapter, civil war has increased since the end of the Cold War and is the most common "face of war" in the contemporary context. According to the Uppsala Conflict Data Project, 90% or more of the armed conflicts since 1989 have been intrastate conflicts.

Civil wars may also "internationalize", drawing in other states or groups outside the borders of the country in which the conflict originates. This may occur as the conflict or its consequences spill over the country's borders or if external parties become involved in the conflict. Good examples include the recent conflicts in Libya (2011, ongoing) and Syria (ongoing), which not only involved homegrown resistance to the dictators in each country (Colonel Muammar Gaddafi in Libya and President Bashar al-Assad in Syria) but soon attracted intervention by others. In Libya, US and NATO forces, along with limited support from other states in the region, intervened to help overthrow Gaddafi, and in Syria, Russia, the US, Iran, and others have engaged in the conflict.

FOR EXAMPLE: THE SYRIAN CIVIL WAR

In the wave of change known as the Arab Spring of 2011, long-standing regimes fell in Tunisia, Egypt, and Libya. However, the Bashar al-Assad regime in Syria managed to push back at its domestic challengers, prompting a civil war that has lasted more than a decade, with hundreds of thousands of dead and more than 13 million driven from their homes. By 2020, with Russian help, the Assad regime steadily defeated its challengers and reasserted its control over most of Syria.

When faced with domestic protests associated with the Arab Spring, both Syrian police and security forces turned on the protesters, but the protesters fought back, prompting harsher reprisals from the regime's defenders. Soon elements of the Syrian military who objected to killing their own citizens defected and created the Free Syrian Army to fight against the regime (Laub 2023). Other anti-Assad rebel groups also formed, often with the support of outsiders. The Islamic Front was supported by Saudi Arabia; the al-Nusra Front was an al-Qaeda-linked group; and the Syrian Democratic Forces comprised militias of Syrian Kurds, Turkmen, Assyrians, and Armenians, along with other Syrian Arabs. The group known as the Islamic State, the Islamic State in Iraq and Syria (ISIS), or the Islamic State in Iraq and the Levant (ISIL), or simply by its Arab initials Da'esh, sought to carve out an Islamic-ruled territory in Syria as well. Further, the United States provided technical support to some rebel groups seen as moderates in the conflict.

The Assad regime fought back, attacking Syrian rebels and rebel-held civilian areas. In violation of international law, the regime used chemical weapons and antipersonnel barrel bombs against civilian areas more than once. The regime had help from Iran, its al-Quds special operations forces, and its client Hezbollah forces from Lebanon, which waded into the war on the regime's side because of religious affinities between the Alawite Assad regime (an offshoot of Shi'a Islam) and the Shi'a-based Iran. Syrian Alawite militias joined in as well in defense of the regime, and Syrian Christians formed their own militias in support of the regime, as they feared an Islamic-themed regime in the future. Further, Russia intervened significantly in the conflict, supporting Assad's military activities and using its air force to pound rebel targets. Russia, a longtime military backer of the Assad regime, has both a naval base and an air base in Syria, along with hundreds of millions of dollars in commercial contracts with the Assad regime (Laub 2023).

The opposition forces are also fragmented by competing goals. Some simply want the Assad family and its entourage gone and a secular or democratic regime installed. Others want to create an Islamic regime (Laub 2023). Supporting the opposition forces, the United States has conducted operations and strikes on Syrian targets, including an attack on a Syrian air base in retaliation for chemical weapons attacks and wants the Assad regime gone. However, the US also wants the Islamic State exterminated. Neighboring Turkey also wants the Islamic State exterminated, but it would like to see Kurdish militias operating near the Turkish border to be eliminated as well, some of which are US allies. Indeed, Turkey aggressively intervened in northern Syria against the Kurds, one of the most effective groups opposing Assad. Iran wants the Islamic State defeated because it sees the group as a Saudi-backed agent, so it cooperates with the United States on that goal, but it pushes back when the US military targets Assad's forces. Russian air forces strike at the Islamic State, but they also strike at rebel forces that the US backs.

After 2018, with Islamic State forces largely defeated, the US sharply curtailed its activities in support of Syrian rebels, while Russia continued its support of the Assad regime. Turkey's intervention in the north in 2018–2019 severely weakened both the Islamic State and Kurdish opposition, and the US commenced withdrawal of most of its forces and activity. While about a third of Syria was still controlled by opposition forces, by 2023, active widespread fighting had ceased, with only sporadic violence in northwestern Syria (Yacoubian 2023).

CONFLICT, CRISIS, AND WAR

We now engage conflict, crisis, and war with each other to gain an overall sense of the ladder of escalation. Figure 2.2 provides one way of bringing these events together. The graphic returns to the ladder of escalation mentioned at the outset of this chapter. Obviously, from one look at it, no one would want a ladder like that! We discuss its features in turn, with the inherently wobbly world it depicts as the bottom line.

Consider the starting point, with a leader being aloof on the roof. No particular conflict is attracting attention. A leader either could initiate, or feel the need to cope with, a conflict started by someone else. Going down the ladder is risky, however. The rather forbidding ladder

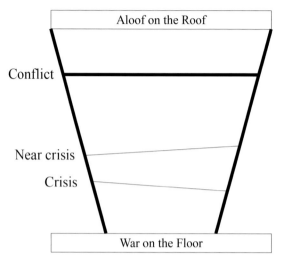

Figure 2.2   The ladder of escalation

is not one that anyone would buy, but instead is imposed by an international system of anarchy and self-help among states. Put simply, the world is dangerous, and each leader must cope with it. The ladder would be much more stable if turned upside down, but the wide top and narrow bottom show a world posing many challenges and possibilities for falling off – meaning escalation of conflict. The rung for conflict is thicker, at least somewhat horizontal-looking, and relatively far above the rungs below it. So being in conflict is not especially dangerous per se but does entail some risk.

What about sliding down from conflict into near crisis? This is a significant drop and, once there, the rung is inherently more dangerous to occupy because it is slanted. The near crisis rung also is much thinner than the one for conflict – it could be a lot easier to break through once coming downward. The rung for crisis also is thin and slanted – and very close to near crisis. Once all the way down to the crisis level, it is easier to imagine things getting worse. Ending up in war, which appears down on the floor, is a very realistic possibility in a world of anarchy.

ANARCHY, CONFLICT, AND COOPERATION

Anarchy is a multifaceted concept. On the surface, it would appear to be associated with disorder and a high potential for violence. Interesting to ponder, however, are the ideas of Taylor (1976) with regard to anarchy and *cooperation*. It is possible to cooperate under anarchy in a state of nature, but the presence of the state creates a tendency to depend upon it for order. If the state suddenly disappeared, natural possibilities for cooperation would no longer be present. Instead, as per intuition, some level of disorder and even violence could be expected to ensue. The exposition from Taylor (1976), which focuses on strategic interaction, brings out the range of possibilities that exist in anarchy as a concept.

SUMMING UP AND MOVING FORWARD

This chapter introduced conflict, crisis, and war as core concepts and issues in the analysis of world politics. International conflict is the most expansive on the list and includes events within which some disagreement is played out over one or more issues. Crisis and near crisis exist in close proximity to each other and may well be the crucial steps on the ladder of escalation. War is the most intense form of conflict and will happen without effective management, in turn, of conflict, near crisis, and crisis.

> **CONSIDER THIS: FROM CONFLICT TO CRISIS TO WAR?**
>
> Conflict between states, and between other significant actors in world politics, is pervasive. Most of these events do not escalate into crises, and even fewer into armed conflict. Thinking about our descriptions of these three events in world politics, and the examples we have offered to help illustrate them:
>
> *What conditions or factors do you think are important to understanding the nature of conflicts, and to explaining why some escalate to crisis or war, while (most) others do not?*

3
The evolution of conflict, crisis, and war

PROLOGUE

More than three decades ago, Political Scientist John Mueller (1990, ix) argued that war, which was "merely an idea" and "not something that is somehow required by the human condition or by the forces of history", has been in a century-long process of disappearing. As Mueller put it (1990: ix), "Conflicts of interest are inevitable and continue to persist within the developed world. But the notion that war should be used to resolve them has increasingly been discredited and abandoned." Moreover, while acknowledging that "war obviously continues to flourish elsewhere" outside of the developed world, "there are reasons … to believe that the developed world's aversion to war may eventually infect the rest of the world as well" (Mueller 1990: ix–x). This trend is "not because [war] has ceased to be possible or fascinating, but because peoples and leaders in the developed world – where war was once endemic – have increasingly found war to be disgusting, ridiculous, and unwise" (Mueller 1990: x). However, Mueller also warns that major war will never be impossible, even among countries of the developed world. Nevertheless, he concludes that "A policy of mindless, Panglossian complacency about major war would be a mistake, but the conditions of our remarkable times do suggest that a degree of wary optimism is justified" (Mueller 1990: xii).[1]

OVERVIEW

Obviously, the decades since Mueller made his argument have offered mixed returns. On one hand, the Cold War confrontation between US- and Soviet-led coalitions, which had defined world politics for decades, concluded without nuclear escalation at the end of the 1980s. Collapse of the unofficial empire centered around the USSR highlighted a wave of democratization around the world. Optimism reached such a high and even exaggerated level that some thought the world to be at the end of history – a permanent triumph of democracy and capitalism (Fukuyama 1992).

---

[1] Professor Pangloss is an excessively optimistic character from Voltaire, in his great satire entitled *Candide*.

However, conflicts, including violent ones, have persisted, and casualties from them have surged after long decades of decline. Events on September 11, 2001 (now known as 9/11), when al-Qaeda terrorists hijacked commercial airliners and used them to bring down the World Trade Center towers and damage other targets in the US, shook the optimistic beliefs reflected in Mueller's argument to their foundation as a new menace – Islamist fanaticism and violence – took center stage. The US and several of its allies went to war against Afghanistan, which had provided the home base for the al-Qaeda terrorists who carried out the 9/11 attacks. Soon after, the US and what it called the "coalition of the willing" waged a controversial war against Iraq, mistakenly believed to be involved with 9/11 and in the process of obtaining weapons of mass destruction. Both wars produced short-term military victories, understood in conventional terms, but also destabilized the countries in question over the long term. Civil wars in both Iraq and Afghanistan ultimately produced results desired neither by the US in particular nor the world community in general.

Yet, even so, war between states has declined, and between developed states it has indeed virtually disappeared. At the same time, intrastate or civil wars have increased significantly, including those that "internationalize" to involve participation by other states. The recent brutal war between Russia and Ukraine, both of whom occupy a gray area between developed and developing states, gives pause as well. So, too, does the horrendous set of events from the Gaza War of 2023. Taken all together, one central takeaway from Mueller's argument and the empirical record of conflict, crisis, and war since he advanced it seems clear: conflict, crisis, and war are persistent, but dynamic, with changing patterns in their nature, scope, participants, location, modes, and more.

This chapter unfolds in five additional sections. The second section provides an overview of the world of war. In the third through fifth sections, we provide an overview of the patterns and trends in conflict, crisis, and war over time. The sixth and final section offers some observations about the overall landscape these trends suggest and sets the stage for our examination of the challenges of modern war in Chapter 4.

IN FOCUS: SCIENTIFIC REALISM MEETS CONFLICT, CRISIS, AND WAR

Map 3.1 from the medieval era is typical of many such graphics from long ago. Beyond a certain distance from the coastline, nothing much could be said with confidence about how things looked or what creatures might be found there. Expressions such as "Here be Dragons" warned mariners of the potential dangers of the unknown in a fanciful way. This shows a common but harmful psychological mechanism at work – the need to "fill in the blanks" in some way when there is no real information to be had. Scientific realism guards against this tendency, which just as easily could creep into the processing of the unknown with regard to conflict, crisis, and war. From a scientific point of view in particular, patience is a virtue. A belief that more of the figurative "map" will be filled in over time is the best possible mind-set to carry into research.

Source: https://www.alamy.com/moskenstraumen-i-carta-marina-1539-olaus-magnus-9 07-moskenstraumen-image185866629.html?imageid=B084ACF3-6614-4F47-BF13-0569 0E591D2E&p=650648&pn=1&searchId=5c3d32ada3fec0735ea19bfc99169bb9&searcht ype=0:

Map 3.1   Here be dragons

A WORLD OF WAR

War of various kinds is a persistent feature of world politics over centuries. Its implications for the survival of states and its enormous costs in lives and treasure have combined to keep war at the center of attention for policymakers and for International Relations scholars seeking to explain it, predict it, prepare for it, and prevent it (e.g., Keohane 2013). Conflict and war have exacted massive costs in lives, material, wealth, and power from those states, groups, and individuals it has involved. According to Levy (1983a), from 1500 to 1975, there were 589 wars exacting some 142 million battle deaths. Four times as many of those deaths (80% of the total) occurred in the 20th century than in the four centuries leading up to it. Not surprisingly, technology is the basic explanation for the massive increase in the lethality of war (McNeill 1982). Along those lines, aerial bombardment and mechanized warfare on land and sea are just the most obvious developments.

Some estimates place global casualties from war at more than one billion and, when both direct and indirect casualties are included, perhaps as many as four billion (e.g., Hedges 2003; Beer 1974; Eckhardt 1991). For an overview of this cost of war, Figure 3.1 shows global deaths in conflicts from 1400–2013 from the research of Roser, Hasell, Herre, and Macdonald (2016). Figure 3.2 shows deaths resulting from conflict and war since 1989 from Malik, Obermeier, and Rustad (2022). Together, both graphics reveal the increasing deadliness of conflict and war over the centuries until about 1950, after which deaths decline until several years into the 21st century, when they accelerate. A system-level factor – Cold War stalemate around the world for the US- and Soviet-led coalitions – can be deployed to help explain some of the downward shift in the deadliness of conflict from 1950 until the new millennium. Confrontations between the evenly matched sides caused a great deal of worry about escalation to nuclear war, but less in the way of casualties than in previous times of full-fledged great power war.

Even the most optimistic observer would have to concede that conflict and war are persistent patterns of world politics (Braumoeller 2019; Mueller 1990). Most conflicts in world politics are resolved without resorting to violence, and when one considers all the many pairs of states that might engage in war, and the many states within whose borders armed strife might occur, war is, in fact, relatively rare, as Poast (2023) and as others (e.g., King and Zeng 2001) have pointed out.

However, as Keegan (2011) argued in *A History of Warfare*, it is a universal phenomenon crossing space and time. By some accounts (e.g., Levy 1983a; Levy and Morgan 1984; Braumoeller 2019), close to 15,000 violent clashes between different groups have occurred over recorded history, with about 600 significant wars taking place since the year 1500. Indeed, using Correlates of War (COW) data, political scientist Paul Poast recently calculated the period 1816–2020 has perfect correlation between years and occurrences of war: at least one war of some kind occurred in every year of the period (Poast 2023). Nevertheless, the participants, locations, types, features, and practices of those wars have varied considerably over time. Moreover, as we just noted, despite its persistence, war is also a relatively rare event.

Recall from Chapter 1 the commitment to analytic eclecticism (Sil and Katzenstein 2010), an approach that is open to combining factors from across theoretical frameworks in order to achieve the best possible explanation. In this chapter, we carry out our analysis of trends and patterns in the spirit of analytic eclecticism. We reference multiple theories along the way, but also keep an eye on maintaining a logically consistent approach toward the explanation of conflict, crisis, and war. Put differently, we access a wide range of ideas to account for what is observed, but try to avoid drifting into self-contradiction.

TRENDS AND PATTERNS IN CONFLICT

As discussed in Chapter 2, we take an inclusive, encompassing view of conflict and define it as "any interaction delimited in time and space, involving two or more international entities (whether states or transnational actors) which possess non-identical preference orderings over two or more sets of alternative choices" (James 1988: 5). This definition treats conflict as an event and allows for a broad range of participants – both states and non-states – and noting "mixed motives" provides for the possibility that adversaries may engage in cooperation and have agreement in some areas even while in conflict. For example, Germany and France objected strenuously to US involvement in the war in Iraq, but maintained allied status in NATO and other forms of collaboration throughout that period and beyond.

As a struggle between clashing interests among the participants in world politics, conflict is pervasive. Indeed, events data compilations such as Conflict and Peace Data Bank (COPDAB) and World Event Interaction Survey (WEIS) collect world politics events and classify them in cooperative and/or conflictual terms – even offering scales (COPDAB) that can represent

CONFLICT, CRISIS, AND WAR IN WORLD POLITICS

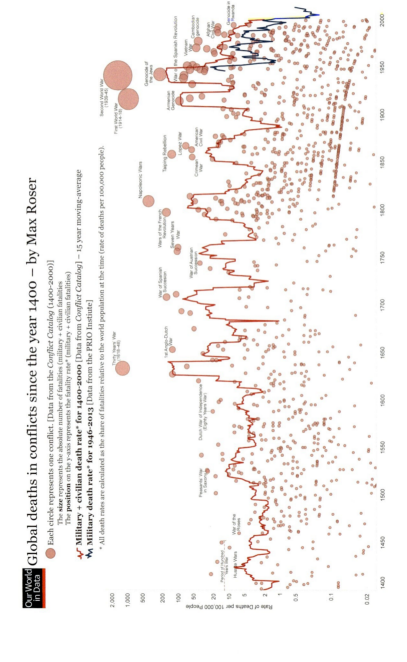

Figure 3.1 Global deaths in conflicts, 1400–2013

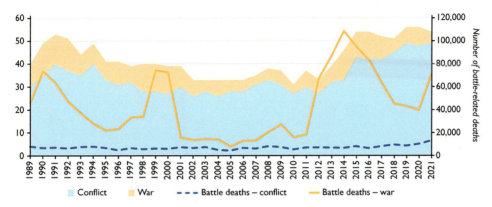

Figure 3.2 Death from conflict and war, 1989–2021

a cooperation-conflict dimension over time. As Goldstein (1992) discusses, the 61 different event categories of WEIS data represent a challenge to efforts to collapse them into a single cooperation-conflict dimension. However, both events datasets are useful in identifying conflict (and cooperation) between pairs of states and a general takeaway from them reinforces the pervasiveness of conflict across the participants in world politics.

What about conflict in a more general sense, especially beneath the level of armed violence? Globalization affects everyone and everything – from individuals all the way up to supranational organizations (Hebron and Stack 2016). Consider, for instance, the Brexit phenomenon. Against expectations beforehand, a referendum in the United Kingdom resulted in approval to leave the EU, a process completed in January 2020. Concerns about the impact of globalization on British identity and ability to act independently – fueled by underlying populist skepticism about globalization – mobilized opinion against staying in the EU. Populism, with its anti-elitist mind-set, can account for any number of conflicts related to supranational organizations and their effects on sovereignty. Opposition in the US to both the UN in particular and trade agreements in general is at a much higher level than in the past, with at least some of this politicization being traced to the rise of populism.

Conflicts that can or do involve the use of force are especially important to both the study of world politics and our focus. The Militarized Interstate Dispute (MID) dataset (Maoz, Johnson, Kaplan, Ogunkoya, and Shreve 2019), now in its 5.0 iteration, captures international disputes from 1816–2014 and classifies them (among other things) into five hostility levels, themselves based on 21 different, rank-ordered kinds of actions during disputes: (1) No militarized action; (2) Threat to use force; (3) Display of force; (4) Use of force; (5) War. According to MIDs data, such conflicts occur over time as shown in Figure 3.3. Since 1992 (through 2014), MIDs data identify 667 distinct disputes, only five of which reached the level of "war" (hostility level 5). The vast majority of these conflicts, however, involved displays or uses of force (levels 3 and 4). Note that many MIDs involve the same participants across multiple events, an observation that leads into discussion of rivalries.

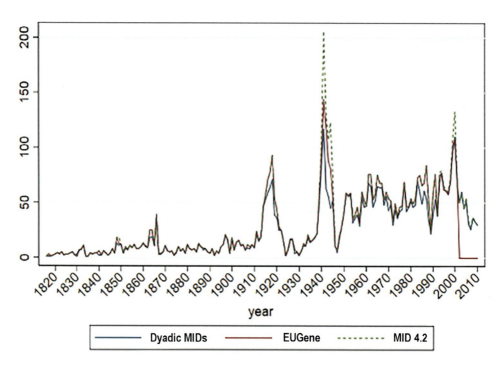

Figure 3.3 MID dyads by year and dataset

Rivalries in world politics have been identified in two fundamentally different ways. One approach is event-based, with the other focusing more on how states perceive each other in strategic terms. From the event-centered point of view, rivalry is "fundamentally about conflicting preferences or goals over some tangible or intangible good(s)" (Diehl and Goertz 2012: 84). Four dimensions combine to identify a rivalry.[2] The first, spatial consistency, focuses on the number and character of actors involved. The standard form for a rivalry to take is an interstate dyad. Duration is the second dimension. Rivalries can be categorized along this second dimension as either long or short term, allowing for some minimal period to ensure face validity. The third dimension of rivalry is behavioral; these interactions are a subset of what takes place between a pair of states in an overall sense and the key trait is militarization. Observed or latent threats with potential to be militarized are essential to concept formation. Standard operationalization of events in a rivalry is through MIDs. Fourth, and finally, conflicts within a rivalry are linked to each other. Path dependence and expectations about the future converge to condition foreign policy decision-making, which reinforces the potential for future strife.

Working within the event-based approach, Diehl and Goertz (2012: 86) implement the Klein, Goertz, and Diehl (2006) operational definition of a rivalry: "a sequence of at least three militarized interstate disputes (MIDs) between the same pair of states in temporal proximity to one another but occurring over an extended period of time (usually over ten years) so as not

---

[2] The rest of this paragraph is based primarily on Diehl and Goertz (2012: 84–85).

to be merely fleeting competitions". As a result, Diehl and Goertz (2012: 86, 105–108) identify 290 rivalries from 1816 to 2001. And how do these events arise? Valeriano (2012) offers a compelling treatment of origins. Key stimulants for rivalry include alliance formation, military buildups, territorial disagreements, and major powers (Valeriano 2012: 80). The preceding factors, moreover, also are significant in sustaining rivalries.[3]

FOR EXAMPLE: INDIA, PAKISTAN, AND THE AYODHYA MOSQUE DESTRUCTION[4]

Pakistan and India have sustained one of the most intense rivalries in the world. Its origins go back to Indian achievement of independence from the British Empire, and the immediate departure of Pakistan, in 1947. The protracted conflict, as the following case summary of a near crisis reveals, includes both material and ideational elements, and is unlikely to be resolved any time soon due to its complexity and legacy of violence.

For three centuries, Muslims and Hindus in India have been in a dispute over the Babri Masjid 16th-century mosque in Ayodhya, a city located in the North Indian state of Uttar Pradesh. Hindus claimed that the holy site, which they call Ram Janmabhoomi, stands at the birthplace of the Hindu deity Ram. Muslims say the claim is spurious and lacks historical evidence. In the mid-1900s, fearing an outbreak of violence between Muslims and Hindus, the government ordered the mosque be locked and denied entry to both groups. After demands from Hindus, the government opened the site in 1986, but prohibited the entry of Muslims. However, the Hindus' ultimate goal was to destroy the mosque and rebuild the Ram temple which had been in place before the mosque's construction in 1528. After winning a majority in the state assembly, the Bharatiya Janata Party (BJP) announced that they would demolish the mosque on December 6, 1992.

On December 6, 1992, thousands of Hindu revivalists destroyed the Babri Masjid mosque, which triggered a near crisis for Pakistan. Four Hindus were killed and falling debris injured at least 100 more. The incident prompted sectarian strife and riots throughout India and in the neighboring countries of Pakistan and Bangladesh. Both countries criticized India for failing to protect Muslims. On December 8, the Indian government condemned the demolition and sent riot police to expel Hindus from the site. On the same day, Pakistan's prime minister, Nawaz Sharif, called for a national strike to protest the mosque demolition. Muslim demonstrators in Pakistan damaged and destroyed dozens of Hindu temples, and nine Pakistanis were killed in the rioting. In Dhaka, Bangladesh, protesters surrounded the Indian Embassy, with hundreds of people reported injured. Meanwhile, violence continued in India, causing hundreds of deaths.

The Pakistani government filed a formal protest to the Indian government through the Indian ambassador in Islamabad. The Pakistani government also appealed to the United Nations and the Organization of the Islamic Conference (OIC). The OIC accused the Indian government of allowing Hindu extremists to demolish the Babri mosque and demanded

---

[3] The factors enumerated in this context are well established in the steps-to-war model from Senese and Vasquez (2008).

[4] The follow summary is based on the description of case 710 from the Near Crisis Project.

that it punish the culprits. Many other Islamic countries denounced the desecration of the mosque and sent protest notes in support of the OIC's condemnation. On December 16, India acquiesced to the demands and set up a commission to investigate the destruction of the mosque, which would eventually find members of India's BJP responsible for the mosque destruction 16 years later. This move decreased state tensions and signaled the end of the near crisis. However, the dispute surrounding the mosque continued for years after, and several groups battled for control over the mosque in the Indian courts. In 2019, the Indian Supreme Court ruled that the land belonged solely to the Indian government. In 2020, Indian Prime Minister Modi initiated the construction of a Hindu temple honoring Lord Ram in place of the mosque.

While this case did not escalate further, it serves as a reminder that the rivalry between India and Pakistan presents an ongoing danger to world peace. At any time, a near crisis could stimulate a pathway through crisis and up to war.

A reliance on event-based conceptualization of rivalry may preclude relationships that can be considered rivalries if that relationship does not include a sufficient number of MIDs (Thompson and Dreyer 2011: 4). Thus, a rivalry may be *attitudinal* in nature to take a different approach. In the attitudinal approach, rivalry can be conceptualized in ideational as well as material terms. "Strategic rivalries", as defined by Thompson (2020: 40), "are interstate relationships in which the parties see their adversaries as competitive but also threatening enemies". With an emphasis on perceptions rather than events, 128 rivalries are identified from 1816 onward (Thompson 2016). Note that the ideational definition is significantly more restrictive; 128 rivalries are designated, in comparison to 290 from the event-based approach over approximately the same amount of time.

One aspect of prior work that is of particular interest here concerns the insight that interstate rivalry may be an effective *substitute* for war outside of the developed world (Thies 2004). For a developing state, Thies (2004) infers, engagement in one or more rivalries can have salutary effects on state extraction. A potentially threatening rival provides the rationale for extending the state apparatus, which includes a military infrastructure that can be used to deter the public from protest or even rebellion. In other words, personnel and weapons acquired ostensibly for external security can be used just as easily to achieve internal ends.[5]

This finding is important to the cases under study because long-term, militarized rivalries can impact perniciously on the home front as well. Rivalries for developing states also have the potential to generate proxy conflicts that do not necessarily entail a MID involving the principal antagonists. Interstate conflicts may even be contrived to justify militarization and ultimately maintenance of a garrison state (Friedberg 2000; Lasswell 1941). At least some of this strife, in addition, inherently is more complex and challenging because it can include ideational as well as material elements (Rubin 2014).

Another way to look at conflicts, specifically in the post-World War II era, comes from the Peace Research Institute of Oslo (PRIO). The PRIO data includes interstate strife as well as conflict that involves states with non-state actors. Focusing on conflicts that involve 25 or

---

[5] A few exceptions, such as weapons of mass destruction, do exist.

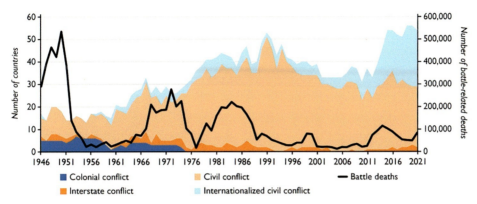

Figure 3.4   Global, state-based conflict trends, 1946–2021

more battle-related deaths, this data show the post-World War II trends in colonial, interstate, civil, and internationalized civil conflicts from 1946–2021, as seen in Figure 3.4. The data show a pattern of increasing overall conflict (both in number of participants and in battle deaths), with 1970, 1989, and 2011 as key points of increase. As we discuss below, conflicts are increasingly civil and/or internationalized civil conflicts since at least the end of the Cold War in 1989.

> **IN FOCUS: INTERNATIONALIZED CIVIL WARS**
>
> A major trend in armed conflict over the past several decades has been the increase in internationalized civil wars in which actors from outside the state of the conflict play a significant role. According to Jenne and Popovic (2017: 1), this role may be to instigate, prolong, or exacerbate the conflict, and the Peace Research Institute Oslo (PRIO) and Uppsala Conflict Data Program (UCDP) stress that such foreign actors may be states and non-state actors who intervene in one way or another in a civil conflict. Such conflicts are particularly troublesome in world politics. As Jenne and Popovic (2017) summarize, they tend to be longer, bloodier, and far more difficult to resolve or end than other civil wars. This is chiefly because the number of veto players – actors who can obstruct an agreement to end the conflict – expands significantly from domestic players factions to the foreign actors involved.

Figure 3.5 shows the pattern of the last 30 years in non-state conflicts, based on PRIO data. According to Malik, Obermeier, and Rustad (2022: 22), non-state conflict is

> the use of armed force between organized groups, neither of which is the government of a state, resulting in at least 25 battle-related deaths per year. Organized groups come in multiple forms: (i) formally organized groups are defined as any non-governmental group of people who have announced a name for their group and are using armed force against another similarly formally organized group, (ii) informally organized groups refers to any group without an announced name, but which uses armed force against another similarly organized group, and (iii) informally organized identity groups are defined as groups which have a common identity along religious, ethnic, national, tribal or clan lines. This category

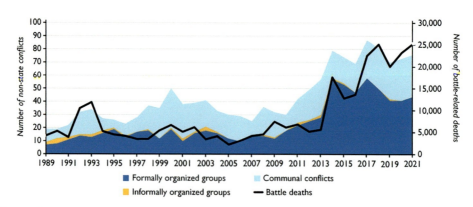

Figure 3.5 Non-state conflicts, 1989–2021

includes conflicts defined as communal, where incompatibilities are based on communal identity.

Here again the trend is toward increase, fueled largely by Islamic State violence beginning in 2011.

One last pass at the patterns of armed conflict since 1946 shows its regional distribution and variation, as seen in Figure 3.6. Viewed in this fashion, the increase in conflict over the time period is geographically concentrated, with Africa and the Middle East seeing the greatest increase. According to Malik, Obermeier, and Rustad (2022: 18), Africa:

> experienced the highest number of unique state-based conflicts (105) during the period 1946–2021, followed by Asia (82), the Middle East (41), Europe (38) and the Americas (27). [since 2010], the number of conflicts in Africa have nearly doubled, from 15 in 2011 to 25 in 2021…. The Americas is the only region to experience a decrease in the absolute number of conflicts over the past ten years, from 2 conflicts to 1.

The contrast between Africa on one hand and the Americas on the other can be explained in a straightforward way in the language of power politics. Based on extensive qualitative and quantitative research, Kisangani and Pickering (2021) demonstrate the extraordinary degree to which Africa is penetrated by outside military interventions. These actions have destabilized border regions and even led to the overthrow of governments, with very high costs experienced by the people of Africa along the way (Kisangani and Pickering 2021). The Western Hemisphere, by contrast, experiences very little intervention because of the hegemonic position of the US. From the standpoint of Power Transition Theory (PTT), it exhibits the pattern of a null case because any effective challenge to the US from within the region is beyond imagination for many years to come (James and Hristoulas 2020).

What can be said, in an overall sense, about patterns of conflict? Multiple data sources confirm that conflict varies over time in terms of amount, actors, and location. The proportion of non-state actors involved in conflict, along with the developing world as a location, is on the

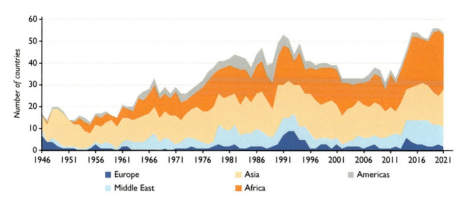

Figure 3.6 Armed conflict by region, 1946–2021

rise. Notable as well are trends that last in some instances for a very long time. Rivalry plays an important role in sustaining conflict throughout the global system.

CRISIS

As we discussed in the previous chapter, the gold standard for data on international crises is the International Crisis Behavior Project (ICB), which defines an international crisis as: "(1) a change in type and/or an increase in intensity of disruptive, that is, hostile verbal or physical, interactions between two or more states, with a heightened probability of military hostilities; that, in turn, (2) destabilizes their relationship and challenges the structure of an international system – global, dominant, or subsystem" (Brecher and Wilkenfeld 1997: 4–5). As of 2017, the ICB Project has identified 487 international crises involving 1,078 crisis actors and a broad range of military-security, political-diplomatic, economic-developmental, and cultural-status issues around the world since 1918 (Brecher, Wilkenfeld, Beardsley, James and Quinn 2023).

Figure 3.7 presents ICB data on the frequency of crises by year since 1918. The obvious fluctuations notwithstanding (e.g., steep drop-offs in frequency in 1920, 1945, and 1965), Figure 3.7 shows a trend upward in crisis occurrence through 1980, followed by a steep downward trend after 1980 and, especially, after 1989. Mediated crises, also shown in Figure 3.7, step up in frequency after 1960, and then step down again after 1990. These patterns make sense in light of the politics of Soviet–American rivalry and the logic of power transition. Crises accumulated under Cold War conditions – confrontations took place between the US and USSR around the globe as client states probed each other for weakness. The danger of World War III came to a peak during the era of approximate equality for the superpower, as PTT would anticipate, but did not transition into a Soviet-led international system. Instead, the US survived the challenge from the USSR and watched its rival go into steady decline (Shifrinson 2018).

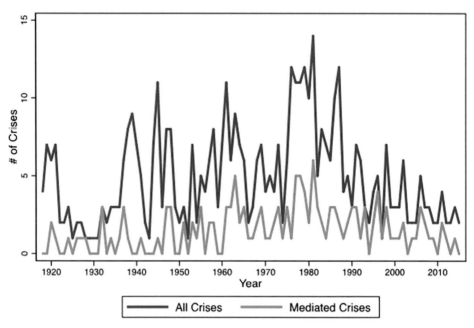

Figure 3.7 International crises, 1918–2017

FOR EXAMPLE: RECENT INTERNATIONAL CRISES

Recent examples of crises in the ICB data from 2017 include the following:

- Serbian Train Incident: As part of the conflict over Kosovo's sovereignty, Kosovo and Serbia experienced a crisis triggered by the dispatch of a Serbian train to Kosovo that displayed provocative Serbian images and slogans such as "Kosovo is Serbia", averted only when the Serbian prime minister ordered the train to be halted (http://www.icb.umd.edu/dataviewer/?crisno=484).
- Shrine Lal Shahbaz Attack: As part of the long-standing conflict between Afghanistan and Pakistan, a crisis occurred when a suicide bomber attacked the Lal Shahbaz shrine in Sehwan Sharif, Pakistan in February 2017, resulting in more than 70 dead. Pakistan blamed Afghanistan for harboring terrorists and failing to control its border region, and the crisis escalated with Pakistani shelling of alleged terrorist sites in Afghanistan and increased border security operations, before a ceasefire ended the crisis in May (http://www.icb.umd.edu/dataviewer/?crisno=485).
- Syria Chemical Weapons II: In April 2017, the US, Russia, and Syria experienced a crisis when the Syrian regime deployed chemical weapons in an attack against its civil war opponents, prompting US cruise missile strikes against Syria, and increased tensions between the US and Russia (http://www.icb.umd.edu/dataviewer/?crisno=486).

- North Korea Nuclear VII: As part of a lengthy series of crisis involving North Korea's pursuit of nuclear weapons and missiles, two North Korean tests of a new intercontinental ballistic missile (ICBM) in July 2017 prompted a lengthy crisis involving North Korea, the US, Japan, and South Korea that lasted until the summer of 2018. In addition to increased tension and a series of threats, the crisis also included expanded military exercises by South Korea and the US, additional missile tests by North Korea (one of which was directly over Japan), and ended with meetings between North and South Korea in April 2018 and the US and North Korea in June 2018, both of which produced joint declarations (http://www.icb.umd.edu/dataviewer/?crisno=487).

These cases are sufficient to bring out some of the most important characteristics of crises in world politics.

Crisis is a global phenomenon. Locations range from Europe, the traditional center of world politics, through to the Korean peninsula and beyond. Non-state actors, most notably terrorists, play significant roles in some cases. Analogous to the concept of rivalry with regard to MIDs is the concept of protracted conflict vis-à-vis international crises. A protracted conflict reflects deep-seated, often identity-related disagreements that play out in a complex way and entail connections to domestic politics and sporadic outbursts of violence (Azar 1990). Note that a case number, such as "VII" for the crisis involving North Korean pursuit of nuclear weapons, indicates the presence of protracted conflict, while other events may stand more on their own.

Data on near crises is being assembled at this time of writing and will match the time frame of the ICB Project: from the conclusion of World War I onward. Near crises come in two varieties. One type is proximate to an international crisis – leading either in or out of a case. The other type is displaced in time from an international crisis. Comparison of the two varieties is expected to provide insight about how international crises begin and end – a key subject area within the study of escalation processes. The data are incomplete at present, so it is not possible to provide graphics that show the distribution of near crises over time and by location.

WAR

Not surprisingly, the nature of war has evolved over time. One way of illustrating some of the changes is to think about the depiction of warfare in films. It is a simple matter to imagine a list of films that depict the shifts from the traditional battlefields of several centuries ago to the more modern clashes on the battlefields of World Wars I and II and on to the complicated military clashes between less-developed indigenous forces and modern armies and the often highly ambiguous contexts of current armed struggles. Consider, as just one point of comparison, *They Shall Not Grow Old* (2018) and *Zero Dark Thirty* (2012). The former is a documentary that depicts the grim life of the trenches in World War I – conventional battlefronts that moved back and forth over short distances but with deadly effect. State-of-the-art technology is used to restore the video to a level of quality that makes the viewer feel as if events are happening right now. The latter movie depicts the long hunt by the US that resulted in the

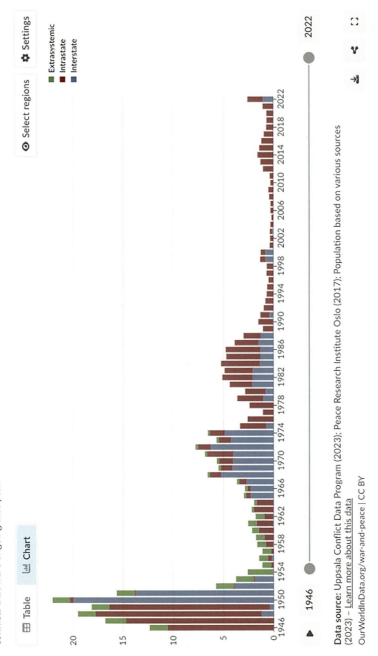

Figure 3.8 Death rates in state-based conflict, 1946–2021

THE EVOLUTION OF CONFLICT, CRISIS, AND WAR

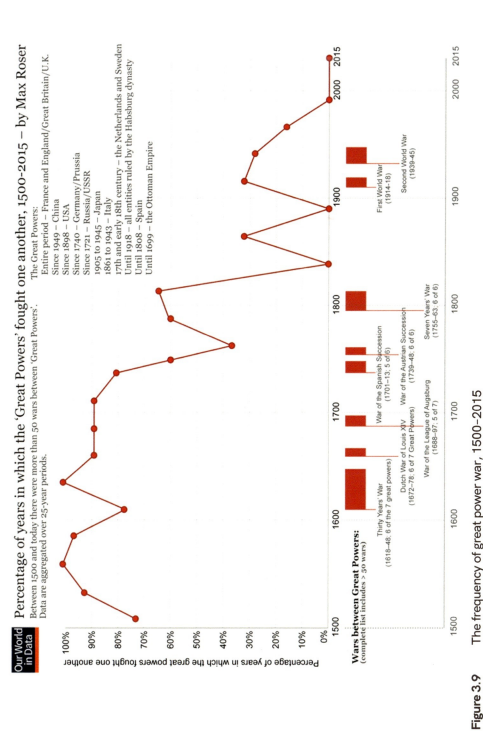

Figure 3.9 The frequency of great power war, 1500–2015

killing of Osama bin Laden, leader of al-Qaeda and the public face of the 9/11 attacks. Both films depict violence, but their many differences reveal the evolution of warfare away from straightforward battle fronts to more ambiguous and even confusing engagements.

Earlier in this chapter, we discussed trends in war's nature – specifically its deadliness. Returning to Figures 3.1 and 3.2. it is apparent that deaths from war – especially state-based war, to use PRIO's terminology – have declined since World War II, even though an uptick has occurred in the past 5–10 years. Figure 3.8 presents another view into that trend from Roser, Hasell, Herre, and Macdonald (2016). Even tracking the four peaks evident in Figure 3.8, corresponding with the Korean War (1950), the Vietnam War (1970 or so), the Iran–Iraq and Afghanistan wars (1980 or so), and the conflicts in Syria, Iraq, and Afghanistan after 2010, the downward trend is clear. Recall too that Figure 3.5 suggests that death from conflicts that are non-state-based have also increased over the past decade. Indeed, Malik, Obermeier, and Rustad (2022, 2016) note that this trend largely accounts for the fact that the decline in the frequency of state-based wars, which have historically accounted for the lion's share of battle-related deaths, has not been accompanied by a decrease in such deaths, which have instead risen.

It helps to understand some of these trends to recognize that the participants of war have changed significantly over time as well. One such change is apparent from Figure 3.9, which shows the dramatic decline in "great power" war over the past six centuries. As that figure suggests, such "major war", surely what Mueller (1990) was targeting in his analysis with which we opened this chapter, has all but disappeared. Indeed, one might suggest that, from the *most likely* participants in war before 1945, great powers are now the *least likely*. One possible explanation resides in technological change, specifically referring to the spread of nuclear weapons (Waltz 1990). Rather than direct warfare, the observed pattern is the fighting of proxy conflicts by client states of the great powers. And note, in particular, that the long-feared World War III between the Soviet- and US-led factions never did materialize.

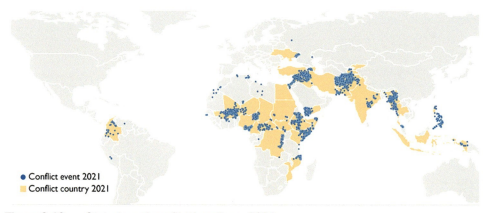

Figure 3.10 State-based conflict locations, 2021

As war has become more limited in recent decades, its location has also evolved. Reviewing Figure 3.6, it is apparent that war is largely and increasingly centered in locations outside Europe and the Americas. Indeed, since World War II, war has predominately been located in an arc across Central and South America, Africa, the Middle East, and South/Southeast Asia. For example, PRIO data on state-based conflicts in 2021are depicted in Figure 3.10. The vast majority of conflict since World War II had been in or between states of the developing world, or between one or more developed states and states or groups in the developing world.

As Figure 3.11 indicates, the same trend in geographic location is evident in non-state strife since 1989 as well. Conflict has shifted away from Europe, which existed for decades as a location of stalemate between the Soviet Union and the US.

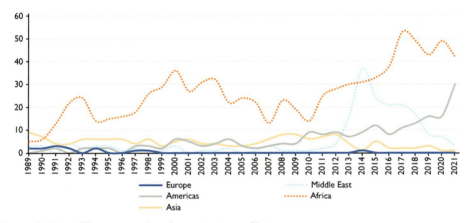

Figure 3.11 The geography of non-state conflicts

Finally, reviewing Figure 3.4, the evolution of the nature of war is also evident, especially in combination with other figures in this chapter. Over time, and especially since 1989, war has become increasingly internal, as civil war has become the most common form of warfare. Indeed, Figure 3.4 shows the growth of civil and internationalized civil wars and the decline – almost disappearance – of interstate and extra-systemic (e.g., colonial) wars. According to the Uppsala Conflict Data Project, 90% or more of the armed conflicts since 1989 have been intrastate conflicts. Even with the current, ongoing wars between Ukraine and Russia, and Israel and Gaza, which began in 2022 and 2023, respectively, in no period of history since the emergence of the state system in the 17th century has the difference between these two types of conflict been so dramatic.

IN FOCUS: CLIMATE CHANGE AND CONFLICT IN THE AFRICAN SAHEL

One of the great challenges facing the global community is climate change. With a focus on the African Sahel states, Raleigh (2010) focuses on the interconnectedness of political marginalization, climate change, and conflict. Figure 3.12 depicts the analysis from Raleigh (2010). The State is the system, with the International System as its environment.

> Within the State, the upper and lower levels correspond, respectively, to government and society. Note that the systemist graphic in this case invites elaboration because it has yet to incorporate connections back and forth between the State and International System.
>
> *Expand the argument in the systemist figure, notably to include linkages back and forth between the International System and the State.*

A final trend in conflict that is worth noting is a shift from conventional to unconventional war over the last half of the 20th century and early 21st century. Although unconventional war is related to civil and extra-state war, its distinguishing characteristics involve participants, tactics, and weaponry. Hence, this shift has been illustrated perhaps most dramatically in the rise of terrorism and the images of commercial airliners crashing into buildings in New York City and Washington, DC, on September 11, 2001; the train bombings in Madrid, Spain, in 2004; the sequence of attacks against tourists and civilians in Mumbai, India, in 2008; and the terrorist strikes in France, Belgium, and the United Kingdom in 2016–2017.

In the now-famous 19th-century study *On War*, Carl von Clausewitz depicted war as a state-centered concept with specific distinctions between governments, military forces, and populations. In this conception, as von Clausewitz wrote, war was "the continuation of politics by other means" and fundamentally tied to the policies and interests of states. Increasingly since 1945, however, armed struggle has involved non-state actors and has blurred, ignored, or rendered irrelevant the distinctions between government, military forces, and population. Weaponry increasingly involves more than typical military arsenals. The civil wars, insurgencies, and terrorism of the post-1945 period are quite different: much more unconventional, involving irregular forces and non-state actors that pose significant challenges because of their nature (see "In Focus: Fourth-Generation War").

IN FOCUS: FOURTH-GENERATION WAR

First used in the 1980s by the US Department of Defense, the term fourth-generation war blurs the distinctions between state and non-state participants, war and politics, combatants and noncombatants (civilians), and battlefields and non-battlefields (see Terriff, Karp, and Karp 2008). At the core of the idea is the decline of the nation-state's monopoly on the means and uses of force, with non-state actors such as terrorists, insurgents, and guerrilla armies increasingly engaged in more unconventional warfare. Fourth-generation warfare is also often highly asymmetric, usually with weaker, non-state participants relying on strategies and tactics that target civilians, nonmilitary infrastructure, and other more vulnerable targets to avoid direct battlefield combat with a state's military forces. In addition, fourth-generation war can involve a wide variety of mostly nonmilitary tactics, including cyberwar and internet trolling, propaganda, misinformation and disinformation, and other actions.

In the current context, cyberwarfare is one of the most important and challenging aspects of unconventional warfare. In 2010, as Iran pursued its covert nuclear weapons program, its facilities, especially the Natanz uranium enrichment plant, began experiencing widespread

THE EVOLUTION OF CONFLICT, CRISIS, AND WAR

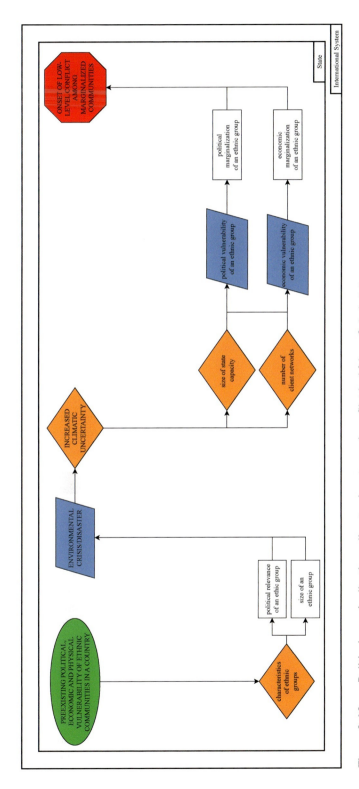

Figure 3.12 Political marginalization, climate change, and conflict in African Sahel states

and unusual failures in the centrifuges used to enrich uranium for weapons development. Not long after, other computer networks in Iran began experiencing strange patterns of failure and unexplained shutdowns. Soon, signs of malicious files began to appear on computers around the world. Ultimately, these problems were attributed to a computer worm called Stuxnet, developed by the US and Israel as apparently the world's first digital weapon and unleashed against the Iranian industrial targets to disrupt and impede the country's nuclear weapons program. Taking advantage of a flaw in the Windows operating system, the worm penetrated computers controlling the operations and caused Iranian centrifuges to malfunction. Unfortunately, Stuxnet soon spread outside its targeted range and was identified on many computer networks around the world, although its harmful operations were narrowly targeted to a precise set of computer software and hardware configurations, and it did little damage outside its Iranian targets (see Zetter 2014).

In the high-speed, interconnected world of the digital age, this new form of warfare has emerged. Cyberwarfare is the attempt by one state or nation to cause disruption, discord, damage, death, or destruction by using computers and other digital devices to carry out digital attacks on the computer systems of another. Hacking and hackers are at the core of cyberwarfare, but the concept refers to the actions of states/nations, or directed by states/nations, rather than those in which individual hackers or criminal groups might engage. However, non-state actors such as terrorist groups may also engage in cyberwarfare.

Most experts regard cyberwarfare as a highly likely component of future conflicts, just as it has indeed been a significant element of the current war between Ukraine and Russia. Such attacks may be directed at government information systems, military and industrial targets, commercial networks and institutions, universities, and hospitals – which are especially vulnerable – and infrastructure such as power/electricity, water, and gas. The weapons of cyberwarfare include such things as phishing attacks and ransomware designed to gain access to computer hardware, accounts, and information systems; viruses and malware designed to corrupt and control computer systems and networks; denial-of-service attacks that make computers or networks unavailable to users; and use of what is known as "zero-day" vulnerabilities or exploits, which are bugs or flaws in software (such as Microsoft's Windows operating system or Office software or Adobe's Flash software) that are unknown to the manufacturer and/or public and are thus open for exploitation because they have not been patched. The intelligence agencies of many countries amass an evolving suite of such weapons and employ them in what seems to be constantly evolving, adapting, and sophisticated ways.

As many as 30 to 60 countries are currently developing cyberwarfare capabilities, according to the US intelligence community. Leading players in the cyberwarfare arena include Russia, China, Iran, and North Korea, along with the US and its friends and allies, such as the UK and Israel. Interesting to ponder are the observations of Valeriano, Jensen, and Maness (2018), who point out that, at least so far, cyber operations have not produced concessions when carried out in isolation. Instead, cyber coercion tends to be more effective when included within an integrated strategy that includes components such as diplomacy and military threats (Valeriano, Jensen, and Maness 2018).

SUMMING UP AND MOVING FORWARD

Overall, the review of the patterns and trends in conflict, crisis, and war over time in this chapter suggests some salient shifts and evolution. Increasingly deadly through World War II, conflict has seen its death toll decline since then. Conflict, crisis, and war have, in many ways, become less centered on "great powers" and more limited, especially since World War II. Increasingly, the locations and participants are in the developing world, and the nature of war since the end of the Cold War at least, and perhaps since the end of World War II, has been increasingly intrastate: civil war, non-state war, and internationalized civil war make up the face of modern war. Conflict, crisis, and war have, therefore, becomes increasingly unconventional and, perhaps, asymmetric.

From the broadest viewpoint, the trends and patterns discussed in this chapter, and summarized in the preceding paragraph, suggest that we can distinguish between and among three, or perhaps four, general eras of warfare since the emergence of the state system in the 17th century (e.g., see Scott, Akbaba, Carter, and Drury 2024):

- The Era of Great Power War, 1648–1945
- The Era of Limited War, 1946–1989
- The Era of Civil War, 1989–2001
- The Era of Unconventional War, 2001–present

In the next chapter, we focus on the most recent years and discuss the challenges of strife in modern times.

> **CONSIDER THIS: MAKING SENSE OF THE EVOLUTION OF CONFLICT, CRISIS, AND WAR**
>
> In this chapter, we have presented a number of dynamics, trends, and patterns in the evolution of conflict, crisis, and war. Considering the evidence presented here:
>
> *What factors and explanations at the individual, state, and system levels of analysis do you think are most helpful in understanding the developments presented to you, and what linkages among them can you make to help make sense of the changes?*

4
The issues

PROLOGUE

Surprising many around the world, the people of the United Kingdom voted to leave the EU in 2016. After a lengthy process, the UK finally left the EU on January 31, 2020 in what became known as "Brexit". Critics of the "Leave" campaign had pointed out repeatedly that the departure likely would lead to economic losses in both the short and long term. Advocates of "Leave" tended to emphasize identity in that debate, arguing that the UK should get out in order to preserve its traditions and avoid becoming fully European.

Debate over Brexit brings out one of the most basic features of political issues. Conflict, along with crisis and war, can be the product of either material or ideational issues (or both) – and things are not always what they appear to be on the surface. Consider, for example, the recent finding from survey research that almost half the supporters of Brexit ("leave the EU") were higher-income British whose wealth likely made them less averse to risk, not lower-income voters commonly expected to support the move (Green and Pahontu 2021). This highly unexpected result, cast at the individual level of analysis, serves as a warning against taking the easy pathway in assessing how and why events occur in the world of conflict, crisis, and war.

OVERVIEW

What roles are played by issues in international conflict, crisis, and war? This chapter seeks a tentative answer to that multifaceted question. Toward that end, we again argue that analytic eclecticism (Sil and Katzenstein 2010) provides the most effective guidance. One reason is the wide range of issues that matter for conflict, crisis, and war. We draw on concepts taken from multiple paradigms, and notably across the previously referenced divide between the material and ideational worlds. Our analysis also crosses and connects the levels of analysis as well, consistent with our argument about the necessity of multilevel linkages and explanations for improved understanding and explanation. This inclusive approach is essential in the quest for knowledge and, per analytic eclecticism, lends itself to greater policy relevance.

This chapter proceeds in five additional sections. The second section focuses on what we know about issues in a general sense as related to conflict processes – an exercise in obtaining breadth of explanation. Sections three and four focus, respectively, on the issues of territory and religion in relation to conflict. Attention to each of these encompassing and important issues provides depth of explanation through a review of reproducible evidence. The fifth section conveys in some detail the insights from *War on Sacred Grounds* (Hassner 2009), a study at the intersection of religion and territory. We convey arguments from that work of scholarship and apply the systemist graphic approach to analyze it. Section six sums up this chapter and leads into Chapter 5, which focuses on systems and conflict.

ISSUES IN GENERAL

In the immediate decades following the horrors of World War II, ostensibly idealistic thinking fell by the wayside and classical realism came to dominate the field of International Relations (IR).[1] Belief in the flawed character of human nature – a will to dominance that guaranteed periodic warfare – resided at the foundation of classical realism, which focused on power politics among sovereign states (Morgenthau 1946). For such reasons, advocates of this approach argued that everything could be subsumed under power as the single issue of world affairs. Yet the historical record proved to be troubling on that point, with states going to war for reasons other than concern about "an impending hegemony or preponderance of power by their main rival" (Holsti 1991: 14). While realism continues to play a central role, its treatment of issues in world politics may be viewed as a starting point rather than a telling of the whole story about conflict, crisis, and war.

Dissatisfaction with classical realism, largely connected to its philosophical rather than scientific character, built steadily as technology advanced; most notably, computers made it possible to carry out rudimentary statistical analysis of increasingly large datasets by the middle of the 20th century. Criticism mounted, with *Power and Interdependence* (Keohane and Nye 1977) emerging as a key challenge to long-standing beliefs based on classical realism. The book notably argued for the importance of interdependence among states as a possible moderating factor vis-à-vis pervasive interstate conflict under anarchy. Pushing back at the core assumptions of realism, Keohane and Nye (1977) credibly introduced the possibility that power might be neither fully in the hands of states nor applicable in the same way from one situation to the next. All of that combined to open the door to the idea that multifaceted issues could be in play, with outcomes in world politics affected by context rather than uniformly reflecting the distribution of power among states.

Essential to movement forward along those lines, the classic work of Mansbach and Vasquez (1981: 28) introduced the idea of moving on "from the issue of power to the power of issues".[2] An innovative sense of how issues play out, based on dimension, type of stake, and the nature of stake proposals, stimulated theorizing well beyond the boundaries of power politics (Mansbach and Vasquez 1981: 57). Mansbach and Vasquez (1981: 59) then offer the resulting

---

[1] Realists successfully defined their liberal intellectual opponents as "idealists" who lacked a grasp of the fundamental aspects of power politics. For an overview of this debate and how it shaped subsequent developments in the field, see Ruane and James (2012: 43–53).

[2] For a compelling account of early efforts toward theorizing about issues, most notably the quest for a typology, see Mansbach and Vasquez (1981: 30–36).

definition: "*An issue consists of contention among actors over proposals for the disposition of stakes among them.*"[3] The stakes are of three kinds: (a) concrete – tangible and divisible; (b) symbolic – representing something of greater value; and (c) transcendent – entirely abstract and focused upon beliefs, prescriptions, or norms (Mansbach and Vasquez 1981: 61–62).

Issue dimensions and stakes combine to create expectations about processes and outcomes that ring true today. Issues with an actor dimension can be expected to produce more symbolic and transcendent stakes, while concrete stakes otherwise become more likely. Concrete versus symbolic and transcendent stakes have a greater likelihood of producing proposals that contain, respectively, relatively equal and unequal distributions of costs and benefits (Mansbach and Vasquez 1981: 66–67). See "For Example: Cod Wars and Cold Wars" for a comparison of two international crises to illustrate the effects of these different issue dimensions and stakes.[4]

FOR EXAMPLE: COD WARS AND COLD WARS[5]

On the night of May 14, 1973, Icelandic gunboats fired on British trawlers, triggering a crisis for Whitehall. On May 16, British fishers threatened to leave the disputed waters if protection could not be assured. London responded on May 19 by dispatching Royal Navy ships to Icelandic waters. This action triggered a crisis for Iceland. The following day, Iceland banned RAF aircraft from landing at the Keflavik NATO base, while protesting to the United Kingdom. Talks between the two prime ministers began on October 2. On November 13 the parliament of Iceland approved an agreement that set aside certain areas within the newly accepted 50-mile limit for British fishers, terminating the crisis for both actors.

Symbolic and even transcendent events greatly complicated the series of crises over Berlin during the Cold War. Consider the case of the Berlin Wall, one of the most prominent in the International Crisis Behavior (ICB) dataset. A crisis for the German Democratic Republic (GDR) and the USSR crystallized at the beginning of August 1961: by that time the flow of East German refugees to the West had reached an alarming level – 100,000 during the first half of the year, including 20,000 in June, which rose to 30,000 in July.

Under growing pressure from the East German leader, Walter Ulbricht, and the specter of an impending collapse of communist power in the GDR, Soviet Premier Khrushchev authorized Ulbricht to erect a wall around West Berlin. Implementation of this decision on August 13 was the major response to the crisis by the USSR and the GDR. This action, in turn, (a) triggered a crisis for France, the United Kingdom, Federal Republic of Germany (FRG), and the US; and (b) terminated the crisis for the GDR because the wall ended the flow of refugees to the West.

---

[3] Italics are in the original.

[4] The accounts that follow for respective cases are based primarily on the summaries in Brecher, Wilkenfeld, Beardsley, James, and Quinn (2023).

[5] Disputes over fishing rights in waters contiguous to Iceland also led to Cod War II, a crisis between Iceland and the United Kingdom that lasted from November 23, 1975 to June 1, 1976. Like Cod War I, this case concluded in an agreement rather than escalation. For details on both cases, see the summaries in Brecher, Wilkenfeld, Beardsley, James, and Quinn (2023).

> With a call on August 16 from West Berlin's Mayor Willy Brandt to the West for effective action, the FRG responded. The FRG legislature held an emergency session the next day. The US, the United Kingdom, and France responded on August 17 and 18 by strengthening the Berlin garrison – 1,500 US troops were rushed to the city. On August 22, GDR forces announced the establishment of a no-man's-land of 100 meters on each side of the Wall. West Berliners were warned to keep clear of that zone. Western forces began to patrol the area to the west while East German forces kept watch over their side. The crisis ended for France, the UK, and the FRG on October 17 when Khrushchev, at the Soviet 22nd Party Congress, withdrew his year-end deadline for the signing of a German peace treaty. For the two superpowers the crisis lingered on another 11 days. A brief but ominous confrontation between US and Soviet tanks from October 25 to October 28 at "Checkpoint Charlie", the crossing point between the US and the USSR sectors of Berlin, re-escalated the interbloc crisis. It was resolved by a tacit agreement between Kennedy and Khrushchev on October 28 for a parallel withdrawal of US and Soviet tanks from a potentially dangerous violent clash.

As the "For Example: Cod Wars and Cold Wars" box suggests, for the USSR and its client state, the GDR, the Cold War crisis over Berlin became nothing less than a struggle for survival of the GDR in the face of massive out-migration. The US and its allies, by contrast, perceived the situation through the lens of human rights; put simply, why should the GDR be permitted to force its citizens to stay there if they preferred living somewhere else? These symbolic and even transcendent stakes go a long way toward explaining why a case like this one became so complex and difficult to resolve, with great danger of escalation to war. By contrast, the dispute over fishing rights in the Cod War I example reached the level of a crisis for Iceland and the United Kingdom, but experienced a more rapid resolution primarily because the main issue had an overwhelmingly material character. Note also the difference along the actor dimension – for the Berlin Wall, the viability of the GDR had come into question, while Cod War I had no such aspect.

With theoretical foundations in place for identification of issues, we can move beyond the limitations imposed by the realist agenda on power politics. Operational matters come to the fore. Significant complexity must be addressed for issues and conflict processes, as Holsti (1991: 17–18) pointed out decades ago:

> Many conflicts involve multiple issues; issues change over time, particularly as a war progresses; disputants do not place the same value, or even identify the same values, as being in contention or jeopardy; some issues are so intermixed that attempts to separate them become arbitrary if not impossible; and weighing the relative importance of different issues injects the investigator's judgment as a substitute for the operating frames of reference of the decision-makers.

As a result, any number of methodological issues may ensue with regard to connecting issues and wars with each other. One example, expressed in the language from Mansbach and Vasquez (1981), is the problem of "different stakes involved for different parties" (Holsti 1991: 46–47). The Berlin Wall case is an exemplar of that type of complexity. "Issues", as Holsti

(1991: 12) summed things up, "are difficult to define and even more difficult to measure". But, it turns out, trying to do so is well worth the effort.

Although assessment of issues within conflict processes faced significant obstacles, remarkable progress can be observed over the course of decades. The Issue Correlates of War (ICOW) Project deserves special recognition for its sustained contributions. Put simply, it represents a successful effort to "collect broader data on disagreements between states about various issues" (Quackenbush 2015: 91). The ICOW Project data include territorial claims (1816–2001) and maritime and river claims (1900–2001) (Hensel and Mitchell 2016: 126). The data collection of the project reflects the consensus position that salience and importance of issues should be incorporated within the study of conflict processes, and the project's researchers created indices for both (i) territorial claims and (ii) maritime and riparian claims as a result (Hensel and Mitchell 2016: 128).

Analysis of ICOW data reveals significant connections. For example, territorial claim salience greatly increases risk of militarized conflict, along with efforts toward peaceful settlement (Hensel and Mitchell 2016: 129). Territorial claims are the most common type of issue and lead to more militarized conflict and wars (Hensel and Mitchell 2016: 133). Note also the finding from Hensel and Mitchell (2016: 135) that wars are more likely for territorial claims with "high intangible salience". This result resonates with what has been said already about the higher average difficulty level of dealing with symbolic or even transcendent issues in comparison to concrete ones. ICOW data continues to generate insights about conflict processes, notably as related to Militarized Interstate Disputes (MIDs).

However, what about the role of issues in connection with near crisis and crisis, already identified as significant events along the path to war? Table 4.1 conveys the coding for ISSUE, which is Variable 65 in the ICB Project data bank. The variable has been coded for near crises as well as crises. For each actor, this variable "identifies the most important initial issue-area" that is perceived.[6] The table displays five general categories, within which are contained subsets of interrelated issues. The military-security and economic-developmental categories are primarily material, while political-diplomatic and cultural-status tilt toward ideational. Territory is under the heading of military-security, while religion appears implicitly within cultural-status in the form of ideology.

Military-security issues constitute an outright majority in Table 4.1 – 143 near crises and 52% of the total. This is in keeping with an underlying truth of realism, namely, that much of what goes on in the world is about the politics of power. At the same time, close to one-half of the near crises pertain to other issues. This is not surprising because critics have pointed out convincingly that realism is not sufficient to tell the full story of conflict, crisis, and war.

---

[6] In cases with multiple issue-areas, the value closest to military-security is coded (Brecher, Wilkenfeld, Beardsley, James, and Quinn 2023). ICB also includes CHISSU (Variable 66), which "identifies any major change in the most important issue-area during the crisis" and codes "the issue-area toward which the change occurred" (Brecher, Wilkenfeld, Beardsley, James and Quinn 2023).

Table 4.1 Issues in near crises

Category	Description	Number and Percentage[a]
Military-security	Territory, borders, access to the sea, free navigation, irredentism, change in the military balance, military incidents, war	143/52
Political-diplomatic	Sovereignty, hegemony, international status, change in international system, colonialism, Cold War	87/32
Economic-developmental	Treatment of property, raw material resources, oil, economic recession, economic pressure, currency problems	33/12
Cultural-status	Ideology, threat to non-material values, internal problems, state of regime, population problems	7/3
Other	Miscellaneous	5/2

Note: [a] The percentages do not add up to 100 due to rounding.

TERRITORY

Among primarily material issues, none possesses more obvious importance than territory as a potential source of conflict. From an evolutionary standpoint, humans have become disposed toward territoriality; it will be occupied and defended as necessary (Vasquez 1995; see also Levy and Thompson 2010: 78, n. 13). For a long time, however, research on militarized conflict had tended to emphasize the international system or characteristics of states, with geographic variables largely on the sidelines (Hensel 2012: 3). This is puzzling because, as Holsti (1991: 57) observed some time ago, the idea of "strategic territory" has existed from Westphalia onward. Recognition of such territory has shaped foreign policy significantly. Consider, for example, Soviet fixation on Poland, the "land bridge" with Germany and an invasion corridor from the West on multiple occasions (Mansbach and Vasquez 1981). The comparatively weaker successor state arguably extended that concern to Ukraine as a result of NATO expansion, with a Russian-initiated war still underway at this time of writing.

Put simply, territory matters, and matters greatly. It evokes "sentiments of national pride and prestige" and often can "symbolize the foundations of the national society" (Holsti 1991: 308). Given its tangible or physical attributes, along with intangible or psychological values, and effects on a state's reputation, territory is highly salient (Hensel 2012: 9). Among the tangible elements are "arable land, subsoil minerals, control of strategic military locations, and so forth" (Mansbach and Vasquez 1981: 198). Intangible aspects can also be important because of indivisibilities and maybe even for reasons of maintaining a reputation for assertiveness (Hensel 2012: 9–11). One of the most memorable instances concerns the persistence of the French in seeking to regain the provinces of Alsace–Lorraine in the Franco-Prussian War of 1870. "In 1914 the French continued to fixate on these 'lost' provinces as symbolic of the *patrie* [i.e., homeland] as a whole", as Mansbach and Vasquez (1981: 245) observe, "and they remained an immovable obstacle in the path of Franco-German reconciliation". Territory, to sum up, is an issue that can be expected to challenge efforts toward conflict management into the foreseeable future.

Evidence overwhelmingly supports the importance of territory in conflict processes, with the steps-to-war model from Senese and Vasquez (2008) as a natural starting point. Data analysis across regions and over time strongly confirms the foundational role of territorial issues along the pathway to war. Territorial issues inherently are more dangerous than other kinds, such as matters of policy or the regime of an adversary. Disputes over territory are even more likely to escalate if handled via conventional realist-based approaches that include armaments and alliances (Senese and Vasquez 2008; see also our discussion of arms/arms races and alliances in Chapter 11).

Hensel (2012) provides a convincing assessment of what has been learned from rigorous statistical analysis about geography and territorial conflict. From 1816 to 2001, over half of MIDs began between adversaries with a shared river or land border, and another 14% started between those contiguous by sea (Hensel 2012: 6). These results are even more compelling because noncontiguous dyads are much more common than contiguous dyads (Quackenbush 2015: 76). Studies of war diffusion, Hensel (2012: 7) observes, also confirm the importance of contiguity.

More than one quarter of MIDs have been explicitly over territorial issues. Territory becomes even more prominent in severe forms of conflict; approximately one-half of all fatal MIDs and full-scale wars are over that issue (Hensel 2012: 12). And the level of conflict over an ongoing territorial claim is increased by characteristics associated with issue salience. Examples would be the presence of shared ethnic or linguistic groups along the border (Hensel 2012: 13).

Indeed, evidence continues to accumulate about the central role of territory in conflict. For instance, based on statistical analysis that combines ICOW data with other compilations for 1816 to 2001, Rider and Owsiak (2021: 191) discover that a strategic rivalry is more likely to develop in a given year "for a dyad disputing territory with power endowments than for a dyad disputing territory without such endowments". Power endowments refer to "either militarily or economically valuable land (or both)" – an operational rendering of strategic territory (Rider and Owsiak 2021: 170).

Territory, to sum up, is primarily a material issue. At the same time, territory can be imbued with symbolic or even transcendent importance, which in turn complicates efforts to resolve conflicts that may arise. Evidence overwhelmingly supports the position that territory is an essential issue within any model of escalation and worthy of further investigation. But, see "In Focus: Issues, Conflict, and War" for a brief survey of other issues historically related and empirically linked to conflict, crisis, and war.

IN FOCUS: ISSUES, CONFLICT, AND WAR

Most studies of war identify territory as the most significant source of conflict among all the actors of world politics. For example, K. J. Holsti (1991) concluded that more than half of the wars over the past three centuries involved conflict over territory, and Vasquez and Henehan (2010) argued that, of all the issues that spark conflict, territorial disputes have the highest probability of escalating to war. However, conflicts and wars can arise from multiple issues and rarely have just one source. Holsti's (1991) study provides a good starting point for other key factors.

- Nation-state creation. The "search for statehood" and independence has been a powerful motivator for conflict and war and has become increasingly important over the past 300 years.
- Ideology. Ideas have been increasingly important to world politics and international conflict. Examples include wars over fascism and communism (World War II, the Cold War) and maybe even the effect of democracy and democratization on relations between states.
- Economics. Many conflicts involve competition for economic resources, markets, and/or transportation. Although Holsti and others argue that such issues have become less central to war in the last century, they are still relevant in many situations (e.g., the 1991 Gulf War).
- Human sympathy: ethnicity, religion, and war. According to Holsti, acting on behalf of others out of sympathy – particularly to protect perceived religious and ethnic kin abroad or for humanitarian purposes – has often been an important factor behind international conflict. India's intervention in East Pakistan (now Bangladesh) in 1971 and the US-led multilateral operations in Kosovo (1999) and Libya (2011) are examples of such instances.
- Predation and survival. According to Holsti, efforts to eliminate another state (often for territorial or identity reasons) have often been at the heart of conflict and war, especially in the 20th century. The Russian invasion of Ukraine is a good example of this.
- Other factors. States have (occasionally) gone to war to defend allies and to defend or restore the balance of power. However, these factors are more important to understanding why states join ongoing wars rather than why the wars begin in the first place.

Holsti's study identifies a range of issues that often motivate war. Overall, he concludes that "relatively abstract issues – self-determination, principles of political philosophy and ideology, and sympathy for kin – have become increasingly important as sources of war while concrete issues such as territory and wealth have declined" (Holsti 1991, 321). This may be quite significant as issues related to territory and wealth are more open to compromise and more readily resolved peacefully than are issues involving statehood, ideology, and identity.

RELIGION

Religion is foundational to identity, with possibilities that include faith, along with agnosticism or atheism. It is clear that religion is at the apex of issues that fit the description of symbolic or even transcendent. What, however, is meant by *religion?* Many definitions have been offered and no effort will be made to sort through the vast literature on concept formation that spans any number of academic disciplines. Applied studies, such as the one at present, take a pragmatic and observational approach. "Religion", according to Hassner (2016: 9), "consists of the practices that surround the sacred, along with the rules, rituals and penalties that attach to them". Lloyd, Haussman, and James (2019: 15), in a study connecting religion with health care, conclude their review "without a formal definition". Brown (2020: 10; see also Fox and Sandler 2004) refers to "pragmatic avoidance" – staying away from an overarching definition in favor of studying religion*s*. And many other studies could be cited that choose the same pragmatic pathway.

Although we cannot adequately cover the rapidly increasing literature on religion and conflict, we do offer an introduction sufficient for context and our subsequent focus on understanding *War on Sacred Grounds* (Hassner 2009), a study at the intersection of religion and territory. After some historical background about religion and world politics, we review ideas about conflict that have found some support from testing, along with a necessarily limited sample of the evidence.

After the Thirty Years War and Treaty of Westphalia, the transnational authority of the Catholic Church no longer existed. Europe transformed into something resembling the modern state system that is familiar today. Religion, as a by-product of that change, receded from prominence and notably, with a few exceptions, did not play a determinative role with regard to war and peace (Holsti 1991: 59). For such reasons, religion resided outside the purview of IR when that academic field crystallized after World War I.

Efforts to formulate and test propositions about religion and conflict appeared sporadically before 9/11, but definitely became more sustained after that date. Consider, as a point of departure, the propositions developed by Fox (2002: 107, 109, 122, 125, 151; see also Hasenclever and Rittberger 2003: 120–122). Religious frames of reference point toward strife by limiting the potential for cooperation via mutual understanding. Challenges to a religious framework can be expected to provoke conflict because of the attendant threat to identity. So, too, will group actions based on different religious frameworks; goals are likely to diverge from each other. A religious frame of reference may include standards of behavior that call for violence in some situations. Grievances can lead to use of religious institutions to mobilize for action, which then facilitates conflict. In addition, religious discrimination and resulting grievances can push a group toward protest and rebellion. Thus, from the outset of this review, it is obvious that religion may bring about conflict through different mechanisms and pathways.

Hasenclever and Rittberger (2003: 110) have identified three approaches to analysis of how faith impacts upon political conflict. First, primordialism sees conflict as cultural, with religion as an independent variable that can lead to realignment and war. Second, instrumentalism emphasizes socioeconomic aspects, with any correlation for religion and conflict deemed to be spurious, and expectation of cleavages and civil wars. Third, and finally, moderate constructivism also emphasizes socioeconomic aspects, but religion is regarded as an intervening variable, and expectations include (i) socioeconomic cleavages, (ii) political conflicts, and (iii) contingent militancy and violence. Once again, religion is seen as capable of factoring into conflict processes in more than one way.

Primordial aspects have been developed further through a focus on religious fundamentalism. Religion is associated with violence, notably through actions by those who claim to be acting against impure influences, and leaders "can harness perceived humiliation to create support for a terrorist movement" (Stern 2003: xix, xx, 18). Along the same lines, fundamentalists are seen to engage in militance to prevent erosion of religious identity and create an alternative to secular life and institutions (Almond, Appleby, and Sivan 2003: 17; see also Fox 2018: 104–107). According to Almond, Appleby, and Sivan (2003: 19), fundamentalists call for religion to be "strong because its enemies are perceived as powerful and potentially overwhelming". Moreover, as Pearce (2006: 51; see also Ghose and James 2006) observes, various religious traditions can be used to justify violence.

Consider, for example, entities such as al-Qaeda and the Islamic State in Iraq and Syria (ISIS). Each of these organizations employed intense violence against those who did not adhere to their distorted reading of Islamic principles, most notably, in relation to the meaning of *jihad*. Fanatical supporters justified their terroristic actions on the interpretation of *jihad* as a call for forcible conversion and, failing that goal, execution of unbelievers. While al-Qaeda and ISIS seemingly have passed from the scene, extremist organizations supported by Iran, among others, continue to wreak havoc, especially in the Middle East and North Africa (MENA). One grievous example is Boko Haram, which has carried out many acts of extreme violence and mayhem in Nigeria (Haynes 2013: 307–313; Idika-Kalu 2023).

Connections for religion with conflict, with an emphasis on those with some support from testing, have been summarized by Fox and Sandal (2011: 83–85; see also Fox and Sandler 2004: 53 and Haynes 2013: 71) to set the agenda for continuing research. Religious differences are associated with higher levels of domestic and international conflict, along with intervention. In addition, ethnic strife is linked to various aspects of religion: legitimacy, institutions, and discrimination. Some connections emerge for religion with terrorism, ethnic conflict, and civil and international wars. Religious worldviews and legitimacy also are linked to strife. Therefore, both religious demographics and content of beliefs are seen to connect with conflict.

Consider, for example, the "Troubles" of Northern Ireland, which escalated toward the end of the 1960s and persisted for decades. Catholics and Protestants engaged in high levels of violence with each other over a set of interlocking issues, within which differing religious and national affiliations figured prominently (Sandal and Fox 2013: 25, 68, 149, 150, 155). Radical elements in organizations such as the Irish Republican Army (IRA) and Ulster Defence Association (UDA) claimed to be acting in defense, respectively, of the Catholic and Protestant communities. Their actions, however, did great harm and created more insecurity rather than less – a process resembling the realist security dilemma but within an intrastate setting.[7]

---

[7] For a detailed development of the concept of a security dilemma within the context of ethnic strife, see Posen (1993).

Religious causes of violence, according to Fox (2018: 112–117), can be divided into four overlapping categories. First, instrumental violence seeks to achieve a political agenda, for example, establishment of a religious state. Boko Haram and ISIS serve as prominent examples. Second, defending the religion refers to violence that derives from "potential centrality to individual and group identities". For example, the IRA in Northern Ireland resorted to violence over the course of several decades, in the name of protecting an Irish Catholic identity from Protestant extremism and biased anti-Catholic intrusions from the British government. Third, doctrines and ideologies may mandate violence. Modern instances are available, but Christianity in the era of the Crusades is among the most memorable. Fourth, seemingly benign religious activities can provoke threats and even acts of violence. One example would be the controversy in New York City about the possible building of an Islamic center in relatively close proximity to the 9/11 memorial site. Taken together, the preceding pathways from religion to conflict and violence bring together, and build on, the primordial, instrumental, and moderate constructivist approaches identified earlier.

Statistical studies of religion and conflict reveal a range of findings that exhibit some overall patterns. Based on Minorities at Risk (MAR) data from the 1990s, Fox (2002: 85–88) finds that religious factors and the presence of Islamic groups are associated with conflict, although the latter would appear to be explained at least in part through pervasiveness of autocratic governments in the MENA. Fox and Sandler (2004: 64) use MAR data to examine all cases of serious ethnic conflict from 1990 to 1995 and obtain important results in connection with religion. International intervention is more likely in religious conflicts; furthermore, third-party states tend to have the same religion as the side on which they intervene (Fox and Sandler 2004: 81).

With the Peace Research of Oslo (PRIO) as the source, Pearce (2006: 45) compiled a dataset of 278 cases of territorial conflict phases from 1946 to 2001. Note that the focus on disputes over territory already creates a higher likelihood of escalation than over other issues. Testing confirms that religious conflicts are more intense than other types, although the evidence is not overwhelming (Pearce 2006: 47–48).

Based on data from the MAR Project for 1990 through 1995, Fox, James, and Li (2009) assess the influence of religion on the degree of intervention in conflict. Ethnic conflicts in the MENA are more likely than those elsewhere to attract intervention, which is in line with the above-noted results from Fox (2002). This pattern is confirmed for other regions – conflicts involving Muslim minorities attract a greater proportion of both military and political intervention as compared to others. It also is noteworthy that "Islamic states in general intervene almost exclusively on behalf of Muslim minorities", while the same is not true with regard to Christian states (Fox, James, and Li 2009: 176). Fox, James, and Li (2009: 176–177) further observe that ethno*religious* minorities are more likely than others to attract political intervention.

Statistical analysis from Fox and Sandal (2011: 87–90) combines data from the ICB and Religion and State (RAS) Projects to learn more about involvement in international crises. The time frame is 1990 to 2002, with the state-year (N = 2249) as the unit of analysis. Religious exclusivity, defined as a state's propensity to support a single religion over others, is the focal point of the study. Intuition might say that state religious exclusivity can be linked to activity in international crises because religion has been politicized and therefore could impact upon foreign policy. This connection is expected to intensify, moreover, within a setting of protracted conflict. Results from the data analysis strongly confirm both expectations (Fox and Sandal 2011: 93–95).

Interesting results emerge from a study of religious discrimination in connection with initiation of, and involvement in, foreign policy crises (Özdamar and Akbaba 2014). The authors assemble data from multiple projects, including ICB and MAR, for 1990 to 2003. Logistic regression analysis confirms a positive connection for religious discrimination at the domestic level with involvement and initiation vis-à-vis foreign policy crises. This is true in the presence of regime type, gross domestic product (GDP), and other standard control variables.

Brown and James (2018a: 1341) combine the Religious Characteristics of States (RCS) and MIDs datasets to study interstate dyads from 1816 to 2010. Following standard practice for such pairings in the conflict processes literature, the dependent variable is "the lower percentages of adherents of each tested religion in the two countries" (Brown and James 2018a: 1362).[8] It is interesting to note that regression analysis reveals that the number of Christians is associated with MID involvement, while datasets that cover a shorter period produce the opposite result (Brown and James 2018a: 1362–1363; see also Brown and James 2018b).

Based on RCS and MID data, Brown (2020: 42–47) carried out statistical analysis on initiation of interstate armed conflict from 1946 to 2010 with directed dyad-year as the unit of observation. The motivating research question is this one: Do religious demographics provide any insight into the first use of force in a MID? The results show the following: "Christianity is firmly negatively correlated with states' propensity to initiate interstate armed conflicts", while Islam is mildly positively correlated, and Buddhism is not correlated (Brown 2020: 73).

Several patterns emerge from the sample of quantitative studies that link religion with conflict. First, only a limited amount of attention focuses on "conflict between the primary actors in global politics: states" (Brown 2020: 13). Second, datasets such as RCS and RAS have facilitated an accumulation of findings about conflict processes in relation, respectively, to religious demographics and how government treats religion. Third, religious conflicts appear to have greater intensity and a higher likelihood of eliciting third-party intervention. Fourth, and finally, specific religions are associated with various aspects of conflict, but with no obvious consistency among the results.

THE INTERSECTION OF TERRITORY AND RELIGION

Territory and religion are not fully separate issue spaces. Consider, for example, the contestation of sacred territory or spaces (Stern 2003: 31; Hassner 2009). Conflict over holy sites can produce a high level of violence; prominent examples include the claims of Hindus and Muslims at Ayodhya that resulted in destruction of the mosque in 1992 and over the Temple

---

[8] Taking the lower of the two values within a dyad is referred to in the literature on conflict processes as the "weakest link" assumption. It is the conventional approach to measurement of dyadic variables throughout the leading journals on conflict processes, such as *Journal of Conflict Resolution*.

CONFLICT, CRISIS, AND WAR IN WORLD POLITICS

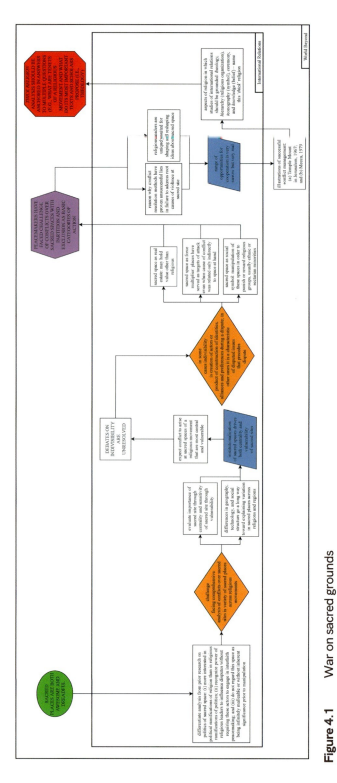

Figure 4.1 War on sacred grounds

THE ISSUES

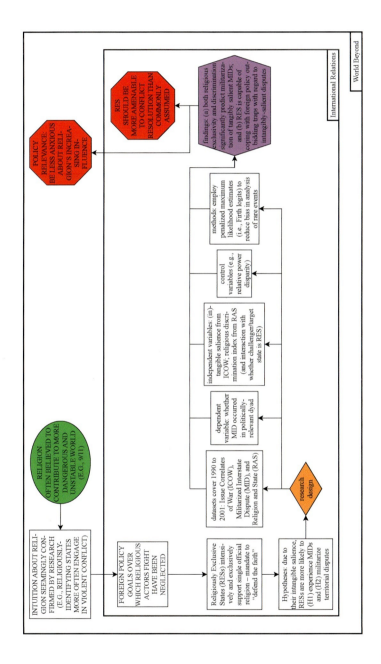

Figure 4.2 Defending the faith

Mount/Haram al-Sharif that led to violence in 2000 (Hassner 2009). To complement the quantitative evidence reviewed for territory and religion, we present an original and interesting qualitative study in systemist graphic form: *War on Sacred Grounds* (Hassner 2009) offers a compelling account of the causes and potential management of conflict over territory that is endowed with religious significance. Tracing the arguments from Hassner (2009) reveals de facto application of analytic eclecticism to obtain knowledge about conflict at the intersection of religion and territory.

Figure 4.1 conveys the arguments from *War on Sacred Grounds* (Hassner 2009) in a systemist format. In Figure 4.1a, the discipline of IR is designated as the system, with the World Beyond as its environment. The macro and micro levels of IR correspond, respectively, to the discipline as a whole and individual scholars within it.

> **FOR EXAMPLE: RELIGION AND MILITARIZED INTERSTATE DISPUTES**
>
> Figure 4.2 conveys the analytical arguments from Zellman and Fox (2020) with regard to the impact of state religious exclusivity on territorial MID initiation.
>
> *After looking it over, do the statistical findings ring true? What additional hypotheses come to mind for additional testing with aggregate data? In addition, are there cases that come readily to mind that would be interesting to review in connection with the findings from this study?*

Figure 4.1b gets underway with "SACRED SPACES ARE BOTH AWESOME AND DREADFUL" → "differentiate analysis from prior research on politics of sacred space: (i) more interested in political ramifications of religion than in religious ramifications of politics; (ii) recognize power of religious leaders to influence disputes without requiring these actors to engage in interfaith peacekeeping; and (iii) do not regard this space as being infinitely malleable or without inherent significance prior to manipulation". As an initial component, the former appears as a green oval.

Analytic eclecticism is clear to see from the outset of the argument. The focus on political ramifications of religion connects with instrumental thinking. Religious beliefs construct sacred spaces – an assertion with a moderate constructivist flavor. There is a primordial aspect as well, manifested in the claim that limitations exist on the malleability of sacred space. In addition to connections with multiple overarching views of the world, concepts from various schools of thought will play specific roles as pathways unfold in the subfigures that follow.

Analysis continues at the micro level in Figure 4.1b with "differentiate analysis from prior research on politics of sacred space: (i) more interested in political ramifications of religion than in religious ramifications of politics; (ii) recognize power of religious leaders to influence disputes without requiring these actors to engage in interfaith peacekeeping; and (iii) do not regard this space as being infinitely malleable or without inherent significance prior to manipulation" → "challenge facing comprehensive analysis of conflicts over sacred sites is variety of sacred places across religious movements". The latter component is divergent and thus appears as an orange diamond. Political culture, geostrategic salience and other factors from across levels of analysis can be expected to play varying roles from one situation to the next

THE ISSUES

Figure 4.1a

CONFLICT, CRISIS, AND WAR IN WORLD POLITICS

Figure 4.1b

THE ISSUES

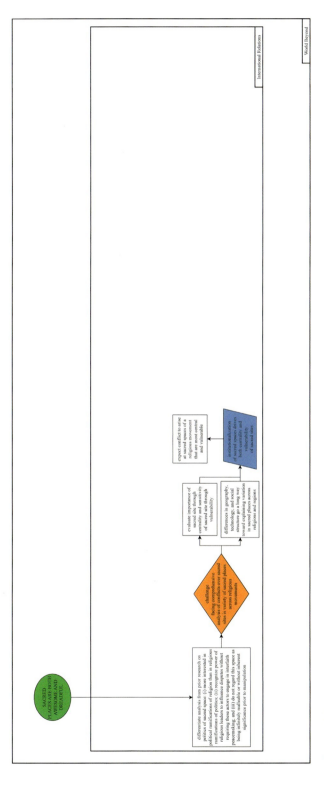

Figure 4.1c

CONFLICT, CRISIS, AND WAR IN WORLD POLITICS

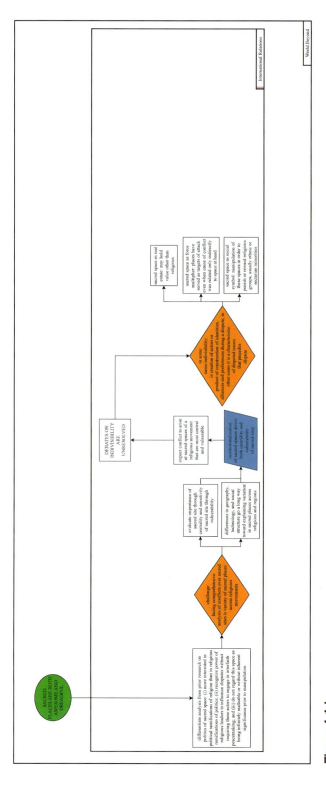

Figure 4.1d

THE ISSUES

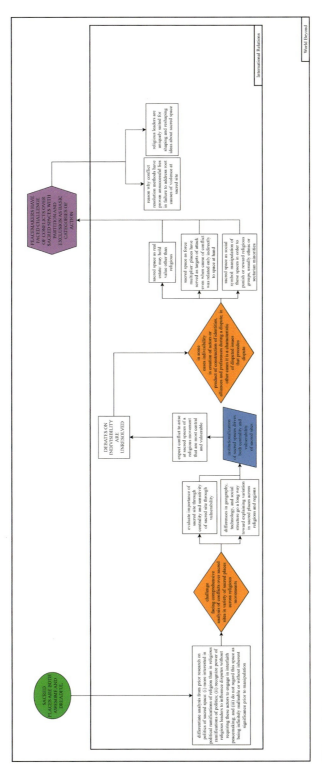

Figure 4.1e

CONFLICT, CRISIS, AND WAR IN WORLD POLITICS

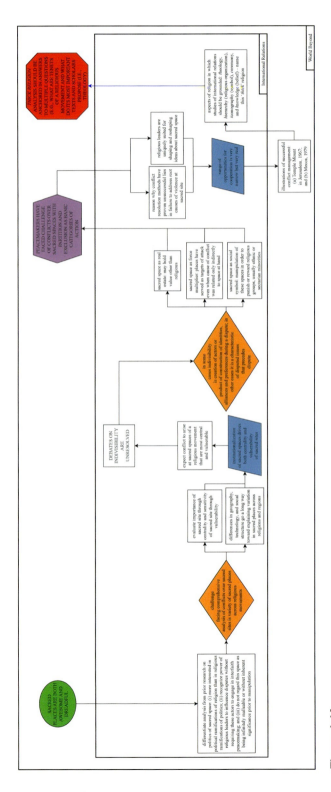

Figure 4.1f

– obviously difficult for any would-be causal explanation. This diversity among potentially relevant concepts also reinforces the comparative advantage of analytic eclecticism.

Figure 4.1c depicts a point of divergence: "challenge facing comprehensive analysis of conflicts over sacred sites is variety of sacred places across religious movements" → "evaluate importance of sacred site through centrality and sensitivity of sacred site through vulnerability"; "differences in geography, technology, and social structure go a long way toward explaining variation in sacred spaces across religions and regions". The tasks for explanation clearly divide into ideational and material categories in the components after the arrow – consider the respective references to feelings of vulnerability and a range of observational items such as geography.

Figure 4.1c reaches a point of convergence with "evaluate importance of sacred site through centrality and sensitivity of sacred site through vulnerability"; "differences in geography, technology, and social structure go a long way toward explaining variation in sacred spaces across religions and regions" → "institutionalization of sacred spaces drives both centrality and vulnerability of sacred sites". The latter, a convergent component, appears as a blue parallelogram.

Institutionalization of sacred spaces can be connected in an interesting way with a prominent concept from behavioral economics: the staying power of the status quo. Bias in assessing the value of an item is stimulated through possession of it, with an upward trend over time (Samuelson and Zeckhauser 1988). Consider that well-confirmed finding in the context of sacred space; attachment to it can be expected to increase on the part of the side in possession, which in turn complicates efforts toward sharing or other forms of compromise. Institutionalization indeed can be expected to move perception of a sacred site toward centrality and vulnerability over time.

Figure 4.1c shows one further connection at the micro level: "institutionalization of sacred spaces drives both centrality and vulnerability of sacred sites" → "expect conflict to arise at sacred spaces of a religious movement that are most central and vulnerable". A highly central and vulnerable site would fit well under the "transcendent" designation from Mansbach and Vasquez (1981). Such a location would serve as a figurative "canary in the coal mine", with the likelihood of adherents perceiving offensive behavior from outsiders to be at the maximum.

Movement from the micro to the macro level occurs in Figure 4.1d with "expect conflict to arise at sacred spaces of a religious movement that are most central and vulnerable" → "DEBATES ON INDIVISIBILITY ARE UNRESOLVED". This assertion brings to mind a central insight from the classic study of negotiation from Fisher and Ury (1983): focus on achievement of goals rather than the defense of specific positions. While that is sound advice, the intense emotions at work in conflict over sacred space push the adversaries in exactly the opposite direction.

Figure 4.1d then shows movement from the macro to the micro level: "DEBATES ON INDIVISIBILITY ARE UNRESOLVED" → "in some cases indivisibility is creation of actors or product of construction of identities, alliances and preferences during a dispute; in other cases it is a characteristic of disputed issues that precedes dispute". As a divergent component, the latter appears as an orange diamond.

Pathways then diverge in Figure 4.1d: "in some cases indivisibility is creation of actors or product of construction of identities, alliances and preferences during a dispute; in other cases it is a characteristic of disputed issues that precedes dispute" → "sacred spaces as real estate: may hold value other than religious"; "sacred space as force multiplier: places have served as targets of attack even when cause of conflict was related only indirectly to space at hand"; "sacred space as social symbol: manipulation of these spaces in order to punish or reward religious groups, usually ethnic or sectarian minorities". Material concerns may accumulate in multiple ways and further complicate efforts to manage an ongoing conflict over sacred space.

Figure 4.1e shows how multiple routes from the micro level of IR come together in the World Beyond: "sacred spaces as real estate: may hold value other than religious"; "sacred space as force multiplier: places have served as targets of attack even when cause of conflict was related only indirectly to space at hand"; "sacred space as social symbol: manipulation of these spaces in order to punish or reward religious groups, usually ethnic or sectarian minorities" → "PEACEMAKERS HAVE FACED CHALLENGE OF CONFLICTS OVER SACRED SPACES WITH PARTITION AND EXCLUSION AS BASIC CATEGORIES OF ACTION". The latter, a nodal component, is depicted with a purple hexagon.

Multiple pathways emerge at the micro level in Figure 4.1e: "PEACEMAKERS HAVE FACED CHALLENGE OF CONFLICTS OVER SACRED SPACES WITH PARTITION AND EXCLUSION AS BASIC CATEGORIES OF ACTION" → "reason why conflict resolution methods have proven unsuccessful lies in failure to address root causes of violence at sacred site"; "religious leaders are uniquely suited to shaping and reshaping ideas about sacred space". Consider, for example, tensions in Israel over the Temple Mount and Haram al-Sharif, holy sites respectively for Jews and Muslims. The problems in managing these essentially coterminous locations without violence can be traced to politicization (Frisch 2011: 34, 96–98). The root causes of mistrust between and among religious groupings in Israel have yet to be addressed successfully, so periodic escalation to violence can be expected to continue in connection with these sacred spaces.

Figure 4.1f shows a point of convergence at the micro level with "reason why conflict resolution methods have proven unsuccessful lies in failure to address root causes of violence at sacred site"; "religious leaders are uniquely suited to shaping and reshaping ideas about sacred space" → "range of opportunities for cooperation is very narrow but very real". As a convergent component, the latter appears as a blue parallelogram. The preceding assertion can be triangulated with the prominent concept of a "win-set" from Putnam (1988). The win-set refers to the subset of options that are satisfactory from the standpoint of leaders bargaining with each other *and* their domestic constituencies. In the context of a highly contested sacred space, the win-set that can satisfy all parties concerned will be small, but religious leaders possess an advantage in trying to find an option within it because their followers will be more likely to trust them over secular politicians.

Movement from the micro level of IR to the World Beyond occurs in Figure 4.1f: "range of opportunities for cooperation is very narrow but very real" → "illustrations of successful conflict management: (a) Temple Mount in Jerusalem, 1967; and (b) Mecca, 1979". The route reenters International Relations with "illustrations of successful conflict management: (a) Temple Mount in Jerusalem, 1967; and (b) Mecca, 1979" → "aspects of religion in which studies of international relations should be grounded: *t*heology, *h*ierarchy (religious organization), *i*conography (symbol), *c*eremony, and *k*nowledge (belief) – name this '*thick*' religion". Taken together, the elements of "thick" religion span the material and ideational worlds.

Figure 4.1f finishes with "aspects of religion in which studies of international relations should be grounded: *t*heology, *h*ierarchy (religious organization), *i*conography (symbol), ceremony, and *k*nowledge (belief) – name this '*thick*' religion" → "*THICK RELIGION* ANALYSIS SHOULD BE ANCHORED IN ANSWERS TO MULTIPLE QUESTIONS (E.G., WHAT ARE TENETS OF A RELIGIOUS MOVEMENT AND WHAT DO ITS MOST IMPORTANT TEXTS AND SCHOLARS PROPOSE (I.E., THEOLOGY))". A natural priority therefore would be to bring each element of "thick" religion into engagement with primordial, moderate constructivist, and instrumental perspectives to move in the direction of more sound policy vis-à-vis conflict management and even prevention.

Additional insights about the nature of the arguments from *War on Sacred Grounds* can be gleaned from the structure of Figure 4.1. Among its 19 components, five fit into either the divergent, convergent, or nodal categories. Thus, the arguments from Hassner (2009) feature a significant amount of contingency. The components are distributed in the following way across locations in the diagram: IR – 14 micro, 1 macro; and World Beyond – 4. The presence of four components in the World Beyond suggests that the argumentation has achieved relevance to policy, as would be expected for a study in the tradition of analytic eclecticism.

> **IN FOCUS**
>
> Reflect carefully on a case of conflict, crisis, or war that you know includes religion to some degree. Perhaps the "Troubles" in Northern Ireland, the bloody violence of the breakup of the former Yugoslavia, or the current violence between Palestinians and Israelis in Gaza come to mind. Apply "thick" religion to provide a comprehensive analysis of that case.
>
> *Does the review seem complete or are there significant aspects of the case that the thick religion framework seems to have missed?*

SUMMING UP AND MOVING FORWARD

International conflict, crisis, and war are associated with a wide range of issues. We gain breadth of explanation from analysis of issues in general. While the realist vision of world politics now is accompanied by many other viewpoints, it retains value in the issue context through a reminder that military-security issues remain important. At the same time, the study of conflict processes has revealed that other issues also can play essential roles along the pathways to escalation. Issues may be primarily material or ideational – or some combination of both – as would be expected from a scientific realist point of view. A review of theorizing and reproducible evidence about two encompassing and important issues – territory and religion – reveals that each is significantly connected with conflict, crisis, and war. This has produced further depth of explanation in each instance. A systemist graphic analysis of *War on Sacred*

Grounds (Hassner 2009), a study at the intersection of territory and religion, shows how these issues can be interrelated within conflict processes.

We turn our attention in the following chapters to understanding conflict, crisis, and war from different levels of analysis. What can each level offer to a comprehensive explanation? Through an investigation of the system level of analysis, that work gets underway in Chapter 5 with focus on system-level explanations.

> **CONSIDER THIS: THE EVOLUTION OF WAR**
>
> *Given our discussion of key trends in the evolution of war in the preceding chapter, have the conflicts since Holsti concluded his study in 1991 reinforced his finding that "relatively abstract issues – self-determination, principles of political philosophy and ideology, and sympathy for kin – become increasingly important as sources of war while concrete issues such as territory and wealth have declined", or do you see important differences?*

PART II
EXPLAINING THE PROBLEM

5
System-level explanations

PROLOGUE

On April 1, 2001, a near crisis began when a US Navy reconnaissance aircraft and a People's Liberation Army (PLA) Navy jet fighter accidentally collided in international airspace over the South China Sea. The accident occurred about 70 miles off the People's Republic of China's (PRC) Hainan Island. (See Map 5.1.) After surviving the incident, the US crew made an emergency landing on the island and the PRC subsequently detained the crew members for 11 days. The PRC's airplane crashed in the ocean, and the pilot did not survive the crash.

Washington and Beijing disagreed over the cause of the accident, when and how to release the US crew and plane, whether the US government should apologize, and the PRC's right to board the US aircraft and learn about its equipment. US officials believed that while the immediate cause of the collision had been accidental contact, this event was precipitated by increased aggressiveness in the PLA's interceptions of US aircraft in international airspace. The PRC government asserted that blame for the accident rested solely with the American pilot whom it claimed had initiated an aggressive turn into the intercepting fighter. The US account of the accident placed blame squarely on the PLA pilot.

On April 11, the US ambassador to China issued a letter to show regret and sorrow without an apology. The PRC accepted the letter and released the US crew but continued to demand that the US stop reconnaissance flights over China. The US and PRC held a meeting to discuss the incident and return of the US plane.

What insights does the way this case played out provide about East Asia in particular, along with international systems in general and the process of escalation? The inconclusive outcome makes sense in terms of the very even balance of capabilities between China and the US as the leading actors in East Asia. For international systems per se, the case is interesting because it shows how even a very dangerous-looking event is not tantamount to escalation.

OVERVIEW

What can a system-based perspective offer to the explanation of international conflict, crisis, and war? This chapter seeks an answer to that question. Among the levels of analysis identified in the classic exposition from Waltz (1959), the system provides the natural starting point for this chapter, while we take up the other now standard levels from Waltz (1959) – state and

Source: https://www.alamy.com/hainan-southernmost-province-of-china-and-surrounding-area-political-map-hainan-island-and-the-paracel-islands-in-the-south-china-sea-image526580637.html?imageid=529F87EE-0EE9-48C9-ABC3-C8023052E4D1&p=183153&pn=1&searchId=fd447e2c9ff839061b5db5d369ef666e&searchtype=0

Map 5.1   Hainan Island

individual – in Chapters 6 and 7.[1] In our view, Occam's Razor, a well-established principle for developing an explanation, offers a useful guide to implementation for levels of analysis. The basic idea of Occam's Razor is to begin with the simplest account and build in complexity only as needed. Since there is one international system, about 200 states, tens of thousands of non-state actors, and over eight billion individual people, the order of work becomes obvious. The system level of analysis offers the potential to explain a lot with a little.

This chapter moves forward in four additional sections. The second section introduces a sample of system-level theories from within the realist school of thought, which has produced by far the most such frameworks. This review offers breadth of explanation vis-à-vis the

---

[1]   Explanations that combine levels of analysis appear in Chapter 10.

causes of conflict, crisis, and war. Section three focuses on one framework: Power Transition Theory (PTT) – a relatively successful system-level theory from beyond the boundaries of realism. In that way, we obtain some depth of analysis as well. The fourth section applies PTT to the evolution of the East Asian system – a region of immense importance with regard to potential escalation of conflict given contemporary developments. In line with analytic eclecticism, while we focus primarily on PTT, we bring realist theories to the analysis of East Asia in a complementary way. Fifth, and finally, we conclude with reflection on the main points of this chapter and lead into the next one.

SYSTEMS, REALISM, AND CONFLICT

Many theories about conflict, crisis, and war are cast at the system level. These frameworks often reside within respective paradigms, while others transcend such boundaries. The causal mechanisms among theories are highly diverse, but the commonality among them is their emphasis on (some) key attributes and structural characteristics of the international system such as anarchy, hierarchy, the distribution of power, and others. These attributes are used to explain recurring patterns of conflict and war, especially such matters as the frequency and likelihood of conflict.

One basic point of difference concerns the anticipated effects of anarchy versus hierarchy in the international system. For purposes of comparison, consider balance of power and long cycle theories, which respectively focus on anarchy and hierarchy (Levy and Thompson 2010: 38–43, 48–50). While balance of power exists in many variants, each emphasizes the desire among states to prevent emergence of a hegemon, with some combination of armaments and allies pursued toward that end. This process played out for centuries in Europe, with each would-be hegemon – from Louis XIV to Adolf Hitler – ending up in defeat against an overwhelming counter-coalition. The long cycle theory, by contrast, focuses on hierarchy at the system level. A leading state, according to the theory, will provide a relatively stable order until global or regional challenges (or both) result in confrontation and even a general war. From the long cycle standpoint, concentration of capabilities into a land-based power is especially threatening and can lead to war with a coalition that includes land and sea powers (Levy and Thompson 2010: 49).

Given the preceding realities, we offer a necessarily limited survey rather than anything resembling a full account of system-level theories. Our survey includes a manageable sample of those theories obtained through implementation of three criteria. First, given the longevity of realism, most theories are contained within it, so our survey will try to provide basic coverage there. Second, we include only those theories with some degree of support from empirical testing in the sample. Third, system-level theories have tended to focus on great power war, so the choices reflect that property. As a result of the criteria, the discussion centers on four realist theories introduced in chronological order within two subsets: (i) dynamic – in which we discuss power cycle and predation; and (ii) static – in which we discuss structural and offensive realism.[2] In each instance, we present a sample of evidence for the theory as well.

Power cycle theory focuses on the operation of the international system as a whole. The theory of power cycles puts forward the idea that great powers in the system pass through waves of increase and decrease in their standing relative to each other (Doran 1971, 1991; Doran and Parsons 1980). The wave for each great power will be different from the others, varying in height and duration, but with the same basic shape. For example, compared to other great powers, the US has exhibited a long and relatively high-level cycle. Cycles of capability feature turning points, where either the direction or pace of movement shifts and creates high uncertainty. A great power's sense of its foreign policy role will lag behind these objective conditions with regard to change in relative capabilities. As a result, either a surplus or deficit of capacity to act will pose a challenge to the leadership in coping with the international system. At such times, according to power cycle theory, the likelihood of great power war reaches its maximum. This is true especially when more than one great power is in proximity to a critical point along its power cycle. A prominent example would be the years leading up to World War I (Doran 1991).

Data analysis offers consistent support to the importance of power cycles, so just a few examples of war-related findings are summarized here. One study focuses on 77 cases of war initiation by a major power – coded by magnitude, severity, and duration. The general hypothesis about proximity to critical points is confirmed across the preceding dimensions (Doran and Parsons 1980: 957, 960). Through testing of a basic hypothesis that links critical points to likelihood of alliance formation, Chiu (2003: 130) produces further support for power cycle theory. Chiu (2003: 130) focuses on critical points from 1814 to 1985 and relies on data for alliances and interstate wars from the usual sources (e.g., Correlates of War (COW)). Data analysis links critical points, but not alliance formation, with the incidence of war (Chiu 2003: 134). This finding is important to power cycle theory because alliances – at the center of so much realist theorizing – appear epiphenomenal by comparison to critical points in accounting for war.

Case studies on war also support power cycle theory. One example concerns Iraq – noteworthy because it provides evidence from beyond the strictly great power subset. Wars involving Iraq with (a) Iran and (b) a US-led coalition occurred in proximity to critical points (Parasiliti 2003). Iraq, for example, "peaked in relative power prior to the Gulf War" and experienced "acute relative decline at the time it invaded Kuwait" in 1990 (Parasiliti 2003: 160). Thus, Parasiliti (2003: 160) accounts for Saddam Hussein's decision in favor of war as a failed adjustment to significant shifts in the strategic environment. Iraq went into relative decline after the war with Iran from 1980 to 1988. The attack on Kuwait soon after reflected concerns about "loss of regional power", such as the share of oil production in comparison to Kuwait, Saudi Arabia, and the UAE (Parasiliti 2003: 160).

---

[2] For a comprehensive evaluation of these realist theories and others that pertain to war, see James (2022). Each realist theory cited in this chapter also is available as a systemist graphic for one or more publications in the VIRP archive (www.visualinternationalrelationsproject.com).

What can be said, in an overall sense, about results from testing power cycle theory? Studies from Yoon (2003), Inoguchi (2003), and various others support the idea and associated evidence from Doran (1989, 1991) that proximity to critical points in the power cycle is associated with conflict processes.[3] Cashman (2013), in particular, observes that studies from Doran have been replicated many times. Inoguchi (2003: 172; see also Doran 2012: 80) observes that the power cycle, given complex and fundamental changes in Asia, will retain significance in the new millennium. Furthermore, a study with results that contradict the association of critical points with war among great powers has yet to appear.

Structural realism, put forward by Waltz (1979), focuses on how the distribution of capabilities at the level of the international system impacts upon its propensity for conflict. States face a situation of self-help and can be expected to engage in power balancing for their own protection. The principal idea about war put forward by structural realism is that bipolarity is more stable than multipolarity. A system with two leading states, as opposed to three or more, will be less prone to break down into highly destructive conflict. Under bipolarity, the two leading states can be expected to match and monitor the efforts of each other. Thus, war becomes less likely than in the relatively more chaotic world of multipolarity.

Evidence from Waltz (1979) focuses on experiences of the great powers, primarily located in Europe, over the course of two centuries. The story of multipolarity is one of complicated alliance systems that form and break down, with attendant uncertainties that make it more difficult to manage conflict and prevent war. With the advent of bipolarity after World War II, major powers no longer fought wars directly with each other. From the standpoint of Waltz (1979: 170), precisely because the two leading states eye each other like scorpions in a bottle, their leaders are able to avert a major war because the system is much simpler to manage. This is most notably true with regard to alliance politics. In a multipolar system, by contrast, balancing can be expected to fail because of free riding, which in turn undermines deterrence of aggression (Levy and Thompson 2010: 33).[4]

IN FOCUS: THE DEBATE OVER SYSTEM STRUCTURE

One weakness of the system structure/polarity argument is that it lends itself to competing, and quite contradictory, interpretations. Consider, for example, the following table (Table 5.1) summarizing arguments about the effects of bipolar versus multipolar power distributions on system stability.

---

[3] Hebron, James, and Rudy (2007) produce evidence that links foreign policy crises and Militarized Interstate Disputes (MIDs) with proximity to critical points.

[4] Structural realism has stimulated a vast literature that includes many critiques; for a summary of those contributions, see James (2022: 364–368).

Table 5.1 Bipolarity, multipolarity, and war

Bipolarity	Multipolarity
More Stable	**More Stable**
Two major powers create a solid balance	More actors increase opportunities for peaceful interactions
War anywhere could become war everywhere	More actors increase the number of states who could oppose an aggressor
Certainty and calculation are easier	
Control over allies is easier. Conflict is only likely between the two major powers	More actors mean more mediators to moderate conflicts
Balance of power is easier to identify and achieve	More actors may slow the rate of arms races
	States cannot focus on only one adversary
	Hostility is diffused
Shifts in the power of most states do not matter	Ambiguity, uncertainty, and unpredictability increase with more actors and complexity
Less Stable	**Less Stable**
Levels of hostility are very high	Opportunities for conflict increase
There are no mediators to moderate conflict between the major powers	Diversity of interests increases
Conflict anywhere can draw in the major powers	Misperception and miscalculation increase in situations of greater complexity and uncertainty
Stalemate between major powers may enable conflicts in peripheral areas	More states mean that unequal distributions of resources are more likely
Clarity and certainty might lead to war	

In terms of empirical evidence, advocates of structural realism cite different outcomes for historical systems in the 20th century. The multipolar world produced World Wars I and II. By contrast, the bipolar system of the Cold War featured various conflicts but terminated without escalation to global war (Waltz 1979). As further supporting evidence, consider a significant asymmetry observed in international crises involving the US and USSR during the Cold War. Analysis of International Crisis Behavior (ICB) data from 1948 to 1985 confirms that the superpower on the defensive tended to come out on top (James and Harvey 1992). This result affirms the underlying idea that bipolarity induced competition within reasonably well-understood boundaries.

What do these competing arguments and evidence about the same explanatory factors suggest about theories of conflict, crisis, and war?

Offensive realism envisions great powers as disposed toward expansion (Mearsheimer 2014 [2001]; see also Levy and Thompson 2010: 35 and Quackenbush 2015: 105). Under conditions of anarchy, intentions do not matter because the existence of capabilities, in and of itself, creates a threatening situation between and among states. Thus, a rational response to this predicament for a great power is to go on the offensive. The more power that can be accumulated, all other things being equal, the higher the level of security that results. Security, however, proves elusive because all of the great powers are thinking the same way. Since relative gains are what matter, it is impossible to be fully secure unless you are the one state that dominates all others (Ruane and James 2012: 60). The result is that great power war can be expected to recur within the international system primarily because of the way in which efforts take place to discourage it through acquisition of capabilities. This feature of the international system accounts for the title of the book from Mearsheimer (2014 [2001]) that puts forward offensive realism, namely, *The Tragedy of Great Power Politics*.

Evidence in favor of offensive realism focuses primarily on major powers, for the most part in Europe, but also including the United States and Japan. Along those lines, the experiences of Italy, which tend to receive less attention in studies that focus on great powers, are covered from 1861 to 1945. Notable also is analysis of Soviet–American nuclear-based rivalry in the Cold War era, which did not culminate in war. Mearsheimer (2014 [2001]) sees the experiences of the great powers over time as quite favorable to offensive realism. Major powers seek to make gains at the expense of others and will go to war to achieve that goal.

Predation theory is the most recent among realist expositions on the causes of war. In a major study, *Rising Titans, Falling Giants*, Shifrinson (2019: 6) puts forward predation theory as an explanation for the degree of conflict observed during times of significant change in relative capabilities. War becomes more likely under such circumstances. Shifrinson (2019) puts forward an explanation for war that focuses on the dynamics of relative capability between and among the great powers. Predation theory begins with the insight that "rising states differ wildly in their approaches to declining great powers" (Shifrinson 2019: 2). The theory assumes, with justification, that leaders rarely possess fully accurate information about the distribution of power (Shifrinson 2019: 3). When considering expansion, a rising state must assess benefits versus cost under conditions of risk. Efforts to maximize power can "elicit retaliation from states with similar concerns about relative power and security" (Shifrinson 2020). War can occur as states react to change in relative capabilities. Policies among rising states therefore will vary by context; there is no deterministic pathway to either peace or war under conditions of strategically significant change in relative capabilities.

Predation theory seeks to "understand and account for a rising state's predatory or supportive policies toward its declining peers" (Shifrinson 2019: 3). The focus is on the politics associated with power shifts. Pathways to, or away from, war reflect strategies adopted by rising states in response to the decline of one or more great power peers. These strategies vary along two dimensions: (a) *goals* pursued by a rising state toward a peer in decline and (b) *means* selected to achieve those aims (Shifrinson 2020). If the declining state is seen to have strategic value and/or a significant remaining level of capabilities, a rising state may seek to prop it up. The intensity of effort can be expected to vary from one situation to the next. Four possible strategies therefore are identified: (a) relegation – negative and more intense; (b) strengthening – positive and more intense; (c) weakening – negative and less intense; and (d) bolstering – positive and less intense.

Evidence from a wide range of cases offers support to predation theory. Examples include (i) the US strategy of weakening, shifting over to relegation, against the USSR during its accelerating decline in the 1980s; and (ii) policies vis-à-vis France and Austria as each moved downward in the mid-19th century, with the German choice of weakening in contrast with Russian and British bolstering (Shifrinson 2019: 521–523). Russia and the United Kingdom placed a higher strategic value than Germany on the continuing membership of Austria and France in the "club". Since all parties could see that France and Austria still maintained significant capabilities, the German policy took the form of weakening rather than an infeasible relegation.

Consider also ongoing land reclamation and military deployments from China in the East and South China Seas (Shifrinson 2018). This activity, as Shifrinson (2018) points out, involves primarily territories that the Chinese government had claimed previously – not an expansion of maritime claims. From the standpoint of predation theory, these policies make sense and are likely to continue. On the one hand, China seeks to gain at the expense of the US from, most notably, its key client states such as Japan. On the other hand, China exists in a crowded and adversarial neighborhood (Shifrinson 2018). The behavior of a rising China therefore is assertive rather than highly confrontational because escalation of conflict with the US would not be desirable for the foreseeable future. In sum, China on the rise pursues a weakening strategy that accurately reflects its geostrategic situation in East Asia.

POWER TRANSITION THEORY

Introduced more than 60 years ago by Organski (1958) in response to the realist-based consensus of theorizing during the Cold War, PTT continues to provide the foundation for one of the most successful programs of research in the field (Organski and Kugler 1980; Tammen, Kugler, and Lemke 2017a and 2017b; Tammen 2000). According to PTT, hierarchy will arise in the international order, with a single state recognized as the leader. The system, therefore, experiences effects from the preponderance of a dominant power as a result. Generally speaking, weaker states will go along with the demands of a leading state, which in turn maintains stability in an effort to preserve its position (Rhamey and Kugler 2020: 45).

What became known as *Pax Britannica*, for example, extended for approximately one century, dating from the final defeat of Napoleon in 1815 to the outbreak of World War I in 1914. The United Kingdom had by far the most powerful navy in the world and used it to promote commerce over the high seas, which in turn reinforced the power of its far-flung empire. While limited conflict occurred, such as the Crimean and Franco-Prussian Wars, Europe did not experience anything close to a system-wide conflagration in the 19th century after the Battle of Waterloo. In line with PTT, as modern Germany emerged as an active challenger and obtained peer status with the United Kingdom from the turn of the 20th century onward, confrontation increased. The Great War ensued in August 1914 because the leader and challenger could not settle their differences otherwise.

PTT focuses on the dynamics of power between the first- and second-place states in the international system. The basic intuition of power transition is that tension rises as the challenger gains ground on the leader. Danger of war is at a maximum in a zone where the difference between the two top states is diminishing – notably within a 20% margin (Rhamey and Kugler 2020: 10). Evenly matched capabilities create the potential for ambiguity about who is at the apex and therefore should be expected to implement and enforce the existing order. PTT is adjacent to realism, but not contained within it. Like realism, PTT focuses on rational action among states as influenced by the distribution of capabilities. However, PTT moves away from realism through its emphasis on the politics of international hierarchy rather than anarchy.

Gradual buildup of potential capabilities can lead to significant changes in power dynamics between the dominant and rising states. In this scenario, escalation is possible and begins within a potential challenger. One scenario, as per above, is that the domestic politics in the rising state are out of line with the existing order; German elites in the early 20th century increasingly resented a colonial system and world economy that worked to the advantage of the United Kingdom. Another possibility is that the dominant power will remain preponderant if the rising state is relatively satisfied and chooses not to challenge the status quo.

PTT thereby acknowledges that the changes in power dynamics do not always lead to war, especially when the rising power is satisfied with the status quo under the leading state (Tammen, Kugler, and Lemke 2017a and 2017b). Power transition studies have shown that dynamics and various situations of parity in capabilities can lead to contradictory outcomes ranging from war to integration. Outcomes will depend on levels of satisfaction and specific indicators of power transition. When the dominant power and the rising power are in parity, the latter does not necessarily challenge the former if both are satisfied with the status quo. In this sense, the dominant power has a key responsibility to create conditions for peace in the international system even as it seeks to entrench its standing at the apex.[5]

Consider the US in the late 19th century, an era where it closed the gap and ultimately surpassed the United Kingdom in capabilities. A key event along the way to a peaceful transition between the two states occurred with settlement of the Alaska boundary dispute in 1903. The United Kingdom took the US side against its Canadian colony in border negotiations – a preventive measure with regard to possible mobilization of public opinion in the rising state in favor of escalating the conflict (James 2021). The settlement removed the last possibly significant territorial issues between the US and the United Kingdom. It is interesting to observe that de facto British leadership continued for some time because of compatible interests *and* the reinforcing effect of a predominantly isolationist mind-set in the US.[6] Another example might be found in the implications of China's rising power in recent decades, as "For Example: A Coming War Between the United States and China?" describes.

FOR EXAMPLE: A COMING WAR BETWEEN THE UNITED STATES AND CHINA?

Recently, political scientist Graham Allison wrote that China and the US were stuck in a "Thucydides trap" (Allison 2017a; see also Allison 2017b).[7] According to Allison (2017b:

---

[5] Critics have pointed out that power transition theorists have failed to pinpoint the structural origins of these different levels of satisfaction toward behavior because of the different assumptions about domestic coalitions (e.g., Schenoni 2018: 471–472).

[6] An authoritative study of the reluctant rise of the US from regional hegemon to status as world leader appears in Zakaria (1998).

[7] The Thucydides trap derives from PTT, referenced already as a long-standing model of how an international system becomes most dangerous when its first- and second-place states are evenly matched in capabilities.

para 3):

> as China challenges America's predominance, misunderstandings about each other's actions and intentions could lead them into a deadly trap first identified by the ancient Greek historian Thucydides. As [Thucydides] explained, "It was the rise of Athens and the fear that this instilled in Sparta that made war inevitable." The past 500 years have seen 16 cases in which a rising power threatened to displace a ruling one. Twelve of these ended in war.
>
> In such a Thucydides trap, when power shifts and a challenger catches up to a dominant leader, even their most basic interactions become more dangerous, and flashpoints or crises can easily spin out of control, leading to military conflict even if neither the challenger nor the dominant leader would have chosen such a course.
>
> China's rapid rise, dramatic economic growth, increasing military might, and growing influence in world politics all make it look like a challenger quickly catching the "top dog". Indeed, in 2019 the University of Sydney's (Australia) United States Studies Centre, went so far as to say "The U.S. is no longer the dominant power in the western Pacific and would struggle to win a conflict against China …. [In fact], the U.S. could lose a war before it starts if, for example, China were to launch a wide-scale, coordinated missile attack against U.S. and allied bases" (Shinkman 2019). When the challenges facing US leadership in world politics are considered, the picture appears even bleaker, especially in the wake of the 2022 Russian invasion of Ukraine, which some observers argue provides cues for future Chinese action against Taiwan. Since many observers note that both the US and China consider their position in the world to be unique and exceptional, warranting leadership and influence, it might be even harder to imagine that one would defer to the other.
>
> *In light of Power Transition Theory and its application by Allison, what factors make a future war between the US and China likely and what factors work against the outbreak of war between the two?*

Contingency is significant within the power transition's outlook. Tammen, Kugler, and Lemke (2017b: 19) observe that war "is not predetermined by structures, but structures set the necessary conditions for war". If the challenger adopts a hostile foreign policy toward the dominant power and the dominant power adopts a similar hostile foreign policy toward the challenger, severe conflict is the likely outcome. "As the defender begins to question the rise of the challenger", according to Tammen, Kugler, and Lemke (2017b: 19), "small increases toward a hostile policy stance produce sharp increases in dyadic conflict. Hence, the structural stage is set for prompting an early conflict initiation and war escalation". With evenly matched capabilities, it becomes relatively easy for each side to imagine that war will produce victory and hence the increased chance of conflict.

While the original PTT focuses on the power and conflict dynamics between a dominant state and a rising challenger in the international system, more recent research has expanded analysis to regional conflicts, civil wars, deterrence and nuclear proliferation, democratic peace, national identity and socialization, and the international monetary system (Tammen, Kugler, and Lemke 2017b). The long-standing success of PTT, along with the availability of a regional variant, makes it an ideal choice for in-depth application to East Asia. Rather than looking at the global system, Lemke (2002) unpacks the logic of PTT within regional hierarchies. Appendix Figure 5A.1 displays the systemist visualization of Lemke (2002) on regions of war and peace. PTT in a regional setting, like at the global level, allows for contingent outcomes. As capabilities shift and questions arise about the hierarchy in place, the playing out of conflict processes can lead to either peace or war.

THE EAST ASIAN SYSTEM

Since its advent in 2013, the Belt and Road Initiative (BRI) has been at the center of Chinese foreign policy. The BRI is emblematic of the rapid rise of China from the late 20th century onward – a point of culmination and symbol of power in East Asia and beyond. In order to obtain insights about where things may be headed for the Sino–US rivalry in East Asia, Zhang and James (2022) have assessed the processes leading up to the BRI in the context of PTT. Zhang and James (2022) apply the principles from Lemke (2002) and show how the regional hierarchy of East Asia has developed over several decades. The period covered is of particular interest because of significant changes in the regional distribution of capabilities between the US as leader and China as challenger. At this time of writing, the jury is still out on whether conflict and crisis – already in plain sight on numerous occasions – will end up in war.

Figure 5.1 shows the analysis from Zhang and James (2022), which tells the story of East Asia in the post-World War II era. The diagram includes 20 components. Within East Asia as the system, there are three micro and 14 macro components, and three components appear in the International System. The diagram is detailed enough to convey the most important developments in the region, but without becoming difficult to comprehend. Frequencies for the respective component types are as follows: initial (2), generic (7), divergent (5), convergent (2), nodal (2), and terminal (2). Given the presence of a total of nine contingencies – adding divergent, convergent, and nodal components together – it is clear that the account of East Asia is not deterministic in character.

Figure 5.1a displays East Asia as the system and the International System as its environment. The micro and macro levels of East Asia, respectively, correspond to actors and interactions among them. Movement from the International System into the macro level of East Asia gets underway in Figure 5.1b with "INTENSE COMPETITION AFTER WORLD WAR II: US AND SOVIET COALITIONS" → "WAVES OF DECOLONIZATION"; "COLD WAR COMPETITION FOR INFLUENCE: MILITARY AND SECURITY ALLIANCES, ARMS RACES, ETC.". The former component is initial and thus depicted as a green oval, while the latter are divergent and appear as orange diamonds.

Early within the Cold War, China became the first non-European communist state. At the time of its revolution in 1949, China did not look anything like a peer state of the US or USSR. The new regime existed as a junior partner within the Soviet coalition, but China played an increasingly important role within the processes after the arrow in the preceding subfigure. China took on a leading role in supporting decolonization around the globe. The former government of China, the Kuomintang, had fled across the Taiwan Strait to the island

SYSTEM-LEVEL EXPLANATIONS

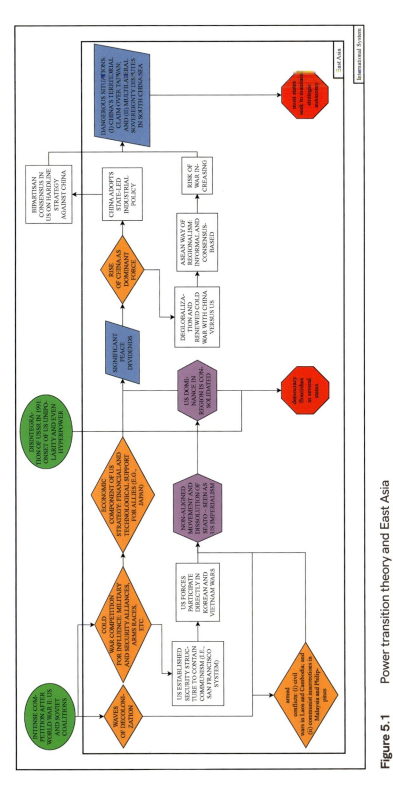

Figure 5.1 Power transition theory and East Asia

Figure 5.1a

SYSTEM-LEVEL EXPLANATIONS

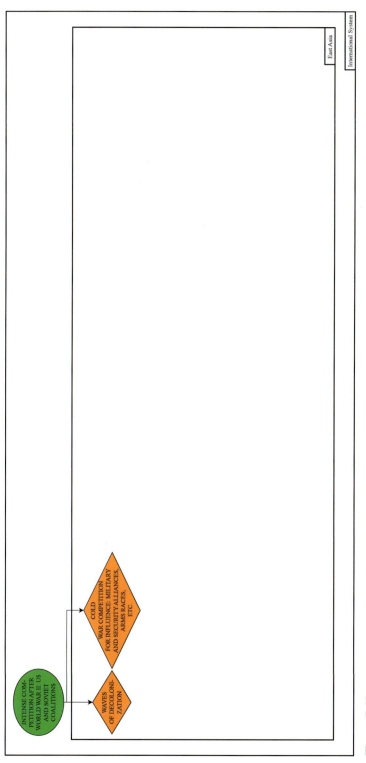

Figure 5.1b

CONFLICT, CRISIS, AND WAR IN WORLD POLITICS

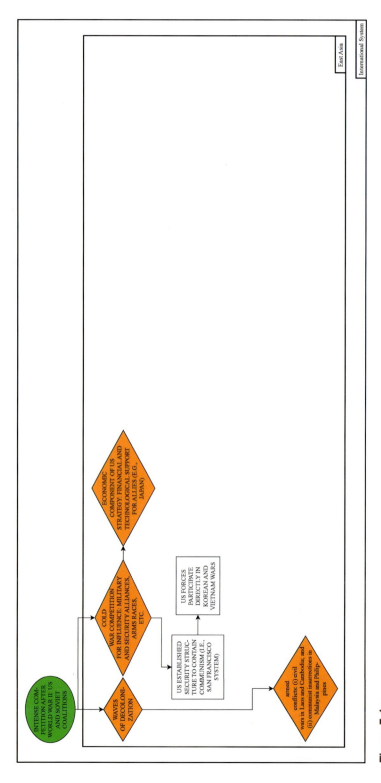

Figure 5.1c

SYSTEM-LEVEL EXPLANATIONS

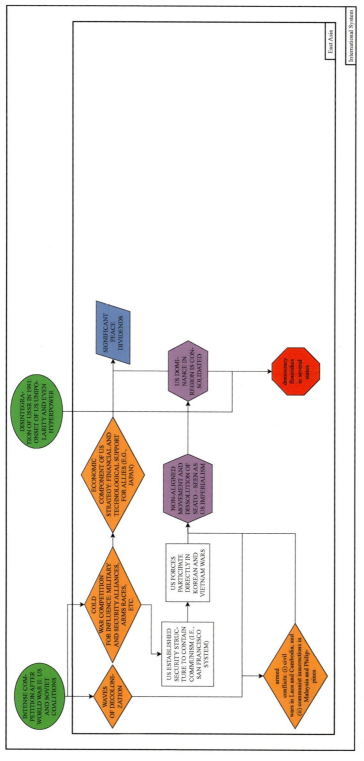

Figure 5.1d

CONFLICT, CRISIS, AND WAR IN WORLD POLITICS

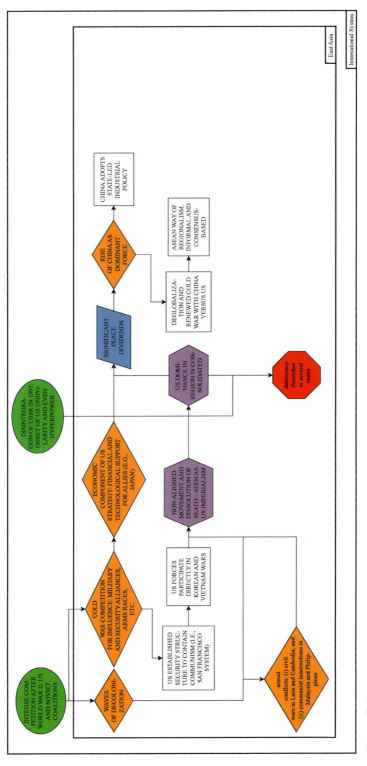

Figure 5.1e

SYSTEM-LEVEL EXPLANATIONS

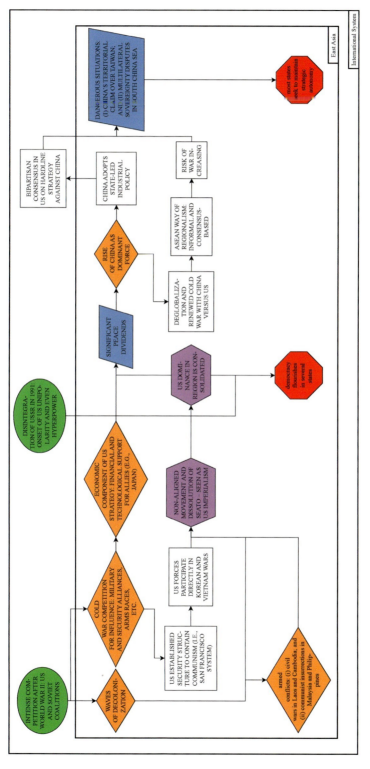

Figure 5.1f

of Formosa, serving as a US outpost from that point onward. Tensions between Taiwan and China escalated on multiple occasions, resulting in cases that are recorded in the ICB dataset.

Multiple routes emerge in Figure 5.1c, with two at the macro level and one from macro to micro. At the macro level, one pathway continues with "COLD WAR COMPETITION FOR INFLUENCE: MILITARY AND SECURITY ALLIANCES, ARMS RACES, ETC." → "ECONOMIC COMPONENT OF US STRATEGY: FINANCIAL AND TECHNOLOGICAL SUPPORT FOR ALLIES (E.G., JAPAN)". The latter component, as a point of divergence, appears as an orange diamond. US support for its allies in East Asia touched on a highly sensitive area for China, which had long memories about humiliation at the hands of imperial powers in general and Japan in particular. Along those lines, one study insightfully described China in oxymoronic terms – as a "fragile superpower" (Shirk 2007).

Another pathway at the macro level proceeds in Figure 5.1c with "COLD WAR COMPETITION FOR INFLUENCE: MILITARY AND SECURITY ALLIANCES, ARMS RACES, ETC." → "US ESTABLISHED SECURITY STRUCTURE TO CONTAIN COMMUNISM (I.E., SAN FRANCISCO SYSTEM)". In response to Cold War imperatives, a hub-and-spokes system developed, with the US at the center and Japan, South Korea, and Taiwan emerging as key allies in East Asia (Zhang and James 2022). This route continues at the macro level of Figure 5.1c with "US ESTABLISHED SECURITY STRUCTURE TO CONTAIN COMMUNISM (I.E., SAN FRANCISCO SYSTEM)" → "US FORCES PARTICIPATE DIRECTLY IN KOREAN AND VIETNAM WARS". The US made enormous commitments to both wars. In each instance, Washington acted on what had become known as the "domino" theory, which held that unchecked aggression would encourage more of the kind and eventually put the homeland in direct danger. To the Chinese, however, US activity in both wars signaled its ongoing hegemonic intentions rather than limited defensive goals.

Figure 5.1c also displays movement from the macro to the micro level: "WAVES OF DECOLONIZATION" → "armed conflicts: (i) civil wars in Laos and Cambodia; and (ii) communist insurrections in Malaysia and Philippines". As a point of divergence, the latter appears as an orange diamond. Across the board, decolonization processes produced conflicts that put China and the US on opposite sides. The strife in Southeast Asia, along with Vietnam as already mentioned, fed into Chinese insecurities about US-led imperialism. Long memories about national humiliation influenced perception of these and other events among both the Chinese elite and society (Shirk 2007; Callahan 2010). Thus, China challenged the US hierarchy in East Asia in limited and primarily ideological ways, long before it obtained anything like matching material capabilities.

Figure 5.1d extends multiple pathways. Pathways at the macro and micro levels reach a nodal point, depicted as a purple hexagon: "WAVES OF DECOLONIZATION"; "US FORCES PARTICIPATE DIRECTLY IN KOREAN AND VIETNAM WARS"; "armed conflicts: (i) civil wars in Laos and Cambodia; and (ii) communist insurrections in Malaysia and Philippines" → "NON-ALIGNED MOVEMENT AND DISSOLUTION OF SEATO – SEEN AS US IMPERIALISM". Seizing upon mixed to bad results for the US in its involvement in conflict processes of various kinds, along with the advent of states that had a mixture of views toward the existing hierarchy, China picked up momentum as a leader within the non-aligned movement. Chinese leaders moved out of the Soviet orbit as the 1960s unfolded and self-designated as a rallying point against US imperialism. The US, by contrast, began to move away from what some labeled "pactomania" and entered a period of reduced involvement in far-flung locations, notably in the aftermath of Vietnam.

Movement continues at the macro level, including an input from the International System, in Figure 5.1d: "DISINTEGRATION OF USSR IN 1991: ONSET OF US UNIPOLARITY AND EVEN HYPERPOWER"; "ECONOMIC COMPONENT OF US STRATEGY: FINANCIAL AND TECHNOLOGICAL SUPPORT FOR ALLIES (E.G., JAPAN)"; "NON-ALIGNED MOVEMENT AND DISSOLUTION OF SEATO – SEEN AS US IMPERIALISM" → "SIGNIFICANT PEACE DIVIDENDS"; "US DOMINANCE IN REGION IS CONSOLIDATED". The first component before the arrow is initial and appears as a green oval, while the components after the arrow, respectively, are convergent (a blue parallelogram) and nodal (a purple hexagon). At the end of the Cold War, the US entered a period of virtually unprecedented prosperity. Global trade and investment increased substantially. A rising economic tide lifted all "boats" in the figurative US-led armada in East Asia.

One route in Figure 5.1d reaches a point of termination at the micro level of East Asia: "DISINTEGRATION OF USSR IN 1991: ONSET OF US UNIPOLARITY AND EVEN HYPERPOWER"; "ECONOMIC COMPONENT OF US STRATEGY: FINANCIAL AND TECHNOLOGICAL SUPPORT FOR ALLIES (E.G., JAPAN)"; "NON-ALIGNED MOVEMENT AND DISSOLUTION OF SEATO – SEEN AS US IMPERIALISM"; "US DOMINANCE IN REGION IS CONSOLIDATED" → "democracy flourishes in several states". The terminal component appears as a red octagon. As the final years of the millennium unfolded, the US took on an increasingly positive image in East Asia – associated with prosperity rather than potentially threatening alliances. Prosperity reinforced democratic institutions in multiple East Asian states. For example, South Korea emerged from decades as a police state into a thriving democracy.

Figure 5.1e extends multiple macro levels pathways, with "SIGNIFICANT PEACE DIVIDENDS" → "RISE OF CHINA AS DOMINANT FORCE". The latter, a divergent component, takes the form of an orange diamond. Market-oriented reforms in China stimulated an amazing period of growth for China, with millions lifted out of poverty (Zhang and James 2022). Over the course of less than two decades, China went from a developing state to approximately peer status with the US at the top of the world economy.

One pathway continues in Figure 5.1e with "RISE OF CHINA AS DOMINANT FORCE" → "CHINA ADOPTS STATE-LED INDUSTRIAL POLICY". As an emerging rival to the US even on a global basis, China began to develop an alternative to what had become known as the "Washington Consensus".[8] The Chinese model of development featured state-driven industrial policies and impressed the world with its well-trained and low-cost labor forces, expanding modern infrastructure, and sustained export-driven growth (Zhang and James 2022; see also Yuan 2015; Feng, Gao, and Yang 2020; Tammen and Wahedi 2020; Gartner, Huang, Li, and James 2021). The BRI takes that framework beyond China and into East Asia in particular and the world in general. The BRI serves, as Zhang and James (2022) point out, as a response

---

[8] Basic components of the Washington Consensus included a commitment to capitalism, lower government spending, and economies open to international trade and investment.

to the pivot or rebalance to Asia proposed by the Obama Administration, along with the subsequent more explicit shift into strategic competition from the Trump years onward.

Another route in Figure 5.1e moves forward with "RISE OF CHINA AS DOMINANT FORCE" → "DEGLOBALIZATION AND RENEWED COLD WAR WITH CHINA VERSUS US". In tandem with its rapid economic rise, China also significantly modernized its military (Shifrinson 2018; Gartner, Huang, Li, and James 2021). With globalization on the wane, economic interdependence also decreased, which open the door to higher levels of conflict.

This pathway is extended in Figure 5.1e by "DEGLOBALIZATION AND RENEWED COLD WAR WITH CHINA VERSUS US" → "ASEAN WAY OF REGIONALISM: INFORMAL AND CONSENSUS-BASED". In the US and elsewhere, social movements began to question the US-led world order, with perception of harmful effects from what had been an increasingly globalized capitalist economy. As the saying goes, "hard times breed hard lines", and Sino–US tensions increased. All of this translated into greater influence for China, notably within ASEAN (Association of Southeast Asian Nations), because of the BRI-based alternative it offered to the US-led world order. In an ironic twist, the Chinese challenge to the US-centered order of East Asia, at least for some time, had an anti-hierarchical nature.

Multiple pathways are extended in Figure 5.1f. One moves out from the macro level of East Asia into the International System: "CHINA ADOPTS STATE-LED INDUSTRIAL POLICY" → "BIPARTISAN CONSENSUS IN US ON HARDLINE STRATEGY AGAINST CHINA". In response to what looked like an attempt to compete with the US around the world through the BRI, along with a threatening military posture vis-à-vis Taiwan, the policy community of the US experienced a dramatic change of viewpoint. A consensus in favor of engagement shifted to bipartisan support for policies that viewed China as a strategic competitor (McCourt 2022). Documents of the US government and military have come to label China as *the* strategic competitor (Zhang and James 2022). A new vision of China in the US increasingly reflected the logic of offensive realism. Rising Chinese military power seems to represent, in and of itself, a commitment to expansionism and ultimately even a takeover of East Asia.

One other pathway moves forward at the macro level of Figure 5.1f: "ASEAN WAY OF REGIONALISM: INFORMAL AND CONSENSUS-BASED" → "RISK OF WAR INCREASING". China cultivated other states through ASEAN, which through the new lens of strategic competition looked like an attempt to undermine the US-led coalition and possibly even replace it with a new one. As per an earlier discussion, this resembles a weakening strategy as described by predation theory (Shifrinson 2018). In addition, the high level of regional activism on the part of Beijing corresponded to the time interval that power cycle theory identifies as a first inflection along the curve (Doran 1991). While China continued to gain ground relative to other great powers, it now would be doing so at a reduced rate. China had settled into a "new normal" after 35 years of high economic growth (Feng, Gao, and Yang 2020). Thus, a sense of urgency could be expected to come about in order to make gains against the US in particular.

Pathways come together in Figure 5.1f with "BIPARTISAN CONSENSUS IN US ON HARDLINE STRATEGY AGAINST CHINA"; "RISK OF WAR INCREASING" → "DANGEROUS SITUATIONS: (I) CHINA'S TERRITORIAL CLAIM OVER TAIWAN; AND

(II) MULTILATERAL SOVEREIGNTY DISPUTES IN SOUTH CHINA SEA". As a convergent component, the latter is depicted as a blue parallelogram.

Among the connections in Figure 5.1f, the last is "DANGEROUS SITUATIONS: (1) CHINA'S TERRITORIAL CLAIM OVER TAIWAN; AND (II) MULTILATERAL SOVEREIGNTY DISPUTES IN SOUTH CHINA SEA" → "most states seek to maintain strategic autonomy". The latter, a terminal component, appears as a red octagon. With the long-standing hierarchy of the US in East Asia openly and even aggressively challenged by China, responses among others in the region can be explained via the logic of PTT. Under such ambiguous conditions – not knowing whether the US would preserve its position at the top or be replaced by China – hedging makes sense. For the most part, in an era of confrontation between the leading and challenging states, others in East Asia have opted pragmatically for neither balancing nor bandwagoning. At least so far, the region is waiting things out.

Interesting to ponder is the possibility of bipolarity in East Asia. Rather than an outright victory for either China or the US, what if something like a dead heat settled into place? From the standpoint of structural realism, this would be the ideal result. The US and China then could manage East Asian politics through an uneasy but, if it would not be too much to hope, stable bipolarity. PTT, by contrast, would see the balance as inherently unstable due to its lack of hierarchy. These opposite views, along with other forecasts that could be added from other theories, serve as a reminder that even the best frameworks from the system level offer an incomplete sense of things where foreign policy is concerned.

IN FOCUS

For purposes of comparison, consider the Caribbean and Middle East as systems. How might each be analyzed via PTT and other theories encountered in this chapter? In what ways do these systems seem different or alike with regard to conflict, crisis, and war?

SUMMING UP AND MOVING FORWARD

This chapter begins the process of examining conflict, crisis, and war via levels of analysis. Economy of explanation accounts for the order of work, which has started with the system level. In the pages of this chapter, we reviewed a sample of theories from the long-standing realist tradition – power cycle, structural, offensive, and predation to provide breadth of explanation. These theories, which focus on either the dynamics or statics of capabilities among states, produce numerous insights about the process of escalation. A complementary depth of explanation is obtained through a focus on one theory, PTT, which also happens to be outside the boundaries of realism. Our application of PTT to East Asia, with its accompanying systemist diagram, lays out a story of how that region has evolved over the course of several decades.

We continue our application of levels of analysis to conflict, crisis, and war in Chapter 6, where our attention turns to the state level. We consider characteristics of government and society and their potential connections with conflict processes.

CONSIDER THIS: UNDERSTANDING THE PATTERNS OF CONFLICT, CRISIS, AND WAR

System-level explanations of conflict, crisis, and war focus on (some) key attributes and structural characteristics of the international system such as anarchy, hierarchy, the distribution of power, and others. Explanations at this level rely on these system-level attributes to explain recurring patterns of conflict and war in a variety of ways. Reflecting on the preceding discussion:

For what patterns of conflict, crisis, and war do system-level theories provide particularly useful or less helpful explanations?

SYSTEM-LEVEL EXPLANATIONS

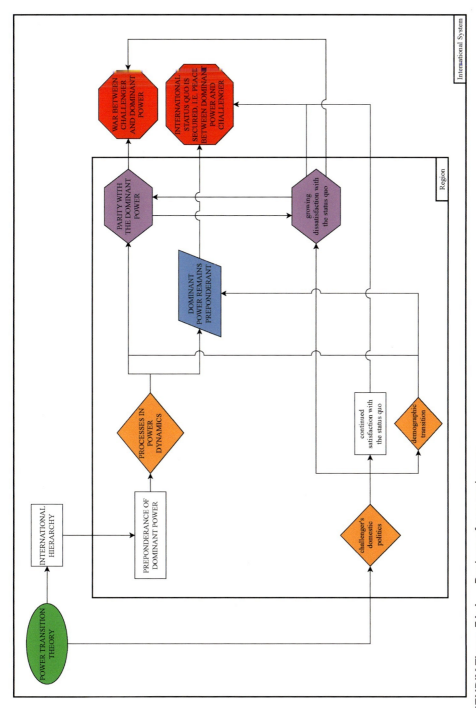

APPENDIX Figure 5A.1 Regions of war and peace

6
State-level explanations

PROLOGUE

North Korea is well established as one of the most troublesome states in the world. With the support of the USSR and China, it started the devastating Korean War that lasted from 1950 to 1953. In the decades since then, North Korea has combined fiery anti-American rhetoric with a campaign of harassment against South Korea. Concern most recently focuses on its potential acquisition of nuclear weapons, since many deem North Korea so irrational that it would have a significant probability of using such capabilities.

Pyongyang, the capital of North Korea, exists as a shrine to the dictators from a single family who continue to rule it. These leaders – Kim Il Sung, Kim Jong Il, and Kim Jong Un – are absolute rulers who enforce what may be the most extreme cult of personality ever seen. Their state reflects the disposition of its leaders: concerned above all else about holding on to power. North Korea therefore exhibits paranoia and xenophobia on an ongoing basis. The dreadful condition of North Korea, most notably in comparison to South Korea, is well illustrated by nighttime satellite imagery, which shows the North in virtually total darkness, while the South features many points of light.

This state clearly is an outlier. It may be the archetype of what Dror (1971) colorfully labeled a "crazy state". Rogue states, to use the more conventional term, tend to be insular dictatorships that show no respect for their peers in the international system and make a mockery of international law. Controversy continues over how to manage the danger posed by such states to international peace and stability. On the one hand, liberal thinking would point toward engagement and negotiation. On the other hand, realists would argue that only a firm approach toward a rogue state will deter its aggression. This debate shows no sign of being over, but also highlights the idea that important aspects of a state's international behavior – including its propensity for conflict and violence – can be attributed to the nature of its internal organization and other national characteristics and conditions.

OVERVIEW

A state-based perspective to understanding conflict, crisis, and war sacrifices some of the parsimony of the system level to add complexity and detail to generate explanations of the participation and war proneness of the principal unit of international relations. While there is just one international system, about 200 states exist, so that trade-off becomes obvious. In Waltz's (1959) classic formulation, this "second image" focuses on conflict, crisis, and war as the outcome of the internal organization and other conditions of states. What does this perspective offer to explanations of conflict, crisis, and war?

This chapter moves forward in four additional sections. The second section introduces a survey of a selection of major state-level theories from multiple schools of thought to establish a broad foundation in both material and ideational terms. The third section focuses on one prominent theory that draws chiefly on the liberal school of thought: Democratic Peace Theory, an influential and central factor in the relatively recent attention to state-level theorizing about conflict and war over the past 40 years or so (Levy and Thompson 2010: 84). The fourth section offers an in-depth deconstruction of a major review essay on regime type, with connections to Democratic Peace Theory and beyond, accompanied by a systemist diagram. We conclude with a fifth section summarizing and reflecting on the main points of this chapter and leading into the next one.

STATES AND CONFLICT

Scientific realism, as introduced in Chapter 1, emphasizes that both the seen and unseen may play important roles in the explanation of conflict processes. Along those lines, for any given state, both material and ideational aspects can be significant for involvement in conflict processes. Chapter 4, on issues, recognized the importance of the material, like territory, and the ideational, like religion. An in-depth review of Hassner (2009), a work at the intersection of the preceding issues, revealed how material and ideational matters can become intertwined and impact significantly on the prospects for cooperation versus conflict.

In his introduction to state-level explanations of war, Cashman (2013: 169) notes that a central starting point for this level of analysis is "that states are not equally violent; great variation in conflict activity exists among the states of the world". Although a central point of realist arguments at the system level is that conflict is normal and war is always possible in an anarchic international system, much empirical evidence from data such as the Correlates of War (COW) Project and many studies that draw from it demonstrate something that state-level theorists consider important and in need of explanation: some states are far more warlike than others and, conversely, some are far more peaceful.

To understand and explain the varying participation and war proneness of the members of the international system, state-level explanations do not look to the structural aspects of the international system. System structure, in whatever form, can be viewed as more or less enabling to conflict, crisis, and war, with any number of potential patterns of interaction. Instead, state-level explanations attempt to explain this variation by directing attention to the states – or units – themselves. The basic argument at this level is that qualities of some states lead them to be more (or less) conflict prone or warlike. State-level arguments thus grapple most directly with the question of which states are the most likely participants in war. At the state level, emphasis is generally placed on various attributes of countries and nations, such as the type and processes of government, economy, or other national/cultural factors, and how these features affect the behavior and interactions of the participants in conflict. In this context, we cover material and ideational aspects in turn.

Material Aspects

As in our previous chapter on the international system, we offer a limited survey rather than a full account of state-level theories. Our selection of theories provides a summary of key lines of argument/explanation, with examples of scholarship and empirical evidence. We start with explanations focused on a broad cluster of national attributes, and target size and power for discussion. Then, we take up explanations focused on the effects of economic systems on conflict and war, targeting interdependence and the "capitalist peace" for discussion. From there, we move to the context of internal political conditions, especially stability/instability, targeting diversionary theory for discussion. We save discussion of the most salient factor – type of government – for the end and take up the high-profile Democratic Peace Theory for discussion in that context.

We begin with a broad cluster of potential explanations, more of a "grab bag" of accounts arising from multiple perspectives and data collection exercises than from unified theoretical arguments. This approach is in line with analytic eclecticism, which advocates for seeking out the best ideas without concern for paradigmatic boundaries.

Consider, to begin, COW data that provides evidence supporting the argument that larger, wealthier, and more powerful states are more likely to engage in war than other states (e.g., Bremer 1980; Small and Singer 1970; Haas 1980). This argument is consistent with several theoretical perspectives, most notably realism. Others have argued that population pressures such as growth, overcrowding, and lateral pressure generated by rising demands for resources lead some states to engage in war (e.g., Choucri and North 1975). Another finding from many studies is that borders may create points of friction that often result in war, a result that dovetails nicely with the centrality of territory as an issue for conflict, crisis, and war we discussed in Chapter 4. As many studies have concluded, states with more borders, or contested borders, engage in war more frequently than those without such contiguity issues, which has made proximity/contiguity a common variable to include in almost any study of conflict.[1]

Another line of argument based on national attributes stresses prior experiences with war. A war weariness argument explains that states that have most recently experienced a significant, costly war are more peaceful in the aftermath because of the impact of those costs and experiences on the population, public opinion, and leaders. For example, after the costly and protracted Vietnam conflict, the United States was often said to be reluctant to commit American troops to another conflict. This "Vietnam syndrome" continues to receive attention and may have been reinforced by subsequent experiences in Somalia (1993), Iraq (2003–present), and Afghanistan (2001–2021). In particular, American leaders appear to be

---

[1] Examples would include Bremer (2000) and Starr and Thomas (2005); see, however, Hensel (2001) and Vasquez (2001) on the importance of territorial disputes conditioning the basic effects of contiguity.

significantly more constrained in their decisions to introduce ground forces into potentially long-term operations (Kalb and Kalb 2011; Mueller 2005).

> **FOR EXAMPLE: LEARNING AND THE OBSOLESCENCE OF WAR?**
>
> In *Retreat From Doomsday: The Obsolescence of War*, John Mueller (1990) introduces another variant of the war weariness argument, pointing to a learning function for developed states that have participated in the major wars of the 20th century. According to Mueller, by the middle of the 20th century, virtually all of Europe, North America, and the developed world elsewhere had recognized this through the experiences of World Wars I and II, and by 1990, this recognition had spread even further. Thus, just as with social conventions such as slavery and dueling, societies learned through experiences that practices like these, and war, were costly, unacceptable, and just plain wrong.

What, then, is the challenge for arguments centered on war weariness and learning as national attributes? Although some COW-based evidence offers limited support of a war weariness effect, much more does not (e.g., Singer and Cusack 1981; Levy and Morgan 1986). Indeed, cross-national data analysis offers little or no support to the idea of war weariness. This may be a product of fading memories among the societies involved in a previous iteration of war (Quackenbush 2015: 294). The jury is out at this point.

Turning to the effects of economic systems on conflict and war, a long history of argument surrounds theorizing about the relationship between the economic structures and practices of states on one hand, and outcomes like conflict on the other. Liberal thinkers such as Montesquieu, Kant, J. S. Mill, and Adam Smith all posited that free market economics and/or free trade reduced conflict and war. In contrast to this commercial liberalism claim, others such as John Hobson (1965) and Vladimir Lenin (1939) argued that capitalism motivated states to compete for resources and markets and resulted in wars between them, especially as imperialism drove them to try to control other parts of the world. Empirical evidence supporting the latter argument has been elusive (Levy and Thompson 2010: 85–92), while the potentially pacific effects of capitalism have been examined by a substantial body of scholarship, with more positive results.

A century or so ago, Norman Angell (1911) argued that capitalism within, and the expansion of trade between, countries raised the costs of war sufficiently to make war between countries increasingly less desirable and likely. Although the subsequent experiences of World Wars I and II appeared to work against Angell's argument, the development of the global economy and its effects on relationships between countries renewed interest in and attention to the effects of economic systems and practices on conflict, crisis, and war. The centerpiece of attention for more than three decades has been on the effects of economic interdependence on conflict.

Economic exchange as a pathway to peace is associated with the philosophy of Immanuel Kant. The core of the contemporary commercial liberalism argument about capitalism and war/peace is that market economics and the connections between states that it fosters reduce incentives for and likelihood of war. In really simple terms, one does not shoot one's customers, as the saying goes; it's bad for business. Variants of this argument focus on the potential role of economic development (e.g., Gartzke 2007; Lake 1992; Lemke 2003), the size/strength of the private sector of a country's economy (e.g., McDonald 2007, 2009), trade interdependence (e.g., Polachek 1980; Weede 1995), the openness and interdependence of financial markets (e.g., Gartzke 2007; Gartzke, Li, and Boehmer 2001), and economic norms and practices, especially in terms of contract-rich versus contract-poor economic systems (e.g., Mousseau 2013, 2018). Factors such as these make war costly and unprofitable (thus increasing opportunity costs) and/or deepen the common interests and preferences of countries, thus minimizing conflict that might lead to the use of force among states (see McMillan 1997; Mansfield and Pollins 2001, 2003; Schneider and Gleditsch 2013 for broad overviews). The general thrust of these variants is that these key economic factors are central to the reduction of militarized conflict between states and help to explain why some states, or pairs of states, are less likely to escalate conflict to war. The argument has been advanced at both the global and regional (e.g., Owen 2012) levels.

IN FOCUS: THE CAPITALIST PEACE AND INTERNATIONAL CRISIS BEHAVIOR

Investigations of the effects of free markets, trade, and other economic exchange on conflict behavior have generally focused on the war proneness of states, and particularly pairs of states. Gartzke and Hewitt (2010) extend the basic argument to the arena of crisis behavior as well. These scholars argue that "development and global markets eventually eliminate resource competition as a motive for war" and also create mechanisms of interaction and alter the interests of participating countries such that interests become more alike and policy differences diminish (Gartzke and Hewitt 2010: 122, 123-125). Applying their argument to crises and drawing on data from the International Crisis Behavior Project from 1950-1992, the authors find support for several key hypotheses on the effect of their version of the capitalist peace on crisis behavior:

1. Once triggered, a crisis is less likely to escalate among globally integrated economies.
2. Crises in economically integrated dyads experience a lower level of violence.
3. Crises in economically developed dyads result in fewer battlefield casualties.

As a result of this empirical support for their argument, Gartzke and Hewitt (2010: 138, 139) conclude that "economic development and market freedoms ... precipitate interstate peace" and "are the more proximate causes of cooperation among states in the modern world".

What might this conclusion mean for efforts to promote cooperation and peace in world politics?

Empirical analysis of the preceding claims about interdependence has provided significant support for the general relationship and to respective explanations. While some studies challenge the relationship (e.g., Barbieri 1996, 2002; Keshk, Pollins, and Reuveny 2004; Kim and Rousseau 2005), a great many others show an inverse connection between interdependence and conflict.[2] Central concerns include issues related to the nature of trade and economic data (e.g., Barbieri 1996) and time order/sequencing of causation (e.g., Keshk, Pollins, and Reuveny 2004). But much more attention has been devoted to whether interdependence/economic factors complement, condition, or supersede other factors.[3] Overall, the balance of evidence appears to indicate that trade and other economic factors underlying interdependence raise costs for and change calculations about engaging in military conflict.[4] Nevertheless, a lively debate continues on the causal mechanisms, dynamics, magnitude, and scope/conditions of this outcome, as well as the relationship between these economic factors and others (such as democracy, which we discuss later in this chapter).

Domestic political conditions are another common state-level factor often associated with war. Broadly speaking, as Hagan (1994: 184) argued, "domestic political systems .... affect what types of leaders can come to power and the orientations to international affairs these leaders are likely to have .... [O]nce a leadership is in power, domestic political processes help to shape its definition of the national interest and its ability to implement it." Some of these conditions may affect the war proneness of states. Among the salient entries in these arguments, Snyder (1991) and others focus on the effects of ruling coalitions and the need to maintain them (see also Oktay 2022 and Kaarbo and Beasley 2008). Rosecrance and Stein (1993) and others highlight the roles of domestic political processes and coalitions in the state's ability to extract resources for national capabilities, especially military power. The connection between domestic political conditions and the rise to power of hardliner leaders is another aspect that may affect a state's propensity to engage in conflict, crisis, and war (e.g., Vasquez 1993). Finally, domestic political changes – especially internal conflict and revolution – may increase a state's propensity for engaging in conflict. Competing elites or newly empowered regimes may look to international conflict to shore up their own political positions, or they may offer inviting targets for other states to attach to try to take advantage of political instability and weakness (see Hagan 1994 for a summary of such arguments).

A key explanation of the relationship between domestic political conditions and processes and conflict, crisis, and war focuses on the role of political instability. Indeed, a major research program has devoted attention to the scapegoat or diversionary theory. Popularized by movies such as *Wag the Dog* and *Canadian Bacon*, this explanation holds that states suffering from poor economic conditions (like high inflation, unemployment, or economic recession or depression) or other internal strife (generated by ethnic or other divisions) are more likely to resort to force outside their borders in efforts to divert attention from those internal problems and generate unity in the face of some external enemy (e.g., Fordham 2017). In effect, leaders seek a "rally 'round the flag dynamic by which support for leaders increases with conflict from

---

[2] See, for example, Weede (1995), Oneal and Russett (1997), Gartzke (2007), Gartzke, Li, and Boehmer (2001), Hegre, Oneal, and Russett (2010), McDonald (2009), Mousseau (2018), and many others.

[3] For instance, see Gartzke (2007), Gartzke, Li, and Boehmer (2001), Russett, Oneal, and Davis (1998), Oneal, Russett, and Berbaum (2003), Hegre, Oneal, and Russett (2010), Mousseau, Hegre, and Oneal (2003), and Mousseau (2009, 2010, 2018).

[4] See McMillan (1997), Mansfield and Pollins (2001, 2003), Schneider and Gleditsch (2013), and Schneider (2022) for reviews of findings at different stages.

'out-group' actors like foreign countries" (Levy and Thompson 2010: 100). On the flipside of this argument, states with such conditions may be attractive targets for attack by others as well (see Chiozza and Goemans 2004; see also Levy 1989a and Butcher 2023 for reviews of this research program). Political problems such as regime unpopularity or unrest (e.g., Meernik 2000; Kisangani and Pickering, 2007, 2011; Pickering and Kisangani 2005, 2010; Tir 2010), economic problems such as unemployment, inflation, or lack of growth (e.g., Ostrom and Job 1986; James and Oneal 1991; DeRouen 1995; Kisangani and Pickering 2011; Mitchell and Prins 2004; Tir 2010), and ethnic division (e.g., Haynes 2016; Butcher and Maru 2018) have all been emphasized as key factors leading to diversionary war behavior.

The driving forces behind diversionary war behavior include multiple possibilities. As Fordham's (2017) review of studies on the topic has noted, these include: (1) in-group/out-group dynamics; (2) agenda setting (to force focus to foreign policy rather than domestic issues); (3) leader efforts to demonstrate competence in foreign policy; and (4) efforts to blame foreign leaders or domestic minorities for internal problems. A variety of domestic contexts also affect the likelihood of a state engaging in diversionary conflict. Some studies have concluded that democracies are more likely to engage in diversionary conflict (e.g., Gelpi 1997) while others have found the opposite (e.g., Enterline and Gleditsch 2000). Sobek (2007), Gent (2009), and Mansfield and Snyder (2005) respectively concluded that autocracies, mixed regimes, and certain types of regimes in transition from autocracy to democracy are more likely to use diversion. Kisangani and Pickering (2007, 2011) found that different types of democracies and different types of authoritarian regimes are more or less likely to resort to diversionary conflict, with leader accountability in each a central factor.

To the preceding factors, Butcher's (2023: 5) summary of the sizable diversionary war literature adds "domestic structures, economic and military capabilities, domestic ethnic cleavages, and even the individual psychology of leaders" as additional factors that can affect a state's likelihood of engaging in diversionary conflict. Both Leeds and Davis (1997) and Smith (1996) introduce strategic interactions to the mix, arguing that leaders facing reelection or "reselection" processes may have increased incentives for diversionary conflict, but fewer opportunities for such behavior as other states recognize the incentives and avoid situations that might lead to diversionary war. Furthermore, the significant body of scholarly literature also includes many studies that point to international and/or external factors (e.g., Mitchell and Prins 2004; Foster 2006 on international rivalries; Tir 2010 on territory; Mitchell and Thyne 2010 on conflict issues) that increase the likelihood of diversionary war (see Fordham 2017; Butcher 2023; Hagan 2017).

Despite the extensive body of scholarship devoted to the explanation, empirical results are somewhat mixed. Across many different methods, models, data, large-n statistical and (fewer) qualitative case studies, studies of the US, other developed countries, developing countries, and cross-national samples, many studies find evidence of diversionary conflict behavior (e.g., Hagan 2017 for a summary), while others do not (e.g., Wolford 2021; Levy and Thompson 2010). While the wealth of studies has refined arguments and conditions under which diversionary conflict is likely (e.g., Fordham 2017), sometimes contradictory findings, complicated domestic–international level interactions, and less-explored causal mechanisms and paths in particular cases suggest the need for further study of both large- and small-n data (Butcher 2023).

Ideational Aspects

Many conflicts focus on ideational matters. Given extensive coverage of the role of religion in Chapter 4, this brief subsection will concentrate on ethnonational identification. While a few states are composed overwhelmingly of one ethnicity – islands such as Japan and Iceland are among those exceptional cases – most members of the international polity are not. The mixture of ethnic identities in a state can create momentum toward either secessionism or irredentism, depending upon the context. The complicated situation of the Kurds provides perhaps the best entrée into such issues. Significant minorities exist in Syria, Iraq, Iran, and Turkey, but there is no sovereign homeland with a Kurdish identity. Kurdish ambitions for statehood, and resistance from those who would lose territory via secession, combine to create ongoing regional instability. Irredentism also is significant in the story of conflict, crisis, and war. Two examples, each connected to a great power, will be sufficient to make the point.

War in Ukraine continues on at this time of writing, with mounting casualties and increasing evidence of a stalemate as the outcome. How, it can be asked, could such a war be unleashed? While all levels of analysis would come into play in a complete explanation, a key element at the state level is about identity – notably, the denial of nationalist aspirations. A systemist graphic from Gansen and James (2022), reveals the key role of a failing state, led by Vladimir Putin, in infecting Russia with anti-Western and expansionist ambitions. After years of oligarchy and kleptocracy under Putin, Russians suffered from a low standard of living and lived with a sense of decline but also nostalgia for former greatness. Putin mobilized anger in society via anti-Ukrainian policies and rhetoric. An irredentist invasion became the ultimate result; Putin effectively made Ukraine the scapegoat for the poor performance of his government. The presence of many Russophones in areas of Ukraine that came under attack provided an ethnonationalist rationale to complement the pursuit of a return to Russian greatness (Gansen and James 2022).

Consider a rather revealing book title: *China: Fragile Superpower*. In this convincing study, Shirk (2007) demonstrates that the Chinese government, while presiding over a superpower in material terms, faces significant ideational challenges that point in the direction of irredentism. Ultranationalists, who focus on the legacy of imperialism in general and hatred of Japan in particular, potentially could force the leadership of China to take aggressive actions abroad over and above anything in line with national interests. A great deal of the insecurity in China focuses on perceived humiliation from the colonial era, most notably in connection with Macau, Hong Kong, and perhaps most intensely, Taiwan.

One of the most intense and dangerous conflicts in the world is over Taiwan. Identity is at the center of this conflict. Put simply, is Taiwan Chinese or not? The answer ends up being not a simple "yes or no". Instead, the rise of China impacted upon Taiwan, which evolved in the direction of a hybrid identity that contains Sinic and other elements, most notably a commitment to democracy (Gartner, Huang, Li, and James 2021). For China, the shift in identification could point toward Taiwan crossing a red line – possibly even a unilateral declaration of independence. To see how the preceding ideational issues can be sufficient to generate intense conflict, consider the example of the International Crisis Behavior (ICB) case known as Taiwan Strait IV.

FOR EXAMPLE: INTERNATIONAL CRISIS – TAIWAN STRAIT IV[5]

A crisis was triggered for the People's Republic of China (PRC) on May 22, 1995 when the US State Department announced that it would issue a visa to allow Taiwan's President Lee Teng-hui to make a private visit to the United States in June, thus reversing the US policy restricting high-level contacts between US officials and Taiwanese leaders, over the objections of Chinese officials. Chinese Foreign Minister Qian argued that the US action violated three joint agreements between China and the US, represented a violation of Chinese sovereignty, and destroyed hopes of a peaceful resolution between mainland China and Taiwan. China cancelled or postponed a series of meetings between US and Chinese officials in subsequent months, but dialogue resumed between the two countries by a variety of officials by September.

The crisis also strained the already troubled relations between Taiwan and China. During Lee's three-day visit to the US in early June, he met with members of the US Senate and House of Representatives and noted that the people of Taiwan were dissatisfied with their marginalized status in the international community. Cross-straits discussions between the PRC and the Republic of China (ROC) were again postponed in early June, and China responded to this crisis by launching a series of military exercises in the East China Sea, lasting from July 21 to July 26. The exercises included a series of tests of M-9 surface-to-surface guided missile tests that were fired only 60 km north of Taiwan's Pengchaiyu Island. These military maneuvers were coupled with fiery rhetoric from the official Chinese news agency Xinhua, which called on China to be willing to spill blood and lose lives in efforts to stop what it considered to be moves by Lee toward potential independence for Taiwan. These military exercises and rhetoric triggered a crisis for Taiwan, which responded on July 27 with a special address from President Lee in which he noted that Taiwan could not be repressed by outside forces.

The cycle of Chinese military exercises and missile tests, followed by statements by Lee that Taiwan would not be intimidated continued through 1995 (notably in August, September, and October), and by early 1996, the PRC had redeployed forces to coastal areas facing Taiwan and had set up additional command structures with responsibility for potential military action against Taiwan. Chinese military maneuvers peaked with war exercises only about 25 miles off the Taiwan coast in March 1996 in anticipation of Taiwan's first democratic presidential elections and were seen as an effort to hurt the electoral chances of President Lee. Despite the threatening tests, the elections were held, as scheduled, on March 23, 1996, and Lee Teng-hui became the first elected president of Taiwan. As scheduled, China's military exercises stopped after the elections, thus ending the crisis for both the PRC and the ROC.

Taiwan attempted to involve the UN in this crisis by submitting an application for Taiwan's membership to the organization, but the application was not approved. The UN

---

[5] The case summary that follows is based on Beardsley, James, Wilkenfeld, and Brecher (2023).

was not a major actor in this crisis, and there were no mediation efforts during the crisis. The US was involved not just in triggering the crisis for the PRC but also by helping to ensure the safety of Taiwan by sending the aircraft carrier USS *Nimitz* to the Taiwan Straits in December 1995, marking the first time US ships had patrolled the area since 1976. Additionally, carrier battle groups were sent to the region in March 1996, during the election period prior to the conclusion of this crisis.

While there are variations in how things play out in the preceding Russian and Chinese cases, one disturbing factor stands out in each instance: the role played by a pervasive sense of humiliation in creating a predisposition to revenge, with violence coming to the fore. In China, there is even an annual Day of Humiliation, on which people are encouraged to bear in mind the legacy of colonialism and occupation. Meanwhile, the state-controlled Russian media does all that it can to blame outsiders for problems that really follow on from government corruption more than anything else. The key role of a sense of humiliation in each instance is disturbing because this feeling is associated quite strongly with a disposition toward genocidal actions. Jones (2017), in fact, cites a sense of humiliation as something close to a *necessary* condition for carrying out genocide.

Assessment of the ideational role in conflict so far has been connected to Type I cognition – fast and emotional in nature (see our discussion of this concept in Chapter 7). Ideas, however, also can contribute to strife through processes associated with Type II cognition – deliberate and analytical in character. Consider, in this context, regime *change*, within which many aspects of a state are changed at once and therefore the result can be quite destabilizing. Revolution, according to Walt (1996), creates both a push and a pull with regard to involvement in conflict. Consider the example of the French Revolution in 1789. The fall of the monarchy created great uncertainty both within France and throughout Europe. Other states, with good reason, had concerns about possible interest in spreading the revolution beyond the borders of France. The motto of the French Revolution – Liberty, Equality, and Fraternity – posed a direct *ideational* threat to the monarchies still in place throughout Europe. On the one hand, France became unstable and its reduced capability – a by-product of revolution at least in the short term – encouraged aggression in order to preempt later efforts at French expansionism (Walt 1996). On the other hand, the new regime eventually did turn expansionist under Napoleon Bonaparte. France ultimately lost a war for supremacy on the continent in the face of an overwhelming coalition assembled against it in 1815.

Consider implications for the world today vis-à-vis ideas and conflict. Rubin (2014) refers to an "ideational security dilemma" in the Arab world. Transnational ideologies, such as those put forward by Saudi Arabia and Iran, pose threats to status quo-oriented regimes that eschew highly directive variants of Islam. Interesting to observe is ideological balancing behavior, akin to what realists have emphasized in the operation of the international system with regard to the distribution of material capabilities (Rubin 2014). Moreover, it is easy to imagine other ideational competitions, such as state-led versus free market development, unfolding and intensifying around the globe.

THE DEMOCRATIC PEACE

At the state level of analysis, perhaps no other factor has been studied more than regime type and its central focus: investigations into the democratic peace thesis. Traceable to Kant's arguments about the possibilities and prospects for a "perpetual peace", the claim that democracies are potentially more pacific in their foreign relations than other countries received early attention from Babst (1964, 1972) and then experienced a resurgence in the early 1980s (e.g., Rummel, 1981; Doyle, 1986). With his influential analysis on the existence of a pacific union among democracies, Doyle (1986) triggered an avalanche of primarily statistical investigations into what one prominent scholar called "the closest thing we have to an empirical law in the study of international relations" (Levy 1989c: 662).

In the four decades since then, there has been an explosion of inquiries into the evidence of and reasons for the relationship.[6] Research designs that link democracy to pacific relations for interstate dyads on an annual basis – the overwhelmingly present unit of analysis in the field – number in the hundreds and perhaps even beyond. Among other things, this vast literature asserts that democracies do not war with one another (e.g., Maoz and Russett 1992; Bremer 1993; Russett 1993; Russett and Oneal 2001), are less likely to threaten or use force against each other (e.g., Russett 1993; Bremer 1993), and are more likely to resolve conflict peacefully (e.g., Dixon 1994; Mitchell 2002). The main, mutually supporting explanations for these patterns center on normative (shared identities and values between democracies) and institutional (the impact of accountability and executive constraints stemming from democratic institutions) causes (e.g., Baum and Potter 2015; Owen 1997; Russett and Oneal 2001; Maoz and Russett 1992, 1993).[7] Although some critics have assailed both the explanations (e.g., Gates, Knutsen, and Moses 1996; Gowa 1999; Rosato 2003) and the evidence (e.g., Layne 1994; Farber and Gowa 1995; Gowa 1999; Spiro 1994), the central claims of the thesis remain formidable despite skepticism from a sizable group of international relations scholars (Gowa and Pratt 2019; see also Reiter 2017 for a review of the claims and critiques of the democratic peace).

Interesting to ponder, as well, is the possibility of an autocratic peace. Peceny, Beer, and Sanchez-Terry (2002) focus on interstate dyads and find that no two military or personalist regimes have gone to war with each other. While not different in likelihood of involvement in Militarized Interstate Disputes (MIDs), dyads composed of single-party states are more pacific than mixed ones. Statistical analyses from Peceny, Beer, and Sanchez-Terry (2002) combine to produce the conclusions that (i) only shared democracy is associated negatively on a consistent basis with MID and war involvement; and (ii) different types of authoritarian regimes vary in their activity within conflict processes.

---

[6] See, for instance, summaries by Lipson (2003), Ray (1995), Russett (1993), Russett and Oneal (2001), Weart (1998), and Chan (2010).

[7] Discussion of causal mechanisms underlying the democratic peace phenomenon remains lively, with many different variables proposed as alternatives to democracy as being responsible for the "heavy lifting". See Choi and James (2007) for an example that emphasizes, among other things, media openness.

STATE-LEVEL EXPLANATIONS

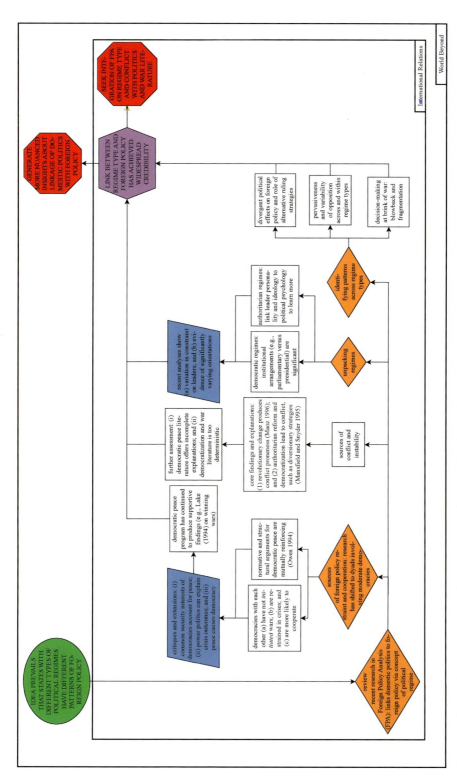

Figure 6.1 Regime type, foreign policy, and international relations

CONFLICT, CRISIS, AND WAR IN WORLD POLITICS

Figure 6.1a

STATE-LEVEL EXPLANATIONS

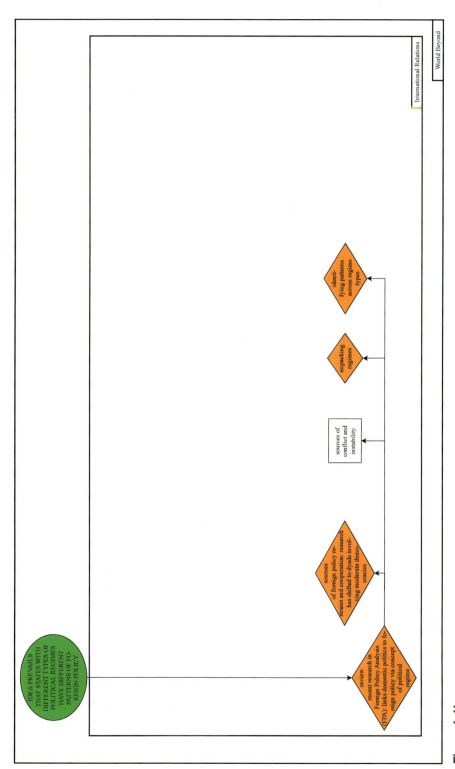

Figure 6.1b

130 CONFLICT, CRISIS, AND WAR IN WORLD POLITICS

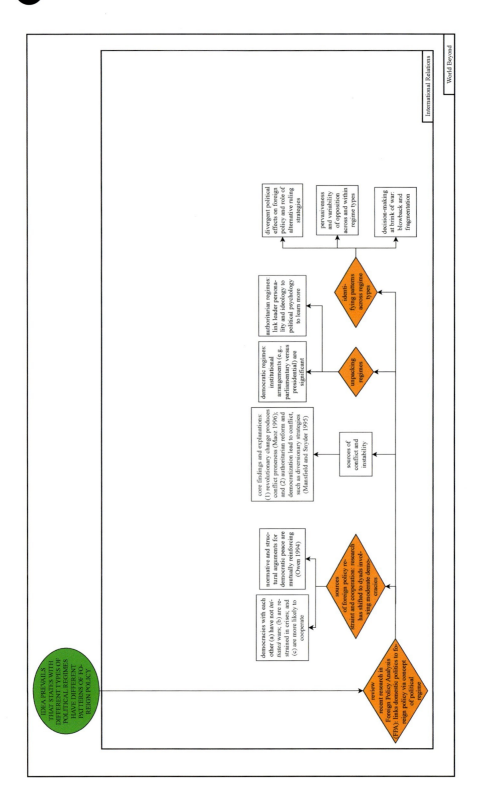

Figure 6.1c

STATE-LEVEL EXPLANATIONS

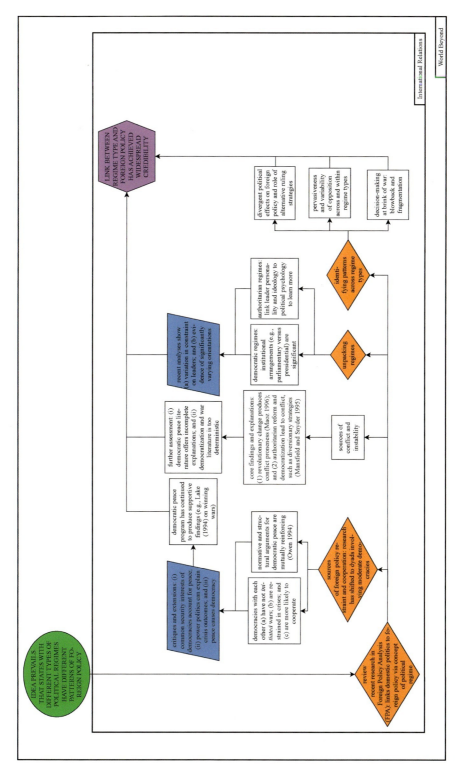

Figure 6.1d

CONFLICT, CRISIS, AND WAR IN WORLD POLITICS

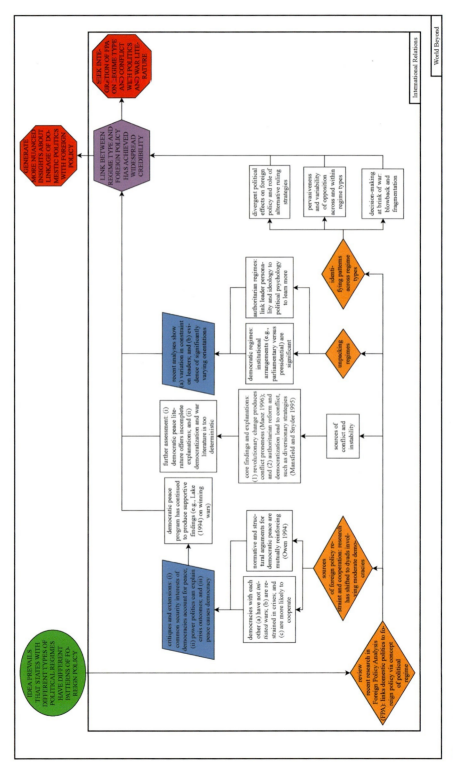

Figure 6.1e

VISUALIZING CONFLICT, THE DEMOCRATIC PEACE AND REGIME TYPE

Figure 6.1, a systemist depiction of Hagan (2010), takes the analysis of the democratic peace in a more encompassing direction. The diagram focuses on regime type, foreign policy, and international relations. The arguments of this graphic provide an excellent summation with regard to how the type of government for a state affects its foreign policy and also, therefore, involvement in conflict processes. Within Figure 6.1, International Relations is the system, with the World Beyond as its environment. The micro and macro levels of International Relations pertain to, respectively, the activities of individual scholars and the discipline as a whole.

Figure 6.1a shows an initial component, depicted as a green oval, in the World Beyond: "IDEA PREVAILS THAT STATES WITH DIFFERENT TYPES OF POLITICAL REGIMES HAVE DIFFERENT PATTERNS OF FOREIGN POLICY". The idea that, say, being a democracy or dictatorship could impact upon both decision-making and actions is widely accepted. A pathway gets underway from the World Beyond into the micro level of International Relations in Figure 6.1b with "IDEA PREVAILS THAT STATES WITH DIFFERENT TYPES OF POLITICAL REGIMES HAVE DIFFERENT PATTERNS OF FOREIGN POLICY" → "review recent research in Foreign Policy Analysis (FPA): links domestic politics to foreign policy via concept of political regime". As a point of divergence, the latter appears as an orange diamond. The rationale for the study by Hagan (2010) is clear; the nexus of domestic politics and foreign policy is a topic deemed worthy of significant attention.

Multiple pathways emerge at the micro level of Figure 6.1b: "review recent research in Foreign Policy Analysis (FPA): links domestic politics to foreign policy via concept of political regime" → "sources of foreign policy restraint and cooperation: research has shifted to dyads involving moderate democracies"; "sources of conflict and instability"; "unpacking regimes"; "identifying patterns across regime types". As points of divergence, three of the four components after the arrow appear as orange diamonds. At this stage of the graphic, four areas of interest have been identified and each will create a route to follow further.

Figure 6.1c depicts movement along one of the above-noted pathways with "sources of foreign policy restraint and cooperation: research has shifted to dyads involving moderate democracies" → "democracies with each other (a) have not *initiated* wars; (b) are restrained in crises; and (c) are more likely to cooperate"; "normative and structural arguments for democratic peace are mutually reinforcing (Owen 1994)". Thus, the cooperative behavior observed between democracies is in line with both ideational and material arguments that create such expectations. A second route continues with "sources of conflict and instability" → "core findings and explanations: (1) revolutionary change produces conflict proneness (Maoz 1996); and (2) authoritarian reform and democratization lead to conflict, such as diversionary strategies (Mansfield and Snyder 1995)". The preceding connection is very much in line with examples provided earlier in this chapter, such as the impact of the French Revolution and Russo-Ukrainian War. The third pathway moves forward with "unpacking regimes" → "democratic regimes: institutional arrangements (e.g., parliamentary versus presidential) are significant"; "authoritarian regimes: link leader personality and ideology to political psychology to learn more". These linkages showcase specific findings about cooperation and conflict with regard to democratic and autocratic regimes. Fourth and last among the continuing routes in Figure 6.1c is "identifying patterns across regime types" → "divergent political effects on foreign policy and role of alternative ruling strategies"; "pervasiveness and variability of opposition across and within regime types"; and "decision-making at brink of war: blowback and fragmentation". The components after the arrow reveal a wide range of patterns across regime types that have emerged from studies of foreign policy and conflict processes.

Figure 6.1d shows four pathways moving forward from the micro to the macro level. Each is followed in turn, prior to the point of convergence that will be reached by all of them.

Starting from left to right, the first route continues with "democracies with each other (a) have not *initiated* wars; (b) are restrained in crises; and (c) are more likely to cooperate"; "normative and structural arguments for democratic peace are mutually reinforcing (Owen 1994)" → "critiques and extensions: (i) common security interests of democracies account for peace; (ii) power politics can explain crisis outcomes; and (iii) peace causes democracy". As a point of convergence, the latter appears as a blue parallelogram. The findings after the arrow show the increasing sophistication of scholarship on regime type as ideas from realism (items i and ii) and potential reverse causation (item iii) enter into theorizing and research designs. This route continues with "critiques and extensions: (i) common security interests of democracies account for peace; (ii) power politics can explain crisis outcomes; and (iii) peace causes democracy" → "democratic peace program has continued to produce supportive findings (e.g., Lake (1992) on winning wars)". This connection reveals how the program of research on democracy and conflict processes continues to yield and confirm innovative hypotheses.

Second among the pathways continuing in Figure 6.1d is this one: "core findings and explanations: (1) revolutionary change produces conflict proneness (Maoz 1996); and (2) authoritarian reform and democratization lead to conflict, such as diversionary strategies (Mansfield and Snyder 1995) → "further assessment: (i) democratic peace literature offers incomplete explanations; and (ii) democratization and war literature is too deterministic". In spite of many interesting contributions, it is clear that the democratic peace literature can be improved in the ways identified.

Third among the routes moving forward in Figure 6.1d is "democratic regimes: institutional arrangements (e.g., parliamentary versus presidential) are significant"; "authoritarian regimes: link leader personality and ideology to political psychology to learn more" → "recent analyses show (a) variation in constraint on leaders; and (b) evidence of significantly varying orientations". As a point of convergence, the latter appears as a blue parallelogram. Once again, research efforts on regime type are seen to be moving forward through identification of nuances that had not previously been considered.

Figure 6.1d moves forward from an orange diamond into multiple pathways with "identifying patterns across regime types" → "divergent political effects on foreign policy and role of alternative ruling strategies"; "pervasiveness and variability of opposition across and within regime types"; "decision-making at brink of war: blowback and fragmentation". These routes feed directly into a nodal component at the macro level: "LINK BETWEEN REGIME TYPE AND FOREIGN POLICY HAS ACHIEVED WIDESPREAD CREDIBILITY". As the contributions and even critiques along preceding pathways confirm, much can be learned about foreign policy through a focus on regime type.

Figure 6.1e shows the final pair of connections: "LINK BETWEEN REGIME TYPE AND FOREIGN POLICY HAS ACHIEVED WIDESPREAD CREDIBILITY" → "SEEK INTEGRATION OF FPA ON REGIME TYPE AND CONFLICT WITH POLITICS AND WAR LITERATURE"; "GENERATE MORE NUANCED INSIGHTS ABOUT LINKAGE OF DOMESTIC POLITICS WITH FOREIGN POLICY". Each of the components after the arrow is a point of termination and thus represented with a red octagon. The first of the two terminal points urges a more integrated approach that blends together areas of research in International Relations that have tended to remain somewhat apart, probably for reasons related to methods. The other point of termination, in the World Beyond, expresses the need for greater insights about domestic politics and foreign policy, which could help in conflict management and prevention of escalation from conflict, through crisis, to war.

> **IN FOCUS: REGIME TYPE AND FOREIGN POLICY**
>
> Review the contents of Figure 6.1. *Do you see errors of omission or commission? What cases come to mind as (dis)confirming examples for the connections displayed in the figure?*

SUMMING UP AND MOVING FORWARD

Although the empirical evidence in support of various explanations at the state level is mixed, the theories provide insights into state-level attributes that may contribute to our understanding of why some states participate in conflict, crisis, and war more or less often than others. Yet explanations at the state level have limitations just as those at the system level do. As Levy and Thompson (2010: 128) argued with regard to the highest level of escalation,

> "War is the product of the actions of two or more states or other political organizations. It follows that to understand the outbreak of war we need to understand why states make certain decisions rather than other decisions. That leads us to an analysis of foreign policy decision-making, which focuses on the individuals and governmental organizations that are empowered to make and implement policies on behalf of the state."

It is to the individual level that we now turn for further examination of the causes of conflict, crisis, and war.

CONSIDER THIS: UNDERSTANDING WAR PRONENESS

In his introduction to state-level explanations of war, Cashman (2013, 169) notes that a central starting point for this level of analysis is "that states are not equally violent; great variation in conflict activity exists among the states of the world". The basic argument at this level is that particular qualities of some states lead them to be more (or less) conflict prone or warlike. Considering the preceding discussion:

What patterns in participation and behavior in conflict, crisis, and war are best and least explained by explanations at the state level of analysis?

7
Individual-level explanations

PROLOGUE

Sir Winston Churchill is one of the most memorable figures in world history – prime minister of the United Kingdom, Nobel Prize winner, and a great many other things. In light of his lifetime of monumental achievements, Churchill might be expected to serve as an exemplar of rational action. Ironically, analysis based on political psychology shows that the cognition of Churchill resembled that of a *romantic* rather than some type of calculating machine. Rathbun (2019) shows that Churchill tended toward Type I rather than Type II cognition. Type I is rapid and emotive, while Type II is deliberate and rational. This served the prime minister well in recognizing, quickly and based on intuition, that Adolf Hitler had ambitions well beyond those stated and largely believed by elites in the West. If left unchecked, or "managed" through fruitless negotiations, Hitler would gobble up Europe and possibly even the world.

Churchill's peers in British politics at the time tended more toward Type II cognition – notably Neville Chamberlain, the architect of the Munich sellout of Czechoslovakia in 1938 – and therefore "missed the boat" altogether in figuring out the German dictator (Rathbun 2019). Cartoonists ridiculed Chamberlain for claiming to have obtained "peace in our time" after the Munich meeting. All of this combines to show that leadership matters and sometimes in ways that are quite counterintuitive.

OVERVIEW

In many ways, the individual level of analysis is the *least* abstract set of explanations about conflict, crisis, and war. This is because the individual level directs our attention to people – especially decision-makers – and their attributes and actions to understand conflict and war. Thus, explanations rooted in Waltz's (1959) "first image" sacrifice the most parsimony and add complexity and detail in the form of characteristics and variations of people to understand decisions to resort to war. What does this perspective offer to explanations of conflict processes?

This chapter moves forward in five additional sections. The next section sets the context of individual-level explanations as they relate to conflict, crisis, and war, introducing two major strands of investigation that dominate those analyses. Two sections follow that offer brief surveys of these two major strands, and a fifth section focuses on one prominent theory as an example and offers an in-depth deconstruction accompanied by a systemist diagram. We conclude with a sixth section summarizing and reflecting on the main points of this chapter.

MAJOR APPROACHES TO INDIVIDUAL-LEVEL EXPLANATIONS

The fundamental premise of individual-explanations is deceptively simple: war is the result of the choices of participants, so comprehending those choices requires attention to the nature and characteristics of the people who make them. As Waltz (1959: 16) put it, in this level "the locus of the important causes of war is found in the nature and behavior of man. Wars result from selfishness, from misdirected aggressive impulses, from stupidity", and perhaps from other individual factors and attributes as well. These explanations turn on the premise that actions and behavior in world politics are essentially bottom-up. System and state-level factors are far from deterministic in this view, while the individual characteristics, worldviews, perceptions, and other characteristics of individuals are behind much variation in conflict behavior. As Levy and Thompson (2010: 129) summarize, individual-level theories "do not deny that system structure and domestic settings frame the problem for state decision-makers", but they do argue that "individual level variables carry significant causal weight". Factors from the individual level therefore serve as a reminder about the amount of contingency that exists in world politics.

> **IN FOCUS**
>
> Churchill's Type I cognitive tendencies come out in his multivolume history of World War II. Consider the title of one volume: *The Hinge of Fate*. People disposed toward Type I cognition tend to focus more on the agency available to individuals as opposed to forces supposedly carrying along history. The title of the above-noted book proves revealing in that sense. Churchill, as one would expect for someone tilting toward Type I rather than Type II cognition, focused on potentially different outcomes that could have occurred if those involved in a series of events had made one or more choices differently.

Theorizing at the individual level has tended to cluster into two main categories. In one category, emphasis is on general aspects of human nature that drive a tendency for human aggression. In another category of individual-level explanations, focus centers on the nature of some humans in particular: the specific characteristics of individual leaders, including their experiences, personalities, perceptions, psychology, and policy preferences.

HUMAN NATURE

Explanations emphasizing human nature generally focus on some version of the argument that, by nature, biology, and/or genetics, humans are inherently aggressive. From philosophers such as St Augustine, Thomas Hobbes, and Reinhold Niebuhr to psychologists and sociobiologists such as Sigmund Freud, Konrad Lorenz, and Edward O. Wilson, scholars have often attributed national violence in the form of war to innate characteristics of human beings. For example, a variety of explanations trace the causes of war to biological factors, often relying on animal research to derive insights into human behavior. In ethology – the study of animal behavior – researchers attribute war to human aggressive and territorial instincts that developed through biological evolution (e.g., Ardrey 1966; Lorenz 1966). In effect, war occurs as a function of human instincts and satisfies some basic needs. However, such arguments suffer from the same limits as the simplistic system-level argument about anarchy: If human nature is inherently aggressive, why is war relatively rare and why are some people and some societies peaceful?

FOR EXAMPLE

One of the most important books in the lexicon of classical realism conveys a basic message about the importance of human nature through its title: *Scientific Man Versus Power Politics* (Morgenthau 1946). Scientific advancement might seem to hold the promise of a peaceful world. Human beings could learn not to fight wars and instead focus on better things. However, according to Morgenthau (1946), no amount of science can overcome the basic will to power that resides in human nature. War, from the standpoint of classical realism, will recur because power politics cannot be "learned" out of existence.

One attempt to answer these questions comes from sociobiologists such as Edward O. Wilson (1975), who combine biological and genetic factors with psychology, anthropology, and sociology to explain war – and its variations – as a consequence of the interaction between genes and the cultural environment. A key idea in this sociobiological approach stresses "phenotypic plasticity", which results in adaptation in "developmental trajectories in response to specific environmental cues" (Fusco and Minelli 2010). In this argument, the genetic potential for aggression is unlocked in some versions of this complex mix and muted in others.

Taking this approach further, others emphasize the effect of societal conditions and practices on learning and behavior, arguing that certain levels/types of societal development, structures, conditions, and/or norms mute instincts for aggression and produce "peaceful societies" (e.g., Dyer 2005; Fabbro 1978; Kelly 2000; Fry 2012). Many such societies have been identified, including Australian Aborigines in Western Australia, the Iroquois confederacy, natives of the Upper Xingu River in Brazil, and, more recently perhaps, the European Union. The Nordic countries are a good case in point: they have not warred with each other for more than two centuries – despite some conflicts and opportunities to do so – and appear to have developed "the concept of social peace based on a culture of conflict resolution and societal solidarity" (Archer 2003: 16).

According to Fry (2012), for example, peaceful societies are associated with (1) an overarching common identity in addition to local identities, (2) a high degree of prosocial interconnectedness among the social units within a system, (3) interdependence among the social units, (4) core values and norms that are non-warring and peace favoring, (5) narratives, rituals, ceremonies, and symbols that reinforce peaceful values, norms, beliefs, and conduct, (6) superordinate institutions, (7) mechanisms for nonviolent intergroup conflict management, and (8) visionary peace leadership. Expectations for obtaining item (8) arguably depend on the functioning of (1) through (7) and vice versa. The people in charge matter and the social milieus that shape their development play a symbiotic role with each other – a virtuous cycle that sustains peace or unfortunately, in some instances, a vicious cycle that produces conflict.

However, studies from a variety of perspectives challenge the preceding arguments as well (e.g., see Cashman 2013: chap. 2 for a summary). In general, though, theorists seeking to explain war at any level of analysis, including the individual level, have tended to move past "human nature" and related arguments as providing limited benefits. As Levy and Thompson (2010: 21) summarize, much like anarchy at the system level,

> an aggregate concept of human nature might serve as a 'permissive condition' for war, in the sense that it allows war to happen, but that does not tell us too much …. The argument that human nature explains both war and peace is unsatisfactory (unless it could explain the conditions under which each outcome is likely to occur).

This important limitation explains why classical realist theories, which focused on human nature as an explanation for conflict, crisis, and war, eventually fell out of favor.

Contemporary strands of research continue to connect with human nature, but with a different point of emphasis than inherent warlikeness. Some feminist scholars have argued that women are more peaceful and cooperative leaders than men. In power, they would therefore be less concerned with national and international security, for example, and more concerned with economic and human security – and economic security would be defined partly as economic equality. Instead of being coercive, women as leaders would engage other countries with aid and diplomacy. More important, they would interact with countries not to gain power but to develop a better relationship that would focus on peace, equal development, and, perhaps, the environment. This perspective is often ascribed to *difference feminists*. This feminist perspective sees men and women as different in their basic nature. These differences can be attributed to genetic or hormonal differences (e.g., estrogen versus testosterone) and/or socially constructed differences (e.g., more boys play competitive contact sports than girls). These basic differences mean that women would be better at negotiating a peace treaty, whereas men would be better at fighting a war. Difference feminists argue that, since only male traits are valued in international relations, there is more conflict in the world. If more women were in leadership roles, then there would be greater balance and peace in the international system.

However, in practice, as women have ascended to lead different countries, they have tended to act much like their male counterparts. That is, women are no less coercive and tough than men when leading a country. For example, Margaret Thatcher, the prime minister of the United Kingdom from 1979 to 1990, was referred to as the "Iron Lady", not because she was engaging, nurturing, and peaceful but because she talked and acted very tough. Thatcher engaged the Soviets with very harsh diplomacy but then convinced her close ally, President Ronald Reagan, that the new Soviet leader, Mikhail Gorbachev, was someone with whom they could negotiate. Up to that point, Thatcher had no intention of negotiating with the Soviets. In 1982, early in Thatcher's tenure, Argentina invaded the Falkland Islands, British-controlled and populated islands approximately 300 miles off the coast of Argentina. Thatcher led a successful and short (74-day) war to reclaim the islands. She made it clear from the start of the invasion that she would not negotiate with the Argentinians at all. It was also widely reported at the time that Thatcher urged George H. W. Bush to take a hard-line, aggressive approach to Iraq's invasion of Kuwait in 1991.

Thatcher may be an archetypal example, but she is by no means the only one. Indira Gandhi of India, Golda Meir of Israel, Benazir Bhutto of Pakistan, Angela Merkel of Germany, Theresa May of the United Kingdom, and others have held the leadership position of their countries. They also tended to behave more like, than different from the men who preceded them. They were tough, did not shrink from conflict, and certainly did not fit an older stereotype of women as peaceful, nurturing mothers who feared conflict.

There are at least two potential responses to the conclusion that the gender of the leader does not matter. First, even though women and men are obviously different, the leadership position – whether it is president, prime minister, or autocratic leader – requires that both men and women act the same way to be successful. Consider women leaders in the developing world: Should we expect their gender to lead to different behavior, or should we expect factors such as poverty and ethnic divisions to cause them to act no differently than the male leaders of the developing world? Some would argue that, regardless of the personal characteristics and preferences of the leader, they must act pretty much like all other leaders or cease to be effective and thus cease being the leader. Bureaucracies, for instance, put constraints on policy implementation (Allison 1971).

A second response to the idea that women leaders are no different from their male counterparts is based on the small number of state leaders who are women. The idea is that in the current self-help, anarchic system, we should not be surprised that women behave in the same manner as men. They are simply following the rules of the game in a competitive and aggressive world system (driven by anarchy, self-help, and other factors) constructed or conceived by men. However, would those rules be different if half or more of the leaders in the world were women?

The speculative nature of this argument is problematic, but there is significant empirical research on the impact of women in other organizations – businesses and corporations, agencies, and even legislative bodies – that suggests that the mere presence of women in those organizations has an impact and that those with significant numbers of women exhibit a different decision-making style and pursue different agendas (McGlen and Sarkees 1993, 1995, 2006). For example, legislatures with more women tend to consider and debate social policy (e.g., medical coverage and regulation) more than economic policy (e.g., tax rates). Some evidence indicates that corporations and other types of organizations with more women in top positions tend to practice more cooperative, participatory, and consensus-based approaches to decision-making. In other words, men and women may prioritize issues differently and thus pursue different agendas when given the opportunity.

One interesting hallmark of this research suggests that there is a sort of critical mass or threshold (about 30%) that must be reached in terms of representation. In organizations in which women constitute less than 30% of the personnel (or leaders), little difference can be identified. In those with more than 30%, some research finds that this critical mass empowers a kind of solidarity in which women's different style, approach, and preferences are evident.

In effect, where there are few women, those in power or leadership tend to conform to the male-dominated context, but where there is a critical number of women, they do not (Dahlerup 1988; Kanter 1977; Phillips 1995; see the UNWomen.org website for more information).

Some fascinating research in this area has begun to tell us what effects gender equality might have on international relations. For example, whether or not women are in leadership positions, do countries that have higher levels of respect for women act differently from those that discriminate against them? The answer is yes – when a country has greater gender equality, it is less likely to initiate a war, although it may still be attacked by other countries. Further, countries with greater gender equality tend to be less likely to have civil wars (Hudson, Ballif-Spanvill, Caprioli, and Emmett 2017). In sum, a vast research agenda on gender is underway in the study of conflict, crisis, and war.

HUMAN EXPERIENCES AND PSYCHOLOGY

If broad individual-level explanations focusing on human nature face limits because of the variability of conflict, perhaps individual-level explanations stressing the experiences and characteristics of some individuals – especially national leaders – provide helpful insights into conflict behavior and its variance. The role of early experiences on the choices of individuals/leaders later in life is one such category of analysis. For example, according to Horowitz, Stam, and Ellis (2015), military experience, age, education, previous occupations(s), family background and parental characteristics and conditions, family wealth, and other factors may have consequences for later behavior and decisions by leaders, with some associated with greater risk and propensity to resort to the use of force. This research team finds that military experience *without* combat experience appears especially important to greater likelihood of the use of force. Such leaders tend to get into crises more frequently than others and are often unjustifiably optimistic about the use of military force, which they initiate more frequently as well (see also Sechser 2004). Older leaders are also more likely to initiate military conflicts, while traumatic childhood experiences (e.g., from family conditions, poverty, and war) may contribute to more aggressive behavior and decisions later in life (see also Horowitz, McDermott, and Stam 2005; Horowitz, Potter, Sechser, and Stam 2018; Horowitz and Stam 2014). In this vein, another example is from the research of Barceló (2020), who finds that leaders with the experience of attending a university in a Western democratic country are less likely than non-Western-educated leaders to initiate Militarized Interstate Disputes (MIDs).

Beyond experiences and background factors such as these, social scientists have developed dozens of approaches that focus on individual personality and psychology in this category of individual-level explanation. As Cashman (2013: 112) sums them up, these factors include

> different psychological needs, different personality traits, cognitive biases inherent in the way the brain processes information, differences in willingness to take risks, different perceptions (and misperceptions) of the environment and of one's opponents, different images of the world and operational codes, and differences in ability to change or adjust present images.

While most of this vast and sprawling literature is not aimed specifically at explaining conflict decisions and behavior, key findings are often quite relevant.

One line of explanation has stressed psychological needs and/or personality traits. Psychological needs are essential emotional and psychological requirements of humans, said to be hierarchical by theorists such as Maslow. In this line of explanation, scholars have concluded that some individuals are more power oriented (e.g., Hermann 1980) or compensate for low self-esteem (e.g., Etheredge 1978; Post 2005) by acting more aggressively. Related to this line of argument are studies focusing on personality traits, which argue that some of these varying characteristics of individuals may lead to more aggressive behavior and preferences (e.g., Gallagher and Allen 2013). Numerous studies indicate that individuals displaying dogmatic, authoritarian, domineering, introverted, risk-acceptant, paranoid, and/or narcissistic personality traits are more likely to embrace the use of force than others (e.g., Rokeach 1960; Etheredge 1978; Post 2005; Winter 2005; Hermann 2005), so leaders with such traits may help to explain conflict behavior (see also Cashman 2013: 54–60 for a useful summary).

Consider a few examples to illustrate these arguments. Studies of US President Lyndon B. Johnson (e.g., Goodwin 1991) suggest that his complicated personality included a domineering side that shaped his Vietnam decisions. Studies of Saddam Hussein find a narcissistic personality driven by a lust for power and conquest that drove his decisions for war from 1980 to 1990 (e.g., Post 1993; Hermann 2005; Walker, Schafer, and Young 2005). Joseph Stalin displayed a paranoid personality, characterized by suspicion and distrust that shaped his behavior before and during World War II and in the Cold War (e.g., Birt 1993).

FOR EXAMPLE: THE STYLE AND PERSONALITY OF DONALD TRUMP

Scholars have examined former US president Donald Trump's volatile and domineering personality and style and its potential consequences. In a recent analysis, Allesandro Nai, Ferran Martinez i Coma, and Jürgen Maier (2019) assessed Trump's personality in the context of more than 100 other political leaders around the world. According to their personality assessment, Trump scored very high on narcissism, psychopathy, and Machiavellianism, and exhibited low emotional stability and a neurotic personality. This assessment is broadly consistent with those of other analysts (e.g., Immelman 2017; McAdams 2016; Sherman 2015).

With that consensus on Trump in mind, let us return to the types of cognition introduced at the outset of this chapter. On the one hand, Trump's style – very Type I at least in its public manifestation – tended to offend and even alienate any number of allies. On the other hand, Trump's bombastic communication may have served as a deterrent to North Korea, at least initially. However, and quite remarkably, after the exchange of insults with Kim Jong Un, Trump became the first sitting president to enter North Korea, and the two leaders subsequently exchanged very friendly letters.

Are Type I leaders able to achieve certain outcomes better than Type II in the competitive international environment?

Some situations would appear likely to favor Type II leaders. For example, President Jimmy Carter enjoyed success in 1978, when he brought together Egypt and Israel to seek a peace agreement. The Camp David Accords, signed by those parties, also created a framework for peace in the Middle East. Given the complexities of the negotiation involved, it is hard to imagine success for a leader prone to Type I cognition. The more nuanced mind of Carter – looking very Type II in approach – worked best in a situation that called for subtle thinking and a high degree of patience.

Similarly, numerous studies suggest that extroverts seek more cooperative outcomes than introverts and that narcissism is usually associated with hostility, aggression, and power-seeking behavior (e.g., Etheredge 1978; Post 2005; Hermann 2005). Finally, Keren Yarhi-Milo (2018: 11) combined a cross-national survey experiment with a statistical study of American presidents from Truman to George W. Bush and case studies of Jimmy Carter, Ronald Reagan, and Bill Clinton to show that leaders with a high self-monitoring trait – individuals who "are inclined to modify their behavior strategically in order to cultivate status-enhancing images" – are more willing to use military options for reputational gains.

Another major line of explanation in the human experiences and psychology category focuses on cognition. We emphasize again that the vast cognition scholarship is generally not specifically aimed at conflict behavior. However, much of it has applications and connections to individual-level explanations of conflict, crisis, and war and, overall, the importance of how individuals think is critical to understanding conflict behavior at this level of analysis. A key starting point is that the nature of human cognition and perception leads people to construct their own reality as they perceive and process the world. According to John Steinbruner (1974: 12–13, 112), "The mind of man [sic], for all its marvels, is a limited instrument" and, given the complexity of the world and the limitations of the mind, the mind "constantly struggles to impose clear, coherent meaning on events". To consider this area, we first address the context of the extensive scholarship on cognition as it relates to political decision-making, and then – in the subsequent section – take up three key areas of research that have important implications for our understanding of conflict, crisis, and war.

Foundations. A central insight of this broad literature is that contrary to the assumptions and premises of the rational actor model that underlies much analysis of decisions and behavior, the human mind works very differently in response to the kinds of limits implicit in the preceding paragraph (see, e.g., Stein 2016). In short, it imposes clarity and tries to make sense of reality through reliance on some common cognitive principles, but these efforts do not always comport with "reality". According to reviews of this extensive literature by Rosati (2000, 2010) and Rosati and Miller (2018), these include (1) the principle of cognitive structures of belief (that the human mind tends to consist of a vast assortment of beliefs that are organized and internally structured, especially around more central beliefs); (2) the principle of selective memory (that people tend to remember certain things better than others, especially the general picture or concept, and be loose with the details); (3) the principle of selective attention and perception (that, although the mind can perceive stable, significant features of the environment, it tends to be selective and incomplete in its attention); (4) the principle of causal inference (that people tend to make inferences about what happened and why based on their beliefs); and (5) the principle of cognitive stability (that the mind tends to keep internal belief relationships stable once formed, especially in the core structure of beliefs). The preceding factors combine, at the very least, to place a figurative asterisk next to any model with rational choice as its point of departure.

Cognitive psychological approaches, such as cognitive consistency theory and schema theory, agree that central beliefs are most consequential. During the 1950s and 1960s, it was popular to view the individual as a "consistency seeker" – motivated to make sense of the world by acquiring and maintaining "coherent systems of beliefs which are internally consistent" (Bern 1970: 13). As a consequence, individuals tend to avoid the acquisition of information that is inconsistent or incompatible with their belief systems, especially their central beliefs, which affects their decisions.

Led by scholars such as Daniel Kahneman, Amos Tversky, and others, a second generation of scholarship emerged in the 1970s describing a more complex cognitive process, viewing the individual as a "cognitive miser" (see, for example, Kahneman 1973; Kahneman, Slovic, and Tversky 1982; Gilovic, Griffin, and Kahneman 2002; Kahneman 2011; and Lewis 2016). According to this view, the minds of individuals are limited in their capacity to process information, so they tend to rely on schemas, heuristics/shortcuts, and other simplifications. Schemas are mental constructs that simplify and structure the external environment, enabling individuals to absorb new information and make sense of the world around them. The more complex and uncertain the environment, the more likely individuals are to rely on schemas and cognitive heuristics – shortcuts in information processing – to make sense of the world and the situation at hand.

The human mind perceives the world and processes information by compartmentalizing and sorting things into relatively simple categories. Such images simplify the world and queue preferences and actions (e.g., Cottam 1994). One common tendency is the formation of "enemy images" – beliefs and schemas of the "other". Indeed, conflict situations often result in mirror images in which the parties each hold diametrically opposite images (a positive and benevolent self-image and a negative and malevolent image of the enemy). Once formed, enemy images tend to be resistant to change.

For example, Holsti's (1967) study of Secretary of State John Foster Dulles focuses on his enemy image of the Soviet Union and his tendency to resist information inconsistent with this image. Holsti argues that Dulles did this by discrediting information that did not fit his image and searching for information that was consistent with his image. He also resorted to reinterpretation and differentiation of information, wishful thinking, and outright refusal to even consider information inconsistent with his image. Dulles also dogmatically advocated the doctrine of massive retaliation against any Soviet aggression. This posture became quite out of touch with strategic and tactical realities because the USSR had achieved approximate equality with the US in nuclear capabilities. A threat of nuclear annihilation over even the "slightest slight" looked increasingly unrealistic and even bizarre with the passing of time and the administration of John F. Kennedy switched to the doctrine of flexible response upon taking office in 1961.

Such black-and-white thinking (e.g., Glad 1983) can contribute to misperception, escalation, intervention, and war. To take one relatively recent example, as a result of 9/11, enemy images appear to have heavily influenced President George W. Bush, as he declared and conducted a global war on terrorism. According to Balz and Woodward (2002), "Bush fashioned a war of absolutes: good vs. evil, with us or against us. He brought a black-and-white mind-set" to the problem at hand (see also Kessler 2003; Thomas 2002). Given the horrendous experience of 9/11, and fear of a possible nuclearized version of it, Bush tended to overvalue any information that pointed toward another disaster on American soil. This caused severe bias in processing information and contributed decisively to the process of escalation leading to the war in Iraq that started in 2003.

Other shortcuts are also evident and consequential. One is a tendency to simplify inferences about causality. As Jervis (1976) put it, "People want to be able to explain as much as possible of what goes on around them. To admit that a phenomenon cannot be explained, or at least cannot be explained without adding numerous and complex exceptions to our beliefs, is both psychologically uncomfortable and intellectually unsatisfying." Such simplifying tendencies heavily reinforce people's perceptions, especially in the case of enemy images. This problem also points toward the necessity of multilevel explanations for conflict, crisis, and war, which we will take up in Chapter 10.

Another important tendency is the use of historical analogies to interpret and make decisions about the present. According to Jervis (1976: 217), "Previous international events provide the statesman with a range of imaginable situations and allow him to detect patterns and causal links that can help him understand his world" since "we cannot make sense out of our environment without assuming that, in some sense, the future will resemble the past". Historical analogies are fraught with danger for decision-makers because they carry with them the tendency to oversimplify, ignore critical elements of context, and shortcut careful analysis (e.g., Stein 2016).

For example, in his examination of analogies and the Vietnam War, Yuen Foong Khong (1992) concluded that the lessons President Johnson and his advisers drew from Munich, Dien Bien Phu, and, most important, the Korean War had a powerful influence on the decision-making process. The use of these historical analogies helped to reinforce the enemy image and predispose the United States toward military intervention. Similarly, according to Goodwin (1991: 100–101), Lyndon Johnson drew heavily on the lesson of Munich in his consideration of the conflict in Vietnam, which led to failure to discriminate between the different situations and contributed to decisions by Johnson to Americanize and escalate the war in Vietnam.

In addition to these examples of shortcuts, numerous other heuristics have been identified, including biases of *representation* (estimating the probability of an event based on how similar it is to a known situation), *availability* (estimating the probability or frequency of an event based on the ease with which instances of its occurrence can be brought to mind), *adjustment and anchoring* (estimating based on an initial value or reference point and/or by focusing on a particular piece of information), *regression to the mean* (failure to consider that natural variation tends to revert to the mean), *confirmation* (seeking information that confirms pre-conceptions), *hindsight* (overconfidence that stems from a "knew it all along" adjustment to the surprise of an unpredictable event), and many others (e.g., Kahneman, Slovic, and Tversky 1982; Kahneman 2011). To cite a prominent example, consider the Bush Administration with regard to focusing on a particular piece of information in the lead-up to the Iraq War of

2003. A report of yellow cake uranium in the possession of Saddam Hussein translated into full-fledged belief in an active nuclear weapons program. This mistaken belief, in turn, caused leadership and public opinion to converge on war as the only safe alternative to allowing a potential WMD (weapons of mass destruction) strike on the US, which still processed events largely within the context of the 9/11 strikes.

In sum, individuals and policymakers rarely formulate decisions through an open intellectual process where goals (and preferences) are clearly ordered, a strong search is made for relevant information, a variety of different alternatives are considered, and the option that maximizes benefits while minimizing costs is selected. The insights of cognitive psychology summarized above suggest that this is simply too demanding and too time-consuming a process for human beings and the human mind (e.g., Tetlock 2006). The cognitive approach and the cognitive patterns of perception and misperception identified may have a profound effect on conflict decisions and conflict behavior. At the same time, some might argue that, analytically, rational choice may serve as a default position, with modifications coming as a result of factors that move decision-making away from its expectations to varying degrees from one instance to the next.

PSYCHOLOGICAL FACTORS AND OUR UNDERSTANDING OF CONFLICT, CRISIS, AND WAR

We now turn to three examples from this area of the individual level of analysis to explore the connections between such psychological factors and our understanding of conflict, crisis, and war.

Example 1: Beliefs and Operational Codes. One approach emerging from the context just summarized focuses on individual beliefs, how they are organized, and their effects on decision-making. Grounded in early work by Leites (1951), George (1969), Holsti (1970, 1977), and Walker (1977), the operational code approach rests on the nature and impact of individual belief systems about political life, from philosophical aspects to instrumental beliefs. Such belief systems are resistant to change, but do change under some conditions, such as dramatic events (e.g., Rosati 2000; Renshon 2008). Studies employing the "opcode" approach seek to identify the foreign policy orientations of leaders and to connect them to their preferences and decisions. According to two major contributors to this approach (Walker and Schafer 2018), it has progressed over more than seven decades through overlapping waves undertaking: idiographic-interpretive studies of particular leaders; nomothetic-typological studies emerging from George's (1969) initial efforts to develop a scientific framework and Holsti's (1977) expansion of George's work into a typological theory; quantitative-statistical studies aided by advances in computer coding and content analysis such as Verbs in Context and Profiler Plus software; and formal modeling studies developing causal connections to decisions and actions.

Many hundreds of analyses employing the operational code approach have been undertaken, and Walker and Schafer (2018) estimate that more 150 world leaders have been studied as scholars attempt to demonstrate that "beliefs play a pivotal role in explaining the process of foreign policy decision making, the ensuing process of strategic interaction between actors engendered by their decisions, and the political outcomes resulting from this interaction process" (Walker and Schafer 2018: 1).

> ### IN FOCUS: GEORGE'S ELEMENTS OF OPERATIONAL CODE
>
> ## THE OPERATIONAL CODE
>
> Philosophical
>
> P-1: What is the essential nature of political life? Is the political universe essentially one of harmony or conflict? What is the fundamental character of one's political opponents?
> P-2: What are the prospects for the eventual realization of one's fundamental political values and aspirations? Can one be optimistic, or must one be pessimistic on this score; and in what respects the one and/or the other?
> P-3: Is the political future predictable? In what sense and to what extent?
> P-4: How much control or mastery can one have over historical development? What is one's role in moving and shaping history in the desired direction?
> P-5: What is the role and chance in human affairs and in historical development?
>
> Instrumental
>
> I-1: What is the best approach for selecting goals or objectives for political action?
> I-2: How are the goals of action pursued most effectively?
> I-3: How are the risks of political action calculated, controlled, and accepted?
> I-4: What is the best timing of action to advance one's interest?
> I-5: What is the utility and role of different means for advancing one's interests?
>
> *Source:* George 1969.

An example of the myriad of studies of operational codes, their nature, development, and effects that connects them to conflict decisions/behavior is the study of George H. W. Bush and Bill Clinton by Walker, Schafer, and Young (1999). They identify operational codes for each president's approach to conflict management (less cooperative and relatively inflexible for Bush; more flexible and cooperative approach for Clinton), and then examine them in connection to US behavior in multiple post-Cold War conflicts involving Panama, Haiti, the Persian Gulf, and Bosnia. These scholars posit that leader "beliefs interact with external conditions and events to provide an explanation of foreign policy behavior" (Walker, Schafer, and Young 1999: 612) and their evidence supports that claim. On the one hand, the research team finds that "The pattern of moves by the United States under Bush's leadership is less cooperative and less flexible – choosing a course of action, sticking with it, and disregarding the opponent's machinations to alter the process no matter what". On the other hand, "the Clinton administration is more cooperative and flexible – responding more to both friendly and hostile moves by the opponent" (Walker, Schafer, and Young 1999: 622). These scholars therefore conclude that "a less cooperative, inflexible president and a more cooperative, flexible president exercised power quite differently but in ways consistent with the stable choice and shift propensities in their respective operational codes" (Walker, Schafer, and Young 1999: 623). To sum up, results from conflict processes will depend on the combination of operational codes among the leaders involved, along with the specific situation they face.

Operational code analysis elaborates on aspects of Type I and II cognition to develop an overall sense of a given leader as an actor in world politics. This suggests an interesting question: what might operational codes look like for those who see themselves as being in a zero-sum relationship with each other – as per the following example focused on bitter rivals.

> **FOR EXAMPLE: THE OPERATIONAL CODES OF BITTER RIVALS**
>
> To say that Hillary Clinton and Donald J. Trump had a bitter rivalry during the campaign for the US presidency in 2016 might even be an understatement. Based on Walker, Schafer, and Smith (2018), Appendix Figure 7.A1 analyzes the operational codes of these opposing candidates in the form of a systemist figure. On the one hand, as would be expected given their negative relationship, Trump and Clinton have some important differences. Trump's task focus score is very low, and Clinton's is relatively higher. In addition, Trump's self-confidence and complexity scores make him closed to information compared to an average president. More interesting, however, are the multiple ways in which the two *resemble* each other: (a) instrumental and philosophical beliefs of the two leaders are less cooperative/more conflictual than over 90% of US presidents; and (b) both are more risk averse than an average president. The preceding point (a), perhaps, would point toward interpersonal conflict, while (b) might point away from it. Taken together, the contents of the figure raise questions about how the years of Trump in office might have played out differently in some ways, but much the same in others, as a result of the operational codes of the president and the alternative candidate in 2016.

Example 2: Misperception and Miscalculation. A second example draws heavily from the insights of the literature on cognitive processing and its limits to emphasize the role of misperception and miscalculation in world politics, an application especially relevant for conflict decisions and behavior. Indeed, there is a commonly argued aphorism that every war involves at least one misperception (Jervis 1988: 677). Jervis (1976) contributed to progress in this area with his thorough survey of the processes of perception and misperception. His synthesis and conceptualization address the role and effects of cognitive consistency for policymakers, the cognitive shortcuts they employ, including historical analogies, how they learn from history, and the common areas of misperception and miscalculation that affect them. Driven in significant part by the cognitive shortcuts described by scholars such as Kahneman and Tversky noted above, key misperceptions center on those involving capabilities (one's own and those of adversaries) and intentions (adversaries) as primary categories (Levy 1983b: 80). Others include misperception of the perceptions and the decision-making processes of adversaries, misperception of future reality and anticipated consequences, misperception of the intentions, capabilities, and responses of third parties, and others (Levy 1983b; Jervis 1988).

Dozens of studies of World War I, World War II, the Korean War, and numerous other conflicts, small and large, have focused on the role both unmotivated (relating to normal cognitive processes) and motivated (related to cognitive and emotional needs) (e.g., Janis and

Mann 1977).[1] Collectively, these studies have identified the role of images and belief systems in generating misperceptions, especially of intentions, but also of capabilities, anchoring and adjustment biases (Kahneman, Slovic, and Tversky 1982), inappropriate historical analogies (e.g., Khong 1992), and situations (e.g., Johnson and Tierney 2011).

Three examples illustrate these analyses of misperception and the linkages to conflict behavior. In addition to a significant study of misperception and the Vietnam War (White 1970), Ralph White's (2004) examination of ten wars in the 20th century identified problematic misperceptions that shaped their initiation and duration. Similarly, Cashman and Robinson's (2007) study of seven 20th century wars concluded that all of them were characterized by consequential misperceptions during the prewar period. Finally, Duelfer and Dyson (2011) apply the misperception lens of cognitive psychology to study the US-Iraq conflict from 1990–2003. They identify a range of misperceptions falling neatly into the categories discussed in the preceding paragraph. These misperceptions stemmed from images and beliefs, various cognitive shortcuts, and other factors that "accumulated over the course of interactions between the United States and Iraq during the period of study, and they contributed heavily to the occurrence of two major military conflicts" (Duelfer and Dyson 2011: 99). Based on such evidence, Saddam Hussein and George W. Bush may have misunderstood each other as much or more than any other pair of world leaders in history.

Example 3: Risk and Prospect Theory. A third example is from what one scholar has called "arguably the most influential behavioral theory of choice in the social sciences" (Taliaferro 2017: 1): *prospect theory*. Originating in the pioneering work of Kahneman and Tversky together (1979, 2004) and with others (Kahneman, Slovic, and Tversky 1982; Quattrone and Tversky 1988), prospect theory focuses on the nature of decision-making under conditions of risk and uncertainty. As Taliaferro (2017: 1–2) summarizes in a recent review of prospect theory's contributions to international relations and foreign policy analysis,

> The theory's best known predictions are that most people are risk averse to secure gains, but risk acceptant to avoid losses; display an extreme sensitivity to real or perceived losses, no matter how trivial the commodity in question; treat highly probable, but uncertain, outcomes as if they were in fact certain; and assign higher values to items already in their possession than to comparable items they seek to acquire

(also McDermott 2004 and Vis and Kuijpers 2018 for reviews of prospect theory's contributions and challenges in the study of international relations). Beginning in the late 1980s, many hundreds of studies have developed and applied the theory for international relations and foreign policy (it has applied to a very wide range of topics across dozens of disciplines and subdisciplines outside Political Science, and to many subfields within it as well).

As Taliaferro (2017) describes, key collections from Farnham (1994) and Stein and Pauly (1993), books by Farnham 1997 and McDermott (1998), and articles by various scholars (e.g.,

---

[1] A few examples include Levy (1990–1991), Van Evera (1999); Jervis (1976, 1988), Lebow (1981), Khong (1992), and Johnson (2004).

Boettcher 1995; Vertzberger 1995; Kowert and Hermann 1997; Levi and Whyte 1997) focused on integrating prospect theory into international relations, largely focused on conflict and security matters. McDermott (1998), for example, applied findings from prospect theory to explain why US leaders engage in more risk-taking when they perceive themselves to be in a domain of losses.

Subsequently, a second wave applied and integrated the insights of prospect theory into a wide range of international relations theories through a diverse set of research designs and methodologies. In terms of conflict behavior, these studies include Davis (2000) on coercion, threats, and reassurances, Boettcher (2004) and Taliaferro (2004a, 2004b) on military intervention, Lobell (2006) on war, and a great many other topics. Through these and other studies, the significance of risk aversion to secure gains, but risk acceptance to avoid losses relative to a critical reference point, has found significant empirical support in experiments, case studies, and large-n statistical studies. For conflict behavior, among other things, prospect theory has helped to shed light on the conditions under which decision-makers might be more likely to engage in risky behavior.

> **IN FOCUS: A SYSTEMIST VIEW OF PROSPECT THEORY ACCORDING TO TALIAFERRO (2017)**
>
> One of the most important developments in political psychology, with significant implications for foreign policy decision-making and action, is prospect theory. Figure 7.1 depicts the authoritative review of prospect theory carried out in Taliaferro (2017). The system in this diagram is International Relations, with the World Beyond as the environment. Within International Relations, the micro and macro levels correspond, respectively, to the activities of individual scholars and the discipline as a whole. Rather than working through Figure 7.1 systematically via subfigures, a few observations will be offered in order to bring prospect theory into focus and stimulate questions about it.
>
> Note the point of departure in the World Beyond: a sense of rising influence for prospect theory in the social sciences. The large plain box at bottom center-left draws attention to the main insights of prospect theory about decision-making. As a modification to rational choice models, prospect theory holds that gains and losses are evaluated relative to a reference point designated by a decision-maker. Under condition of perceived gains (losses), a leader is likely to become less (more) acceptant of risk. With regard to designation of a reference point, there is an endowment effect – something already possessed is valued more than otherwise. Taken together, the preceding properties can help to explain departures from standard rational choice models, which emphasize maximization of self-interest based on a straightforward calculation of expected value. Prospect theory points toward nuances that otherwise might persist as anomalies for the study of decision-making about conflict, crisis, and war.
>
> *Apply the contents of Figure 7.1 to cases not mentioned in it. How can prospect theory help to explain decisions and actions that otherwise might seem puzzling?*

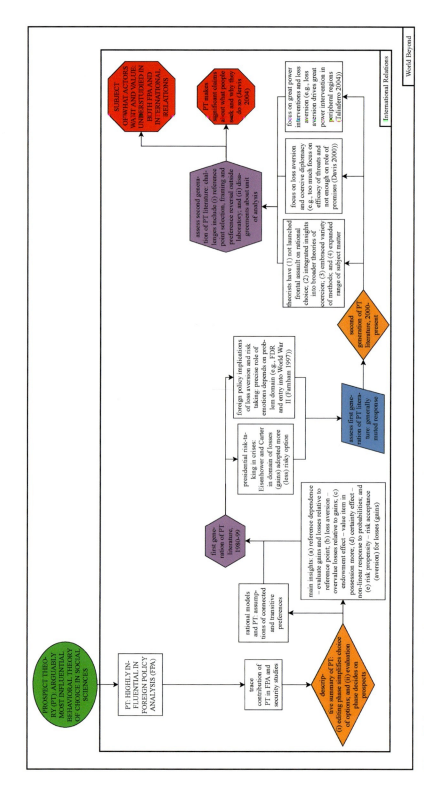

Figure 7.1 Prospect theory and foreign policy analysis

SUMMING UP AND MOVING FORWARD

If system-level explanations are potentially powerful and attractive because they are relatively simple, as we discussed in Chapter 5, they are often very general and more successful at explaining broader patterns, such as system-level conditions under which war is more or less frequent (or more or less intense). These accounts are generally less helpful in explaining the participants and other specific aspects of wars. As we reviewed in Chapter 6, state-level explanations sacrifice parsimony to improve explanation of why some states participate in war more or less often than others. In this chapter, our review suggests that analysis at the individual level has contributed most to understanding the decisions and actions of particular states by focusing on the individuals who make those decisions.

While sweeping analyses of human nature appear to explain broad patterns of war with simple ideas (e.g., human aggression), they have proven less helpful when put to the test. By contrast, the focus on human experiences and psychology has yielded significant insight into leaders/policymakers and their conflict decisions/behavior. Yet, though some have applauded these contributions as a "cognitive paradigm" (e.g., Rosati and Miller 2018: 4; see also Steinbruner 1974 and Tetlock 1998), Cashman (2013: 113) reminds us at the end of his review of the explanations and contributions of the individual level of analysis that

> none of the ideas we have encountered here add up to a fully developed theory of war. We do not as yet have a psychological or cognitive theory of war … Nevertheless, these individual-level variables are often important enough that if they are omitted from our explanations we will fail to understand the reason for war.

In sum, the key factors on which individual-level analyses focus are almost certainly interconnected themselves, and they almost certainly play out in varying ways in the small-group and state-level contexts of most foreign policy decisions.

For example, the groupthink argument suggests that the characteristics of some decision groups turn the particular mix of personalities and group structure into a situation in which the participants get locked into a single way of thinking and ignore relevant information. In certain situations, this phenomenon can lead to decisions to use force. President Kennedy's decision to invade the Bay of Pigs in 1961 and Johnson's decision to escalate US involvement in the Vietnam War are classic examples of groupthink. Another good example may be the US decision to go to war in Iraq in 2003 under George W. Bush as well. In that case, Badie (2010) argues that the president and most of his advisers were convinced that war was the only logical choice and refused to consider seriously other options (Badie 2010). When such group contexts are paired up with leader characteristics or experiences, they could reinforce each other. Moreover, different regime types probably connect to these factors as well, with individual characteristics of leaders probably more important to understanding war in regimes in which such individuals are more powerful and less constrained by structures and processes of accountability.

CONSIDER THIS: WHEN DO INDIVIDUALS MATTER?

According to Levy and Thompson (2010: 128), "War is the product of the actions of two or more states or other political organizations. It follows that to understand the outbreak of war we need to understand why states make certain decisions rather than other decisions. That leads us to an analysis of foreign policy decision-making, which focuses on the individuals and governmental organizations that are empowered to make and implement policies on behalf of the state."

What aspects or patterns of participation and behavior in conflict, crisis, and war are best and least explained by explanations at the individual level of analysis?

INDIVIDUAL-LEVEL EXPLANATIONS

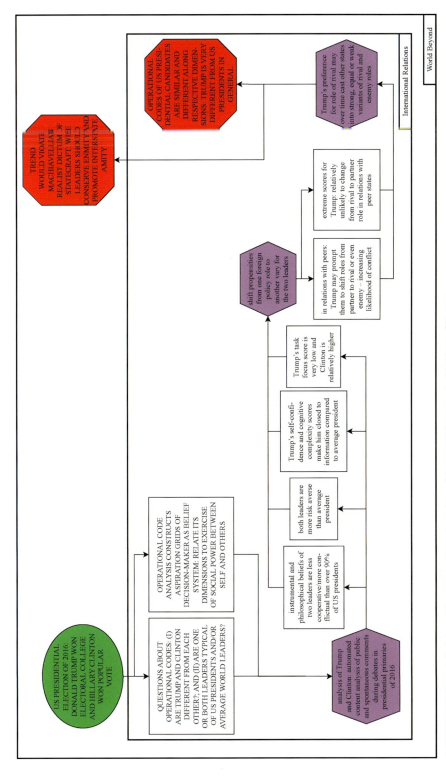

APPENDIX Figure 7.A1   The operational codes of Donald Trump and Hillary Clinton

8
Understanding crises

PROLOGUE

Over six decades ago, a defining moment in the Cold War occurred in Berlin, remembered today as the epicenter of confrontation between the US and USSR. By August 1961, migration out of Soviet-controlled East Berlin had accelerated to the point at which Soviet leadership feared for the survival of its client state, the German Democratic Republic (GDR). The USSR responded by building a barrier that became known as the Berlin Wall, which prevented citizens of the GDR from fleeing into the Western-supported Federal Republic of Germany (FRG). The international crisis known as the Berlin Wall reached its peak in late October 1961, when Soviet and American tanks squared off at "Checkpoint Charlie", the name given to the crossing point between East and West Berlin. While the crisis over the Berlin Wall did not result in war, the sight of Soviet and US tanks in confrontation conveyed a dangerous situation that might have escalated all the way to a nuclear calamity.

Fast forward to the new millennium and it is possible to see both continuity and change with regard to international crises. While the Cold War is over, echoes of its East–West main axis of conflict remain in place. Russia, at this time of writing, escalated a crisis with Ukraine into a full-scale war in February 2022 that still is underway. Other states, such as Sweden and Finland, joined NATO out of concerns about further Russian acts of aggression in the region. At the same time, international crises outside of the great power domain are more common than in the past. Crises in the Global South often unfold completely beyond any concerns about competition in the Global North. For example, identity-related tensions that produced international crises such as Sudan-South Sudan – 2011 reflect local conditions, in that instance related to conflict over religion among other issues.

OVERVIEW

For the preceding reasons, understanding international crises requires a comprehensive view. Although these events are variegated over location and time, a unified approach to the study of crisis is possible. Accessing the concept, formation, and data of the well-established International Crisis Behavior (ICB) Project provides a path toward breadth and depth of understanding.

This chapter proceeds in six additional sections. The second section focuses on the nature of international crises and the bringing about of project-based research on that subject. The three sections that follow focus on research findings from the ICB Project. Section three probes the origins of international crises, with trigger violence as one example. The fourth section focuses on processes such as violent crisis management. Section five considers the outcomes and legacies of international crises, for instance, the likelihood of victory and recurrence. The sixth section profiles an international crisis, the Soleimani Assassination – 2019, in light of the results from sections three through five. The seventh and final section sums up what has been accomplished and leads into the next chapter.

THE NATURE OF INTERNATIONAL CRISES AND PROJECT-BASED RESEARCH

With the advent of nuclear weapons and onset of the Cold War, it became obvious that crisis interactions would be affected. "Academic attention", as Beardsley, James, Wilkenfeld, and Brecher (2020) observe, "moved toward the study of *crisis* in response to tendencies during the Cold War toward dangerous escalation in a world armed to the teeth and faced with potential nuclear destruction". Nuclear war became unthinkable on the one hand but possible on the other hand if the superpowers failed at any point in crisis management (Brodie 1959; Kahn 1960; Schelling 1960).

During the Cold War, crises in world politics took place within certain boundaries, as Murauskaite and Astorino-Courtois (2023: 57) observe:

> With the red line of a nuclear exchange clearly established, *probing and shaping* behavior continued on the sidelines, with adversaries and their proxies using lesser forms of confrontation to identify the limits of the unacceptable and test the strength of alliances, as well as the level of actual commitment to various verbally professed policies and threats.

At the same time, events still could get out of hand – beyond the control of even the US and USSR. A prominent case study of the Korean War revealed how misperceptions on the US side of the conflict provoked a dramatic Chinese entry into, and intensification of, the ongoing conflict (Whiting 1960). As per the title of the case study, *China Crosses the Yalu*, huge numbers of troops began to cross the river and engage with UN forces from late October 1950 onward. This created the potential for further escalation and appears as an intrawar crisis, Korean War II – 1950, within the ICB dataset.

Systematic research on crises began, as therefore would be expected in response to the nuclear era, with the theory and practice of deterrence (Schelling 1960; Russett 1963). Put simply, how could crisis escalation to nuclear war be prevented? The frightening events of the Cuban Missile Crisis in 1962 accelerated interest in subjects such as bargaining (Young 1968), competing and complementary approaches toward analysis of crisis management (Allison 1971), and the practice of "coercive diplomacy" (George, Hall, and Simons 1971). Interdisciplinary borrowing, notably from psychology, advanced the study of crisis decision-making through the discovery of significant challenges from misperception, groupthink, and other now familiar factors (Holsti 1972; Janis 1972; Jervis 1976). Team-oriented efforts to understand crises came into being as well (Hermann 1972).

From a social scientific point of view, the significant dangers posed by international crises called for a project-based approach based on reproducible evidence. When it came into being in 1975, the ICB Project answered that call. Research based on aggregate data and case studies from that project made it possible to accumulate and disseminate knowledge about crises in world politics. A wide range of hypotheses about decision-making and other aspects of crisis have been tested using ICB datasets. Patterns have been identified with respect to the onset, processes, and outcomes and legacies of crises (Beardsley, James, Wilkenfeld, and Brecher 2020). Taken together, the corpus of work from ICB conveys academic value and policy relevance.

ICB Project data continues to be the most prominent in research on international crises. While other studies of crisis provide valuable insights, we feature research based on ICB Project data and case material in this chapter. (Research designs often incorporate variables from other datasets together with those of ICB, so we recognize and include those sources in at least an indirect way.) Recall from Chapter 2 that ICB continues to provide the standard definitions for international crisis and foreign policy crisis. An international crisis disrupts processes and challenges the structure of either the system as a whole or one of its subsystems. This type of event includes the experiences of all actors involved. A foreign policy crisis refers to the perceptions and actions of a specific state when its leaders perceive a threat to basic values, finite time for response, and a higher probability of escalation.

Consider, for example, Sudan-South Sudan – 2011, an international crisis that focused on whether a new state would emerge after years of seething conflict. Actors in this case included both states and international organizations, in varying status associated with their degrees of activity. Sudan and South Sudan participated as foreign policy crisis actors. The US had a low level of involvement, while the African Union served as a mediator and the UN allocated an observer group.

After the Cold War, and especially in the new millennium, crises are shifting toward a combination of state and non-state actors. The politics of identity often spill over and stimulate cross-border tensions and interstate conflict (Beardsley, James, Wilkenfeld, and Brecher 2020). For example, the Sudan-South Sudan case can be traced to secessionism. On July 9, 2011, the people of southern Sudan voted for independence. The crisis came soon after; violence broke out in the Abyei region and sovereignty over it remains disputed to this day.

Most recently, "gray zone" activities have come into prominence and add significantly to the complications attached to international crises. The gray zone is a major emerging feature of the international system, described as "a space between war and peace where major powers spar with each other indirectly or through the actions of their proxies" (Wilkenfeld and Quinn 2023: 80). Gray zone activities are part of larger challenges that come from a combination of activities that threaten a defender's interest by "clouding intent and attribution" (Murauskaite and Astorino-Courtois 2023: 72–73). Such actions, which create ambiguity and heighten risk of misperception, can include use of proxies, low-level cyberattacks, and covert operations (Murauskaite and Astorino-Courtois 2023: 70–71).

Consider, in the preceding context, the international crisis known as the Russo-Georgian War – 2008. In the pre-crisis period, Russia backed South Ossetian and Abkhazian separatist movements. Self-designated Russian "peacekeepers" moved into Georgian-populated areas of Abkhazia and a difficult-to-trace bombing took place in South Ossetia. Russia triggered a crisis for Georgia by moving troops toward battle areas inside its borders on July 7, 2008. These murky events combine to show an instance of gray zone activities at work.

Wilkenfeld and Quinn (2023: 100) offer a good summation of the visible tendencies of international crises over time:

> In sum, there is an increasing tendency toward nebulousness, stasis, and non-resolution of issues in international crises: a steady increase in ambiguous outcomes over time; an increase in the proportion of crises that have simply faded and ended with most actors dissatisfied during the post-Cold War period; and tension escalation hovers at around 50% as the most common post-crisis outcome in the post-Cold War period.

The ICB Project maintains relevance, even allowing for the evolving nature of international crises, because of its comprehensive conceptualization and data collection. The concepts of international crisis and foreign policy crisis, respectively, focus on events and perceptions. ICB data collection, moreover, includes the activities of state, non-state, and transnational actors. For such reasons, ICB continues to serve effectively as the basic source for research on crises.

Studies based on concept formation and data from the ICB Project, over the course of a half-century, have produced a vast amount of knowledge about crises in world politics. Several comprehensive reviews of the Project are available to be consulted with regard to its findings about (a) onset; (b) processes; and (c) outcomes and legacies (Brecher 1999; Brecher, James, and Wilkenfeld 2000; James 2004, 2019; Beardsley, James, Wilkenfeld, and Brecher 2020; Iakhnis, Neumeier, van Wijk, and James 2020; Beardsley, James, and Wilkenfeld 2025). We base the following three sections of this chapter on material gleaned from the preceding sources. The tabulations that appear focus on the findings from data-based studies that have produced statistically significant results. Our discussion points about the results focus, as relevant, on (a) range; (b) classification as material, ideational, or both; and (c) connections to research programs such as neo-Kantianism.

Before moving ahead, a few qualifications are in order. First, what follows is a limited subset of all findings from the ICB Project, but sufficient to be representative of the insights gleaned from its research. Second, we do not provide a complete list of the specific studies that report any given result; these can be identified through consultation of the review essays that have been used to construct the tables that follow. Third, ICB also has produced a considerable number of case studies, both book and article-length, but it would be challenging to aggregate the results of this research in the way that follows. Fourth, it would require quite a bit of space to show how variables are coded, so we do not include that information.[1] Coding, however, can be accessed from studies included in the aforementioned review essays. Fifth, and finally,

---

[1] When findings are integrated into the systemist graphic analysis of a specific international crisis later on in this chapter, some material about coding will be provided as relevant.

the tables in the sections that follow contain results that are designated by respective authors as statistically significant – a distinction in kind rather than by degree.[2]

> **IN FOCUS: GOING BEYOND A STATE-CENTERED VIEW OF CRISIS**
>
> Much has been learned about crises in world politics via research carried out, primarily with ICB Project data, for a half-century. At the same time, this scholarship has focused overwhelmingly on the experiences of states, notably those experiencing a foreign policy crisis. However, other concerns exist. For example, how might human security be integrated into the research agenda? Human *insecurity*, as Iakhnis, Neumeier, van Wijk, and James (2020) point out, is an integral part of virtually any crisis. *Could health and other aspects of human security be integrated into future research on crises?*

ORIGINS

Table 8.1 displays the findings from ICB-based research about the onset of crises. The columns of the table correspond to levels of analysis, characteristics, and findings. Levels of analysis in this table (and Tables 8.2–3) are largely familiar, but adjusted somewhat in light of the way in which research findings about crises are distributed in practice. International system and state appear in the usual way, complemented with two other levels of analysis: (i) interstate dyad and (ii) society and individual. Important datasets and statistical results from them, used in tandem with ICB, frequently are structured in terms of interstate dyads. In addition, this table combines individual decision-makers and members of society into a hybrid level that focuses on agency.

Three aspects of crisis onset appear in the third and final column of Table 8.1 that covers findings. The first aspect concerns the likelihood that an international crisis will occur. Whether a state will initiate a foreign policy crisis for another state appears second. The third aspect focuses on the presence of trigger violence at the outset of an international crisis. If a characteristic of a crisis is associated significantly with a given aspect in at least one aggregate data analysis, a check mark appears. Each aspect of the findings about onset is reviewed in turn.

Likelihood of a crisis is most heavily studied among aspects of onset and characteristics have been identified from all levels of analysis. Relevant factors range all the way from polycentric system structure to a shorter time in office for a US president. The former is relatively complex – a system with two superpowers but other centers of independent decision-making – and therefore more difficult to navigate. The latter, a trait of the US specifically, essentially focuses on possible effects from lack of experience among its leadership in system management. Each of these characteristics has been found to increase the probability of an international crisis.

Both material and ideational factors can affect the probability of an international crisis breaking out. On the material side, the risk of a coup might lead to an international crisis

---

[2] In other words, results significant at one level (e.g., 0.05) are treated as equivalent to those at another (e.g., 0.01) for the purposes of this review.

Table 8.1 Research findings about the onset of international crises

Level of analysis	Characteristic	Likelihood	Initiator	Trigger violence
International system	polarity – polycentric system (i.e., two superpowers and other independent decision centers)	✓		
	expected utility for initiator relative to target is greater than or equal to zero		✓	
Interstate dyad	protracted conflict setting	✓		✓
	opportunity case – only one adversary is a crisis actor			✓
	mixture of regime types; fewer common memberships in international organizations; lower level of economic development	✓		
State	state religious exclusivity; risk of coup; shorter time in office for US president	✓		
Society and individual	lower effective number of political parties and lack of media access; latent hawkishness of leader		✓	
	shorter time in office for US president	✓		

either due to vulnerability or attempted diversion on the part of state leadership. A protracted conflict, in which intensely hostile emotions play an ongoing role, represents the ideational side of crisis outbreak.[3] So, too, does government imposition of religious exclusivity (i.e., insisting upon adherence to one type of faith), which may signal either a truculent regime or serve as a provocation toward other states, in either instance making a crisis more likely than otherwise.

Some dyadic characteristics associated with the likelihood of crisis are connected to ongoing programs of research. Toward the opposite end of neo-Kantianism is the observed mixture of regime type, fewer common memberships in international organizations, and a lower level of economic development. These dyadic characteristics are expected to dispose states toward

---

[3] Protracted conflict refers to a situation in which adversaries have a relationship of sustained hostility. Negative images and mutual mistrust represent the norm within a protracted conflict (Brecher 2018).

involvement in international conflict, in the present context meaning crisis – a reversal of pacifying effects confirmed via neo-Kantian research for democracy, international organization membership, and economic interdependence.[4]

With regard to taking on the initiator role in a crisis, existing research once again points us to relevant material and ideational characteristics. When expected utility for initiator relative to target is greater than or equal to zero, an obviously material factor is at work – this may be seen as the essence of the rational choice model. A lower effective number of political parties and lack of media access also create material conditions that could facilitate initiation of a crisis. Under those conditions, an aggressive leader would not face the inhibiting effects of a vigilant party system and media, with resulting greater likelihood of triggering a crisis for other states. On the ideational side, latent hawkishness of a leader is a characteristic that obviously points toward a state taking on the initiator role.

This time in association with trigger violence, protracted conflict once again plays a significant and intuitively obvious role as an ideational characteristic. A sustained relationship of hostility and mistrust creates a disposition toward violence. In material terms, an opportunity case – meaning that only one adversary is a crisis actor – is linked to trigger violence. A sense of vulnerability for the noncrisis actor may well be lacking and thus inhibitions against use of violence against an adversary are reduced as a result.

FOR EXAMPLE: RANN OF KUTCH 1965

A crisis over territory between India and Pakistan, one of many in their protracted conflict since 1947, lasted from April 8 until June 30, 1965. Ever since the process leading to independence, Pakistan had claimed the northern part of the Rann of Kutch. Crises were triggered for India and Pakistan on April 8, 1965 when each attacked the other's police post in the disputed territory. The question of "who attacked first?" remains disputed to this day. While the conflict de-escalated, its violent origin is in line with expectations for how crises will begin in the context of a protracted conflict. A full-scale war broke out between India and Pakistan later in that same year.

PROCESSES

Table 8.2 summarizes results of research from the ICB Project with regard to processes within international crises – in other words, what happens after the origin and before the outcome. The first and second columns once again correspond to level of analysis and characteristics. In this table, the findings pertain to an extensive range of processes. Perceived gravity of threat appears first. The second column focuses on whether mediation or negotiation becomes less

---

[4] A low level of economic development is not the same as absence of interdependence, so the parallel with neo-Kantianism is inexact. However, prosperity is a factor adjacent to interdependence within the vast literature on neo-Kantianism, so the comparison is not out of bounds.

Table 8.2 Research findings about the processes of international crises

Level of analysis	Characteristic	Findings				
		Higher gravity of threat	Mediation or negotiation less likely	Severity of violence	Centrality of violence	Violent crisis management
International system	non-state triggering entity					√
	absence of international organization with economic leverage		√	√		
Interstate dyad	protracted conflict setting			√		√
	contiguity; power discrepancy; non-nuclear actors			√		
	lower proportion of democracies					√
	opportunity case – only one adversary is a crisis actor	√				
	rivalry without settled border	√	√	√		
State	lower percentage of women in legislature			√	√	√

Level of analysis	Characteristic	Findings
Society and individual	ethnic dimensions	√
	societal unrest; mass violence; civil war; strikes, riots, demonstrations (and territorial issues); higher decision-maker stress; absence of female leader; gender inequality	√
		√
	leader with previous experience in social movement; US president high in belief in ability to control events	√
		√
	democratic leader scoring relatively high in distrust, nationalism, need for power, 1	√

likely to occur. Severity and centrality of violence, respectively, appear third and fourth. Fifth, and finally, is violent crisis management.

With regard to higher gravity of threat, ideational factors come to the fore. Existence of an opportunity case once again plays a material role – the threat experienced by a single targeted actor is likely to be greater, on average, in such an obviously asymmetrical situation. Ethnic dimensions, in which identity is at issue, contribute to higher gravity of threat in an ideational way. Interesting to note is one further characteristic that spans the material-ideational divide: rivalry without a settled border. Identified already as a key factor in research on territory and conflict, this is the *only* characteristic that appears across all findings in the table about the processes of international crises.

Mediation or negotiation become less likely under conditions of a rivalry without a settled border. A lock-in effect, disposing the crisis participants against third-party efforts at conflict management, would seem more likely under conditions of rivalry and conflict over territorial boundaries. A non-state triggering entity, as an ideational characteristic, has the same effect. Such actors, by default, are more difficult to include in, and/or reluctant to accept, mediation or participation in negotiations.

Severity of violence is the most heavily researched among processes in international crises. Multiple material characteristics are associated with greater severity of violence. Contiguity, power discrepancy, and nonnuclear actors are significant dyadic factors. A difference in power, along with contiguity, would facilitate use of violence through easier opportunity for use. Without the presence of a nuclear actor, violence might rise to more severe levels due to reduced worries about the consequences of escalation.

Rivalry without settled borders, a material-ideational hybrid characteristic, appears once again at the dyadic level. Related to that observation is the presence of several indicators in conjunction with territorial issues: societal unrest, mass violence, civil war, strikes, riots, and demonstrations. Conflict over territory is difficult to manage on its own and therefore more severe violence can be expected when the situation is complicated by domestic conflict in one form or another.

> **FOR EXAMPLE: KASHMIR II – 1965**
>
> One of the most prominent instances of rivalry without settled borders involves India and Pakistan. Multiple crises and even full-scale war have occurred over the course of decades, with the disputed Kashmir region at the center of things. The Kashmir II crisis for India was triggered on August 5, 1965 when Pakistani "freedom fighters" began infiltrating Kashmir. These forces hoped to create a large-scale uprising against Indian control over most of the former princely state. India responded on August 25, sending several thousand troops across the 1949 Kashmir Cease-fire Line. India succeeded in capturing most of the areas through which the infiltrators had come and thereby triggered a crisis for Pakistan. The latter responded on September 1 by dispatching an armored column across the cease-fire line in southern Kashmir and threatening the vital road linking the capital city of Srinagar with the plains of India. India's major response was to invade West Pakistan on September 5. On September 4 and 6, the UN Security Council called for a cease-fire and the withdrawal of armed forces; India and Pakistan accepted later on that

> month. The protracted conflict continued, however, with no end in sight with regard to the disputed territory of Kashmir.

Among ideational factors, protracted conflict and ethnic dimensions once again come into play. It is interesting to note that, at the state level, a lower percentage of women in the legislature also is associated with severity of violence. Effects at the level of society and individual point in the same direction; severity of violence is associated with gender inequality and absence of a female leader. Taken together, these factors point toward the potential constraining effects on violence that inhere within a liberal society.

Several characteristics from the level of society and individual that point toward higher severity of violence are associated with respective research programs. The long-standing program of research on decision-making can be connected with higher decision-maker stress, a leader with previous experience in a social movement, and a US president with a high belief in ability to control events (BACE). The connection of stress with greater violence is obvious by intuition – more risk of even unwanted escalation. Activity in a social movement could make a leader more ideological than pragmatic in disposition, which in turn would increase the likelihood of violent confrontation. The same can be said for the likely effects of a high BACE for a US president – less pragmatic than otherwise and more likely to become involved in violence through either use or provocation. With regard to the neo-Kantian program of research (or perhaps instead adjacent to it), note the absence of an international organization with economic leverage. More severe violence becomes likely without the constraining effects of such third parties.

Findings about centrality of violence form a subset of those for severity of violence. Rivalry without a settled border, a leader with previous experience in a social movement, and a US president high in BACE once again carry great weight as explanations.

For violent crisis management, a non-state triggering entity is a significant ideational characteristic. Non-state actors, on average, can be expected to operate under more limited constraints than even autocratic states. A rivalry without a settled border makes another appearance as a material-ideational combination, while protracted conflict does so from the ideational side. A connection with the neo-Kantian research program is made via a lower proportion of democracies.

With regard to the program of research on decision-making, the relevant characteristic is a democratic leader scoring relatively high in distrust, nationalism, and need for power. All of these traits, by intuition, point away from pragmatism and toward a confrontational and even violent approach toward crisis management.

OUTCOMES AND LEGACIES

Table 8.3 shows the findings from ICB research on the outcomes and legacies of international crises. The first and second columns again refer to levels of analysis and characteristics. Outcomes and legacies appear in the third column. The outcome-related aspects include likelihood, respectively, of victory and war. For legacy, the focus is on increase in tension and recurrence of crisis.

Table 8.3 Research findings about the outcomes and legacies of international crises

Level of analysis	Characteristics	Likelihood of victory	Likelihood of war	Increased tension or recurrence[a]
International system	polycentrism; economically weak region; number of participants; third party actors; heterogeneity of participants; proportion of nondemocracies involved; greater number of issues; ethnic or irredentist conflict; territorial issues; major power activity; violent trigger; no superpower threat involved		√	
	absence of facilitative type of mediation			√
	absence of mediation; absence of UN or regional organization involvement			√
	international organization supports democracy	√		
Interstate dyad	lower number of nuclear actors; positive or zero expected utility for initiator versus target; initiator has greater capability than target; initiator coalition with more capabilities than target coalition; contiguity; proximity to home territory		√	
	nuclear superiority	√		
	protracted conflict; lower number of joint international organization memberships			√

Level of analysis	Characteristics	Findings		
		Likelihood of victory	Likelihood of war	Increased tension or recurrence[a]
State	private military mobilization; proximity to date of independence; low political constraint (and ethnic dominance)		√	
	nuclear capability	√		
Society and individual	increase in latent conflict for initiator (and positive expected utility)		√	

Notes: [a] Increased tension refers to whether there is another international crisis with the same participants in the next five years. Recurrence may include cases that take place outside of that time interval.

For likelihood of victory, significant material characteristics include nuclear capability and superiority. These are basic aspects of capability, in absolute and relative terms, which seem naturally associated with success from confrontation in a crisis. On the ideational side, and also with a link to the neo-Kantian research program, is the presence of an international organization that supports a democracy. This approximates an interaction effect from two elements of neo-Kantianism.

For likelihood of war, relevant material characteristics at the level of the international system include polycentrism, a greater number of participants, an economically weak region, major power activity and no superpower threat involved. With its relatively high complexity, polycentrism would make efforts to avert escalation inherently more challenging, and the same can be said for a crisis situation with a greater number of participants. An economically weak region might be more warlike due to a lower attachment in general to the status quo. Major powers are more capable of fighting wars. The absence of a superpower threat would tend to reduce concerns about escalation to war.

Significant material traits at the dyadic level associated with likelihood of war include lower number of nuclear actors, positive or zero expected utility for initiator versus target, an initiator with greater capability than its target, contiguity, and an initiator coalition with more capabilities than the target coalition. All of the preceding metrics connect together with rational choice calculations and the realist sense of power politics.

At the level of society and the individual, an increase in latent conflict for the initiator (and positive expected utility) contributes significantly to the likelihood of war.[5] Taken together, these traits point toward diversionary action on the part of the leadership – going to war in an opportune situation in order to cope with problems at home – which we discussed in some detail in Chapter 7.

With regard to the ideational side, significant characteristics at the level of the international system include heterogeneity of participants, ethnic or irredentist conflict, and third-party actors. Each of the preceding ideational factors in place makes war more likely– all point toward greater intensity, complexity, or both as challenges to keeping the peace. At the state level, proximity to date of independence is a relevant trait. This is in line with intuition that a regime becomes more stable in any number of ways as its existence continues.

Both material and ideational aspects, as per the analysis from Hassner (2009) in Chapter 4, inhere within territory. Thus, it is possible to identify two hybrid characteristics in relation to likelihood of war: territorial issues and proximity to home territory. Territory is at once a resource with objective value and the basis of emotional attachment. A third hybrid characteristic is low political constraint and ethnic dominance. The ability to act on behalf of an overarching ethnic identity, perhaps even in an impulsive way leading to war, would be enhanced.

> **IN FOCUS**
>
> Protracted conflict between India and Pakistan has produced any number of international crises and even full-scale war. Moreover, late in the 20th century, the dyad became nuclear-equipped, as Pakistan obtained the same weapons status that India achieved decades earlier. The most recent international crisis between these adversaries, which involved a suicide bombing, took place in 2019. *In light of such events, what do the findings from Table 8.3 suggest about the prospects for constructive change in the India–Pakistan rivalry? What might be said of the findings from Table 8.3 in this context?*

Two characteristics associated with the likelihood of war can be connected with the neo-Kantian research program: one directly – war becomes more likely with a higher proportion of non-democracies involved – and the other indirectly – private military mobilization. Democracies, on average, would have less capability of mobilizing privately for possible military action.

Two traits can be connected with the program of research on decision-making: violent trigger, along with the number of issues. A violent beginning to a crisis creates greater challenges to decision-makers in managing escalation. The same effect can be anticipated as the number of issues increases – greater complexity makes crisis management more difficult and increases the likelihood of war.

With regard to increased tension or recurrence, protracted conflict appears once again as an ideational characteristic. A crisis is more likely to be seen as an episode in a multiparty series as opposed to the final say about anything. Breaking the chain of crisis becomes a very tall order once a protracted conflict is in place. Other ideational elements include the absence

---

[5] Identified in James (1988), latent conflict refers to economic problems, such as inflation, which could become manifest and threaten the stability of those in power.

of mediation (and facilitative type of mediation in particular), along with absence of UN or regional organization involvement, and a lower number of joint international organization memberships. International organizations can provide ideas – perhaps thinking outside of the proverbial "box" – with the possibility of helping adversaries to avoid playing out the same conflict in multiple iterations.

AN INTERNATIONAL CRISIS IN PROFILE: THE SOLEIMANI ASSASSINATION – 2019

Following the United States's withdrawal from the Iranian Nuclear Deal, the US and Iran experienced an international crisis from June 18, 2019 to January 8, 2020. The crisis culminated in the assassination of Iranian General Qasem Soleimani and retaliatory Iranian airstrikes. After a summary of the crisis in words, a systemist graphic presentation follows and connects with previously summarized findings about onset, processes, and outcomes and legacies.

Problematic relations for Iran and the US with each other can be traced back most readily to events in 1953. The government of Prime Minister Mohammad Mosaddegh challenged major power oil interests by threatening to take Iran down a more independent pathway. The US overthrew Mosaddegh and installed Mohammad Reza Pahlavi, the Shah of Iran, and Iran became a pro-Western state but also a brutal dictatorship. Iranians suffered under the SAVAK, the Shah's secret police and intelligence service. Toward the end of the 1970s, the power of the Shah weakened, and an expansive coalition supported the Iranian Revolution in 1979. The Revolution, however, ultimately led to an Islamic Republic – one very much at odds with the established international order in general and the US in particular. Over the decades that followed, Iran supported terrorism. In addition, and most worrisome to many in the international community, evidence mounted that Iran had a program underway to develop nuclear weapons.

In July 2015, the United States, Iran, and several other world powers signed the Joint Comprehensive Plan of Action (JCPOA) to dismantle and freeze elements of the Iranian nuclear weapons program.[6] On May 8, 2018, United States President Donald Trump announced that the United States would withdraw from the JCPOA and sanction Iran in a campaign to place "maximum pressure" on the country. Trump and other Republican leaders had been critical of the Obama-era deal because (i) some of the restrictions on the Iranian program had sunset clauses and (ii) it became more difficult to deter Iran from supporting violent non-state actors engaged in fighting against the US and its regional partners.

Tensions heightened after Trump's announcement to leave the JCPOA. Iran responded by boosting uranium enrichment in defiance of the JCPOA's terms. On April 15, 2019, the Trump Administration designated the Islamic Revolutionary Guard Corps, a branch of the Iranian military, as a foreign terrorist organization (FTO). This action stands out as the first time the US labeled part of another country's governmental apparatus as an FTO. On June 13, 2019,

---

[6] The following description of the background to, and events of, the crisis is based primarily on the case summary from Brecher, Wilkenfeld, Beardsley, James, and Quinn (2023).

two oil tankers were attacked near the Strait of Hormuz, about a month after four commercial ships were damaged in the same area. The United States blamed Iran for the attacks, with Trump calling the country "a nation of terror".

After the US announced that it would order 1,000 additional troops to the region, a crisis for Iran began on June 18, 2019. The announced deployment responded to alleged Iranian attacks on ships in the Strait of Hormuz. Several days later, on June 20, Iran shot down a US military drone, a Global Hawk, which the US claimed was operating in international waters. This action both triggered a crisis for the US and constituted Iran's major response to the increased US troop presence. On June 22, Trump unveiled a new suite of sanctions against Iran as the US's major response to the crisis.

Violent and nonviolent crisis management techniques followed on. After a series of escalating official public statements by both actors, unsuccessful attempts at coming to a resolution took place through the United Nations Security Council (UNSC). On December 31, 2019, Iran backed an assault by a Shiite militia on the US embassy in Iraq.

Tensions peaked on January 3, 2020, when US forces assassinated Qasem Soleimani, commander of the Iranian QUDS Force. The attack occurred while Soleimani was visiting Iraq. The US had deemed Soleimani to be the intellectual architect of the Iranian asymmetrical warfare doctrine.

Iran retaliated for the death of Soleimani with a series of missile attacks aimed at US military bases in Iraq on January 8, 2020. On the same day, Iranian forces also accidentally shot down a passenger aircraft, Ukraine International Airlines Flight 752 departing from Tehran, resulting in 176 people killed. Ayatollah Khamenei had promised a greater response, citing the missile strikes as insufficient, yet neither adversary took further escalatory actions. The crisis terminated for the US and Iran on January 8, after the Flight 752 tragedy.

Discussions on the escalating situation took place at the UNSC. However, no resolutions came to pass from those talks. Russian delegates voiced their concerns about a growing US presence in the region during these talks and asked for all parties to show restraint in the matter. The European Union and League of Arab States, among others, sent delegates and participated in the talks, but these organizations took no further action. Also relevant to this case, the US and Iran experienced a separate international crisis during this period, related to an attack, claimed by the Houthi rebels, on the Abqaiq oil field in Saudi Arabia.

A Systemist Graphic Analysis

Figure 8.1 conveys a systemist graphic account of the preceding international crisis. The graphic also includes the historical background to the Soleimani Assassination case. Iran is the system, with the International System as its environment. The macro and micro levels of Iran refer, respectively, to government and society. Subfigures show how events unfolded, with references along the way to findings about the onset, processes, and outcomes and legacies compiled in the preceding section. In addition, we also reference the contents of Table 8.4 in the narrative. Table 8.4 offers a profile of the Soleimani Assassination – 2019 case in connection with the findings from Tables 8.1–3. The first column of the table corresponds to crisis phase – onset, processes, and outcomes and legacies. The second column conveys aspects and

172 CONFLICT, CRISIS, AND WAR IN WORLD POLITICS

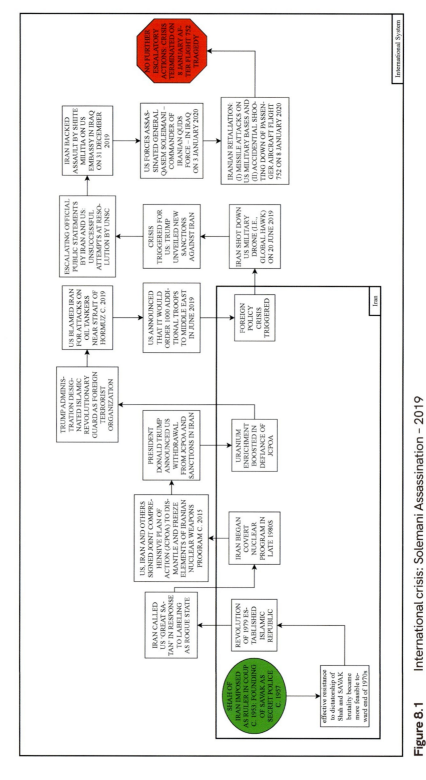

Figure 8.1   International crisis: Solemani Assassination – 2019

details – for example, within onset, the US is in the role of initiator. The third and final column lists the characteristics that are present and how many are missing in relation to a given aspect of crisis.

Table 8.4 Profile of an international crisis: Soleimani Assassination – 2019

Phase	Aspects and details	Characteristics present and number of characteristics missing
Onset	Likelihood	mixture of regime types; fewer common memberships in international organizations; state religious exclusivity, 4
	Initiator – US	expected utility for initiator relative to target is greater than or equal to zero; latent hawkishness, 1
	Trigger violence – non-violent military	[ ]^a, 2
Processes	Higher gravity of threat – threat to influence	[ ]^a, 3
	Mediation or negotiation less likely – UNSC and multiple regional organizations involved	[ ]^a, 2
	Severity of violence – minor clashes	power discrepancy; lower percentage of women in legislature; absence of female leader; gender inequality; leader with previous experience in social movement; US president high in BACE, 13
	Centrality of violence – violence preeminent	leader with previous experience in social movement, US president high in BACE, 1
	Violent crisis management – multiple techniques including violence	lower proportion of democracies; democratic leaders scoring relatively high in distrust, nationalism, and need for power, 1
Outcomes and legacies	Likelihood of victory – US sees win	
	Likelihood of war	third party actors; heterogeneity of participants; proportion of non-democracies involved; major power activity, positive expected utility for initiator versus target; initiator has greater capability than target, 16
	Increased tension or recurrence	UN and regional organization involvement; lower number of joint international organization memberships, 1

Note: ^{a} Empty brackets indicate that none of the characteristics is present.

CONFLICT, CRISIS, AND WAR IN WORLD POLITICS

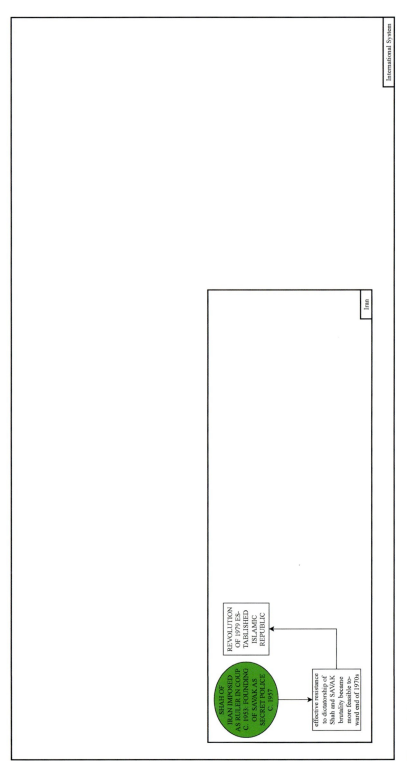

Figure 8.1a

UNDERSTANDING CRISES

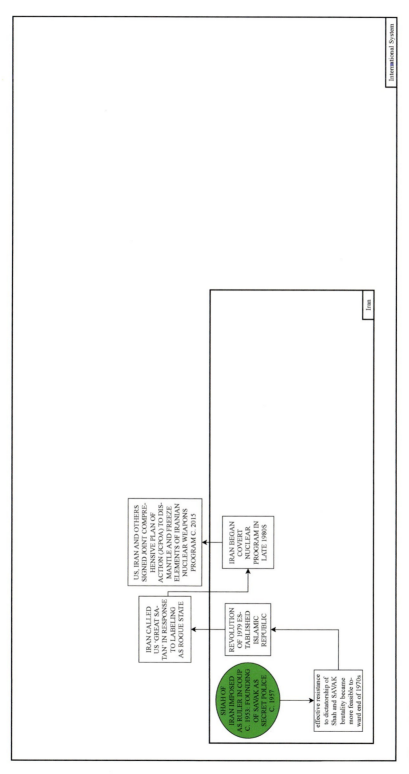

Figure 8.1b

CONFLICT, CRISIS, AND WAR IN WORLD POLITICS

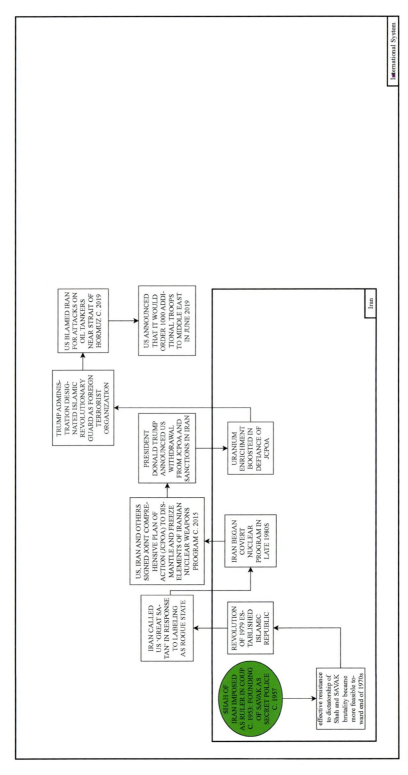

Figure 8.1c

UNDERSTANDING CRISES

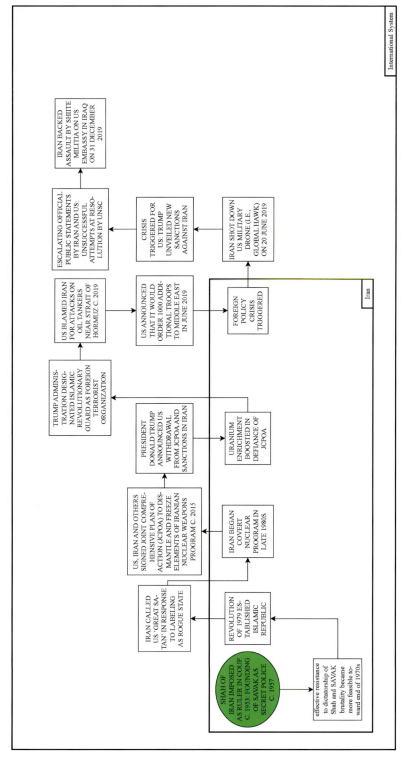

Figure 8.1d

CONFLICT, CRISIS, AND WAR IN WORLD POLITICS

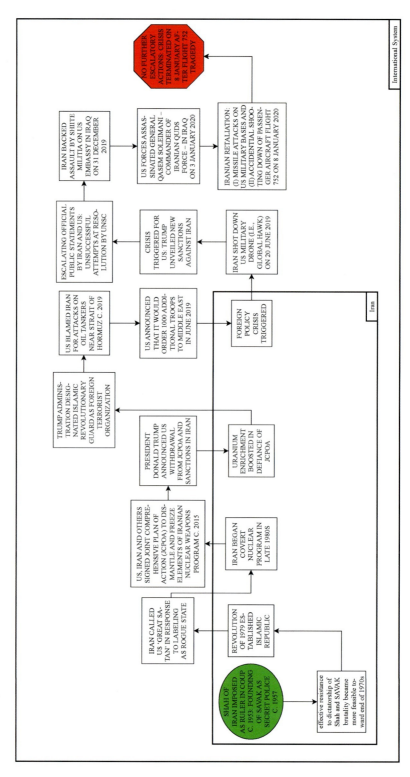

Figure 8.1e

Figure 8.1a shows a point of origin with "SHAH OF IRAN IMPOSED AS RULER IN COUP C. 1953: FOUNDING OF SAVAK AS SECRET POLICE C. 1957". This initial component appears as a green oval. Iran under the Shah became a client state of the US – a member of the Central Treaty Organization (CENTO) alliance and ardent opponent of the USSR in the Cold War. However, aside from those within the favored coalition around the Shah, Iranians increasingly tended to see his rule as serving US interests more than their own. Moreover, the SAVAK obtained a well-earned reputation for brutality in enforcing the Shah's regime.

Figure 8.1a shows movement from government to society: "SHAH OF IRAN IMPOSED AS RULER IN COUP C. 1953: FOUNDING OF SAVAK AS SECRET POLICE C. 1957" → "effective resistance to dictatorship of Shah and SAVAK brutality became more feasible toward end of 1970s". President Jimmy Carter won the election in 1976 and put greater emphasis on human rights over realpolitik in US foreign policy. This impacted Iran directly as the Shah, under US pressure, began to liberalize his regime. The pathway continues with "effective resistance to dictatorship of Shah and SAVAK brutality became more feasible toward end of 1970s" → "REVOLUTION OF 1979 ESTABLISHED ISLAMIC REPUBLIC". Reforms from the Shah turned out to be too little, and too late, to satisfy the population. A broad coalition of political opponents came out into the open and overthrew the Shah in 1979. However, a faction among the revolutionaries quickly seized power and imposed an Islamic Republic on the rest of the population.

Figure 8.1b shows the route moving into the international system with "REVOLUTION OF 1979 ESTABLISHED ISLAMIC REPUBLIC" → "IRAN CALLED US 'GREAT SATAN' IN RESPONSE TO LABELING AS ROGUE STATE". The new Islamic Republic and the US embarked upon a poisonous relationship when militants took over the US embassy in November 1979 and held staff hostage until the end of the Carter Administration in January 1981. This ICB crisis led into any number of negative rhetorical exchanges and even some violence, such as the shooting down of the Iranian passenger airplane in 1988 by the Vincennes, a US guided missile cruiser.

Figure 8.1b shows the return of the pathway into Iran: "IRAN CALLED US 'GREAT SATAN' IN RESPONSE TO LABELING AS ROGUE STATE" → "IRAN BEGAN COVERT NUCLEAR PROGRAM IN LATE 1980S". The US already saw Iran as a rogue state, in support of Islamist radicals such as Hezbollah and seeking to undermine Western interests in the Middle East. Iran, for its part, looked at nuclear weapons as a potential deterrent against attacks from the US or Israel. While Iran paused the nuclear program after the US-led invasion of Iraq in 2003, it did not come to an end. The route continues with "IRAN BEGAN COVERT NUCLEAR PROGRAM IN LATE 1980S" → "US, IRAN AND OTHERS SIGNED JOINT COMPREHENSIVE PLAN OF ACTION (JCPOA) TO DISMANTLE AND FREEZE ELEMENTS OF IRANIAN NUCLEAR WEAPONS PROGRAM C. 2015". Quarreling over the nuclear program between Iran and the US, along with other states and the International Atomic Energy Agency (IAEA), characterized events into the 2010s. After long negotiations, the JCPOA came into being, although not without controversy. Critics worried that the Agreement lacked sufficient enforcement mechanisms and would do little of practical value to prevent a nuclear-armed Iran.

Figure 8.1c shows movement of the route within the international system: "US, IRAN AND OTHERS SIGNED JOINT COMPREHENSIVE PLAN OF ACTION (JCPOA) TO DISMANTLE AND FREEZE ELEMENTS OF IRANIAN NUCLEAR WEAPONS PROGRAM C. 2015" → "PRESIDENT DONALD TRUMP ANNOUNCED US WITHDRAWAL FROM JCPOA AND SANCTIONS IN IRAN". In line with the skeptics, who tended toward a realist rather than liberal viewpoint, President Trump pulled the US out of the JCPOA. The pathway moves back into Iran with "PRESIDENT DONALD TRUMP ANNOUNCED US WITHDRAWAL FROM JCPOA AND SANCTIONS IN IRAN" → "URANIUM ENRICHMENT BOOSTED IN DEFIANCE OF JCPOA". Iran proceeded in an incremental but unmistakable way toward the goal of obtaining weapons grade material.

Figure 8.1c shows the route shifting into the international system: "URANIUM ENRICHMENT BOOSTED IN DEFIANCE OF JCPOA" → "TRUMP ADMINISTRATION DESIGNATED ISLAMIC REVOLUTIONARY GUARD AS FOREIGN TERRORIST ORGANIZATION". In April 2019, the Trump Administration signaled its impatience with Iran through the FTO designation for the Islamic Revolutionary Guard, referring directly to its support and promotion of terrorism. The pathway continues with "TRUMP ADMINISTRATION DESIGNATED ISLAMIC REVOLUTIONARY GUARD AS FOREIGN TERRORIST ORGANIZATION" → "US BLAMED IRAN FOR ATTACKS ON OIL TANKERS NEAR STRAIT OF HORMUZ C. 2019". The attack on the tankers in June 2019 raised tensions between Iran and the US to an even higher level. This link and others before it, taken together, illustrate the processes of gray zone conflict as described earlier in this chapter.

Figure 8.1c reveals a further shift upward in intensity of interaction: "US BLAMED IRAN FOR ATTACKS ON OIL TANKERS NEAR STRAIT OF HORMUZ C. 2019" → "US ANNOUNCED THAT IT WOULD ORDER 1000 ADDITIONAL TROOPS TO MIDDLE EAST IN JUNE 2019". This military deployment by Trump had special meaning because he had been so emphatically opposed to such actions while a candidate for the presidency.

Figure 8.1d shows the transition into an international crisis: "US ANNOUNCED THAT IT WOULD ORDER 1000 ADDITIONAL TROOPS SHIPS TO MIDDLE EAST IN JUNE 2019" → "FOREIGN POLICY CRISIS TRIGGERED". With the crisis underway, consider the contents related to onset in Table 8.4. With regard to likelihood of crisis, three characteristics (e.g., mixture of regime types) are present and four are absent. The initiator is the US, and two characteristics are present, with one absent. Finally, the trigger of the case is nonviolent military. Note that neither of the characteristics associated with a violent trigger is present. Taken together, the preceding data suggest that the case is in no way unusual – for example, very likely to have occurred in light of its characteristics.

Conflict between Iran and the US escalated, as depicted in Figure 8.1d: "FOREIGN POLICY CRISIS TRIGGERED" → "IRAN SHOT DOWN US MILITARY DRONE (I.E., GLOBAL HAWK) ON 20 JUNE 2019". An angry US claimed that the drone had been shot down over international waters. The pathway continues with "IRAN SHOT DOWN US MILITARY DRONE (I.E., GLOBAL HAWK) ON 20 JUNE 2019" → "CRISIS TRIGGERED FOR US: TRUMP UNVEILED NEW SANCTIONS AGAINST IRAN". Announced on June 22, the sanctions aimed to prevent top Iranian officials from using the international banking system.

Figure 8.1d shows the route moving forward with "CRISIS TRIGGERED FOR US: TRUMP UNVEILED NEW SANCTIONS AGAINST IRAN" → "ESCALATING OFFICIAL PUBLIC STATEMENTS BY IRAN AND US: UNSUCCESSFUL ATTEMPTS AT RESOLUTION BY UNSC". The pathway continues with "ESCALATING OFFICIAL PUBLIC STATEMENTS BY IRAN AND US: UNSUCCESSFUL ATTEMPTS AT RESOLUTION BY UNSC" → "IRAN BACKED ASSAULT BY SHIITE MILITIA ON US EMBASSY IN IRAQ ON 31 DECEMBER 2019".

Figure 8.1e shows further movement in the international system with "IRAN BACKED ASSAULT BY SHIITE MILITIA ON US EMBASSY IN IRAQ ON 31 DECEMBER 2019" → "US FORCES ASSASSINATED GENERAL QASEM SOLEIMANI – COMMANDER OF IRANIAN QUDS FORCE – IN IRAQ ON 3 JANUARY 2020". The pathway continues with "US FORCES ASSASSINATED GENERAL QASEM SOLEIMANI – COMMANDER OF IRANIAN QUDS FORCE – IN IRAQ ON 3 JANUARY 2020" → "IRANIAN RETALIATION: (I) MISSILE ATTACKS ON US MILITARY BASES AND (II) ACCIDENTAL SHOOTING DOWN OF PASSENGER AIRCRAFT ON 8 JANUARY 2020". The last connection is the penultimate one in the series, so this is a good point at which to pause and look at the processes of this case.

Table 8.4 reveals that the adversaries in the case perceived a threat to influence – about halfway along the continuum. None of the characteristics associated with higher gravity of threat is present. With regard to mediation or negotiation, the case features involvement by both the UN and multiple regional organizations. Neither of the characteristics associated with the absence of mediation or negotiation is present, so the activity of those international organizations would not be unexpected. The adversaries experienced minor clashes; an examination of characteristics reveals six present (e.g., US president high in BACE) and 13 absent, which would seem in line with intuition against higher severity of violence or none at all. Violence is preeminent in the case, with two characteristics present (e.g., US president high in BACE) and one absent. Crisis management features multiple techniques including violence; three associated characteristics are in place (e.g., lower proportion of democracies) and one is not.

Figure 8.1e adds the final connection: "IRANIAN RETALIATION: (I) MISSILE ATTACKS ON US MILITARY BASES AND (II) ACCIDENTAL SHOOTING DOWN OF PASSENGER AIRCRAFT ON 8 JANUARY 2020" → "NO FURTHER ESCALATORY ACTIONS: CRISIS TERMINATED ON 8 JANUARY AFTER FLIGHT 752 TRAGEDY". As a terminal component, the one after the arrow appears as a red octagon.

Table 8.4 shows that the US perceived that it won the case. Two traits associated with likelihood of victory (e.g., nuclear superiority) are present and one is absent in this case. War did not occur; the balance between characteristics present (e.g., third-party actors) and absent, respectively, is six versus 16. Finally, in the strict sense, it is too early within the ICB coding scheme to say whether tension has increased, because a five-year period must elapse prior to assessment. However, at this time of writing, war between Hamas and Israel rages on in Gaza, while shipping through the Strait of Hormuz continues to be disrupted by Houthi rebels. The adversaries in these interconnected ongoing conflicts are linked in various ways to the US and Iran, so it seems likely that tension ultimately will be coded as on the rise for the Soleimani international crisis.

Looking back across the categories of onset, processes, and outcomes and legacies, the profile of the Soleimani Assassination case is in line with intuition. It is not possible to identify an anomaly, meaning an aspect that is significantly out of line with associated characteristics. The fine-grained data from ICB, showcased in this international crisis, creates the opportunity for those interested in the relationship of the US with Iran to study it in depth. At the same time, this case can be compared with hundreds of others in the ICB dataset in order to pursue breadth of understanding.

IN FOCUS

Problems between the US and Iran did not end with the assassination case above. Later that same year, an international crisis, Abqaiq Oil Strike, involved the US, Iran, and Saudi Arabia. This case focused on the gray zone conflict involving the Houthi rebellion, sponsored by Iran, and taking place in Yemen. The rebellion, in a state neighboring Saudi Arabia, foreshadowed concerns in the US and beyond about the Houthis and other Iranian proxies at this time of writing. Most notably, the Houthis engaged in rocket attacks against Israel at various times during the Gaza War. *In light of such ongoing events, what policy recommendations might be made to reduce the loss of human life within that regional setting?*

SUMMING UP AND MOVING FORWARD

Understanding international crises requires a comprehensive review of onset, processes, and outcomes and legacies. A review of evidence from the ICB Project reveals the breadth of what is known about material and ideational characteristics across levels of analysis – international system, interstate dyad, state, and society and individual – impact upon crises. Factors identified by prominent research programs – decision-making and neo-Kantianism – prove to be significant in accounting for various aspects of crises in world politics. A systemist graphic analysis of the Soleimani Assassination, an international crisis that took place in 2019, has provided depth of understanding. Chapter 9 will focus on understanding civil wars.

CONSIDER THIS

As we described in Chapter 3, crises grew more and more frequent from about 1980 and then, especially after 1989, experienced a steep downward trend in occurrences. Given the nature and explanations of crisis onset, processes, and outcomes and legacies, and the changing participants discussed in this chapter:

What factors help to understand the trends and changes over the past two or three decades?

9
Understanding civil wars

PROLOGUE

One of the worst humanitarian disasters in living memory came about as a result of the ongoing civil war in Syria. Estimates of casualties reach about 600,000 since the war began in 2011, with more than 5.4 million living as refugees abroad, over 6.9 million internally displaced, and approximately seven in ten Syrians in need of humanitarian assistance.[1] Refugees in large numbers have fled to Turkey, Jordan, and Lebanon, creating complications for those already troubled societies. Syrian President Bashar al-Assad controls about 70% of Syrian territory and, with Russian support, is battling with a coalition of Islamist militants in the northwest. Kurdish and Turkish-backed forces also fight with each other in areas along the northern border of Syria. Over the course of years, various efforts to obtain a diplomatic solution to the civil war have yet to succeed, and there is no end in sight.

How could such awful things happen and continue on to this day? Along with other Arab states, Syria experienced pro-democracy protests in the spring of 2011. The corrupt dictatorship of al-Assad responded with increasingly violent measures to shut down demonstrations, but by September 2011, organized rebel militias – and most prominently the Free Syrian Army – engaged in regular combat with Syrian government forces. The strife had a sectarian quality from the outset because Assad ruled in favor of the minority Alawites and against the interests of the Sunni majority. Conflict escalated and more significant actors became involved, notably the US, EU, Arab League, Iran, and Russia. Turkey, Saudi Arabia, and Qatar made efforts to fund and arm rebel factions, which aggravated an already violent conflict. Assad, with the goal of deflecting criticism away from his brutal regime, attempted to portray all of his opponents as in league with Sunni Islamic extremism and foreign co-conspirators. Chemical weapon attacks took place in 2013 and the violence and chaos of the many-sided conflict continued in subsequent years to exact a high price in terms of both human life and material destruction. In sum, cases such as this one draw attention to the menace of civil war and thereby make it a priority to obtain greater understanding in order to manage and possibly even head off these lethal events.

---

[1] The information conveyed in this prologue is taken from Council on Foreign Relations (2024a) and Britannica (2024a).

OVERVIEW

Since the end of World War II and especially since 1989, as Lobell and Mauceri (2004: 1) and many others note, most wars have been internal rather than interstate. Many analysts describe civil wars as "perplexing phenomena" that continue to challenge both individual states and the international community (e.g., Lounsbery and Cook 2011: 73). Some of these armed conflicts have persisted for decades, with resulting massive loss of life (Buhaug, Gates, and Lujala 2009; Regan 2002). One estimate, for example, is that 127 civil wars in 73 states resulted in 16.2 million battle deaths and displaced over 50 million people from 1945 to 1999 (Taydas, Enia, and James 2011: 2627–2628). The massive loss of life and other suffering caused by the warfare in Syria, as per above, is a case in point. Civil wars also rage on today in Colombia, Afghanistan, Iraq, Uganda, and elsewhere around the world. For such reasons, civil war has garnered increasing attention in the study of conflict processes (Cunningham, Gleditsch, and Salehyan 2009).

Interest in civil war increased dramatically after the collapse of the USSR and associated states at the turn of the 1990s. Some of the former communist states changed peacefully into a variety of regimes, while others experienced significant internal conflict and even civil war. Research on civil war focused on the traumatic experiences of Eastern Europe, expanded worldwide, and findings accumulated.

Explanations for civil war converged into two now-familiar categories: greed and grievance (Collier and Hoeffler 2004; Dixon 2009a: 713; Taydas, Enia, and James 2011: 2629). Greed refers to rebellion directed toward personal gain, notably with regard to lootable resources such as diamonds. These explanations see civil war as a product of material self-interest on the part of insurgents (Taydas, Peksen, and James 2010: 196). Oil, to cite a prominent example of a lootable resource, seems to be especially dangerous in its association with civil war (Dixon 2009a: 722), contributing to its reputation as "the devil's excrement". Grievance, by contrast, focuses on efforts to rectify real or perceived injustice, for instance, to reduce or even end discrimination based on religion (Basedau, Fox, and Zellman 2023). The emphasis in grievance-based studies is on "psychological processes and factors with potential to create discontent among citizens" (Taydas, Enia, and James 2011: 2631). Comprehensive review essays from Dixon (2009a, 2009b) reveal that a combination of factors related to greed and grievance seem necessary, although still insufficient, to explain the occurrence and other properties of civil wars. As per the study of international crisis recounted in Chapter 8, research on civil war has identified a range of relevant material, ideational, and hybrid (i.e., a mixture of material and ideational) characteristics.

Scholarship has evolved beyond the initial dichotomy of greed and grievance. A more inclusive concept, "opportunity", which takes into account that factors beyond greed can facilitate violent action, is referenced commonly in studies of civil war (Taydas, Enia, and James 2011: 2630). It seems promising to take a further step toward comprehensive theorizing through a combination of opportunity with willingness – corresponding to the prominent framework for analysis from Most and Starr (1989). This way of thinking sees any action that occurs as a combination of the ability to act with the desire to do so. When we turn to a review of research findings about civil war in a later section of this chapter, our analysis focuses on roles played by material, ideational, and hybrid factors, as per the assessment of international crises in Chapter 8.

This chapter moves forward in four additional sections. The second section focuses on the meaning and an approach toward analysis of civil war. Section three examines data-based research on the origins of these lethal conflicts. The fourth section creates a systemist diagrammatic representation of what is known about the onset of civil war. Section five reviews what has been accomplished in this chapter and leads into the next one.

THE MEANING AND AN APPROACH TOWARD ANALYSIS OF CIVIL WAR

Table 9.1 lists a sample of definitions for civil war, along with respective sources. While many other works could be listed, those that appear in the table offer a useful summary of the main characteristics associated with civil war. First, civil war is a type of conflict that includes an adversarial relationship between a government and one or more rebel groups. Second, there is some variation in intensity when designating a civil war – both in terms of overall level of casualties as well as per unit of time. Third, there is "substantial similarity in the samples of every study of civil war" (Dixon 2009a: 707), even if case listings fall short of being identical with each other. More in-depth discussion of the studies cited in the table (and beyond) would bear out that point. Fourth, and finally, aggregate data analysis of civil war has produced generally reliable results. Observe that a review of 647 statistical coefficients in a major study of civil war onset (reported in Dixon 2009a: 723) revealed only *one* such number to be "both significant and opposite in apparent effect from another". From a practical standpoint, there is a consensus on the meaning of civil war, even if there are nuances among various studies when formal and operational definitions are offered.

Decades of systematic evidence have accumulated about the origins of civil war, so analysis could follow any number of directions. Several specifications therefore should be offered before moving ahead with a review of the research findings. First, a sample rather than a population of literally thousands of studies provides the basis for what is reported in the section that follows. At the same time, the research that *is* included has appeared in highly regarded publication outlets and recognizes the work of leading scholars.[2] Second, the research results are taken from statistical studies that tend to use the same relatively small number of highly regarded datasets, which facilitates comparative analysis. Third, research that covers domestic conflict in a more encompassing manner, with civil war as one aspect, is included within some of the studies above. Fourth, in some instances, findings reported in a discussion of academic literature from a given publication have been cited (e.g., Bakke and Wibbels 2006) and the presence of review essays by Dixon (2009a, 2009b) greatly expands the number of statistical

---

[2] The studies include Fortna (2004a, 2004b, 2015), Bakke and Wibbels (2006), Buhaug, Gates, and Lujala (2009), Cunningham, Gleditsch, and Salehyan (2009), Dixon (2009a, 2009b), Regan (2009), Taydas, Peksen, and James (2010), Akbaba and Taydas (2011), Lounsbery and Cook (2011), Taydas, Enia, and James (2011), Lounsbery (2016) and Toft (2021).

Table 9.1 Definitions of civil war

Definition	Source
An armed conflict that caused more than 1,000 battle deaths (total); that represented a challenge to the sovereignty of an internationally recognized state; and occurred within the recognized boundary of that state; that involved the state as one of the principal combatants, and in which the rebels were able to mount an organized military opposition to the state and to inflict significant casualties on the state	Doyle and Sambanis (2000) cited in Fortna (2004b: 276)
Incidents of violence involving states and rebel groups that generate at least twenty-five casualties in a given calendar year, over some incompatibility classified as control over the central government or territorial autonomy/secession	Eriksson and Wallensteen (2004); Gleditsch et al. (2002) cited in Cunningham, Gleditsch and Salehyan (2009: 579)
Conflict that (1) involves fighting between a state and a non-state group who seek to take control of a government, to take power in a region or to use violence in order to change government policies to achieve certain goals; (2) killed at least 1,000 people overall, from both sides, with a yearly average of at least 100 and (3) killed at least 100 people on average from each side (including civilians attacked by rebels)	Fearon and Laitin (2003) cited in Taydas, Peksen, and James (2010: 202)
An intrastate armed conflict between a government and non-state actor operating within its area of sovereignty resulting in at least 200 battle-related deaths in a given year	Regan (2002) cited in Lounsbery and Cook (2011: 80)
A universe of cases in which a group has a serious enough perceived grievance against the state to launch a violent rebellion in which some groups choose to use terrorism as part of their repertoire of tactics whereas others do not	Fortna (2015: 521)

studies included in the analysis. Fifth, specific details about data collection and coding of variables, along with statistical significance, are available from either individual studies or the works cited in Dixon (2009a, 2009b). Sixth, we present results at the most general level, so we refrain from diving into nuances.[3] Seventh, and finally, we exclude significant results for some characteristics because of a relatively high degree of uncertainty about how cause and effect might work vis-à-vis a given aspect of civil war.[4]

---

[3] For example, some of the findings about onset of civil war pertain to federal or semi-federal states in particular (Bakke and Wibbels 2006).

[4] With regard to onset of civil war, we do not include the following characteristics: primary commodity exports neither very high nor low; high population density; lower level of social (ethnic

Consider first the material factors that impact upon opportunity for civil war. At the level of the international system, a neighboring state at war could offer a safe haven and/or base of operations for insurgents – a strategic factor. Civil wars in Rwanda, Burundi, and the Congo that began in the 1990s readily come to mind. Each case of civil strife included significant cross-border activities involving insurgents from the point of onset onward (McDoom 2020).

Within the state, mountainous terrain, a geographic characteristic, would enhance opportunity because of the obstacles that government forces might experience in attempting to put down a rebellion. The civil war in Chechnya from 1994–1996 serves as an example here. While not all of the region is mountainous, the terrain meeting that description presented great challenges to Russian forces in efforts to prevent and then quell the rebellion.

With regard to opportunity in connection with demography, a larger population creates a reservoir of potential fighters and makes government control of the state inherently more difficult. Perhaps the most obvious example is China, which experienced a civil war that produced a communist regime as the outcome in 1949: by 1945, China already had a population of over 500 million. Another state-level factor, this time government-related – institutional weakness of bureaucracy – enhances the opportunity for insurgent action in an obvious way. Referring once again to the Chinese civil war, Maoist revolutionaries faced off against the notoriously ineffective government of the Kuomintang (KMT) that came to power when Japanese occupation came to an end with defeat in World War II (Britannica 2024b).

Last among the purely material-based factors that affect opportunity for civil war is one within society and geographic in nature: a territorial base of insurgency that is separated from the capital city by land or water. To once again reference the Chinese case, the Maoist upstarts had bases in the north and quite distant from the capital of Peking, today known as Beijing. Their distance from KMT strongholds in Peking and other urban areas enhanced prospects of survival and later success for the communist insurgents.

Some material characteristics impact upon willingness to fight a civil war. At the state level, economic factors include low per capita income, lack of economic growth, and soil degradation. Consider, for instance, Sierra Leone, which experienced a civil war from 1991 to 2002. When the war began, Sierra Leone ranked among the poorest states in the world, with its citizens living on an estimated $1.80 per day (Graff, Lewis, and Rice 2006). With regard to lack of economic growth, the years prior to civil war in the Ivory Coast tell an awful story; according to Graff, Lewis, and Rice (2006), per capita income dropped to $650 in 2000 and the conflict lasted from 2002 to 2007. In many poor states, suboptimal practices in agriculture damage the soil and add to ongoing challenges of governance. Soil degradation can be expected to get even worse once civil war is underway, as in the case of Lebanon from 1975 to 1990 (Kallio 2015).

IN FOCUS: THE CAPABILITY APPROACH

Civil wars can be very costly in terms of human life. One way to think about civil war prevention concerns the "capability approach" developed by Amartya Sen (1985), a Nobel laureate in economics. Sen argues that the focus of public policy should be shifted from aggregate indicators such as GDP (gross domestic product) toward measurement of things that matter directly to people. Emphasis should be placed on enhancing the capabilities of people, in order to achieve their goals, and thereby increase overall satisfaction with life.

> *In reflecting upon the capability approach, should it be seen as potentially helpful in civil war prevention or perhaps too utopian to consider?*

Government-related characteristics related to willingness, also within the state, include the degree of corruption (e.g., bribes) and lack of rule of law and order (e.g., strength and inequality of legal system). Yemen, still embroiled in civil war, is a good case in point. Transparency International (2024), a standard source of data on governance, ranked Yemen 161st in its worldwide survey when the civil war got underway in 2014. With rampant corruption, many people might become more disposed toward insurgency – either out of lost hope for reform of the regime or simply seeking personal gain.

With regard to ideational factors, two affect willingness and both reside at the level of society. These characteristics are demographic in nature and pertain to identity: ethnic dominance and heterogeneity. The breakup of Yugoslavia, which led to a series of wars from 1991 to 1995, had numerous identity-related aspects (Kaufman 2001). The quest for Serbian ethnic dominance tells one part of the story, with a resort to extreme acts of violence in the quest for control over territory in which others, such as the Croats, currently lived. Ethnic diversity tells another part of the story; in addition to Croats and Serbs, the former Yugoslavia also included Montenegrins, Macedonians, Muslim Bosnians, and Slovenes. Even without Serbian efforts toward reinforcement of ethnic dominance beyond numbers alone, the likelihood of civil strife would have been high because of the challenges posed for Yugoslavia in seeking to manage significant ethnic diversity after the collapse of a long-standing dictatorship. Many would become willing to take up arms in a situation that increasingly resembled the "security dilemma" at a subnational level (Posen 1993). In other words, the fear of aggression by one group against another easily could turn into a self-fulfilling prophecy, leading to war in the same way as with states in the international system.

One hybrid characteristic (i.e., with both material and ideational aspects) affects willingness. At the state level is a government-related factor – discrimination against societal groups (e.g., religious minorities) – as a precursor to civil war. One of the most prominent examples of discrimination – affecting employment, housing, and other essential aspects of life – concerns the condition of Catholics in Northern Ireland in the years leading up to what become known asthe "Troubles" from 1969 onward. After sustained protests failed to persuade the authorities to engage in meaningful reform, Catholics lost hope for peaceful change (Walter 2022). As a result, extremist factions on the Catholic side became willing to use violence. Protestants retaliated and civil war soon became an entrenched way of life.

Several material characteristics are associated with both opportunity and willingness. Two factors from the state-level focus on history: previous conflict and the absence of a distinct civil war in the previous year. Sudan serves as an example of how previous conflict can set the stage for new iterations of civil war. From 1955 to 1972, tensions between northern and southern Sudan erupted into civil war over demands from the latter for later autonomy. Sudan also experienced intense conflict over Darfur in the 2000s and the echoes of these and other previous rounds of strife can be heard in the violence of the civil war today. With regard to the absence of a distinct civil war in the year before outbreak, implications for both opportunity and willingness are obvious. If a civil war had occurred so close beforehand, resources available (i.e., opportunity) and disposition toward (i.e., willingness) fighting likely would be at greatly reduced levels.

One further state-level characteristic is government-related and relevant to opportunity and willingness: a lower value for the Quality of Institutions Index (i.e., combined score for corruption, rule of law and order, and bureaucratic quality). Any number of states could be noted, but Somalia is among those most obviously referenced. By 1991, Somalia had become a failed state, with no effective governance and clan-based factional infighting as the rule rather than the exception. The lack of a functional government enhanced the opportunity for insurgency, along with willingness among the population to take the risk of seeking to overturn the regime in pursuit of personal gain or a better life for people in general.

Poverty, a material and economic trait of society, also is linked to opportunity and willingness. Somalia once again becomes an obvious point of reference. Those with very little or nothing to lose have no obvious attachment to the status quo and are available to be mobilized by leaders who promise, even with little credibility, to make things better. Somali clan leaders created predatory forces out of youth who otherwise had essentially nonexistent prospects.

One hybrid and demographic characteristic in society, the absence of mass education, also enhances opportunity and willingness. Sierra Leone, virtually bereft of an educational system as an obvious by-product of its intense poverty, once again can serve as an illustration (Østby and Urdal 2010). A low level of education creates a greater opportunity for insurgent leaders to persuade people to follow them, whether out of an espoused ideology or personal charisma. Potential followers might be more willing to engage in a violent insurgency due a general lack of knowledge and resulting proneness to listen to those with extreme views directed against the government.

Two ideational factors connect with both opportunity and willingness. Each is state level and government-related: anocracy and regime instability. Along those lines, consider the experiences of the Dominican Republic in the 1960s in the account from Regan and Bell (2010). After the assassination of President Rafael Trujillo in 1961, the Dominican Republic moved away from democracy and simultaneously experienced major political instability. Civil war ensued and the US intervened to restore some level of stability in 1965.

With the review of findings about the onset of civil war in place, what can be said about the contents of Table 9.2 as a whole? We summarize the distribution of characteristics across (a) levels of analysis; (b) type – material, ideational, or hybrid; (c) correspondence to opportunity, willingness, or both; and (d) dimension (e.g., geography). This helps to identify both accomplishments of the data-based research upon which Table 9.2 is based and priorities for further work.

With regard to levels of analysis, the distribution of characteristics is as follows: international (1), state (14), and society (5). The obvious priority for expansion of research is at the international level of analysis, in line with the long-standing insight from Gourevitch (1978) about potentially significant effects coming into the state from abroad. Note once again the absence of the individual level among levels of analysis.

For type of characteristic, the dispersion is material (13), ideational (4), and hybrid (3). The mostly material basis of explanation undoubtedly reflects the sustained influence of the greed and grievance frame of reference that originated with Collier and Hoeffler (2004). Further explanation of ideational aspects also is in line with the point above about looking more at individuals in accounting for civil war.

With regard to the roles played by characteristics, the distribution is opportunity (5), willingness (8), and hybrid (7). There already is solid coverage of both opportunity and willingness, so placement of characteristics into a well-integrated model emerges as a priority.

Dimensions are dispersed as follows: government (7), demography (4), economy (4) history (2), geography (2), and strategic (1). While five of the corresponding disciplines are referenced more than once, the strategic dimension appears just a single time. This observation returns once again to the relatively limited role of the international level of analysis in existing data-based studies of civil war onset. In addition, note the absence of *psychology* – the dimension that would correspond most readily to the individual level of analysis.

What can be said in an overall sense about the statistical findings conveyed in Table 9.2? On the one hand, great progress has been made in identifying characteristics that impact regularly and significantly upon the likelihood of civil war. On the other hand, Dixon (2009a: 723) observes that statistical models of civil war onset exhibit "low predictive power". One reason might be the need to consult additional variables in order to increase the variance explained by statistical models, which in turn could help with the ability to anticipate the onset of civil war. Of course, those variables may be out there already, and an expanded version of this chapter might locate them, but for now the observation from Dixon (2009a) will be regarded as remaining accurate about the performance of data-based research about civil war onset. A natural next step, therefore, is to fit the characteristics identified through statistical research so far into an initial model of civil war onset. To borrow a phrase from Winston Churchill, what follows should be regarded as more akin to "the end of the beginning rather than the beginning of the end".

A SYSTEMIST GRAPHIC ANALYSIS OF CIVIL WAR ONSET

With an assessment of aggregate findings about civil war in place, we turn our attention to a potential way of fitting things together into a model. A systemist graphic approach facilitates telling a story about cause and effect with regard to the onset of civil war. This might be done in various ways, given the state of the academic literature, because there is no "standard model" for the origins of civil war (Dixon 2009a: 719). The 20 characteristics included in Table 9.2, therefore, can be assembled into an initial model that goes beyond regression equations. The systemist graphic pursues cause and effect within the network of variables that previously have been designated as "independent" in statistical models of civil war onset.

Figure 9.1 is an initial effort to bring together the results from statistical testing in a visual way. The graphic shows the State as the system, with the International System as its environment. The macro level of the State corresponds to its properties as a whole (e.g., government), while the micro level focuses on society. A series of subfigures will be used to facilitate analysis of the contents.

UNDERSTANDING CIVIL WARS

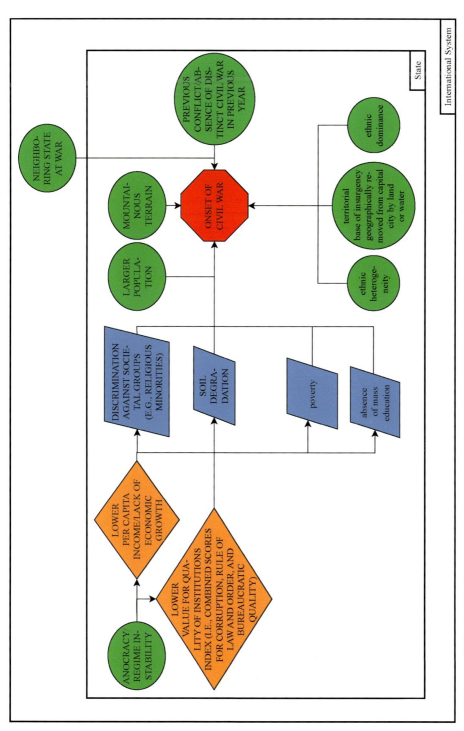

Figure 9.1 Civil war onset

CONFLICT, CRISIS, AND WAR IN WORLD POLITICS

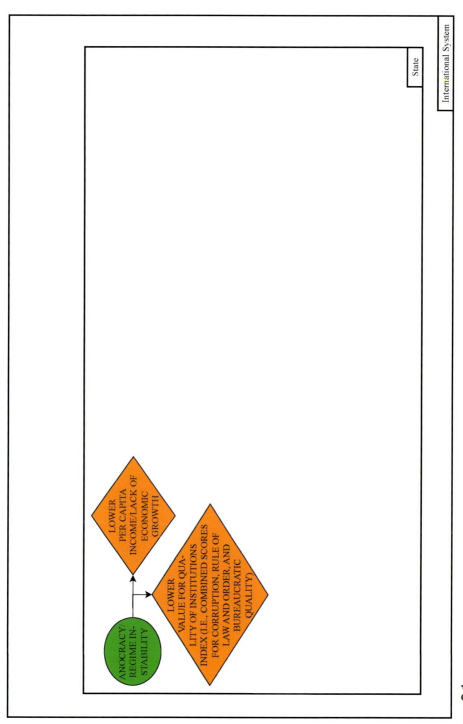

Figure 9.1a

UNDERSTANDING CIVIL WARS

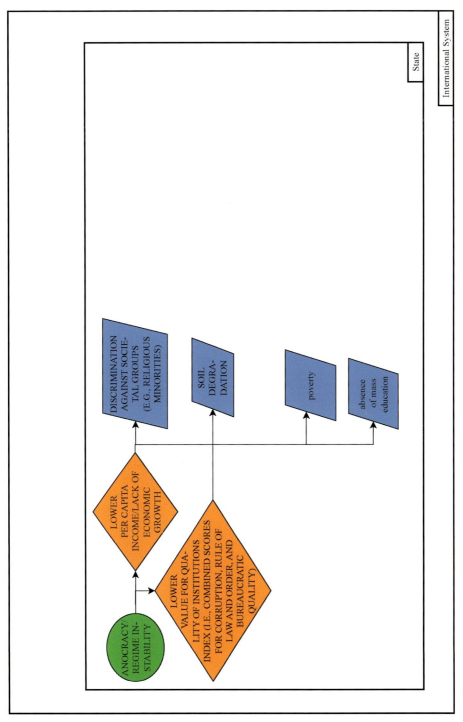

Figure 9.1b

CONFLICT, CRISIS, AND WAR IN WORLD POLITICS

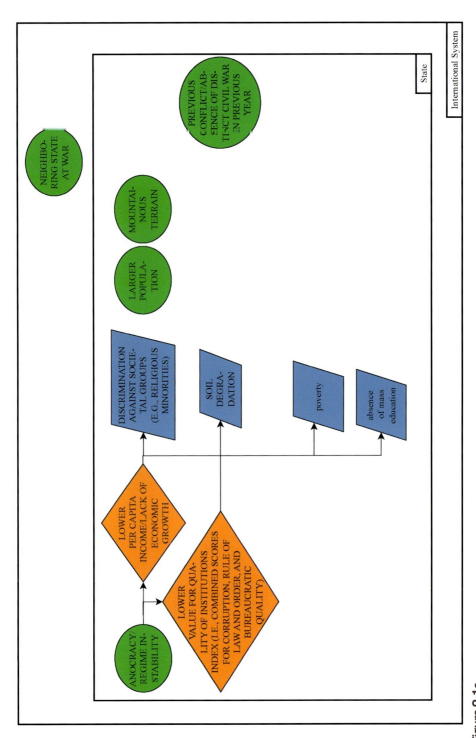

Figure 9.1c

UNDERSTANDING CIVIL WARS

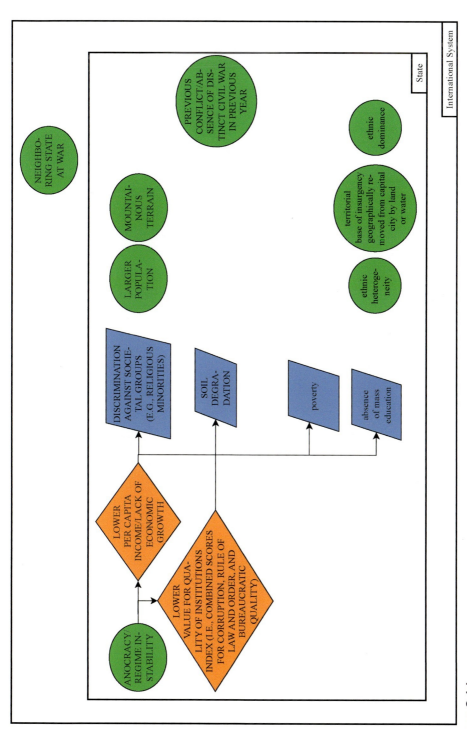

Figure 9.1d

CONFLICT, CRISIS, AND WAR IN WORLD POLITICS

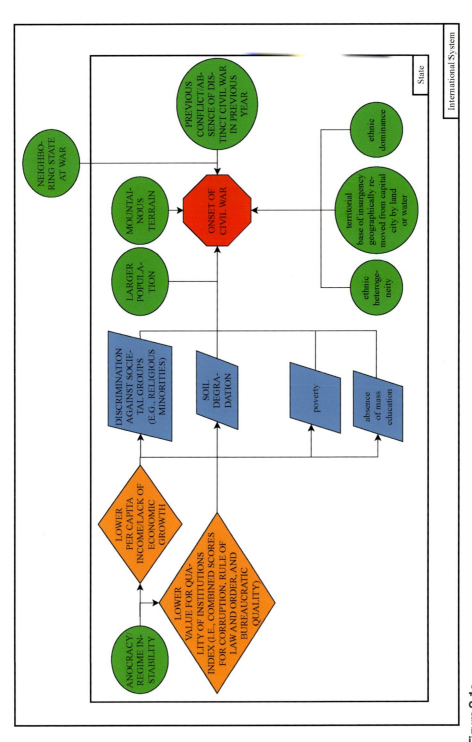

Figure 9.1e

Figure 9.1a puts multiple pathways in motion at the macro level: "ANOCRACY/REGIME INSTABILITY" → "LOWER PER CAPITA INCOME/LACK OF ECONOMIC GROWTH"; "LOWER VALUE FOR QUALITY OF INSITUTIONS INDEX (I.E., COMBINED SCORES FOR CORRUPTION, RULE OF LAW AND ORDER, AND BUREAUCRATIC QUALITY)". The initial component before the arrow takes the form of a green oval. The components after the arrow, as points of divergence, appear in the form of orange diamonds. The connections are from undesirable aspects of government – either a "halfway house" between democracy and autocracy and/or an unstable regime – to unfortunate effects, respectively, on the economy and governance. In economic terms, both static (per capita income) and dynamic (growth rate) aspects point in the wrong direction, which would follow on naturally in the presence of a shaky regime. The overall quality of governance, as well, would be expected to suffer.

Pathways come together at the macro and micro levels in Figure 9.1b: "LOWER PER CAPITA INCOME/LACK OF ECONOMIC GROWTH"; "LOWER VALUE FOR QUALITY OF INSITUTIONS INDEX (I.E., COMBINED SCORES FOR CORRUPTION, RULE OF LAW AND ORDER, AND BUREAUCRATIC QUALITY)" → "DISCRIMINATION AGAINST SOCIETAL GROUPS"; "SOIL DEGRADATION"; "poverty"; "absence of mass education". As points of convergence, each component after the arrow is depicted as a blue parallelogram. Pernicious aspects of government and the economy combine to produce harmful effects at the macro and micro levels. For the state, damage occurs to both population and territory. Within society is witnessed an impoverished standard of living and suboptimal provision of a key public good – education.

Several components create a basis for civil war at the macro level in Figure 9.1c: "MOUNTAINOUS TERRAIN"; "POPULATION"; and "PREVIOUS CONFLICT/ABSENCE OF DISTINCT CIVIL WAR IN PREVIOUS YEAR". An additional component from Figure 9.1c appears in the international system: "NEIGHBORING STATE AT WAR".

Within society, three components appear as green ovals in Figure 9.1d: territorial base of insurgency geographically removed from capital city by land or water; ethnic dominance; and ethnic heterogeneity.

All pathways come together in Figure 9.1e: "DISCRIMINATION AGAINST SOCIETAL GROUPS"; "SOIL DEGRADATION"; "poverty"; "absence of mass education"; "MOUNTAINOUS TERRAIN"; "POPULATION; "PREVIOUS CONFLICT/ABSENCE OF DISTINCT CIVIL WAR IN PREVIOUS YEAR"; "NEIGHBORING STATE AT WAR"; "territorial base of insurgency geographically removed from capital city by land or water"; "ethnic dominance"; "ethnic heterogeneity" → "ONSET OF CIVIL WAR". As a point of termination, the component after the arrow takes the form of a red octagon.

With the graphic exposition in place, several observations can be made about its properties to help to set priorities for further research. First, with regard to structural completeness, two basic types of systemist linkage are missing: (i) within the micro level of the State as a system; and (ii) from the State as a system into its environment, the International System. These abeyances, in substantive terms, refer to processes at the level of society and how a state experiencing civil war might impact upon the world beyond its borders. A second point concerns how the components in the figure are distributed by location, with the numbers being as follows: International System (1), State – macro level (9); and State – micro level (5). This distribution further reinforces the need for attention to the international level of analysis. Third, consider dispersion of component by type: initial (8), convergent (4), divergent (2), and terminal (1). On the one hand, the story told is not deterministic – not the present of six points of contingency when the divergent and convergent components are added together. On the other hand, there are no generic components, which reveals that the initial attempt to fit characteristics from Table 9.2 together has produced very short sequences leading into civil war as the point of termination. Along those lines, consider the contents of subfigures 9.1c and 9.1d. A total of seven initial components connect directly with civil war; how that takes place through additional steps is a story waiting to be told.

While it is beyond the scope of this chapter to respond authoritatively to research priorities identified via the systemist graphic exercise, a major work of scholarship (Jenne 2015) provides illustrations of what type of exchange between quantitative and qualitative research might prove to be productive for understanding civil war. Jenne (2015) applies the concept of *nested security* to gain analytical purchase with regard to cases of civil strife in Europe over the course of decades. The nested security model focuses on how "conflicts at higher levels tend to have a *disproportionate* impact on conflict dynamics at lower levels" (Jenne 2015: 34). Forces from the global and regional level, such as hegemonic power shifts and trans-state networks, respectively, can be expected to impact upon the playing of politics within a given state (Jenne 2015: 33). Therefore, as Jenne (2015: 33) sums things up, nested conflicts are best treated as "complex conflicts with both domestic and international components". An examination of the historical record of European cooperative conflict management, with cases that range from (a) German minorities in Czechoslovakia in the years between World Wars I and II through to (b) Albanians in Kosovo during the post-Cold War era produce overwhelming support for the model of nested security. In sum, the nested security framework, with its emphasis upon how global and regional factors can impact upon intrastate conflict, serves as an exemplar from qualitative research that reinforces the systemist argument in favor of a full specification of causal linkages across levels of analysis.

While nested security is one model among many that focus on conflict processes, its findings are especially relevant to future data-based studies of civil war onset. A greater focus on how factors beyond the state impact upon its prospects for civil war – including both the regional and global environments – could increase significantly the ability to anticipate these destructive events. A more complete story also would involve details about how civil wars reverberate back into the international system.

SUMMING UP AND MOVING FORWARD

Civil wars in Somalia, Iraq, Colombia, and elsewhere continue to plague the world. The initial step toward managing and even preventing such conflicts is to achieve enhanced understanding of those events. Based on the findings of data-based studies, much has been learned about the onset of civil war. Material, ideational, and hybrid factors combine to account for the origins of these intense conflicts. Characteristics have been identified that contribute to opportunity, willingness, or both in regard to civil war onset. In addition, characteristics identified via statistical research correspond to at least six dimensions, with history and geography as two examples. A systemist visualization brought those characteristics together as components of an initial model of crisis onset. The diagrammatic exposition identified a number of priorities for further theorizing and research about civil war, perhaps most notably pursuit of additional connections between the state and international system.

Chapter 10 focuses on multilevel explanations for conflict, with attention directed to the American Civil War – a case from long ago with significant reverberations into the present. Chapter 10 culminates in a comparative analysis of findings from this chapter with what emerges from a review and analysis of the American Civil War. The analysis draws upon the contents of Table 9.2. Along those lines, we briefly identify points of continuity and difference through examination of a 19th-century civil war in connection with results from aggregate data analysis of more recent and contemporary cases.

CONSIDER THIS: CIVIL WAR AS THE FACE OF MODERN CONFLICT

In Chapter 3, we suggested that historical and empirical patterns show that war since 1989 has essentially been intrastate and unconventional. Given the analysis in this chapter:

What factors best explain why civil war is the "face of modern conflict"?

APPENDIX

Table 9.A1 Research findings about the processes of civil wars

Level of analysis	Characteristics	Findings	
		Violence	Duration
International system	Occurrence prior to end of Cold War		√
	Proximity of conflict to border		√
	Military intervention	√	√
State	Higher population		√
	Lower income per capita; Poverty and income inequality		√
	Lootable resources (e.g., gemstones and petroleum in conflict zone)		√
	Absence of coup d'etat		√
Government-insurgent dyad	Greater number of dyads		√
	Low mobilization and arms-procurement capacities for insurgents; Weaker insurgents; Insurgents have territorial control; Insurgents engage in terrorism		√
	Insurgents do not have a legal political wing		√
Society	Distance from capital (i.e., location in periphery)		√
	Weaker rebels		√
	Religion as central to conflict	√	√
	Polarized ethnic groups		√
	Non-territorial issues	√	√

Table 9.A2 Research findings about the outcomes and legacies of civil wars

Level of analysis	Characteristics	Findings				
		Insurgent success	Insurgent change	Insurgent splintering	Consent-based peacekeeping	Stable peace
International system	Military intervention on behalf of insurgents	√				
	Peacekeeping mission					√
	Mediation		√	√		
	Lack of military intervention on behalf of insurgents			√		
State	Mountainous terrain with many borders	√				
	High level of economic development					√
	Size of military forces; decisive victory					√
	Length of conflict				√	
	Length of conflict up to a certain limit			√		
	Annual intensity of conflict		√	√		
	Outcome is stalemate rather than decisive victory				√	
Government-insurgent dyad	Strength of insurgents (e.g., numerical advantage); non-use of terrorism	√				
	Length of conflict	√				

Level of analysis	Characteristics	Findings
Society	Previous group change event; lack of previous mediation	✓
	Previous mediation	✓
	Smaller size of opposition	✓
	Issues of territory	✓
	Absence of identity-based conflict	✓
	Non-territorial issues	✓
	Lower death toll	✓
	Weaker insurgents	✓

Levels of analysis for the origins of civil war correspond to the international system, state, and society. This scheme of organization reflects what is observed within the data-based academic literature about the onset of civil war. The individual level of analysis is conspicuous by its absence from statistical research – an interesting contrast with the significant focus on psychological traits of leaders witnessed in the treatment of international crises in Chapter 8 and war in general in Chapter 7. In order to obtain a sense of how leadership factors into the playing out of civil strife, qualitative works of scholarship would need to be accessed instead. For example, Jenne (2015: 123–126) provides an account of European civil war that includes material on the role played by Slobodan Milošević during his time as head of the League of Communists of Serbia in the 1980s and beyond. We devote further attention to the individual level of analysis at a later point in this chapter when a systemist graphic is implemented to provide an overall sense of onset for civil war.

FOR EXAMPLE

In at least some instances, it is virtually impossible to imagine a revolution without its leader. One such case is that of Cuba in 1959. Set in the context of the economic weakness, political corruption, and working-class discontent of Batista's Cuba, Fidel Castro effectively employed a nationalistic populism to appeal to and mobilize opposition to the regime. At first presenting a moderate and less ideological image, Castro united opposition and only shifted to more radical rhetoric and stances after solidifying his support. His personal charisma, machismo, and compelling speeches were key features in his success. Although the story of the Cuban Revolution cannot be reduced to a single leader, it is equally true that it is hard to identify a revolutionary movement more associated with one person. Castro ruled Cuba from the successful revolution in 1959 to his death in 2008.

As in Chapter 8, we focus on material, ideational, or hybrid traits in this analysis of characteristics relevant to civil war. While theories and individual hypotheses about civil war have been tested, the literature on aggregate data analysis does not manifest a connection with overarching frameworks in the same way that it did in the previous chapter. Rather than identifying characteristics with potentially paradigmatic categories like greed or grievance, we devote attention to the *range* of factors from across a number of disciplines that have been accessed in systematic research on civil wars. Then, we link the characteristics to the following set of dimensions: geography, demography, history, economics, government, and strategic. Finally, we also connect the characteristics to opportunity, willingness, or some combination of them. While Chapter 8 on international crises covered onset, processes, and outcomes and legacies, we take up the latter two subjects in Chapter 10, although we provide a few reasons about "why and how?" in the concluding section of this chapter.[5]

---

and religious factionalization); intergovernmental strength of nationally governing party when ethnic regions are governed by opposition party; and lower ethnic regional concentration combined with smaller central government grants.

[5] Appendix Table 9.A1 focuses on statistical findings about processes, while Appendix Table 9.A2 does the same thing for outcomes and legacies. As per note 4 concerning onset, some charac-

ORIGINS OF CIVIL WAR

Table 9.2 conveys the results from data-based research on the origins of civil war. The columns refer, respectively, to levels of analysis and characteristics.[6] Characteristics that are underlined refer to those included in the comprehensive review essay from Dixon (2009a).[7] The substantive focus of the statistical analysis in the table is the likelihood of onset for a civil war.

Table 9.2 Research findings about the onset of civil wars

Level of analysis	Characteristics
International system	Neighboring state at war
State	Mountainous terrain
	Soil degradation
	Anocracy; regime instability
	Lower per capita income
	Larger population
	Lack of economic growth
	Previous conflict; absence of distinct civil war in previous year
	Degree of corruption (e.g., bribes)
	Lack of rule of law and order (e.g., lower strength and impartiality of legal system)
	Institutional weakness of bureaucracy
	Lower value for Quality of Institutions Index (i.e., combined scores for corruption, rule of law and order, and bureaucratic quality)
	Discrimination against societal groups (e.g., religious minorities)
Society	Territorial base of insurgency geographically removed from capital city by land or water
	Ethnic dominance; ethnic heterogeneity
	Absence of mass education
	Poverty

teristics are excluded because of relatively high uncertainty about cause and effect. For processes, higher democracy score (in connection to violence) and lower ethnic and linguistic fractionalization (in connection to duration) are excluded from Appendix Table 9.A1. One characteristic, very long or short conflict (in connection to insurgent change), is left out of Appendix Table 9.A2 for outcomes and legacies.

[6] The absence of findings from the government-insurgent dyad level undoubtedly reflects this factor becoming a focal point of research about processes, outcomes, and legacies – in other words, deemed relevant once a civil war is underway. The contents of Appendix Tables 9.A1 and 9.A2 support that assertion.

[7] The characteristics from Dixon (2009a, 2009b) are those, based on results from the studies reviewed, that had been designated as either high or medium in confidence. The same notation is used in Appendix Tables 9.A1 and 9.A2.

10
Multilevel explanations

PROLOGUE

South Carolina seceded from the US in December 1960, the first of 11 states to do so over the course of several months. A key local issue concerned the remaining Union (i.e., US) forces in that state – what would happen to them? The commanding officer of the Union garrison at Fort Moultrie in South Carolina, Major Robert Anderson, followed an order from Washington to defend government property against any forthcoming secessionist attacks. He therefore moved his personnel to the more defensible Fort Sumter in the Charleston Harbor, depicted in Map 10.1. The fate of Fort Sumter would set a precedent, as what became known as "Secessionitis" took hold, and the Confederate States of America (CSA) formed in February 1861. Under the command of Brigadier General P. G. T. Beauregard, Confederate forces directed artillery fire toward Fort Sumter on April 14, 1861. With that action, ordered by President Jefferson Davis of the fledgling CSA, what has become known as "the" Civil War got underway. On April 14, after a sustained bombardment by superior CSA forces, Anderson surrendered the fort. Support for war in both the North and South became overwhelming after Fort Sumter changed hands. It became obvious that neither the Union nor the Confederacy would be willing or able to put forward a compromise that could satisfy the other. Differences would have to be settled through a resort to arms.

By the time the war concluded in April 1865, over 600,000 Americans had died, with another 750,000 wounded (Miller and Pohanka 2000: 12). Massive physical destruction took place as well, especially toward the end of the war in the CSA. How, then, did such a terrible thing happen? And why do civil wars continue to erupt around the world?

OVERVIEW

The American Civil War provides an excellent opportunity to connect explanations of conflict and war across levels of analysis. While many other civil wars have occurred throughout history, the one in the US in the mid-19th century occupies a special place. Social scientists continue to study the Civil War, even more than 150 years after its conclusion. Why did such a conflagration occur along geographic lines? This question is direct and simple, but many thousands of pages have been used in trying to answer it. Academic journals even focus specif-

Source: https://www.alamy.com/stock-photo-bombardment-of-ft-sumter-charleston-harbor-south-carolina-177529906.html?imageid=7CF95DC0-B140-47C1-BC12-6A8863241B81&p=645468&pn=2&searchId=227c0f1f8fa0a03c2a6ebfe826ed24b3&searchtype=0

Map 10.1   Fort Sumter and the American Civil War

ically on the American case, for example, *Civil War History* and *The Journal of the Civil War Era*.

The main reason for such attention is that the war accelerated the rise of the US to the top of the world pecking order, first in material terms and later on with regard to replacement of Great Britain in a leadership role. The restored Union, as a result of the Civil War, had industrialized at a much faster rate than otherwise. By the time the war had ended, the military forces of the United States rivaled those anywhere in the world in terms of overall size and technological advancement. While demobilization occurred quickly, the US had demonstrated the ability to create formidable military forces and could do so again.

Controversies continue over the highly complex causes, processes, outcomes, and legacies of the American Civil War, so it is a natural focal point in turning to multilevel explanations. The Civil War defies any simple account based on a single event or even level of analysis. As will become apparent, factors from the international system, state, and individual levels are required to provide a compelling explanation for that lethal conflict.

Work unfolds in six additional sections. The second section offers a comprehensive sense of cause and effect that is grounded in the philosophy of Aristotle, placed in a social scientific framework via Kurki (2008). Section three offers a necessarily abbreviated account of the multifaceted events leading up to the Civil War. The fourth section applies the framework of Kurki (2008) to the case at hand through a systemist visualization. Section five conveys lessons for the contemporary study of conflict processes – an exercise in the logic of discovery. The sixth section compares the findings about the Civil War to the results based on aggregate data analysis that have been reported in Chapter 9. The seventh and final section reflects on what has been accomplished and leads into the next chapter.

A COMPREHENSIVE SENSE OF CAUSE AND EFFECT

The concept of causation is fundamental to scientific inquiry.[1] Recall from Chapter 1 that the most basic requirements for assignment of cause and effect – covered in any textbook on research design – are correlation, temporal order, and nonspuriousness. If a putative cause is absent much of the time when the effect is observed, that raises questions, at the very least, about its necessity. It therefore is essential to find correlation – preferably, nearly constant conjunction between the appearance of cause and effect. Temporal order also obviously is required – a cause must precede its presumed effect. Finally, and most complicated, is nonspuriousness. What if a cause is associated with, and precedes in time, its would-be effect? Is that enough to establish causation? The answer is "no" because something else – observed together with the cause on a regular basis – could be the genuine explanation for the effect. The goal of research is to distinguish genuine from spurious causes. While it is not possible to conduct an experiment toward that end for events outside of a laboratory, the closest approximation is to cast the net widely in the search for causal factors.

A framework that recognizes the existence of *types* of causes is essential to a rigorous, compelling account for an event. The need for a broad conception of causation goes all the way back to the philosophy of Aristotle, which designated (1) two basic types of causal conditions; and (2) two sub-types of each. Kurki (2002, 2008) offers an authoritative translation of Aristotle's ideas into a modern social scientific framework. The two basic types of causal conditions are

---

[1] The principal source for this section is the authoritative treatment of cause and effect in International Relations (IR) from Kurki (2008).

(a) constitutive or intrinsic; and (b) active or extrinsic (Kurki 2008: 220). An intrinsic cause is "that which is within the thing being caused, that which continues to be present in a thing through constituting it" (Kurki 2008: 220). This refers to an inherent characteristic of a state or other entity. For instance, a state might be island-based, such as Australia and Indonesia. By contrast, as Kurki (2008: 220) observes, an extrinsic cause "is that which is not within the being, but which lends an influence or activity to the producing of something". This refers to action. An example would be the building of the Great Wall of China as a highly visible designation of its border. The difference between intrinsic and extrinsic causes might be compared to potential versus kinetic energy in the domain of physics.

Within category (a) of intrinsic cause are the sub-types of material and formal, while category (b) of extrinsic cause encompasses the efficient and final sub-types. Importantly, and following Aristotle, any convincing story about cause and effect must incorporate *each* of the preceding types. The Aristotelian approach "directs us towards a multifaceted understanding of causal powers in the social world" (Kurki 2008: 223). We introduce each main category and its sub-types in turn.

Consider first material causes. As Kurki (2008: 221) argues, nothing exists without materiality and the:

> material possibilities of substances are shaped by their internal structure (form), often on multiple levels. A gun, for example, has certain material powers in relation to how it has been shaped (its form) as well as arising from the substance out of which it is shaped (a wooden gun has different properties from a silver one).

Material causes are primary and essential for any explanation – envisioned as limiting, enabling, or conditioning (Kurki 2008: 221, 223). In the case of the silver and wooden guns just noted, a common intrinsic and material trait would be that each can fire (or not, if purely decorative), while a difference would be the likely much higher price of the former in comparison to the latter.

Consider a further illustration of material cause with regard to weapons – a comparison of American and German tanks during World War II. All tanks on both sides had metal construction, the ability to support infantry movements, and sufficient firepower to open up fortified positions. At the same time, the German Panther would likely win a confrontation against the American Sherman with a single tank on each side. Superior armor and other traits favored the Panther over the Sherman. Greater numbers, not individual matchups, ultimately favored the US in tank battles against Germany (Zaloga 2008). Thus, variation can exist in terms of intrinsic material potential across individual units of observation that fall under a more general heading.

Formal causes also appear within the intrinsic category. The reference is to the conceptualization from Aristotle that focuses on what shapes or defines matter – the constitution of things "by defining meanings and relations, rather than by acting as moving sources of change" (Kurki 2008: 221). Formal causes pertain to arrangements – structure rather than process. Moreover, as Kurki (2008: 223) observes, the formal designation provides "a useful way of framing the causal role of ideas, rules, norms and discourses in the social world". Put simply, formal causes are about the context for interaction. Regime type is an important example; recall from previous chapters how much is known about the differences between combinations of democracies and autocracies with regard to cooperation and conflict.

Consider protracted conflict as an instance of formal cause for events in world politics. When two states are in a sustained confrontation with each other, leading to a series of international crises and possibly even war, this process is defined as a protracted conflict (Brecher and Wilkenfeld 1997, 2000). Adversaries in a protracted conflict exhibit higher levels of distrust, along with greater disposition to violence and escalation, and any number of other undesirable things (Brecher 2018). By contrast, as Brecher (2018) observes, international crises that take place in a "one off" context are more likely to be resolved with lower levels of violence and escalation. The presence or absence of protracted conflict is a formal cause of international crises per se and various properties of them.

Efficient cause is the first of two sub-types in the extrinsic category. It refers to sources of change – the primary movers that put into motion the potential that exists (Kurki 2008: 222). Efficient causality, according to Kurki (2008: 222), "is fundamentally embedded within and in relation to other types of causes and cannot in itself explain anything". This contrasts with the tendency among many theorists to emphasize the "pushing and pulling" sense of cause and effect (Kurki 2008: 219). Immediate circumstances leading to an outcome therefore tend to be emphasized at the expense of a more complete explanation. Within a full-fledged account of something that has happened, efficient cause recognizes the role of agency (Kurki 2008: 225). The proverbial case of the "last straw", which causes a person to become angry enough to respond to a series of perceived provocations, perhaps will come to mind most readily here as an illustration of efficient cause.

Consider, as an example of an efficient cause, the Japanese surprise attack against the US on December 7, 1941. The assault against Pearl Harbor led to a declaration of war by the US the next day. President Franklin Delano Roosevelt described December 7 as a day that would "live in infamy". The Pearl Harbor attack therefore stands as an obvious efficient cause for US entry into World War II. At the same time, the events of December 7 represent a point of culmination for many previous developments across the Pacific Ocean. Confrontations between Japan and the US had been building up for a long time before Pearl Harbor. The US embargo on oil and gasoline exports to Japan from August 1941, for example, escalated the conflict significantly. The Empire of Japan, based on a chain of relatively small islands, had very little in the way of natural resources, so the US embargo represented a serious threat to its ambitions. Other events just as easily could be added along the pathway to Pearl Harbor to provide a more complete explanation.

Final cause is the second of two extrinsic sub-types. The reference here is to purposes and ends that direct mechanistic processes (Kurki 2008: 222). As Kurki (2008: 226) points out, final causes "give intentionality the fundamental role that it deserves in social explanation".[2] Put simply, people act with purpose. For instance, why open up a bank account? The intention is

---

[2] Final and formal causes can relate to each other in important ways. These categories overlap, for instance, with regard to reasons given for an action (Kurki 2008: 227). Purposes and intentions can be symbiotic with each other.

to engage in economic exchange – making and receiving payments – in a way that is practical. The final cause of the bank account is witnessed via the filling out of cheques and deposit slips.

Consider the rivalry between India and Pakistan in connection with final cause. The international crisis known as the India-Pakistan Nuclear Tests (Beardsley, James, Wilkenfeld and Brecher 2023) got underway in May of 1998. India conducted a pair of nuclear tests and Pakistan responded with five of their own. The case de-escalated as a result of sanctions on the adversaries imposed by the US and its key allies. In this situation, the acquisition of nuclear weapons for the purpose of intimidating the adversary stands out as a final cause of the international crisis.

Comprehensive, Aristotelian specification of cause and effect is in line with the principles of scientific realism, analytic eclecticism, and systemism put forward in Chapter 1. First, with regard to scientific realism, note that the categories of causation span the material and ideational worlds. Kurki's (2008) framework features both intrinsic characteristics and observable extrinsic actions. Second, and in line with analytic eclecticism, the goal of comprehensive explanation implicitly transcends paradigmatic boundaries. To account for an event, each of the four causal sub-types must be referenced, with no restrictions on content. Third, and finally, the framework from Kurki (2008) is systemist; structure and agency play interactive roles. Sample explanations from Kurki (2008: 218–230) are seen to move readily back and forth between and among levels of analysis. For the preceding reasons, the framework from Kurki (2002, 2008) is ideally suited to join forces with systemism in the quest for multilevel explanations.

One qualification should be offered before looking specifically at the series of events leading up to the Civil War and then applying the Kurki (2002, 2008) framework to it. On the surface, a chronology of events would appear to include only extrinsic causes. Actions, not intrinsic characteristics, are included in such a list. However, once taken, actions have outcomes. These results, in turn, can play the role of material or formal causes. Take, for example, the volcanic eruption on the island of Krakatoa in 1883, possibly the loudest event in recorded history. The series of explosions, culminating on August 27, destroyed about two-thirds of the island and had other long-standing effects as well.[3]

While an intense event in and of itself, the new landscape resulting from the volcanic eruption of 1883 could occupy the role of a material or formal cause in the explanation of some later development. The same is true of events on the list of those covered in the following section. It is possible for any given event in the chronology to be either an intrinsic or extrinsic cause, depending on whether the time frame is the past or present.

IN FOCUS: INTEGRATING MATERIAL AND IDEATIONAL REALITIES

In *The Idea of History*, Collingwood (1946) asserted that history cannot be conceived of in purely material terms. All historical processes contain at least some degree of interpretation. At the same time, it is important to maintain a grasp of material reality, in order not to slide into a discussion that is purely about opinions and unguided by evidence. One

---

[3] For a fascinating account of the Krakatoa eruption, see Winchester (2005).

> way of achieving such a balance, as argued in this book, is to adopt scientific realism in combination with analytic eclecticism. After the preceding review of cause and effect from Kurki (2008), does that seem convincing to you?

CIVIL WAR IN THE UNITED STATES

Many pages would be required to provide a comprehensive history of the events that led up to the Civil War in April 1861. Outstanding works of scholarship are available for consultation and we have referenced their contents to provide a necessarily brief history of how the conflagration came about.[4] What follows is a review of events leading up to the Civil War, with occasional overlap in time along the way. While obviously it always is possible to go further back in history to include more potentially relevant events, or offer greater detail about those already included, the excellent sources used to undergird this account make it unlikely that anything consequential is not referenced in at least some minimal way.

Slavery existed in the Western Hemisphere long before the arrival of Europeans. Those taken in battle during warfare among Aboriginals, in some instances, could expect to live out their years in slavery. Importation of slaves by Europeans began in the territory that became known as the US in 1619. Slavery continued to exist in each of the 13 colonies at the time of the American Revolution. Significantly, the ratified Constitution of 1788 contained the Fugitives from Labour Clause (Article IV, Section 2, Clause 3), better known as the Fugitive Slave Clause. The Clause required that anyone who escaped from one state into another be returned if they had been "held to Service or Labour" in their original location. While the Clause made no explicit reference to slavery, all parties knew quite well what it meant in practice.

Efforts to limit harm from slavery proceeded at a glacial pace. For example, the US restricted and banned importation of slaves, respectively, in 1794 and 1808. These actions reflected pressure from the anti-slave trade movement, with origins in Great Britain under the memorable leadership of the parliamentarian William Wilberforce (Hague 2008). At the same time, countervailing forces attempted to sustain slavery where it already existed. The Fugitive Slave Act in February 1793 stands out among such measures in Congress. Those who had made their way to free territory still would be counted as slaves and subject to being returned to their masters. The Act put the original Fugitives from Labour Clause into operational form; it referred explicitly and coercively to an obligation among citizens to aid the recovery of slaves as permanent property of their masters. The legislation even counted the children of fugitive slave mothers as slaves as well. The fact that the measure passed through the House 48–7 revealed the relative weakness of the anti-slavery movement in the initial decades following the American Revolution.

---

[4] These works include Genovese (1969), Potter (1976), Fehrenbacher (1978), Woodward (1981), Carden (1986), Freehling (1990, 1992, 2008), Freehling and Simpson (1992), Miller and Pohanka (2000), Lakwete (2005), Hague (2008), Green (2009), Gudmestad (2011), Chernow (2017), Croon (2018), Phillips (2018), Powell (2021), and Daut (2023).

Spanish, and later on, French overseers exploited the slave population of Haiti through gold mining over the course of centuries. The slaves in Haiti rebelled in 1791 and ultimately achieved independence in 1804 – a powerful response to colonialism and the institution of slavery all at once (Daut 2023). Haitians found the continuation of slavery by the French in other locations, such as Guadeloupe, to be abhorrent. Events in Haiti elicited anxieties among slave owners in the US about whether rebellions might be forthcoming there as well. Southerners felt a mounting threat, along the same lines, from Northern abolitionists.

Slavery disappeared in what became known as the North primarily due to lack of economic viability. The same thing might have occurred in the South, but technology intervened. Eli Whitney invented the Cotton Gin in 1794. Southern mechanics took the original wire-toothed gin from Whitney and changed it over into the saw gin (Lakwete 2005). All at once, slavery became more profitable than before because of much higher efficiency from the harvest of cotton. The cotton gin "enabled slaves to pick 20 times more cotton than previously" (Miller and Pohanka 2000: 13). In addition, transportation via steamboats from 1812 onward contributed to the success of the cotton-based economy (Gudmestad 2011). The number of slaves in the South increased dramatically from that point onward and production of cotton skyrocketed. "King Cotton" became the centerpiece of the Southern economy (Miller and Pohanka 2000: 27). Furthermore, slavery played a significant role in an emerging Southern mind-set and identity (Genovese 1969). Exports of cotton to Great Britain became substantial and politically important at a later date when the European powers faced the question of whether to side with the North, South, or neither side in the sectional conflict.

With the Louisiana Purchase from France in 1803, US territory more than doubled in size (Miller and Pohanka 2000: 12). Intense conflict over the balance of power between slave and free states came to the fore in 1819, as Missouri sat on the brink of admission to the US as a free state. If that occurred, the free states would have a majority in the Senate. The ensuing crisis ultimately produced what became known as the Missouri Compromise of 1820. When Massachusetts agreed to give up control over a large expanse of its northern territory, that entity came into the Union as the free state of Maine. Missouri entered with it, but as a slave state, which preserved the numerical balance – 12 states each for free and slave. The uneasy agreement also prohibited slavery in territory that had come with the Louisiana Purchase. Specifically, slavery would not be permitted beyond parallel 36°30° west and north of Missouri. Given its complicated nature, the Missouri Compromise had little chance of providing a sustainable answer to the question of slavery.

William Lloyd Garrison published the first issue of *The Liberator* on January 1, 1831. This newspaper served as a rallying point for abolitionists and an ongoing offense to slaveholders. *The Liberator* worked in tandem with Frederick Douglass, who had been born a slave but gained his freedom and became the "voice of freedom" – eventually, the most memorable of all abolitionists (Miller and Pohanka 2000: 28). Anti-slavery petitions to Congress accumulated over the course of the years that followed. Defenders of slavery responded to abolitionist pressure with the Pinckney Resolutions of 1836. One resolution, which became known as the "Gag Rule", prohibited slavery-related petitions. It is revealing that all of the Pinckney Resolutions passed, with even the Gag Rule achieving a margin of 117 to 68. In 1840, the House passed additional legislation that prohibited reception of anti-slavery petitions, but that only seemed to provoke rather than shut down abolitionists.

Economic woes took center stage in the events leading up to the Nullification Crisis of 1832–1833. Administered by the John Quincy Adams Administration in 1828, a protectionist tariff raised hackles in multiple states, with an intense reaction from South Carolina in particular. The measure even became known as the Tariff of Abominations. A follow-up tariff in 1832 from the Andrew Jackson Administration did not significantly help the situation and raised anger to a level in South Carolina where status in the Union itself shadowed discussions of what would come next. A state convention voted to declare both tariffs null and void within its confines.

Congress responded with a bill authorizing the president to use force in order to obtain compliance with the tariffs. Vice President John C. Calhoun and Henry Clay, a Senator from Kentucky who had obtained national prominence from multiple runs at the White House, worked out a compromise on the tariff. While that quelled talk in South Carolina about leaving the Union, it did not resolve the underlying question of ultimate authority over policy. South Carolinians increasingly feared abolitionists and their leaders tried to prohibit public exchanges about what became known, euphemistically, as the "peculiar institution" (Freehling 1992). Slavery lurked in the background, and increasingly the foreground, of further debates over federal authority versus the rights of states.

Events in the 1840s showed that tensions over slavery had not gone away, in spite of ongoing Southern efforts to repress the issue. Northern opposition to slavery had increased and Congress eliminated the Gag Rule in December 1844. The House vote of 108 to 80 fell primarily along a North–South axis. While the Senate might maintain a balance, the larger and more rapidly increasing population of the industrializing North caused its margin in House seats to increase significantly over the South. Immigration from Europe, especially Ireland and Germany, increased dramatically (Miller and Pohanka 2000: 15). The majority of immigrants coming to the US looked for work in the North rather than the South because of overall economic growth and resulting opportunities, which served to increase the difference in size of population.

Founding of *De Bow's Review* in 1846 exemplified reaction in the South to the intensifying campaign in the North against slavery. The magazine openly advocated for secession as a response to the growing economic power of the North, which had industrialized dramatically in comparison to the still largely agricultural South. It is interesting to note that in the "war of words", advocates of slavery and its critics often made references to the Bible. Churches in the South and North emphasized different points in the scripture and some even broke into separate branches during the 1840s and 1850s over slavery as a force for good or evil (Carden 1986). It is important to add that the US of the 19th century featured a much higher level of religiosity than today, so conflict within churches mattered greatly in weakening national cohesion.

From its origins along the Eastern Seaboard at the time of the Revolution, the US had expanded significantly in territory, most notably the Louisiana Purchase of 1803. The United States annexed Texas in 1845, and the Mexican War of 1848 added further to the size of the US (Miller and Pohanka 2000: 18). Both free and slave economies stood to profit from access to the new territory. Inexpensive land in the west made it possible for many to own a farm who otherwise could not do so. Slaveowners also could see potential for crops such as cotton to grow on the newly available land.

Most notably in relation to new territories won from Mexico in the recently concluded war, the Compromise of 1850 consisted of a series of actions designed by Congress to manage the issue of slavery. The complex agreement included admitting California as a free state, allowing the New Mexico and Utah territories to decide on slavery, and various other measures. Perhaps most significant in terms of later impact would be the imposition of a much stronger Fugitive Slave Act, which outraged Northerners who now would be required to help return escapees to the South. On the other side, the South increasingly worried that Washington would continue meddling with slavery and possibly even seek to eliminate it.

Harriet Beecher Stowe published *Uncle Tom's Cabin* in serial form and then as a novel in 1852. The story, which highlighted the violence embedded within the institution of slavery, had a massive impact throughout the country. The book raised consciousness about the evils of slave owning, which contradicted long-standing defenses of the peculiar institution based on it being the natural order of things. Debates over *Uncle Tom's Cabin* aggravated the existing tensions between South and North.

Stephen A. Douglas, the prominent Senator from Illinois, put forward a bill in 1854 that intended to open up settlement of farmlands in the west, notably through expansion of rail lines. The bill, however, included a provision for deciding the issue of slavery through votes held in respective territorial legislatures. Opinion in the North crystallized against the bill because it effectively overturned the Missouri Compromise and opened the door to westward expansion of slavery. The Kansas–Nebraska Act of 1854 further intensified conflict, notably in Kansas. What became known as "Bleeding Kansas" ensued, as pro- and anti-slavery forces fought bitterly and foreshadowed strife that would follow on at the national level a few years later. The structure of the political system changed as well, with greater divisions among Democrats and the founding of the Republican Party as an amalgamation of those with varying degrees of opposition to slavery.

Among the many violent events over the years of Bleeding Kansas, one stands out: the Pottawatomie Massacre of 1856. The reason is that the atrocity signaled the entry of John Brown into the battle over slavery. Brown, an abolitionist with messianic tendencies, took the lead in killing five pro-slavery men on May 24, 1856 at Pottawatomie Creek. Reactions to that act of violence served to further divide the North and South against each other. For example, the pro-slavery Lecompton Constitution passed in 1857, but obviously as the result of widespread voter fraud in Kansas. This measure, however, did not survive when, at the suggestion of President James Buchanan, a vote on it took place in Kansas. Kansans rejected the Lecompton Constitution overwhelmingly and divisions increased within the Democratic Party, which struggled to paper over increasing differences between members in the North and South.

Around the time of the massacre led by John Brown, a shocking event took place in the Senate. Senator Charles Sumner of Massachusetts gave a speech on May 19, 1856 that attacked slavery in general and Senator Andrew P. Butler of South Carolina in particular. Preston S. Brooks, a relative of Butler, beat Sumner with a cane on May 22 and very nearly killed him.

This series of events further reinforced the sectional conflict. Northerners saw the event as evidence of barbarism in the South. Southerners supported Brooks, with newspapers openly congratulating him on acting against radical abolitionism and sending canes to replace the one broken in the assault. Members even began to carry weapons into Congress.

Still infamous even centuries later, the Dred Scott Case of March 1857 further inflamed Northern opinion against slavery (Fehrenbacher 1978). Dred Scott had been a slave, eventually purchased by an army surgeon, John Emerson, and moved to free territory. After the death of Emerson, Scott sued for his freedom and saw the case go all the way to the Supreme Court. The decision of the Court, to return Scott to slavery on the basis of lacking the rights of citizenship, horrified the North. Opposition to slavery increased to ever-higher levels in the North, which in turn made Southerners feel under attack for their way of life.

George Fitzhugh published an inflammatory book in 1857, *Cannibals All!*, which offered an unapologetic defense of slavery. He argued that slavery served to stabilize society in the South and that all parties benefited from that institution. The North, through enslavement of factory workers, presumably could achieve the same goal. This book built upon the steady drumbeat of *De Bow's Review*, which urged the South to be wary of Northern power based in financial interests. In addition, *Cannibals All!* came out at the time of the Panic of 1857, a serious economic downturn that caused more of the Southern elite to seek some distance from the interests of the North.

Ironic and fascinating, the Lincoln–Douglas debates of 1858 played a significant and multifaceted role. The irony is that Abraham Lincoln lost the Senate race to Stephen A. Douglas, but ended up winning the presidency against him two years later.[5] The series of debates brought the issue of slavery into even greater national prominence because of the sharply contrasting positions of the Democratic and Republican candidates on its expansion in particular. Douglas, a Democrat, tried to sit in the middle on the issue through endorsement of the principle of popular sovereignty in the territories. Lincoln, a Republican, came to national prominence through the debates (Miller and Pohanka 2000: 30). He condemned slavery as immoral but did not call for abolition. Instead, he emphasized the need for containment of the practice rather than diffusion into territories acquired by the US.

John Brown, a central character in the story of Bleeding Kansas, moved into a new theater of battle. He organized an attack carried out on October 16, 1859 at Harper's Ferry, Virginia. Brown hoped to arouse and arm slaves against their masters. Instead, Brown and his small team of raiders, 22 all told, became holed up in the local armory. In yet another twist of fate, US Marines quickly and easily defeated the invaders. (The irony in this instance refers to who led the Marines against Brown: Colonel Robert E. Lee, who went on to become the most memorable general in the CSA.) The hanging of John Brown in December 1859 further divided the nation. Southern leaders framed the attack as one that signaled forthcoming efforts to end slavery once and for all (Miller and Pohanka 2000: 19). The demise of Brown even inspired composition of "The Battle Hymn of the Republic", which glorified Brown as a martyr and became the Northern theme song in the Civil War.

---

[5] In that era, state legislatures still decided upon Senate races. Controlled by Democrats at the time, the legislature of Illinois elected Douglas.

Harper's Ferry also had an important impact in the South: the rise of an effective militia system. While most Southerners did not own slaves, whites came together in patrols to enforce the institution of slavery. Local militias became more numerous and akin to professional soldiers after the attack at Harper's Ferry. All of this contributed further to emergence of a Southern identity that featured the institution of slavery and an ability to defend it by force.

When the election of 1860 came around, the Democratic Party stood hopelessly divided over slavery. The final straw turned out to be the demand for a slave code in the territories; Democrats in the North and South parted ways over that matter in particular. Douglas tried to be the "candidate of regional compromise" but could not unite the Democratic Party (Chernow 2017: 118). Lincoln won the Republican nomination for president, in all likelihood, because he "offended the fewest" in a difficult situation (Chernow 2017: 118). Lincoln, not even on the ballot in states that joined the CSA, won the presidency. Elected in a four-way contest and with just 40% of the vote, Lincoln entered into office facing what still is remembered as the greatest national crisis in history. Lincoln, at the time, occupied a moderate stance on the overarching issue of slavery. In line with the official Republican Party position, the President-elect did not openly support abolition, but instead opposed expansion of slavery into newly acquired territories.

What would Lincoln do? Southerners initially took a "wait and see" approach, but radicals soon won the day in one capital after the next (Woodward 1981; Freehling and Simpson 1992; Freehling 2008; Chernow 2017; Croon 2018). Secessionitis spread quickly. South Carolina left first, on December 20, 1860, and ultimately 11 states joined the CSA by the spring of 1861. The CSA stood for equal rights among states rather than people. President-elect Lincoln denounced secession and called it illegal. Opinion in the North clearly opposed secession and wanted to preserve the Union. A crisis over federal property in the CSA quickly ensued and the events at Fort Sumter, noted at the outset of this chapter, brought on the war.[6]

FOR EXAMPLE: GETTING TO YES

Getting to Yes (Fisher and Ury 1991) is one of the most influential works of all time on the subject of negotiation. A basic insight from that volume is that it is more productive to focus on achievement of *interests* rather than to hold a particular *position*. In other words, successful negotiation requires creativity rather than stubbornness.

With that in mind, could the Civil War have been averted through more effective negotiation? Or did it simply have to occur?

---

[6] All but forgotten is the cannon fire directed against the steamer, *Star of the West*, early on January 9, 1861. The attack came from The Citadel, a military school in Charleston, with the intention of preventing the vessel from bringing supplies and reinforcements to Fort Sumter (Miller and Pohanka 2000: 40). Given that the Union did not react to the attack on the ship, it is not granted any causal status.

A SYSTEMIST CAUSAL ANALYSIS OF THE CIVIL WAR IN THE UNITED STATES[7]

Table 10.1 organizes the preceding history of events leading up to the Civil War along two dimensions: connection to type of cause and level of analysis. The events appear in chronological order along the rows of the table. The columns contain, for each respective event: (i) the type and sub-type of associated cause; and (ii) level of analysis at which it resides. There are 19 intrinsic (3 material, 16 formal) and 2 extrinsic (1 efficient, 1 final) causes among the types and sub-types. Across levels of analysis, the totals are system (4), state (11) and individual (6). The formal and the state, respectively, are predominant numerically among sub-types and levels of analysis. The struggle leading up to the Civil War, in an overall sense, can be characterized as something that took place primarily within the borders of the US. Each of the causal sub-types will be covered with some attention to placement in levels of analysis as well.

Events that contributed to intrinsic material causes include two that pertain to the acquisition of territory (Louisiana Purchase; Annexation of Texas and Mexican War) and one that focuses on military capability (John Brown attacks Harper's Ferry – rise of militia system in the South). Expansion of the US created the potential for the fight over slavery to diffuse into new locations. Military readiness of the South increased as an unintended side effect of John Brown's quixotic attack on Fort Sumter.

Since 16 events contributed to intrinsic formal causes, it is helpful to subdivide these into the state and individual levels of analysis. Each subset is considered in turn.

Eleven events occur at the state level: Fugitive from Labour Clause in ratified Constitution and Fugitive Slave Law Passed; Missouri Compromise; Nullification Crisis; Pinckney Resolutions and Gag Rule passed in Congress; Congress repeals Gag Rule; Compromise of 1850 and expanded Fugitive Slave Act; Kansas–Nebraska Act; Preston Brooks attacks Charles Sumner on Senate floor; Supreme Court upholds Fugitive Slave Act in ruling on Dred Scott case; Lincoln–Douglas Senate debates in Illinois; Abraham Lincoln elected president. These events crystallized into an incoherent federal system brimming over with confrontation. Legal and even physical battles over slavery, together with legislative packages that resembled "Rube Goldberg" contraptions, created an institutional design that all but had to come apart.

Five events take place at the individual level: William Lloyd Garrison begins publishing *The Liberator*; founding of *De Bow's Review*; Harriette Beecher Stowe publishes *Uncle Tom's Cabin*; Pottowatomie Massacre carried out by John Brown; George Fitzhugh publishes *Cannibals All!*. Four of these items show how the battle over slavery played out in the written word, while two are about physical actions taken against adversaries. The five events combine to show the context that existed as war became imminent – a situation that resembled protracted conflict at the international level but carried out in the society of one country.

With just two events, it is much easier to cover the extrinsic causes of the Civil War. Secession of 11 states to form the Confederate States of America (CSA) is the final cause. Secessionitis

---

[7] James (2022: 177) provides a paragraph-long introduction to how the categories from Kurki (2002, 2008) could be applied to the case of the Civil War.

Table 10.1 Events leading to the civil war: an inventory of causes

Event	Year	Constitutive/Intrinsic		Active/Extrinsic		Level of analysis		
		Material	Formal	Efficient	Final	System	State	Individual
Fugitive from Labour Clause in ratified Constitution and Fugitive Slave Law Passed	1788, 1793		✓				✓	
Louisiana Purchase from France	1803	✓				✓		
Missouri Compromise	1820		✓				✓	
William Lloyd Garrison begins publishing *The Liberator*	1831		✓					✓
Nullification Crisis	1832–3		✓				✓	
Pinckney Resolutions and Gag Rule passed in Congress	1836		✓				✓	
Congress repeals Gag Rule	1844		✓				✓	
Founding of *De Bow's Review*	1846		✓					✓
Annexation of Texas and Mexican War	1848	✓				✓		
Compromise of 1850 and expanded Fugitive Slave Act	1850		✓				✓	
Harriett Beecher Stowe publishes *Uncle Tom's Cabin*	1852		✓					✓
Kansas-Nebraska Act	1854		✓				✓	

Event	Year	Type		Level of analysis		
Preston Brooks attacks Charles Sumner on Senate floor	1856	✓		✓		
Pottowatomie Massacre carried out by John Brown	1856	✓				✓
Supreme Court upholds Fugitive Slave Act in ruling on Dred Scott case	1857	✓		✓		
George Fitzhugh publishes *Cannibals All!*	1857	✓				✓
Lincoln-Douglas Senate debates in Illinois	1858	✓			✓	
John Brown attacks Harper's Ferry – rise of militia system in the South	1859		✓			✓
Abraham Lincoln elected president	1860	✓			✓	
Secession of 11 states to form the Confederate States of America (CSA)	1860–1	✓	✓			
CSA attacks Fort Sumter	1861	✓		✓		
All events together	1788–1861	3	16	1	4	11	6

spread among states that saw it as a means to achieve their common and overarching goal: to preserve the institution of slavery. When the CSA attacked Fort Sumter, that constituted the efficient cause of the war – the point of no return.

Consider how the series of events come together to form an overall sense of what brought about the Civil War. Material causes reside in the expansion of territory within which to dispute the status of slavery, along with military readiness of the institution's defenders in what became known as the Confederacy. Confrontation built up in both government and society over the course of decades and created an increasingly difficult context within which to manage the issue of slavery – the formal cause of eventual escalation to war. The attack on Fort Sumter, the efficient cause, demonstrated that neither side could put together a compromise that would satisfy the other. The final cause, formation of the CSA, followed on from the objective among slave states to preserve the peculiar institution.

Figure 10.1 assembles the events from Table 10.1 into a systemist graphic account of the Civil War. The system is the United States, with the International System as its environment. The macro and micro levels of the United States, respectively, are government and society. In this context, note that society corresponds to the individual level of analysis.[8]

Among the 21 components in the diagram, the distribution among respective roles is as follows: initial (1), generic (12), divergent (2), convergent (4), nodal (1), and terminal (1). Adding together the divergent, convergent, and nodal categories yields seven points of contingency along the way. The diagram therefore tells anything but a deterministic story – note especially that the points of convergence tend to come toward the end of the process.

With regard to levels of aggregation, the components are arranged as follows: International System (i.e., Environment) (4), US government (i.e., Macro level of System) (11), and US society (i.e., micro level of System) (6). Among the eight basic linkage types from systemism – Macro → Macro, etc. – seven appear in Figure 10.1. Missing from the graphic is Environment → micro – that is, a connection to American society from the International System. This gap may reflect the state of communication technology in antebellum America more than anything else – early in the railway era and before invention of the telephone. For example, foreign governments seeking to influence the outcome would have very little 'reach' into American society.

Subfigures 10.1a–f will tell the story of the events leading up to the Civil War. The first subfigure covers the two decades at the end of the 18th century, while those after it focus on each subsequent ten-year interval.

Figure 10.1a displays an initial component as a green oval at the macro level of the system: "'FUGITIVES FROM LABOUR' CLAUSE INCLUDED IN RATIFIED CONSTITUTION (1788) AND FUGITIVE SLAVE LAW PASSES CONGRESS (1793)". The US got underway with a basic contradiction in place: a commitment to freedom and equality but also the practice of slavery. The Fugitive Slave Law represents just the first in a series of increasingly complicated arrangements designed to preserve slavery without destroying the country.

---

[8] As per other chapters, the individual level also can refer to in-depth analysis of leading figures, such as a head of state or foreign minister.

MULTILEVEL EXPLANATIONS

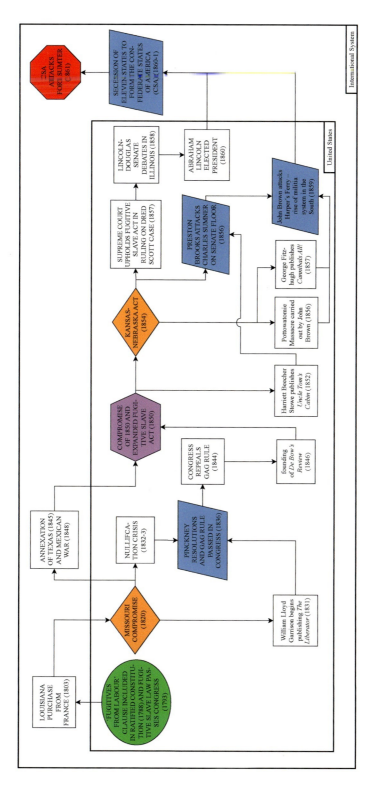

Figure 10.1 Events leading up to the civil war

CONFLICT, CRISIS, AND WAR IN WORLD POLITICS

Figure 10.1a

MULTILEVEL EXPLANATIONS

Figure 10.1b

CONFLICT, CRISIS, AND WAR IN WORLD POLITICS

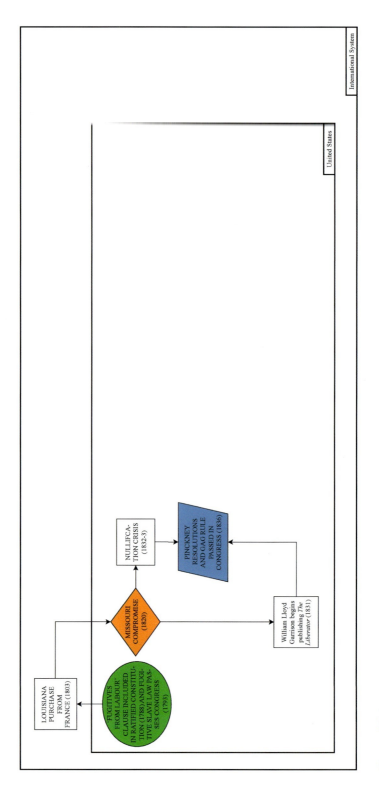

Figure 10.1c

MULTILEVEL EXPLANATIONS

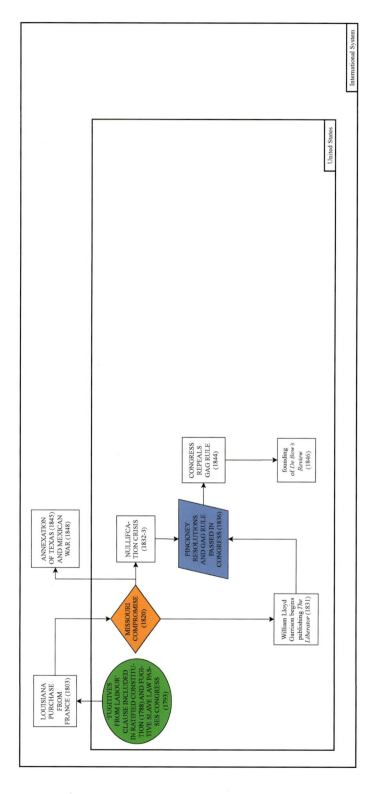

Figure 10.1d

CONFLICT, CRISIS, AND WAR IN WORLD POLITICS

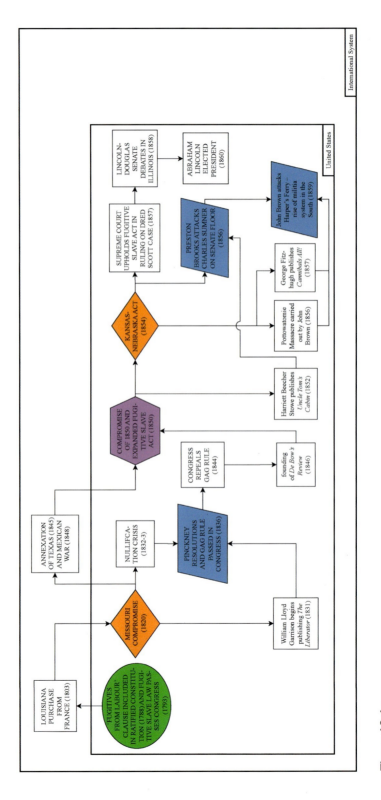

Figure 10.1e

MULTILEVEL EXPLANATIONS

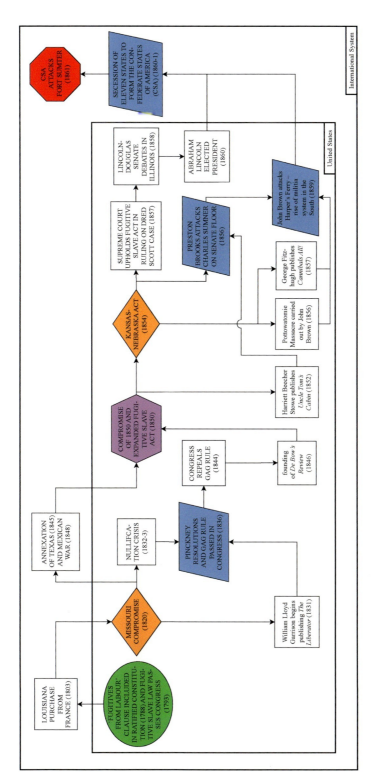

Figure 10.1f

Figure 10.1b shows a connection from the macro level of the system into the environment: "'FUGITIVES FROM LABOUR' CLAUSE INCLUDED IN RATIFIED CONSTITUTION (1788) AND FUGITIVE SLAVE LAW PASSES CONGRESS (1793)" → "LOUISIANA PURCHASE FROM FRANCE (1803)". Given the incoherence embedded in the system via slavery, the acquisition of a vast territory from France created the potential for new conflicts to emerge over how that land would be used. The pathway reenters the macro level of the system with "LOUISIANA PURCHASE FROM FRANCE (1803)" → "MISSOURI COMPROMISE (1820)". As a point of divergence, the latter appears as an orange diamond. The contents of the Missouri Compromise pointed toward the rising power of abolitionism and steps taken to contain the strife inherent in territorial expansion.

Pathways diverge in Figure 10.1c: "MISSOURI COMPROMISE (1820)" → "NULLIFICATION CRISIS (1832–3)"; "William Lloyd Garrison begins publishing *The Liberator* (1831)". The Compromise of 1820 satisfied opinion on neither side of the slavery issue. South Carolina, in the Nullification Crisis, came out into the open in supporting the rights of states over the authority of the national government, with the issue of slavery barely in the background at that point. Meanwhile, opposition to slavery intensified in the North, with *The Liberator* both signaling that shift and encouraging direct action against the peculiar institution.

Pathways come back together at the macro level in Figure 10.1c with "NULLIFICATION CRISIS (1832–3)"; "William Lloyd Garrison begins publishing *The Liberator* (1831)" → "PINCKNEY RESOLUTIONS AND GAG RULE PASSED IN CONGRESS (1836)". As a point of convergence, the latter appears as a blue parallelogram. In an attempt to manage rising conflict over slavery in both the federal system and society, Southern representatives shut down debate over the subject in Congress.

Events move forward in Figure 10.1d at the macro level with "PINCKNEY RESOLUTIONS AND GAG RULE PASSED IN CONGRESS (1836)" → "CONGRESS REPEALS GAG RULE (1844)". The reversal on the Gag Rule reflected a shift toward the North in the Congressional balance of power that permitted and even encouraged open criticism of slavery as an institution. This route shifts to the micro level with "CONGRESS REPEALS GAG RULE (1844)" → "founding of *De Bow's Review* (1846)". With debate over slavery legalized in at least one House of Congress, advocates of slavery attempted to defend it at the level of society. A market emerged for publications such as *De Bow's Review*.

Figure 10.1d also shows movement into the environment with "MISSOURI COMPROMISE (1820)" → "ANNEXATION OF TEXAS (1845) AND MEXICAN WAR (1848)". The Missouri Compromise had anticipated territorial expansion of the prosperous and dynamic, but still slaveholding, country as it moved forward in the 19th century. It remained to be seen whether the somewhat rickety "house" that Congress constructed in 1820 could remain standing in the face of rapidly accumulating new lands and forthcoming quarrels over them.

Figure 10.1e sees pathways coming together at the macro level: "ANNEXATION OF TEXAS (1845) AND MEXICAN WAR (1848)"; "founding of *De Bow's Review* (1846)" → "COMPROMISE OF 1850 AND EXPANDED FUGITIVE SLAVE ACT (1850)". As a node, the latter appears as a purple hexagon. New territories and tensions over slavery created pressure in the federal system, with the Compromise of 1850 as a complicated attempt to once again keep everyone in the figurative "house". Most notable among the legislative pieces from that time is expansion of the Fugitive Slave Act, which met with opposite reactions in the South and North.

Routes continue on in Figure 10.1e at the macro and micro levels with "COMPROMISE OF 1850 AND EXPANDED FUGITIVE SLAVE ACT (1850)" → "KANSAS–NEBRASKA ACT (1854)"; "Harriett Beecher Stowe publishes *Uncle Tom's Cabin* (1852)". As a point of divergence, the first component after the arrow appears as an orange diamond. Based on events so far, it should come as no surprise that efforts toward compromise succeeded in neither government nor society. The attempt to preserve a balance between free and slave states with the Kansas–Nebraska Act simply opened a new battlefront. Meanwhile, the publication of *Uncle Tom's Cabin* served as a stunning moral indictment of slavery, to which even more Northerners demanded a response.

Movement at the macro levels appears in Figure 10.1e with "KANSAS–NEBRASKA ACT (1854)" → "SUPREME COURT UPHOLDS FUGITIVE SLAVE ACT IN RULING ON DRED SCOTT CASE (1857)"; "PRESTON BROOKS ATTACKS CHARLES SUMNER ON SENATE FLOOR (1856)". As a point of convergence, the latter component after the arrow appears as a blue parallelogram. After the Kansas–Nebraska Act, conflict over slavery further intensified. Southerners responded angrily with further legislation and even a symbolic beating of abolitionism carried out in the halls of Congress itself.

Routes in Figure 10.1e also move from the macro to the micro levels with "KANSAS–NEBRASKA ACT (1854)" → "Pottowatomie Massacre carried out by John Brown (1856)"; "George Fitzhugh publishes *Cannibals All!* (1857)". With the Kansas–Nebraska Act able to satisfy neither side in the slavery debate, actions in society became even more intense. The physical violence of John Brown and intellectual extremism of Fitzhugh are two sides of the same coin.

Figure 10.1e depicts further movement from the micro to the macro level: "Harriett Beecher Stowe publishes *Uncle Tom's Cabin* (1852)" → "PRESTON BROOKS ATTACKS CHARLES SUMNER ON SENATE FLOOR (1856)". Publication of *Uncle Tom's Cabin*, which intensified the emotions undergirding the anti-slavery movement, stands out as the figurative "exclamation point" among statements that enraged many Southerners. The beating of Sumner by Brooks expressed mounting anger toward abolitionists in a violent manner that resulted from the triumph of emotion over reason.

Pathways come together in Figure 10.1e with "PRESTON BROOKS ATTACKS CHARLES SUMNER ON SENATE FLOOR (1856)"; "Pottowatomie Massacre carried out by John Brown (1856)"; "George Fitzhugh publishes *Cannibals All!* (1857)" → "John Brown attacks Harper's Ferry – rise of militia system in the South (1859)". The component after the arrow, a point of convergence, takes the form of a blue parallelogram. The list of confrontational events before the arrow resulted in the doomed action from Brown that appears after it. Northern interest in a compromise over slavery virtually disappeared after the hanging of Brown. On the other side, Southerners increased their capacity for protection against potentially more effective efforts to free the slaves in the future.

Further connections appear at the macro level of Figure 10.1e: "SUPREME COURT UPHOLDS FUGITIVE SLAVE ACT IN RULING ON DRED SCOTT CASE (1857)" →

"LINCOLN/DOUGLAS SENATE DEBATES IN ILLINOIS (1858)". The Dred Scott case, which reinforced the institution of slavery, reverberated into the electoral system. With the high-profile Douglas as the incumbent Senator, and the articulate Lincoln as the challenger, their debates over slavery took on national prominence. Figure 10.1e shows the macro pathway moving further along with "LINCOLN/DOUGLAS SENATE DEBATES IN ILLINOIS (1858)" → "ABRAHAM LINCOLN ELECTED PRESIDENT (1860)". Abraham Lincoln became a viable candidate for president as a result of his performance in the Senate debates two years earlier. His views, seen as moderate along the political spectrum of 1860, went just far enough to unite anti-slavery opinion and win the presidency.

Several routes come together at the macro level of the system in Figure 10.1f: "ABRAHAM LINCOLN ELECTED PRESIDENT (1860)"; "John Brown attacks Harper's Ferry – rise of militia system in the South (1859)" → "SECESSION OF ELEVEN STATES TO FORM THE CONFEDERATE STATES OF AMERICA (CSA) (1860–1)". The latter, as a convergent component, appears as a blue parallelogram. Slavery had become so fundamental to Southern identity that the states with that institution left the Union in spite of very little evidence about how Lincoln would govern.[9] The sense of threat that had escalated dramatically after the Brown raid caused the South to see government action to abolish slavery as inevitable, so secession seemed like the only option left on the table.

Connections conclude in Figure 10.1f with "SECESSION OF ELEVEN STATES TO FORM THE CONFEDERATE STATES OF AMERICA (CSA) (1860–1)" → "CSA ATTACKS FORT SUMTER (1861)". As a terminal component, the latter appears as a red octagon. Since Lincoln already stated that he would not respect secession, the CSA attacked in order to obtain what it regarded as rightful control over property within its newfound borders.

LESSONS FOR TODAY

While not intended to be representative of cases in general, assessment of cause and effect for the Civil War still can be informative. The Civil War is arguably the most heavily studied case of its kind and thus holds special interest with regard to the logic of discovery. The theoretical points that follow are raised for further consideration. Some of the items listed below already have been introduced in other contexts within previous chapters.

First, among the subfigures 10.1a–f, note the increasing density of interaction as measured in the number of components introduced for each decade (i.e., prior to the very short period of 1860–1): a (1), b (2), c (3), d (3), e (9), f (3). Essential events go from 1 to 9 in number across the decades leading up to the Civil War. A point to bear in mind, with regard to anticipating the onset of a civil war in general, is the likelihood of increased activity across the board. Both instances of conflict, and management of it, may gather momentum in a process that culminates in civil war.

---

[9] Several border states, within which slavery persisted, did not leave the Union. An answer to the question of why some slaveholding states did not join the CSA is beyond the scope of this exposition.

Second, consider the role of the endowment effect, which focuses on how people become more attached to something once they have obtained it (Samuelson and Zeckhauser 1988). Owners of slaves in antebellum America, if abolitionists succeeded, would be required to give up valuable property. With the passing of time, attachment to the institution of slavery built up in the South – a sense, and even a right, of possession. In other circumstances, either physical property or status possessed by one group might be challenged by another and that could seem quite threatening. The endowment effect could make it more difficult over time for those in a favored position to agree to concessions, which in turn would increase the likelihood of escalation to civil war.

Third, the concepts of Type I and II cognition would seem relevant once again, as per discussion of leadership in Chapter 7 (Rathbun 2019; see also Kahneman 2011). As described by Rathbun (2019), Type I and II cognition, respectively, are (I) rapid and emotional and (II) deliberate and analytical. It is striking how events leading up to the Civil War reveal a dramatic shift from Type II to I. Events such as the publication of *Uncle Tom's Cabin* and the beating of Sumner by Brooks are just two corresponding examples from the escalating confrontations of the 1850s that culminated in the attack on Fort Sumter.

While not exhaustive, the preceding ideas may have much wider application than beyond the case at hand with regard to accounting for the causes of civil war. Introduction of these points about the cause of one civil war is intended to encourage creative thinking about why such destructive events happen in general. This observation invites comparison with aggregate findings about civil war from Chapter 9.

THE AMERICAN CIVIL WAR AND RESULTS FROM AGGREGATE DATA ANALYSIS

How does the Civil War compare with cases of such strife in general? A review of Table 9.2 from Chapter 9 suggests that six state level, and two society level, characteristics can be connected with events from the Civil War. Based on Table 10.2, what follows is intended more as illustration than definitive analysis. The review of characteristics and events should stimulate debate about possible errors of omission and commission in placing the events of the Civil War in the context of more general aspects of explanation identified in the preceding chapter.[10]

Anocracy and regime instability can be identified with the following events: Nullification Crisis; Missouri Compromise; Pinckney Resolutions and Gag Rule passed in Congress; Congress repeals Gag rule; Compromise of 1850 and expanded Fugitive Slave Act; Kansas–Nebraska Act; Lincoln–Douglas Senate debates in Illinois; Abraham Lincoln elected president. The battle over slavery at the state level is a clear reflection of anocracy – an incompletely formed democracy that excluded many people, most notably slaves – and serves as the embodiment of regime instability.

---

[10] It is understood that some events from the Civil War might be just as easily connected with another characteristic instead. The enumeration below, as noted already, is intended as a starting point for further discussion.

Table 10.2 The Civil War and results from aggregate data analysis

Level of analysis	Characteristics	Events from Civil War
State	Anocracy; regime instability	Missouri Compromise; Pinckney Resolutions and Gag Rule passed in Congress, Congress repeals Gag Rule; Compromise of 1850 and expanded Fugitive Slave Act; Kansas–Nebraska Act; Lincoln-Douglas Senate debates in Illinois; Abraham Lincoln elected president
	Larger population	Louisiana Purchase from France; Annexation of Texas and Mexican War
	Previous conflict	Nullification Crisis; Preston Brooks attacks Charles Sumner on Senate floor; Pottowatomie Massacre carried out by John Brown; John Brown attacks Harper's Ferry – rise of militia system in the South
	Absence of distinct civil war in previous year	None
	Lack of rule of law and order (e.g., lower strength and impartiality of legal system)	Fugitive from Labour Clause in ratified Constitution and Fugitive Slave Law Passed; William Lloyd Garrison begins publishing *The Liberator*; Supreme Court upholds Fugitive Slave Act ruling on Dred Scott case; Secession of eleven states to form the Confederate States of America (CSA); CSA attacks Fort Sumter
	Discrimination against societal groups	Fugitive from Labour Clause in ratified Constitution and Fugitive Slave Law Passed; Founding of *De Bow's Review*; Harriett Beecher Stowe publishes *Uncle Tom's Cabin*; George Fitzhugh publishes *Cannibals All!*
Society	Absence of mass education	Founding of *De Bow's Review*; George Fitzhugh publishes *Cannibals All!*
	Poverty	Fugitive from Labour Clause in ratified Constitution and Fugitive Slave Law passed

Another characteristic associated with civil war in general is size of population. Multiple events significantly increased the population of the US in the years leading up to the Civil War: Louisiana Purchase from France; Annexation of Texas and Mexican War. These developments played an aggravating role with regard to the issue of slavery in particular – would that institution be permitted to spread beyond its current boundaries? Emotions ran very high in responding to that question.

Previous conflict also is connected to civil war. One event at the state level is relevant here: Preston Brooks attacks Charles Sumner on Senate floor. Note also the intense conflict underway in society as well: Pottowatomie Massacre carried out by John Brown; John Brown attacks Harper's Ferry – rise of militia system in the South. These acts of violence took place, it is worth noting, relatively close to the outbreak of the Civil War. Note, however, the *absence* of such conflict in the year preceding the Civil War's outbreak – a trait also in line with aggregate findings.

Lack of rule of law and order comes out in any number of events at the state level: Fugitive from Labour Clause in ratified Constitution and Fugitive Slave Law Passed; Supreme Court upholds Fugitive Slave Act ruling on Dred Scott case; Secession of eleven states to form the Confederate States of America (CSA); CSA attacks Fort Sumter. The former two items reveal the erosion of a national consensus on law and order, while the latter two constitute the final stages of its breakdown.

Discrimination against societal groups (state level), along with Absence of mass education and Poverty (society level), are characteristics that can be linked to several events: William Lloyd Garrison begins publishing *The Liberator* (1831), Founding of *De Bow's Review* (1846), Harriett Beecher Stowe publishes *Uncle Tom's Cabin* (1856), and George Fitzhugh publishes *Cannibals All!* (1857). These publications all focused on the intense discrimination, in the form of slavery, carried out against Blacks. In a state without mass education, these publications mattered significantly in intensifying elite opinion on both sides of the issue.

Many of the characteristics listed in Table 10.2 do not appear in the preceding list. This should not be seen as a refutation of aggregate data findings about the onset of civil war. Instead, it is affirmation that multiple pathways can be followed in reaching civil war as an outcome. The US case features some aspects more than others.

SUMMING UP AND MOVING FORWARD

With an emphasis on development of multilevel explanations, this chapter has focused on one of the most famous events in world history – the American Civil War. To manage the complexity of an event such as the Civil War, the framework from Kurki (2002, 2008) on cause and effect has been introduced. This scheme of organization includes both intrinsic and extrinsic elements of causation – respectively inherent properties and actions. When applied to the Civil War in tandem with levels of analysis, the framework performs effectively. All four types of cause – material and formal (i.e., intrinsic) and efficient and final (i.e., extrinsic) – can be found along the pathway to the Civil War. In addition, these causes span the standard levels of analysis – international system, state, and individual – and therefore constitute a multilevel explanation. The accomplishments of this chapter lead naturally into those that follow. Chapter 11 will focus on management of conflict by states, while Chapter 12 will do the same thing for transnational and non-governmental organizations.

> **CONSIDER THIS**
>
> The case of the American Civil War illustrates some ways in which causal explanations at multiple levels of analysis link together to provide a fuller, more complete understanding of how and why conflict, crisis, and war occur. Considering the review of major explanations of conflict, crisis, and war at the system, state, and individual levels (chapters 5–7):
>
> *Can you develop one or more multilevel linkages that connect key arguments or factors across levels to provide what you believe to be more complete explanations than any one at a particular level?*

PART III
COPING WITH THE PROBLEM

11
Taking matters into their own hands: state-based approaches to managing conflict, crisis, and war

PROLOGUE

As the threat of Russian invasion increased in 2021 and 2022, the US responded with multiple efforts, first to prevent the action, and then to counter it. President Joe Biden, Secretary of State Antony Blinken, and Defense Secretary Lloyd Austin reached out repeatedly to their counterparts in Europe in a diplomatic campaign to gain support and agreement among North Atlantic Treaty Organization (NATO) members and the European Union (EU) to resist Russian aggression and provide economic and military aid to Ukraine to strengthen its ability to fight back. US and other Western diplomats also engaged in efforts to persuade Russian President Vladimir Putin to refrain from military action, including threatening economic sanctions to punish Russia. After these efforts failed and Russia began its invasion in February 2022, the US led NATO and the EU to provide extensive military aid, training, and intelligence to Ukraine, which proved essential to its ability to withstand the initial wave of the Russian invasion, and then to counterattack late in 2022 to reverse most of those initial gains.

This episode illustrates a range of state-based efforts to managing conflict, crisis, and war. In the run-up to the 2022 invasion and after, states engaged in diplomacy, efforts to build a coalition of support and rely on an alliance to prevent and resist, the threat and application of sanctions, the use of military aid and force, and application of a broad package of sanctions against Russia. Russia and Ukraine used their military forces, one to invade and achieve its expansionist, predatory goals, and the other to defend itself against attack. A broad array of countries joined together to support Ukraine in its efforts to defend itself. Many additional actions involved other players and avenues, including international organizations and non-governmental organizations, but the efforts of states were front and center throughout.

OVERVIEW

In this chapter, we consider those actions states take to address conflict, crisis, and war. As we have established in the early chapters, the interests and objectives of states and other players are often different, leading to conflict and, sometimes, to crisis and war. In the formally anarchic structure of the international system, the absence of authoritative central institutions in world politics often makes coordination and cooperation difficult, prompting fear from the players that their interests will not be protected unless they take action themselves. For states, this self-help incentive triggers a range of strategies and approaches to managing conflict, crisis, and war. States carry out diplomatic relations and engage in bargaining and negotiation. Virtually every state seeks to build military power and many actively use it to resolve conflict. They frequently turn to alliances to expand their power and protect themselves from threats and enemies. States also try to manage and control the acquisition and use of military power, engaging in a variety of efforts to control the accumulation, spread, and use of military might.

As we shall see, these efforts may or may not be effective. A wide variety of factors contribute to these varied outcomes, but one central aspect warrants our attention at the outset – the security dilemma. Led by the seminal work by Butterfield (1951), Herz (1951), and Jervis (1976, esp. ch. 3; 1978), the challenge of the security dilemma has long been a linchpin in studies of conflict and cooperation in world politics. As Herz (1951: 157), who coined the term, wrote:

> Groups and individuals [in the anarchic international system] … must be … concerned about their security from being attacked, subjected, dominated, or annihilated by other groups and individuals. Striving to attain security from such attacks, they are driven to acquire more and more power in order to escape the effects of the power of others. This, in turn, renders the others more insecure and compels them to prepare for the worst. Because no state can ever feel entirely secure in such a world of competing units, power competition ensues, and the vicious circle of security and power accumulation is on.

Thus, as states seek to manage conflict, crisis, and war – to provide for their own security, to protect their interests, and to pursue their objectives in the anarchic arena of world politics – their efforts often generate reactions from others that result in greater insecurity or threats to interests/objectives.

According to Robert Jervis (1978), six key elements – which together encompass both material and ideational aspects – underlie the security dilemma: (1) its foundation in the anarchic structure of international politics; (2) the role of states' uncertainty and fears about each other's present and future intentions; (3) its unintentional outcome of defensive actions; (4) its result in the decrease of one's own security as an unintended and self-defeating outcome; (5) its self-reinforcing, spiral dynamic; and (6) its potential for producing unintended and tragic results – war – while not being the case of all war. The security dilemma is thus a paradoxical situation in which the actions of a state to be secure often end up creating even greater insecurities.

Stemming from the anarchic structure of world politics – the absence of a central coercive authority creates self-help incentives for states, who turn to diplomacy, economic coercion, the acquisition of military power, alliances, the use of force, and other instruments to protect themselves from real and potential threats and to pursue their perceived interests in the face of real and potential conflicts. Unfortunately, such actions may threaten others, who respond accordingly, so engaging in them may result in producing action-reaction cycles leading to more conflict, crises, and even war. Each state may take actions it sees as defensive and non-threatening, but such actions often alarm others and could cause exactly what each is trying to avoid. These observations call back to the very unsafe appearance of the Ladder of Escalation in Figure 2.2 – so many ways to fall off – and very challenging to climb down safely.

With this context as a key starting point, Chapter 11 unfolds in an additional ten sections. Following this introductory section, we summarize the use of diplomatic tools to prevent, mitigate, and resolve conflict, crisis, and war in sections 2–3, and turn to the use of economic coercion in sections 4–5. Section 6 discusses defense, deterrence, and alliances. Sections 7–8 then turn to uses of force short of war to resolve conflict. Sections 9–10 consider arms control and disarmament. Section 11, the final one, offers summary insights and leads into Chapter 12. For each topic, we provide description and context of the state-based approach in question, and then briefly review what research reveals about their uses, effects, and consequences for conflict, crisis, and war. As will become apparent, the sections appear in ascending order of intensity with regard to the techniques under review.

DIPLOMACY AND NEGOTIATION: DEFINITION AND CONTEXT

States (and others) regularly resort to diplomacy to manage conflict, crisis, and war. The appeal of conflict resolution through communication, bargaining, and negotiation is intuitive: to paraphrase Winston Churchill, "jawing" is better than fighting. For centuries, states have relied on diplomats and emissaries to communicate and engage in efforts to manage conflict and crises and to prepare for, avoid, and end wars.[1] Diplomacy generally involves bargaining (a term usually meaning more competitive and conflictual diplomacy) and/or negotiation (a term usually meaning more collaborative problem-solving) over some issue of conflict in pursuit of common interests. In the modern state system, every country relies on diplomats who serve abroad in their foreign affairs ministries, in embassies in the capital cities of foreign countries, in consulates in major cities of foreign countries, in other missions abroad, and in international organizations (IOs) such as the United Nations who represent and negotiate on behalf of their country or employer. Such individuals may include the highest-ranking officials of a country (the head of state or of government) and foreign ministers, ambassadors, envoys, and other lower-ranking personnel. Now, non-governmental organizations and private individuals also engage in diplomacy.

For diplomats on each side of a dispute, the key to success is to find a solution to which both sides can agree. As Fisher and Ury (1991) wrote decades ago, the other side should have something to say "yes" to – a benefit that appears desirable and enables them to avoid appearing as if they just gave in to demands. In effect, diplomats try to fashion proposals that encourage their counterparts to see that they have interests in and benefits from their adoption.

---

[1] Broad historical examinations of diplomacy, negotiations, and its nature and evolution include Berridge (2015), Hamilton and Langhorne (2011), Henriksen (1986), Magalhães (1988), Sending, Pouliot, and Neumann (2015), Kremenyuk (2002), Plantey (2007), Rathbun (2014), and Starkey, Boyer, and Wilkenfeld (2005).

Imagine a hypothetical conflict between two states, as depicted in Figure 11.1. As the figure suggests, each state has its maximum demand, or ideal preference for an outcome, and diplomacy is involved in communicating those preferences. Each state also has its bottom line, or resistance point, which is the minimum it will accept at the outset of the diplomatic interaction. Part of diplomacy is trying to learn what that resistance point for the other side is, while protecting your own. Between the two resistance points is a settlement gap: the distance between the minimum demands of each side. How far apart the two sides are in this gap greatly affects the possibility of a successful diplomatic resolution to the conflict.

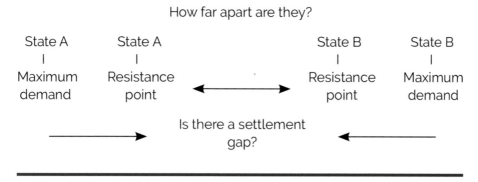

Figure 11.1   The structure of negotiation (adapted from Lauren et al. 2007)

> **FOR EXAMPLE: ARE SOME "SETTLEMENT GAPS" UNBRIDGEABLE?**
>
> At this time of writing, Israel appears to be in the late stages of prosecuting its war against Hamas. The descent of the Israel-Palestine protracted conflict into intense violence once again invites speculation about a settlement gap. Put simply, are there conflicts where one does not exist, and is Palestine versus Israel the prime example? Any solution with the potential to last would seem to have obvious requirements, such as two independent states, guarantees from leading powers who are trusted by each side respectively, and so on. Yet a settlement involving such components remains elusive. And efforts from third parties such as the United States appear to be of limited impact as well. *Why?*

Finding ways to close the settlement gap and cooperate over common interests and resolve issues of conflict is the art of diplomacy. Obviously, persuasion might be involved, as might threats. Either or both sides might introduce a wide variety of "carrots" (rewards such as foreign aid) and "sticks" (punishments such as sanctions or threats of force) to stress common interests and/or potential costs of failing to resolve the matter. Diplomats might also try to use a linkage strategy to connect other issues to the resolution of the current one. For example, one state might agree to another state's preference on trade if the second state moves closer to the first on human rights. Diplomacy is often bilateral, between the parties to a dispute, but increasingly, multilateral diplomacy is common (e.g., Muldoon and Fagot Aviel 2020).

The parties to this conflict might even invite in a third party or parties to try to help them reach agreement. An early and notable example is from 1906 when US President Theodore

Table 11.1 Types of third-party diplomacy

Approach	Behavior	Example
Good offices	A third party provides a place for the two sides to negotiate	Norway and the 1993 Oslo Accords
Mediation	A third party organizes the talks and proposes possible options to settle the dispute, but no settlement is forced on the participants by the third party	US President Jimmy Carter and the 1978 Camp David Accords
Arbitration	The participants present information and views and agree in advance to accept an option developed by and determined by the third party	The UN-sponsored 1996–1999 Brčko arbitration, in Bosnia-Herzegovina
Adjudication	In a court-like proceeding, the participants present their positions to the third party, who acts like a judge and decides which of the positions is "correct". The participants agree in advance to abide by the third party's decision.	The International Court of Justice in the 1984 Nicaragua v. United States of America on Military and Paramilitary Activities in and against Nicaragua

Roosevelt won the Nobel Peace Prize for mediating the 1905 war between Russia and Japan. In general, there are four main types of such third-party diplomacy: good offices, mediation, arbitration, and adjudication, as shown in Table 11.1. Progressing from good offices to adjudication, the parties to the dispute relinquish more and more control over the outcome. Moreover, the nature of the third party is of special importance, ranging from strict neutrality to the conflict to one having important interests at stake.

DIPLOMACY AND NEGOTIATION: USES, EFFECTS, AND CONSEQUENCES

Diplomacy and negotiation are central approaches to international relations and conflict resolution, employed to sustain cooperation, manage conflict, control crises, and avoid or end war. According to one scholar, they are the "engine room" of international relations (Sharp 1999: 34). A sprawling literature has explored diplomacy's development over time, its role in a wide variety of international issues, its practices and practitioners, and its outcomes.[2] What do empirical studies tell us about its outcomes, especially with respect to conflict, crisis, and war?

According to a review by Butler and Boyer (2017), the outcomes of bargaining and negotiation are highly dependent on the characteristics of, and variation in, at least four key factors:

1. The Contextual Environment. As Butler and Boyer (2017: 2–4) summarize, variation in the international context over time (including historical matters, the distribution of power, and globalization and its many features and effects) plays a key role in both the nature and results of diplomacy. Additionally, crises are critical contextual or situational factors as well, and a large body of literature has examined crisis bargaining and negotiation (e.g., Snyder and Diesing 1977; Beardsley et al. 2006; Wilkenfeld et al. 2005). Finally, as Butler and Boyer (2017: 8) note, "cultural factors associated with national identity play a major role as a result of their impact on communication styles, which in turn have a significant effect on the exchange of information and, by extension, the behavior of negotiators and mediators".
2. Key Actors. The nature and outcomes of bargaining and negotiation depend substantially on the participants. Long the province of states, differences in role, power, and position are key factors (Butler and Boyer 2017: 4–5). However, the dramatic expansion of diplomacy to include IOs, regional organizations, non-governmental organizations, substate actors, and even private (multinational) corporations and individuals has significant consequences for the conduct and consequences as well (Butler and Boyer 2017: 5–6).
3. Issues and Stakes. Both the character and the number of issues, and the stakes they involve (both "real" and perceived, at home and abroad), affect negotiation and bargaining processes and outcomes. In addition to the effects of multiple issues (which provide opportunities for linkage strategies but also increase the complexity of the bargaining, and the number of actors involved, which also adds layers of complexity in the form of stakes, preferences, and processes), according to Butler and Boyer (2017: 8–9), scholarly research shows that three additional factors are critical. These factors are: (a) "the extent to which a negotiator's position on one or more issues is ideological in nature"; (b) "the degree to which negotiators desire comprehensive or partial 'solutions'"; and (c) "the degree to which proposed 'solutions' to the issue(s) at hand are salient, and register amongst all parties in order to foster a shared bargaining space crucial to a successful negotiated resolution".
4. Processes and Strategies. Finally, Butler and Boyer (2017: 11–14) suggest that a host of variables involving process, timing (e.g., elapsed time, iterations, and time pressures), signaling, and competitive versus collaborative approaches also affect the outcomes of bargaining and negotiation.

Like the literature on diplomacy, an extensive body of scholarship has examined the processes of bargaining and negotiation and their outcomes, far too broad for us to review in any detail

---

[2] For entry points into this broad literature, see Berridge (2015), Hamilton and Langhorne (2011), Henriksen (1986), Magalhães (1988), Sending, Pouliot and Neumann (2015), Kremenyuk (2002), Plantey (2007), Rathbun (2014), Starkey, Boyer and Wilkenfeld (2005), and the many works by Neumann on the topic (e.g., Neumann 2005, 2012, 2013, 2020; Neumann and Halvard 2013).

in this chapter.[3] However, a few key observations highly relevant to conflict, crisis, and war warrant at least some brief attention. Perhaps a good starting point is Trager's (2016: 221) observation that "processes of negotiation between state representatives provide information about what issues states are willing to fight for and what issues they consider less important". Building on Schelling (1960, 1966) and Jervis (1970, 1976), an extensive literature on credibility, signaling, audience costs, and their nature and consequences in diplomacy (e.g., Fearon 1994a, 1994b, 1995; Powell 1988, 2002; Sartori 2002; Tomz 2007) has developed and identified the importance of patience, reputation, and the like (see Trager 2016: 208–217 for a summary). As Schelling (1960) stressed, both threats and promises/assurances are part of this signaling process and may be more or less effective depending on how costly or credible they are.

Other scholarship explores the complications arising from the individual-level aspects of bargaining and negotiation processes. It may be true, as some scholars conclude, that democracies are more able to generate costly signals due to the audience costs associated with democratic accountability, but the cultural, cognitive, and affective elements of human behavior and interaction sometimes make diplomatic threats counterproductive, escalating conflict and increasing the chances for war (e.g., Jervis 1976; Stein 1991; Lebow and Stein 1989; Odell and Tingley 2013: 151–152) or generating understanding and empathy (e.g., Holmes and Yarhi-Milo 2017). As Trager (2016: 219) summarizes

> Threats may provoke for many reasons, including that they confirm negative images about the threatening state that already exist in the target state. But the form of a demand may matter as well in that it influences the affective response. Framings that are humiliating or appear to deny 'voice' to threatened states, for instance, may make it harder for threatened states to back down.

The insights of prospect theory, which we summarized in Chapter 7, are also relevant on this point, and leader responses may be riskier (with respect to conflict) in some situations than in others.

The role of third-party diplomacy is also the subject of substantial analysis, with complicated results (see Trager 2016 and Kydd 2010 for summaries): biased mediators may be more effective in some cases (e.g., Kydd 2003), unbiased mediators appear more effective in others (e.g., Favretto 2009; Smith and Stam 2003; Kydd 2006), and some argue that they are mostly ineffective (Beardsley 2011). In some situations (e.g., civil war/ethnic conflict), their involvement may even exacerbate the violence (e.g., Kuperman 2008; Kydd and Straus 2013). Related to this, a considerable body of work stresses the importance of "ripeness" in the successful outcome of third-party mediation (see Hancock 2001). This insight depends on the idea that the settlement of violent conflicts through diplomacy, especially third-party diplomacy, is more likely to succeed at some times than at others. Central to the idea is the importance of a "hurting stalemate" in which costs are high to both sides but a path to victory is not perceived as possible for either. Developed in large part through the work of Zartman (1995, 2000;

---

[3] For reviews, see Boyer and Butler (2017), Butler and Boyer (2017); Odell and Tingley (2013), Trager (2016); and Weiner and Sharp (2017).

Zartman and Touval 2007), Haass (1990), Bercovitch (1996), and Stedman (1991), among others, some studies of post-Cold War conflict resolution have offered empirical support for the argument (e.g., Butler and Boyer 2017: 14).

> **IN FOCUS: PRINCIPLES FOR EFFECTIVE MEDIATION**
>
> According to the UN guide for effective mediation (United Nations 2012), eight fundamentals are at the core of effective mediation: Preparedness; Consent (of the parties); Impartiality; Inclusivity; National ownership; Adherence to international law and normative frameworks; Coherence, coordination and complementarity of the mediation effort; and Quality peace agreements.
>
> *Based on what we know from scholarly research, how useful is this guidance?*

ECONOMIC COERCION: DEFINITION AND CONTEXT

To manage conflict, crisis, and war, states also may turn to economic coercion, a step beyond more diplomatic means, but short of force. An economic sanction is a policy that reduces the economic exchange between two states for a political goal. Part of economic statecraft (e.g., Baldwin 1985), as Cilizoglu and Early (2021: 2) summarize, "economic sanctions entail the threat or use of governmental policies designed to adversely affect the economic welfare of their targets in order to weaken them, stigmatize them, punish them, or compel a change in their behavior". Economic statecraft and the use of sanctions have a long history, appearing in the writings of individuals such as Sun Tzu, Plato, Aristotle, and Alexander Hamilton, and in the practices of countries for centuries.

> **FOR EXAMPLE: CIVIL WAR BLOCKADES**
>
> During the American Civil War, an incident at sea had the potential to bring Great Britain into the fight on the side of the Confederacy. On November 8, 1961, at an early stage of the war, the USS *San Jacinto* intercepted *The Trent*, a British mail ship. The Union ship took two Confederate envoys from *The Trent* into custody yet released them very quickly after intense British protest. On the one hand, the Union hoped to use its naval superiority to blockade the Confederacy and wreak havoc on its economy and therefore also war-fighting capacity. On the other hand, as President Lincoln put it, "One war at a time" showed a pragmatic sense about the limits of power. The Union's economic statecraft in the form of a blockade had some effectiveness, but it had to be implemented in a manner that would not extend the conflict outward and stimulate hostile involvement of a great power with particularly formidable capabilities at sea.

In general, a state can impose an economic sanction on another state in four basic ways, which can also be combined into more comprehensive approaches.

1. Import and Export Sanctions. The most common type of sanction is a trade sanction that cuts the exchange of goods between the two countries. In trade sanctions, the sanctioning state (referred to as the sender) reduces or cuts off completely either (a) goods and services coming from the sanctioned country (referred to as the target) – these are import sanctions (boycotts) – or (b) goods and services being sold to the sanctioned country – export sanctions (embargoes). Sixty-nine percent of all sanctions include import or export restrictions (Hufbauer et al. 2009). Import sanctions hurt businesses in the target country by not allowing them to sell their goods in the sender country. Export sanctions tend to cause production problems in the target country because of restricted parts and supplies and may cause prices to rise there because there are fewer products being sold.
2. Aid Sanctions. Assuming it provides such assistance, the sanctioning state can reduce or eliminate foreign aid to a target. For example, in 2017 the US threatened to suspend aid to Pakistan and actually withheld military aid to Egypt. Other examples include the 1974 law (the Jackson–Vanik Amendment) that required the US State Department to certify that all countries receiving any type of aid not engage in human rights violations, and the 1976 US law requiring that all countries receiving aid not be involved in supporting terrorist groups.
3. Financial Sanctions. Financial sanctions freeze the movement of assets (e.g., money in bank accounts) of government officials, business elites, or the government of the target country. These are increasingly common in the globalized and highly interconnected international economy of today and are often referred to as "smart sanctions" because they seek to punish individuals responsible for a regime's behavior, rather than the state's population as a whole. For example, when Iranian students stormed the US Embassy and took hostages in 1979, President Carter froze all Iranian bank accounts in the United States, denying the Iranian government access to about $12 billion in assets. In 2011, the Arab League imposed financial sanctions against Syria, for the Assad regime's violent crackdown against Arab Spring dissenters. Following the 2022 Russian invasion of Ukraine, the US and EU froze the assets of over 1,900 individuals and entities in Russia, including President Vladimir Putin, his closest supporters, many Russian oligarchs, and even Putin's rumored mistress, former Olympic gold medalist gymnast Alina Kabaeva (Parker 2022). Such sanctions have since become more difficult to impose in the globalizing world economy because of the proliferation of offshore banks in places such as Bermuda, Antigua, Barbuda, the Cayman Islands, Cyprus, and elsewhere.
4. Third-Party Sanctions. A fourth type of sanction threatens a third country that is doing business with the main target of the sanctions. Third-party sanctions are levied against a third-party state to keep that state from doing business with the primary target of the sanctions. For example, the 1996 Helms–Burton Act in the US directed the United States to sanction other countries doing business with Cuba – the target of the sanctions was Cuba, but countries like Canada, Spain, the UK, or others were punished for their economic ties. Similar efforts were aimed at countries doing business with North Korea in recent years.

Two final observations help complete the context. First, as we noted, these sanctions can be combined into total or comprehensive sanctions that essentially cut off all economic connections with the target. Two examples are the sanctions campaigns against South Africa and Rhodesia (now called Zimbabwe) during the time of their apartheid regimes. In both cases, a white minority ruled the country, and when called on to open the political system to all citizens of the state, both refused. The UN mandated comprehensive sanctions against each country, and slowly almost all other countries began to follow the UN mandate. Second, sanctions can be unilateral – imposed by one country against another – or multilateral – imposed by many countries against the target. Multilateral sanctions may be imposed by like-minded states together, or IOs may call for and coordinate them (more on the role of IOs in Chapter 12).

ECONOMIC COERCION: USES, EFFECTS, AND CONSEQUENCES

Highly appealing – and increasingly so in recent decades – to states as a coercive policy instrument short of the use of force, sanctions have a complicated record in practice (e.g., Cortright and Lopez 1995). According to Rowe's (2018: 1) summary, "sanctions comprise a versatile instrument of statecraft that states use to do many things, including to change the behavior of target regimes; avoid the recourse to force; make force more effective; impose costs for unwanted policies; signal disapproval of others' actions; or build and reinforce norms of acceptable behavior". This complex array of potential goals makes the effectiveness of sanctions somewhat difficult to measure.

States may engage in economic coercion through sanctions for a wide variety of reasons, including ideational goals such as supporting democracy and human rights and symbolic purposes such as sending signals about acceptable behavior. Many of these purposes are directly related to conflict, crisis, and war, however. The senders of sanctions often impose them to weaken the target state's military and economy. The basic idea is that the sanctioning country wants to weaken the target before attacking (or being attacked). Thus, the sanctions have a distinct security objective and are often used as a prelude to war. Sanctions may also be used to destabilize a government, often in hopes of changing the leadership, type of government, or its policies.

Further, states often use sanctions to try to limit the proliferation of nuclear weapons. Canada has taken the lead several times, starting in the 1970s by sanctioning India and Pakistan for proliferation and the EU (known as the European Community at the time) and Japan for a failure to maintain nuclear safeguards. Other states such as Australia and the United States have also used sanctions to stop countries from developing nuclear weapons. The sanctions by the United States and the EU against Iran are a prime example of these efforts. After 2005, the UN authorized sanctions against Iran because Tehran rejected international inspections of its nuclear program. Leading the sanctioning effort, Europe and the United States cut off trade and investment with Iran, moving to lift the sanctions only after Iran agreed to limit and end its nuclear programs in the 2015 accords with the UN's Permanent 5, the EU, and Germany. Since 2018, the US has reimposed, or attempted to reimpose, many of these sanctions against Iran after withdrawing from the 2015 accords.

In this context, how effective are sanctions? As we noted, gauging the effectiveness of this instrument to manage conflict, crisis, and war has challenged scholars and policymakers, in part because of the many purposes to which sanctions may be aimed. For example, if sanctions are symbolic statements meant to provide signals, then assessing their "impact" is one thing (e.g., Drury 2001), but if they are meant to change or compel behavior, then compliance with the demand is the essence of effectiveness. Most empirical assessments of the effectiveness of sanctions focus on their success in bringing about desired changes in target behavior. Unfortunately, even the most positive of these empirical analyses indicate that sanctions work less than 40% of the time, and perhaps as little as 5% (e.g., Hufbauer et al. 2009; Elliott 2009; Pape 1997, 1998; Baldwin 1999/2000; Baldwin and Pape 1998; Morgan, Bapat, and Kobayashi 2014). Thus, despite the increasing appeal of sanctions as a policy tool, first in the post-World War II/Cold War context, and then in the more recent post-Cold War/globalization context in which targeted or smart sanctions aimed at individuals rather than countries have proliferated (e.g., Cilizoglu and Early 2021), they suffer from a "sanctions paradox" (e.g., Drezner 1999).

Many reasons underlie this limited effectiveness. Target states may find ways to adapt domestically to sanctions, and they may develop alternate trade/economic partners – including black-market avenues – to evade their restrictions and mute their impact (e.g., Early 2015; Cilizoglu and Bapat 2020; Early and Peksen 2019). Moreover, states imposing sanctions may fail to engage in the necessary enforcement and monitoring efforts (e.g., Drury 2001; Early 2015, 2016; Morgan and Bapat 2003). Yet, a shift has occurred over time. During the Cold War and early post-Cold War years, most sanctions were aimed at the national level, targeting countries not individuals. The assessments of sanctions effectiveness noted above generally focus on these sanctions and this period. Since 2000, as sanctions have become increasingly "smart" and common (see, for example, Cortright and Lopez 2002; Bierstecker, Eckert, and Tourinho 2016; Early and Cilizoglu 2020; Cilizoglu and Early 2021), and targeted at individuals rather than states, some evidence indicates they have become more effective, while still "working" (only) about a third to half the time (e.g., Bierstecker, Eckert, and Tourinho 2016; Rosenberg et al. 2016; Early and Preble 2020). As Cilizoglu and Early (2021: 11) conclude, some recent studies "suggest that the success rate of modern economic sanctions is higher than the success rate of sanctions episodes from the 20th century". This trend, in all likelihood, points toward some level of learning among those imposing sanctions, perhaps most importantly becoming more aware from past experience about when that option should be eschewed.

Last, we note that, beyond the sanctions-related paradox, there are significant dilemmas associated with the use of sanctions, some of which involve elements of the security dilemma. For one, much research indicates that the cost of sanctions, especially those targeted at countries rather than individuals, tends to hurt civilian populations much more than regimes, not only by imposing economic and other hardships that populations bear, but also by triggering repression by regimes against their populations (e.g., Peksen 2009, 2011; Perry 2022; Wood 2008; Jadoon and Early 2024; Lektzian and Regan 2016; Peksen and Drury 2009, 2010), especially against women and minorities (e.g., Drury and Peksen 2014; Perry 2022). They also may not weaken the leadership of targeted countries, as many sanctions are intended, and might even strengthen it (e.g., Allen 2005, 2008). Imposing sanctions on targets has also inflicted economic costs on the senders as well, harming their economies, with the effects of the 1980 US grain embargo on the Soviet Union (specifically the harm on American grain exporters) as a case in point. Finally, some research indicates that sanctions may be most effective at the threat stage but are less effective when imposed. For example, K. Chad Clay (2018) concludes that threats to impose sanctions for human rights abuses may result in improvement, but the imposition of sanctions probably results in worsening human rights performance. Of course, the dilemma is clear: As Clay (2018) notes in his research, if threats to impose sanctions are never carried out, eventually the threats will not work either.

> ### IN FOCUS: SENSITIVITY, VULNERABILITY, AND SANCTIONS
>
> *Power and Interdependence* (Keohane and Nye 1977) stands as one of the most influential books of all time in the field – one of the founding works in international political economy. Among the concepts introduced in that volume, and quite relevant in pulling together ideas about sanctions, are sensitivity and vulnerability. Sensitivity refers to how much of an impact an action might have on an actor, while vulnerability is about the degree to which effects can be handled without harm. In the context of sanctions, sensitivity and vulnerability have obvious points of relevance. As a starting point, it would make little sense to attempt sanctions against a target state known to have little sensitivity with regard to losing access to certain kinds of imports. Things get more complicated, however, with regard to vulnerability. If there is likely to be sensitivity, to what degree does vulnerability – a key to successful sanctions – also exist? Can the target state effectively find a way to do without, or substitute for, whatever would be missing from its economy after the imposition of sanctions? The concepts of sensitivity and vulnerability combine to provide an overarching theoretical approach to analysis of sanctions.

DEFENSE, DETERRENCE, AND ALLIANCES

For centuries, states have accumulated military capabilities to deter potential attackers, defend against attacks, and extend power and influence, exemplifying the words of a Roman scribe who wrote "If you want peace, prepare for war" (*si vis pacem, para bellum*). To do so, states generally have two basic options: building their own military might and forging alliances to increase military capabilities. As state-based approaches, both avenues have complicated effects on conflict, crisis, and war.

Defense: Definition and Context

Throughout history, most states have expended considerable resources on military and security forces. With the exception of a few microstates (such as Vatican City and others in the Pacific Ocean), Costa Rica, Iceland, and Grenada, most countries maintain military forces. Table 11.2 shows the top ten countries by their military expenditures in 2022 by both dollar amount and share of global military spending. This list includes the most powerful countries in the world, topped by the United States, which accounts for 39% of global military spending, three times that of its closest competitor, China, and ten times more than Russia.

Table 11.2 Top ten countries in military spending, 2022

Country	US$ (billions), current $ and share of global total
United States	877 (39%)
China	292 (13%)
Russia	86.4 (3.9%)
India	81.4 (3.6%)
Saudi Arabia	75 (3.3%)
United Kingdom	68.5 (3.1%)
Germany	55.8 (2.5%)
France	53.6 (2.4%)
South Korea	46.4 (2.1%)
Japan	46 (2.1%)

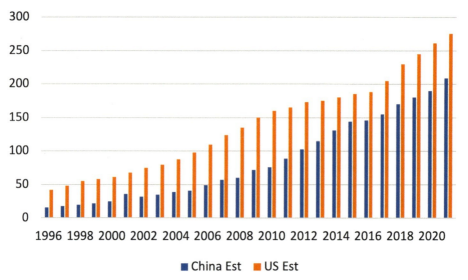

Figure 11.2   Top ten countries in military spending, 2022

Source: Tian et al. (2022).

FOR EXAMPLE: CHINA'S MILITARY SPENDING

China is the largest country in the world by population, either first or second largest by size of economy, and fourth largest by territory. Although China has internal security concerns and faces conflict over the future of Taiwan and with many of its neighbors over maritime claims in the South and East China Seas, it is not involved in any wars. Yet, as

Figure 11.2 shows, according to official Chinese reports, Chinese defense spending has long been accelerating and essentially doubled from 2010 to 2020. Independent reports from the Stockholm International Peace Research Institute (SIPRI) suggest that Chinese defense spending is both higher and growing more quickly than official figures indicate. China's priorities for this massive increase in military capabilities are also revealing: ballistic and cruise missiles, submarines, new aircraft carriers (China has two aircraft carriers in service and its third is nearing completion), electronic warfare (including cyberwarfare) capabilities, high-tech weapons such as stealth aircraft, and increasingly sophisticated information technology and command, control, and communications capabilities. Why is China devoting such considerable resources to the acquisition of military power? A recent statement by Chinese President Xi Jinping is instructive: in 2023 Xi Jinping warned his top security administrators that China must "adhere to bottom-line thinking and worst-case scenario thinking" (quoted in Gan 2023).

States typically devote sizable portions of their resources to their militaries to counter threats and to gain or maintain power. Indeed, from some perspectives, military power is necessary to deal with the inevitable conflicts that arise in the dangerous, anarchic world. Traditionally, much of the money spent on defense has gone to building larger and larger armed forces. Indeed, the number of military personnel in a given state has long been an important measure of military might, but it is far from the only factor. Such things as military technology and less tangible factors such as troop quality and training, leadership, reputation/resolve/will, motivation, loyalty, and morale are also important to the capacity of military forces for defense and deterrence.

For example, at the time of the 1991 Gulf War, Iraq had the world's fourth largest army, but that did little for Iraq as technologically superior forces led by the United States quickly overwhelmed the poorly trained and unenthusiastic Iraqi forces. Similarly, in the second war in Iraq in 2003, the Iraqi army significantly outnumbered US forces, but those numbers again did little good in the face of US military technology and tactics. Even more recently, the numerical advantages of the Russian military over Ukraine's military forces have proved less important than the equipment, motivation, training, and leadership shown by Ukrainian forces.

In terms of size, technology (with "smart weapons" and the "revolution in military affairs" merely among the most recent versions of competition to assemble the most effective and capable military forces), quality, and many other dimensions, these efforts have always been highly consequential for the security dilemma. The historical record indicates that states seek military power and advantages to cope with security concerns and address potential and actual conflicts, crises, and wars. But decades of research into this approach have focused on the potential for arms races between states to emerge, and on their implications for conflict, crisis, and, especially, war.

Defense Consequences: Arms Races, Conflict, Crisis, and War

According to Sample (2021: 63), "few specific questions about war causation and conflict processes have attracted so much public attention and academic inquiry as that of the impact of arms races on the likelihood of war". Conceived of as a stimulus-response process with significant implications for the security dilemma, a good starting point for the examination of arms races and their consequences is work by Richardson (1960; see also Choucri and North 1975; Zinnes 1976), who stressed the action-reaction dynamics of the competition. According to Richardson (1960), the central factors driving arms races are the nature and level of grievances between countries, the military capabilities of the competitor (and its trajectory of acquisition), and one's own military capabilities (and the relative balance with the competitor). These factors combine to produce a competitive reciprocal process of military acquisition, with classic, oft-studied historical examples including the great power arms races preceding World War I and the Cold War arms race, nuclear and otherwise, between the US and the Soviet Union.

How do such arms races affect conflict, crisis, and war? Historically, it appears that most wars are not preceded by arms races, but many – though not all – arms races do escalate to war. However, in what would seem to be a classic illustration of the security dilemma at work, substantial empirical evidence demonstrates that "arms races are associated with a higher probability of states getting into militarized disputes and escalating those conflicts to war rather than deterring war" (Sample 2021: 66). In one seminal early study, Wallace (1979) concluded that ongoing arms races contributed to the escalation of militarized disputes to war. Others challenged Wallace's findings (e.g., Weede 1980; Diehl 1983, 1985; Fearon 1994b) but two decades of work by Sample (e.g., 1997, 1998, 2002, 2014, 2018; see also Sample 2021 for a summary/review) reinforced the finding that arms races lead to the escalation of militarized disputes to war within a five-year window, especially before 1945, while nuclear arsenals after World War II largely eliminate that relationship because of the potentially devastating costs of nuclear war. Sample's work also supports the role of arms races as part of Vasquez's (2011) steps-to-war thesis in which territorial claims play the primary and initial role.

Deterrence: Definition and Context

In the context of strategies of defense and acquisition of military might to contend with conflict, crisis, and war, a stunning revolution occurred with the beginning of the nuclear age in August 1945. After the United States used two atomic bombs against Japan at Hiroshima and Nagasaki, developing and deploying nuclear weapons became a significant aspect of military power with dramatic consequences. The existence of nuclear weapons transformed the ways strategists thought about defense, war, and the role of military might in conflict, crisis, and war.

While the acquisition of military power previously had a deterrent function, as did alliances, threat of sanctions, and other tools of foreign policy, the nuclear age changed the nature of deterrence, and nuclear weapons assumed a primary place in its applications. As US strategist Bernard Brodie (1946: 76; see also Brodie 1978) stated shortly after World War II, "thus far the chief purpose of our military establishment has been to win wars. From now on its chief purpose must be to avert them. It can have almost no other useful purpose". In effect, the prospect of nuclear annihilation transformed war – especially great power war – by making it, and the conflict and crises that might lead to it, far riskier (a state, in particular its civilian population, can be destroyed without being defeated on the battlefield). Consequently, direct military confrontations between countries deploying nuclear arsenals diminished considerably. Despite the high-stakes tensions of the Cold War, for example, the United States and the Soviet Union never directly confronted one another militarily, and the fear of a nuclear war during the 1962 Cuban Missile Crisis drove home the potential consequences of this technological revolution.

The essence of nuclear deterrence is to possess sufficient nuclear arsenals to prevent another state from taking an undesired action, either through threat of inflicting unacceptably high costs (punishment) on the adversary in the event of the action, or by ensuring that the action itself cannot succeed if undertaken (denial) (e.g., Morgan 1983; Schelling 1966). Thus, in one sense, the context of the nuclear age is not very different from previous ages: as we have described, over the centuries, states have amassed military might to keep adversaries from attacking them.

Scholars, policy analysts, and military strategists often distinguish between direct and extended deterrence and between immediate and general deterrence. As Fuhrmann (2021: 105) summarizes, these two dimensions (who is being protected – oneself or one's allies; has a conflict or provocation started) create four types of deterrence. In the absence of an existing conflict/provocation, general or (direct) deterrence involves the use of retaliatory threats to discourage attacks against the state making the deterrent threat, while extended deterrence involves retaliatory threats to discourage attacks against allies and friends of the state making the deterrent threat. In the case of existing conflict/provocation, immediate deterrence involves the threat to retaliate against attackers who are believed to be actively considering specific military operations against the target, which is readying itself to respond. Immediate extended deterrence, by contrast, involves threats to retaliate in defense of friends/allies.

After World War II, nuclear deterrence was a central part of the defense strategies of both the United States and the Soviet Union. Not only did these countries build increasingly large and powerful arsenals for direct deterrence of each other; they also made commitments to extend their nuclear umbrellas to important allies. For the United States, for example, Europe, Japan, and others were included in the extended deterrence commitment, while the Soviet Union included its allies in Eastern Europe and elsewhere.

Immediately after World War II, when the United States was the sole nuclear power, and even after the Soviet Union had acquired nuclear weapons but could not use them against US territory, the United States could make nuclear threats more freely. As the nuclear arms race accelerated and the Soviet Union expanded its nuclear arsenal to match and, in some ways, to exceed that of the United States, brinkmanship and the underlying strategy became far too risky to maintain.

From the early 1960s to the end of the Cold War, the basis of deterrence for both sides became what was known as mutually assured destruction (MAD). This approach amounted to a "you shoot, I shoot, and we are both dead" threat that rested on the stability of a basic nuclear stalemate and made conflicts very dangerous. In terms of deterrence, MAD rested on the ability of both sides to field a secure, second-strike capability of sufficient size to destroy a significant portion of the other side's society, usually in what was known as counter-value targeting (or targeting cities and industrial centers), no matter what kind of attack was directed against them. That is, even if one side unleashed a counterforce strike designed to destroy nuclear arsenals and other war-fighting abilities, the other side would still be able to retaliate with a devastating second strike in return. Stability in this relationship ensured no first-strike advantage for either side and thus effective deterrence (Morgan 2018a).

IN FOCUS: DR. STRANGELOVE

Dr. Strangelove or: How I Learned to Stop Worrying and Love the Bomb is considered one of the greatest satirical movies of all time – a brilliant dark comedy. (Spoiler alert – in case you decide to watch the film before reading further.) The movie, from 1964, came out in the aftermath of the Cuban Missile Crisis and pokes fun at the concept of "MAD" by showing how things could go terribly wrong and produce nuclear annihilation in spite of all precautions in place. A deranged American military officer – acting outside of the chain of command – somehow is able to order a preemptive nuclear strike on the Soviet Union. Frantic efforts ensue to stop this, but one plane gets through. Unknown to the US, the USSR had in place the "Doomsday Machine": a device that, if activated, would trigger so many cobalt bombs that the surface of the earth would be rendered uninhabitable for over 90 years. Even one nuclear weapon used against the Soviet Union would be sufficient to trigger the doomsday device, so when the rogue plane successfully drops its bomb, the world as it had been known comes to an end – precisely the outcome that all of the weapon building had been intended to prevent.

At its heart, the nuclear arms race that dominated the Cold War was an action-reaction cycle of competition to ensure that no weapons gains of the other side could eliminate this fundamental second-strike, or MAD, capability. Both the United States and the Soviet Union developed increasingly powerful and accurate nuclear weapons, deploying them on land (intercontinental ballistic missiles, or ICBMs, as well as medium- and short-range missiles), through the air (as gravity bombs and, later, cruise missiles), and across the sea (as submarine-launched ballistic missiles, or SLBMs). The Anti-Ballistic Missile Treaty (ABM) of 1972 was even concluded to limit the ability to defend against missiles in order to help ensure the stability of a second strike.

As the Cold War wound on and yielded to the post-Cold War context, a series of new concerns arose with respect to nuclear might. First, states with nuclear arsenals felt the need to possess weapons in quantities and with capabilities (explosive power, accuracy) sufficient to ensure the ability to retaliate against an attack. Ensuring a second-strike capability became critical, and the action-reaction cycle of arms competition between the major nuclear powers ensued.

Second, acquiring nuclear capabilities became important to other countries as well. The United Kingdom, France, and China followed the United States and the Soviet Union and developed their own nuclear arsenals, in part to ensure that they could deter nuclear strikes themselves with the threat of retaliation, and in part to ensure that they had a seat at the table with the major powers. These five states were the first official nuclear weapons states, but they have been joined by India (1974) and Pakistan (1998), which publicly tested nuclear devices, and Israel, which has not publicly acknowledged possession of nuclear weapons but is widely believed to have an arsenal of approximately 90 weapons. North Korea first tested nuclear weapons in 2006 and has done so multiple times since then. It is suspected of possessing sufficient material for about 30 to 40 nuclear weapons and in 2017 claimed to have achieved the ability to make warheads small enough to be placed on missiles. In this context, nonproliferation, or efforts to prevent the spread of nuclear weapons and weapons materials to other states, became a major issue as well (see Map 11.1). In addition to efforts to construct international agreements and institutions such as the International Atomic Energy Agency (1957), the Nuclear Non-Proliferation Treaty (NPT) (1968), and the Comprehensive Nuclear Test-Ban Treaty (1996), a variety of efforts – from the offering of benefits and rewards to more coercive measures, including military operations – have been undertaken to prevent other states from gaining nuclear capabilities.

Finally, grappling with the potential of non-state actors, including terrorist groups – to acquire the capabilities to build and deliver nuclear weapons either in traditional warheads or through other makeshift devices such as dirty bombs and suitcase bombs – became an increasingly serious concern. Such concerns also called into question the feasibility of deterrence in the case of non-state adversaries such as terrorists.

Deterrence and Conflict, Crisis, and War

Led by strategists such as Bernard Brodie and Thomas Schelling, among others, deterrence is commonly understood to rest on three components. First, for a state to be able to deter a potential aggressor, it must have the necessary military capability to retaliate in a damaging way. Second, a state must make a commitment – a threat that a certain action will result in retaliation. Third, a state must somehow demonstrate its will – to convince the target that such a retaliation would be carried out if necessary. Hence, credibility rests on capability and on will or intention. As Huth (1988: 4) argued, this established two essential requirements as foundations for effectiveness: "(1) military capabilities sufficient to inflict substantial costs on a potential attacker, and (2) the will or intention to use those capabilities if necessary" (see also Zagare 1990; Zagare and Kilgour 2000).

Thousands of pages have been devoted to the examination of how to achieve credible deterrence threat, and to the conditions under which deterrence is likely to succeed or fail. As Fuhrmann (2021) summarizes, empirically, the answer is that it depends considerably on contextual factors. For one, although far from conclusive, while the logic of deterrence suggests that nuclear deterrent threats might be relevant to any kind of conflict, empirical research indicates that effectiveness is greater in high-level conflict than in low-level conflict (e.g., Huth, Bennett, and Gelpi 1992; Jervis 1989), and higher between pairs of nuclear states than between nuclear and nonnuclear pairs, although nonnuclear opponents of nuclear states may exercise greater restraint in crises (e.g., Rauchhaus 2009; Bueno de Mesquita and Riker 1982; Asal and Beardsley 2007; Beardsley and Asal 2009a, 2009b; Geller 1990). Additionally, as Schelling (1966) argued, extended deterrence is more difficult, less effective, and more subject to contingencies than general or direct deterrence, which empirical studies by Russett (1969), Huth and Russett (1984), and Huth (1988, 1990) support. Fuhrmann's (2021) summary also identifies contingencies related to nuclear capabilities, posture/strategy, and the nuclear taboo,

254 CONFLICT, CRISIS, AND WAR IN WORLD POLITICS

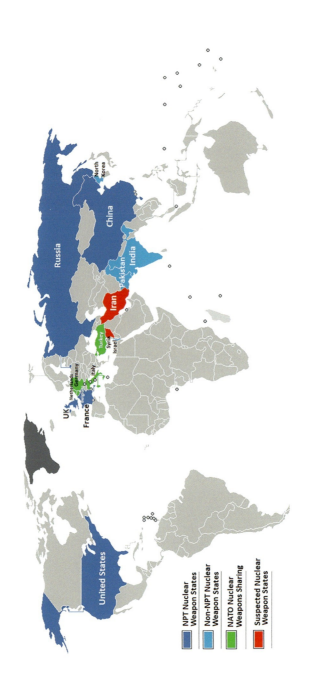

Source: https://en.m.wikipedia.org/wiki/File:Nuclear_weapons.png

Map 11.1 Nuclear weapons states, 2020

while Stein (1991) stressed the importance of combining reassurance with deterrent threats in order to avoid conflict spirals.[4]

> **IN FOCUS: DETERRENCE AFTER THE COLD WAR?**
>
> The "long postwar peace" (Gaddis 1986) after World War II has been credited by many scholars and policymakers to the Cold War nuclear standoff between the United States and the Soviet Union. Since the end of the Cold War, more and more questions have arisen about the continued relevance and efficacy of nuclear deterrence in the dynamic context. There are many reasons for this concern.
>
> 1. The nuclear weapons "club" is getting more members. As of 2023, the Federation of American Scientists estimated that, while only five states had nuclear weapons during most of the Cold War, nine states now control more than 12,500 nuclear warheads. Some of these states are decidedly hostile to the status quo, including Iran, an expansionary Russia, and a North Korea that believes only nuclear weapons and missiles can protect its regime from the US. Although the logic of deterrence may prevail among these states and generate stability based on fear of mutual destruction, scholars such as Scott Sagan (Sagan and Waltz 2002) argue that proliferation greatly increases the possibility of nuclear accidents, theft of nuclear weapons, or other purposeful uses of the weapons.
> 2. States have increasing concerns about the relevance of deterrence for smaller-scale attacks, including those by a single bomb or missile. This has led some countries – led by the United States and Israel – to continue to develop the capability to shoot down incoming missiles, which also has implications for deterrence. An obvious example, underway at this time of writing, concerns missile attacks on Israel by Iranian proxy actors such as Hezbollah.
> 3. In the post-Cold War world, deterrence increasingly applies to conventional weapons as well, and history suggests that this kind of deterrence is even more difficult to maintain. Put simply, the security dilemma is alive and well.
> 4. In the post-Cold War World, the most common "face" of war is civil or intrastate war or unconventional war, as we discussed in Chapter 3. The related increase in the importance of non-state actors in conflict calls into question the continued relevance – and even possibility – of meaningful deterrence. The basic idea behind deterrence is that, if attacked, the state can counterattack and badly hurt the original attacker, but that formula is complicated by non-state actors whose location is more fluid and difficult to identify. If states can't legitimately threaten a counterstrike, deterrence is difficult, if not outright impossible.

Finally, empirical studies by George and Smoke (1974), Lebow (1981), Stein (1987), and Morgan (2003) provide insights into deterrence failures. These studies highlight the role of challenger risk and cost (in part of inaction) calculations, defender interests and commitments and the challenger perceptions of these things, and domestic political calculations in deter-

---

[4] See also Danilovic and Clare (2017) and Morgan (2018b) for relevant reviews.

rence failures. They also highlight the ability of challengers to design and undertake controlled, low-level actions to accomplish *fait accompli*, limited probes, and controlled pressure to defeat deterrent threats and cause deterrence failure. Russian attacks on Georgia and the Crimean region of Ukraine in recent decades are among the most obvious illustrations.

Alliances: Definition and Context

Building one's own military power is a major internal avenue for addressing crisis, conflict, and war, but states often seek external help by forging alliances with others to counter threats and increase strength. The logic of this approach is straightforward: because states often must coordinate with other states to ensure their own security and to address conflict, crisis, and war, they may join together for common interests and to face common enemies, making a formal commitment to cooperate for specific purposes, such as mutual defense. In general, alliances involve commitments to collaborate in offensive military operations (e.g., the Soviet–German pact prior to the outbreak of World War II) or defensive commitments to come to each other's aid in the event of an attack (e.g., the NATO alliance). Such alliance commitments often serve as deterrents to potential attackers and improve a state's ability to defend itself from potential attack if it were to occur but, just as in the case of efforts to build one's military power, this approach is affected by and has implications for the security dilemma.

Alliances are driven by a variety of dynamics (e.g., Weitsman 2017; Leeds and Morgan 2018). A foundational dynamic involves the security dilemma, where anarchy, uncertainty, and the pursuit of capabilities to protect against attack or domination, or to project power, lead states to join together, while other states respond in kind to such efforts by others (e.g., Snyder 1984; Vasquez 1993; Senese and Vasquez 2008). Alliance formation thus also involves attempts to pool power and capabilities to address conflicts and meet common threats, and/or deter potential attackers, and it helps states to coordinate plans and actions if conflicts escalate to crisis and war (e.g., Kenwick and McManus 2021).

Other dynamics are also involved.[5] One is protection, in which smaller states might ally with more powerful ones to gain help and support in the face of conflict with a dangerous neighbor, adversary, or rival. In recent years, NATO expansion – at least in the sense of the desire of countries formerly in the sphere of the Soviet Union – may be understood in part from this perspective, as can the current desire of Ukraine and Georgia to become part of NATO, and the decision of Sweden and Finland to join NATO after the Russian invasion of Ukraine in 2022.

Second, a bandwagoning dynamic may be at work, in which a state allies with a much more powerful state to gain benefits from the prospective success of that state in conflict, crisis, war, or even influence more generally (Waltz 1979; Wright 1942). Bandwagoning may result from the calculation that opposition to the more powerful state (by itself or by others) is unlikely to succeed or from the calculation that the opportunity to share in the benefits of the stronger state's pursuit of power is compelling, whether those benefits involve payoffs from the stronger

---

[5] See, for example, Weitsman (2017), who discussed balancing, tethering, bandwagoning, and hedging.

state or a share of any spoils of war that might ensue. A good example is the behavior of Central European states, such as Hungary and Romania, in the years around the start of World War II, when they joined with Nazi Germany. A more recent example was the several smaller European states that sided with the US-led invasion of Iraq in 2003 in direct opposition to Germany and France. Bandwagoning involves *unequal exchange* because the smaller and more vulnerable state makes concessions to the larger power and accepts a subordinate role (Walt 1987: 282).

Finally, alliances might be driven by balancing dynamics where states join with others to counter the power or threat of another (Walt 1987; Waltz 1979). In this dynamic, alliances are most likely to form when power imbalances emerge. As one state's power grows, it presents a potential threat to others, which may join together to counter the first and more (or potentially more) powerful state. Shared concerns over the possible threat posed by the growing power of the first state can lead the others to *balance* against it by making an alliance. The alliance between France and Russia in the years before World War I reflected their concern with the rising power of Germany, as did the British decision in the same period to abandon its historical role as offshore balancer to join France and Russia to counter the rising challenge of Germany. Similarly, one interpretation of the NATO alliance uniting the United States, Canada, and most Western European states emphasized the need to counter the Soviet threat in Europe, and more recently, the threat of an expansionist Russia.

> **FOR EXAMPLE: ALLIANCES AND NOSTALGIA FOR THE COLD WAR?**
>
> In 1990, political scientist John Mearsheimer (1990) argued that the end of the Cold War would soon produce regret. In particular, he argued that the Cold War's end would result in the return to multipolarity in Europe and the end of the NATO alliance, a key contributor to stability and peace among European states. NATOs demise would be accompanied, he predicted, by the emergence of additional European nuclear powers and something more like the destructive and violent behavior of the 1648–1945 period than the relative peace in Europe after 1945. What assumptions and causal inferences underlie Mearsheimer's argument, and how has it fared in the 35 years since its publication? To stimulate thinking about responses to that question, have a look at Figure 11.3. In this diagram, based on a book from 2018, Mearsheimer builds on his previous work and offers a critique of the liberal world order that ensued in the decades after the Cold War.
>
> *What do you think about the combination of Mearsheimer's analyses from then and now?*

Other motivations and dynamics may also be at work, however. The preceding dynamics tend to see alliances as temporary arrangements to meet threats. NATO, for example, might be understood as alliances made necessary by the need to counter the Soviet Union during the Cold War, but likely to weaken in the absence of the original threat. However, other perspectives such as those from liberal and constructivist paradigms view alliances as based on cooperation, common values and identities, and mutual interests, and thus expect them to be more enduring (e.g., Weitsman 2017; Williams 1998; Williams and Neumann 2000). The NATO alliance provides a nice illustration. The persistence – and expansion – of NATO after

258 CONFLICT, CRISIS, AND WAR IN WORLD POLITICS

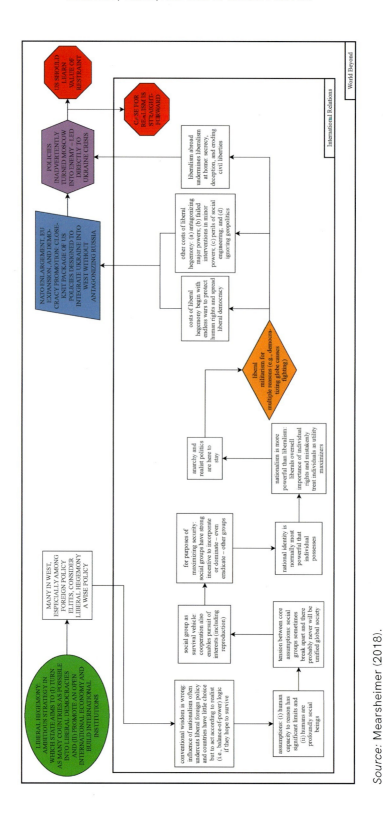

Source: Mearsheimer (2018).

Figure 11.3 The great delusion: liberal dreams and international relations

the end of the Cold War, despite the collapse of the Soviet Union, might therefore rest on the cooperative links and shared values and interests that have helped it persist and evolve.

Alliances and Conflict, Crisis, and War

As mechanisms for states to help themselves to provide for security and manage conflict, crisis, and war, do alliances deter or incite conflict and violence? Are they avenues for peace or causes of war? The sizable body of empirical research on the effect of alliances on conflict, crisis, and war is complicated and suggests that the answers are highly contingent on context and the nature of the alliances.

Aided by the development of systematic data on alliances in the Correlates of War (COW) project over several waves (e.g., Singer and Small 1966; Holsti, Hopmann, and Sullivan 1973; Gibler and Sarkees 2004) and the Alliance Treaty Obligations and Provisions (ATOP) Project (Leeds et al. 2002; Leeds and Mattes 2007), numerous scholars have sought to determine their effects on conflict and war, with contradictory results that provide support for both the avenues for peace and the causes of war inferences. As avenues of peace, the logic rests largely on the deterrent nature of alliances. Early empirical studies such as Singer and Small (1968) and Levy (1981) concluded that alliances are associated with peace. As cause of war a major part of the logic is summed up by Weitsman (2017: 9): "the formation of an alliance, by triggering the security dilemma, will culminate in a counterbalancing alliance, and increased alliance polarization, which in turn will heighten the possibility of misperception, hostility, and the likelihood of war" (Kaplan 1957; Wright 1965; Holsti, Hopmann, and Sullivan 1973). Following this logic, numerous scholars found empirical evidence that alliances increased conflict and war (e.g., Siverson and King 1979; Wayman 1990) and play a key role in the escalatory "steps to war" causal chain (e.g., Vasquez 1993; Senese and Vasquez 2008). In spite of these contradictory findings, much research agrees that alliances contribute to the expansion of war once they fail to deter conflict and militarized disputes begin, as alliance partners join in on one side or the other (e.g., Siverson and King 1979; Siverson and Starr 1991; Huth 1998).

Part of the reason for the contradictory results is the role of context, which some scholars have stressed to help reconcile the competing findings. Indeed, the effects of alliances are highly contingent on a wide variety of contextual factors. For example, a number of studies have concluded that the effects of alliances vary by historical context, with more war-causing effects prior to World War II and more peace-inducing effects after (e.g., Levy 1981; Senese and Vasquez 2008). Other factors related to the strategic context such as geography, the nature of the dispute, and levels of hostility also generate variation on the effects of alliances (e.g., Kenwick and McManus 2021). Furthermore, the nature of the alliance commitment also appears to matter, as Leeds (2003) concluded: alliances committing a state to the defense of another when attacked reduce the likelihood of the initiation of militarized disputes, and thus deter. Conversely, alliances that commit a state to aiding the initiator of a militarized dispute or to remain neutral in such an event increase the likelihood of militarized disputes (see also Johnson and Leeds 2011). Finally, newly formed alliances (especially in the context of a conflict or militarized dispute) appear to have more war-inducing results than existing alliances, which are more stabilizing (e.g., Kenwick and McManus 2021; Kenwick, Vasquez, and Powers 2015;

Kenwick and Vasquez 2017). In short, as an approach to managing conflict, crisis, and war, alliances may or may not be effective.

USING FORCE: DEFINITION AND CONTEXT

In conflict, crisis, and war, states may use force in a variety of ways. According to the Militarized Interstate Dispute (MID) data these uses include:

- *Threats of force* – including threats to blockade, to forcibly occupy territory, to declare war, and to use force, including nuclear weapons or other weapons of mass destruction
- *Displays of force* – including placing forces (including nuclear forces) on alert; mobilizing armed forces; public displays or operations of land, air, or naval forces in or outside a state's territory; and purposeful border violations with military forces (without combat)
- *Uses of force* – including blockades, occupation of territory or seizure of material or personnel, small-scale military clashes or raids (with less than 1,000 total battle deaths), and declarations of war
- *Interstate war* – involving sustained military combat resulting in more than 1,000 total battle deaths

How can states apply their military power through these means to obtain security? In general, we can identify at least three (in addition to deterrence, which we discussed earlier) main uses that may translate military power into security.

Defense

Just like it sounds, the defensive use of force means having the ability to fight off an attack, to deny an attacker a victory. Defense involves deploying and using military force to protect oneself, ward off an attack, and minimize damage from the attack to the greatest extent possible (Art 1980). As we discussed earlier in this chapter, the key to gaining security in this strategy is to build sufficient, usable military capabilities to fight off an attack. Defensive force can also contribute to deterrence, as the more substantial, clearer, and more obvious the defensive capabilities are, the greater the likelihood that a potential attacker will refrain from attacking in the first place. And yet in the event of an imminent or actual attack, defensive force improves a state's ability to be secure by fighting off the attack.

Prevention and Preemption

The preventive and preemptive uses of force are related to defense in many ways. The central idea behind both is that there is a threat facing the state, against which it is best to strike first before an attack can be unleashed. Preventive and preemptive uses of force are based on the view that, in some situations, the best defense is a good offense. What is the difference between preemption and prevention? The strategies are not very precisely defined and are highly controversial and subject to political argument as well. In general, preemption occurs when the threat of attack is *imminent*, that is, expected within a matter of weeks, days, or even hours; prevention occurs when the threat is seen as *inevitable*, that is, expected sometime in the more distant future (Art 1980: 6). Both preemptive and, especially, preventive uses of force are highly controversial because they involve using force first, which is sometimes hard to distinguish from outright aggression.

Compellence

The fourth strategy for using force to gain security is compellence, also often referred to as coercive diplomacy because it blends diplomacy with the use of force to achieve its ends (e.g., George, Hall, and Simons 1971). Thomas Schelling (1966) characterized compellence as the use of military force to stop a foe from doing something it was already doing or to force it to start doing something it was not yet doing. To do so, the state engaging in compellence undertakes military actions that will stop only when its adversary engages in the desired response.

Compellence may be the easiest strategy to evaluate in terms of success, but it is the hardest strategy to use. It is successful when the adversary (target) stops (or starts) doing what was demanded by the state deploying the force. However, because compellence requires the target to act, usually very publicly, in response to a combination of threat and punitive action, it also tends to trigger concerns about prestige, reputation, and losing face. Consequently, it may trigger resistance and escalation, or even strategic withdrawal followed by future challenges that threaten a state's security in new, even more serious ways.

For some perspectives, uses of force such as these, and the underlying centrality of military might on which they rest, are at the core of security, power, influence, and efforts to manage conflict, crisis, and war. As Robert J. Art (1980: 35) aptly summarized:

> The efficacy of force endures. For in anarchy, force and politics are connected. By itself, military power guarantees neither survival nor prosperity. But it is almost always the essential ingredient for both. Because resort to force is the ultimate card of all states, the seriousness of a state's intentions is conveyed fundamentally by its having a credible military posture. Without it, a state's diplomacy generally lacks effectiveness.

USES OF FORCE AND CONFLICT, CRISIS, AND WAR

Since we have discussed the nature, evolution, and causes of war in its many forms in detail in previous chapters, here we focus on a few issues regarding empirical research into its outcomes and its uses as a tool to address conflict short of full-scale war.

First, given its prominence as an approach to conflict, how does the use of force fare in terms of securing a state's objectives? We have previously noted challenges and consequences of the acquisition of arms in our discussion of arms races earlier in this chapter. States choosing to use force face similar challenges. A significant body of empirical research suggests that states initiating violent conflict are unlikely to achieve their aims. According to multiple studies over time, initiators of war were about as likely to fail as to succeed prior to the 20th century. Since then, initiators have become significantly less likely to win the wars they start (e.g., Lebow and Valentino 2009; Wang and Ray 1994). Moreover, they tend to fare worse the longer a war continues (e.g., Slantchev 2004).

There is some variation, however, based on regime type, as several studies have found that democracies may be more effective in war (e.g. Biddle and Long 2004), and appear more likely to prevail in the wars they initiate than authoritarian regimes (e.g., Reiter and Stam 1998; Filson and Werner 2004), though this may be specific to particular time periods (e.g., Bennett and Stam 1998) and may be highly context-dependent and only apply to lower-level disputes and not larger interstate wars (e.g., Reed and Clark 2000; Renshon and Spirling 2015). This may also derive from and depend in part on individual-level factors and variations among leaders (e.g., Jervis, Lebow, and Stein 1984; Lebow 2003). Thus, there does not appear to be an advantage for "first-movers" when it comes to resort to war as a way to address conflict.

In more limited uses of force (e.g., the first three categories of the MIDs categorization), the empirical record is less clear. Some research suggests that states who move first to issue and/or escalate threats and limited uses of force (displays, etc.) in conflict and crisis situations have tended to prevail (e.g., Maoz 1983), although the outcomes may be more nuanced than this simple representation (e.g., Leng 1983). Similarly, an initiator advantage appears to exist for more limited uses of force as well, perhaps especially for democracies (e.g., Gelpi and Griesdorf 2001; Renshon and Spirling 2015). Case evidence from classic studies such as Blechman and Kaplan (1978), Blechman and Wittes (1998), Sisson, Siebens, and Blechman (2020), and Zenko (2010) reinforce both the prospects for and challenges of limited, political uses of force such as these, finding that they are successful under certain conditions and about half the time.

Second, since the time of Clausewitz, the connection between the use of force, political objectives, and diplomacy has been embraced by practitioners and scholars alike. As we noted above, this has led to what Schelling (1966), George, Hall, and Simons (1971), George (1991), and others have called compellence or coercive diplomacy. Combining threats to do harm with more positive inducements to change behavior, coercive diplomacy has been a mainstay of efforts to cope with conflict and manage crisis (e.g., Jakobsen 2020; Sperandei 2006). However, as one recent summary concluded, "Coercive diplomacy is a hard-to-use, high-risk strategy with a low success rate – especially with respect to solving crises without any use of force. Success hinges on a favorable context, skillful diplomacy, and psychological factors beyond the coercer's control" (Jakobsen 2020: 1). Indeed, an extensive body of evidence, mostly in the form of case studies from the Cold War (e.g., Schelling 1966; George, Hall, and Simons 1971; George 1991; Jentleson 1991; Blechman and Kaplan 1978; Sechser and Fuhrmann 2017) and post-Cold War (George 1991; Stein 1992; Art and Cronin 2003; Treverton 2000; Sisson, Seibens, and Blechman 2020; Sechser and Fuhrmann 2017) finds coercive diplomacy to be highly context-dependent, ripe for evasion by its targets, and resistant to success in practice. Scholarly studies by Leng (1983), Hensel (1999), and Prins (2005), among others, conclude that coercive strategies like this are prone to escalate violence. As Jentleson (1991) concluded, in its applications, more limited goals (such as foreign policy restraint) are far more likely to succeed than more expansive ones.

ARMS CONTROL AND DISARMAMENT: DEFINITION AND CONTEXT

The final avenue for managing conflict, crisis, and war in our discussion in this chapter involves the application of diplomacy to the challenge presented by the practice of states to seek military power to secure themselves in a decentralized, dangerous world. As we have discussed in this chapter, the acquisition (and use) of military might for deterrence, defense, and war often generates insecurities and action-reaction dynamics that can escalate out of control. Threats develop or are heightened, points of conflict and crises emerge, and problems of uncertainty, trust, and understanding spread. Coping with these challenges has led states and other actors to engage in efforts to construct agreements for disarmament or arms control to control or eliminate weapons and/or areas/practices of military activity. From some perspectives, such agreements might address security dilemmas, reduce uncertainty, and control or avoid arms races and the threats that arise from the accumulation of military might.

Arms control and disarmament are related but distinct approaches to security and conflict. Disarmament stresses the elimination (or, at least, the drastic reduction) of weapons; arms control generally stresses restraint or regulation of the amount, type, positioning, or use of weapons. Although some advocates of arms control see it as an opportunity to make progress toward more general disarmament, historically disarmament movements have tended to involve the public, social movements, and non-governmental organizations more often and more extensively than states or their leaders. Aside from involuntary disarmament forced on a defeated state by the victors (e.g., Rome's forced disarmament on Carthage in the 3rd century; Napoleon's forced disarmament of Prussia in the early 19th century; and forced disarmaments of defeated enemies by the allies after both World War I and World War II, all of which were short-lived as the defeated states soon found ways to rearm and often to retaliate), disarmament efforts have not led to much success.

In the late 19th and early 20th centuries, efforts in The Hague conferences (1899 and 1907) and the world disarmament conference of the 1930s embraced disarmament goals but produced few tangible results. The Hague conferences mostly restricted the use of certain kinds of weapons, and the 1930s endeavor collapsed under the tensions of that period and the rise of German power. The advent of the nuclear era and devastating power and destructiveness of nuclear weapons led many to push for disarmament in the form of their elimination. For example, the US-proposed Baruch Plan to establish a UN Atomic Development Authority (ADA) to take control of all nuclear energy activities and manage nuclear disarmament collapsed under US–Soviet disagreement. Subsequent official efforts toward nuclear disarmament generally followed suit.

Still, nuclear disarmament efforts have been led by the publics of various states, social movements, and non-governmental organizations within and across national boundaries. For example, it was significant public pressure in the United States and Europe, in part by mothers concerned about contaminated milk, that led the Soviet Union, the United States, and Britain to conclude the 1963 Partial Test Ban Treaty, which eliminated testing in the atmosphere and seas. Another good example is the antinuclear movement that spread in the early 1980s. Prompted by increased tension between the United States and the Soviet Union and plans to expand nuclear arsenals and the deployment of missiles in Europe, as well as the collapse of arms control talks, antinuclear demonstrations erupted in the United States and across Europe. Citizens, scientists, and religious organizations (including the Catholic Church) advocated for control, reduction, and eventual elimination of nuclear weapons. In the United States, the nuclear freeze and nuclear disarmament movements conducted large-scale demonstrations and lobbied American policymakers to take steps to curtail the nuclear arms race. In Germany, antinuclear groups pressured the government to oppose the expanded deployment of American nuclear missiles. Although unsuccessful in achieving their central goals, these and other groups brought pressure to bear that contributed to the resumption of arms control talks between the United States and the Soviet Union and the conclusion of the Intermediate-Range Nuclear Forces (INF) Treaty in 1987.

Even more recently, the 60th anniversary of the United States' use of atomic bombs against Japan in 1945 prompted public demonstrations calling for nuclear disarmament. In 2008, Norway convened an International Conference on Nuclear Disarmament; in 2009, US President Barack Obama called for a nuclear-free world; and in the wake of the 2011 Fukushima nuclear disaster in Japan, some renewed efforts for nuclear disarmament occurred as well. However, states thus far have resisted nuclear – or any other type of – disarmament. Arms control remains the more productive result.

To be sure, arms control and disarmament overlap when arms control efforts target specific types of weapons for elimination. Moreover, arms control and disarmament both rest in part on the idea that controlling weaponry and the competition to acquire it will make states more secure, stabilize arms competitions and the uncertainty they involve, and improve their ability to manage conflict. As it developed, principally in the 20th century, arms control, in particular, is committed to establishing limits and stability in the military competition between countries, to reduce uncertainty and promote trust and cooperation (Lamb 1988: 20). Advocates argue that, as an avenue to address and manage conflict, crisis, and war, controlling the escalatory spiral of weaponry in this fashion contributes to better management of the security dilemma. See In Focus: Arms, Arms Control, and War for some additional discussion.

IN FOCUS: ARMS, ARMS CONTROL, AND WAR

According to Robert Jervis (1993: 239), "If the main objective of arms control is to make war less likely, then any theory of arms control must rest on a theory of the causes of war." Seeking security through the acquisition of arms or through arms control and disarmament depends in part on whether one views weapons as a cause of war. *Spiral theorists* believe that the anarchic environment of world politics leads otherwise peaceful actors to arm themselves out of fear and uncertainty (Lamb 1988: chap. 10). As the security dilemma suggests, others react by arming themselves, leading to increased tension and an action-reaction cycle in which arms are acquired in greater amounts. Eventually, this cycle "spirals out of control and some incident touches off a war no one really wanted" (Lamb 1988: 181). *Aggressor theorists*, in contrast, believe that some states are naturally warlike, requiring other states to be prepared to fight to protect themselves and punish the aggressor (Lamb 1988: 183).

Spiral theorists thus argue that arms cause war by contributing to misperception, fear, and insecurity. Arms control and disarmament are therefore vital, as they promote communication and cooperation and help prevent or break the spirals that lead to war. The most extreme spiral theorists will advocate unilateral disarmament measures as signals of peaceful intentions. For aggressor theorists, such actions are foolish. Instead, they argue that military strength is a necessary deterrent to aggressors. Arms control is undesirable, even dangerous, because it may create vulnerability or a false sense of security. Spiral theorists view shows of strength by aggressors as escalatory steps in the conflict spiral, while aggressor theorists view conciliatory actions like disarmament as dangerous acts of appeasement likely only to encourage aggressors (Lamb 1988: 1184–1185). In some ways, this argument is not that different from the debate over allowing guns to be carried on college campuses; some see that as inherently dangerous, and others see it as necessary to protect oneself from evildoers.

Arms control policies are heavily influenced by the particular theories state leaders embrace, whether they recognize it or not. British Prime Minister Neville Chamberlain was driven by a simple spiral theory in his efforts to head off war in Europe before World War II, while other European leaders tended to be influenced by aggressor theories in the run-up to World War II, competing with each other to demonstrate resolve and deploy military force. One or the other of these approaches have guided American presidents (and probably their Soviet, then Russian, counterparts) for the past 70 years. Often disputes among leading diplomats and foreign policy advisers based on these competing perspectives have resulted in challenges, delays, and even failures in efforts to negotiate.

What do you think?

Table 11.3 lists major arms control agreements since World War I, and Table 11.4 shows the basic aspects of arms control, identifying the key features of participants, purposes, and types. In terms of participants, arms control can be unilateral, although instances in which a single state has voluntarily refrained from acquiring weapons are highly unusual and often only temporary. Bilateral agreements between rivals and competitors are more common but are frequently limited in their impact. Unless the world is essentially bipolar, as during the Cold War between the United States and the Soviet Union, the broader effect of bilateral agreements can be limited. Multilateral agreements, which range from just a few participants to arrangements involving most states, are potentially more far-reaching (depending on the number of participants) but are also much more difficult to achieve because of the multiple perspectives and interests involved, as well as the difficulty in monitoring and verifying compliance.

Let's focus on the types of agreements and consider a few examples:

- *Rules of war* seek limits on the occurrence and acceptable practices of war. For example, in 1928 the Kellogg–Briand Pact tried to outlaw war, and the treaty establishing the League of Nations also banned aggression among its members. The Geneva Conventions of 1864, 1906, 1929, and 1949 sought to establish rules for the treatment of wounded and captured soldiers, as well as civilians, during times of war. The Hague Conventions of 1899 and 1907 established limits on the use of weapons and war crimes.
- *Communication and administration* focus on improving cooperation and communication to reduce tension between participants. For example, the 1962 "Hot Line"

Table 11.3 Major arms control treaties since World War I

Treaty	Focus	Members
1922 Washington Naval Agreements	Limits major naval vessels	Multilateral
1925 Geneva Protocol on Chemical and Biological Weapons	Bans use of chemical and biological weapons	Multilateral
1959 Antarctic Treaty	Bans military activity in Antarctica	Multilateral
1963 Limited Test Ban Treaty	Bans nuclear tests except underground	US, UK, USSR; others joined later
1967 Outer Space Treaty	Bans nuclear weapons in space	US, UK, USSR; others joined later
1967 Treaty of Tlatelolco	Establishes nuclear weapons-free zone in Latin America and the Caribbean	Multilateral
1970 Nuclear Non-Proliferation Treaty	Bans acquisition of nuclear weapons by non-nuclear states	Multilateral
1972 Strategic Arms Limitation Treaty I	Limits nuclear weapons arsenals	US, USSR
1972 Anti-Ballistic Missile Treaty	Limits strategic missile defense systems (terminated in 2002)	US, USSR
1972 Seabed Arms Control Treaty	Bans nuclear weapons on ocean floor	US, UK, USSR; others joined later
1974 (1990) Threshold Test Ban Treaty	Limits size of nuclear tests	US, USSR
1975 Biological Weapons Convention	Bans all biological weapons	Multilateral
1977 Strategic Arms Limitation Treaty II	Limits nuclear weapons arsenals (never ratified)	US, USSR
1986 Treaty of Rarotonga	Establishes nuclear weapons-free zone in South Pacific	Multilateral
1988 Intermediate-Range Nuclear Forces Treaty	Bans intermediate-range nuclear forces from Europe (terminated in 2019)	US, USSR

Treaty	Focus	Members
1992 Treaty on Conventional Armed Forces in Europe	Limits key categories of conventional weapons for NATO and Warsaw Pact forces	NATO; Warsaw Pact
1994 Strategic Arms Reduction Treaty I	Reduces nuclear arsenals (expired in 2009)	US, Russia
1996 Comprehensive Nuclear Test-Ban Treaty	Bans all nuclear explosions (not in force)	Multilateral
1997 Treaty of Bangkok	Establishes nuclear weapons-free zone in Southeast Asia	Multilateral
1999 Ottawa Treaty on Anti-Personnel Mines	Bans land mines	Multilateral
2002 Treaty on Open Skies	Protects unarmed aerial surveillance	Multilateral
2003 Treaty of Moscow	Limits number of deployed nuclear warheads	US, Russia
2008 Treaty of Semipalatinsk	Establishes nuclear weapons-free zone in Central Asia	Multilateral
2009 Treaty of Pelindaba	Establishes nuclear weapons-free zone in Africa	Multilateral
2010 Convention on Cluster Munitions	Bans cluster bombs	Multilateral
2011 New Start (Strategic Arms Reduction Treaty)	Reduces existing active nuclear arsenals by 50%	US, Russia
2014 Arms Trade Treaty	Regulates international trade in conventional weapons	Multilateral: 130 signatories, 89 ratifications

agreement established a dedicated communications link between the United States and the Soviet Union in the aftermath of the Cuban Missile Crisis, which was updated in the 1980s to include more modern communications and the establishment of nuclear crisis centers in both countries.

- *Confidence-building measures* involve arrangements for transparency and information sharing on military matters to reduce the fear and uncertainty that often occur. Agreements to share information on military exercises and troop movements, allowing inspections and observers, and a variety of other restraints that promote openness, transparency, and predictability are at the core of this type of agreement. In the 1970s and 1980s, for example, the Conference on Security and Co-operation in Europe and its

Table 11.4 Participants, purposes, and types of arms control

Participants of arms control	Purposes of arms control	Types of arms control
Unilateral Bilateral Multilateral	Reduces likelihood of conflict and war Reduces likelihood of uncontrollable war Reduces resources devoted to armaments Controls proliferation of weapons of mass destruction Establishes and reinforces restraints on violent behavior Contributes to progress toward disarmament	Rules of war Communication and administration Confidence-building measures Geographic agreements Quantitative limitations Qualitative limitations Horizontal proliferation control

Source: Adapted and summarized from chapters 2 and 3 in Lamb (1988).

successor, the Organization for Security and Co-operation in Europe, established agreements to provide for advance warning of military exercises by rival NATO and Warsaw Pact forces and to allow observers from the other side, all in order to lessen the tension between the two blocs.

- *Geographic agreements* limit or ban military activities and arms competitions in specific locations. For example, in 1959 the United States, the Soviet Union, and others agreed to the demilitarization of Antarctica to avert competition and conflict over military bases and activities there. Similarly, the 1967 Tlatelolco and Outer Space Treaties banned the placement of nuclear weapons in Latin America and in outer space, respectively, and the 1971 Seabed Arms Control Treaty did the same for the ocean floor. At present, there are five agreements establishing nuclear-weapons-free zones throughout the world: Latin America (Tlatelolco); the South Pacific (the Treaty of Rarotonga); Southeast Asia (the Treaty of Bangkok); Africa (the Treaty of Pelindaba); and Central Asia (the Treaty of Semipalatinsk). However, only the Latin America treaty has the full compliance of all the official nuclear powers: the United States has not agreed to the South Pacific or Africa agreements, and none of the nuclear powers have agreed to the Southeast Asia or Central Asia accords.
- *Quantitative limitations* establish some numerical limits on arsenals or some part(s) of them. For example, the Washington Naval Agreements of 1922 and the London Naval Treaty of the next decade set limits for Britain, France, Italy, Japan, and the United States on the number of battleships and cruisers allowed to each party, based on tonnage limitations. The Strategic Arms Limitation Talks (producing SALT I in 1972 and SALT II in 1979) set limits on the number of nuclear weapons delivery vehicles that the United States and the Soviet Union could develop. The Strategic Arms Reduction Talks (START) initiated in the 1980s by US President Ronald Reagan and Soviet President

Mikhail Gorbachev resulted in a 1991 agreement (START I) that limited the two sides to 6,000 total nuclear warheads and 1,600 total delivery vehicles (e.g., ICBMs, SCBMs, and bombers). In 2011, the United States and Russia concluded and ratified the so-called New START treaty, which reduced nuclear delivery vehicles by half, to 800, and limited deployed nuclear warheads to 1,550.

- *Qualitative limitations* control types of weapons, not just numbers. The 1987 INF Treaty between the United States and the Soviet Union eliminated an entire class of nuclear weapons from the two sides' arsenals for 30 years before it was abandoned. Similarly, the 1997 Chemical Weapons Convention prohibited the development, production, acquisition, stockpiling, retention, transfer, or use of chemical weapons by its 190 members.
- *Horizontal proliferation control* limits the spread of weapons and weapons technology beyond states that currently possess them. The best-known example of this type of agreement is the 1968 (1970) NPT, which was extended indefinitely in 1995. This agreement, which currently has 191 members, limits nuclear weapons to the five official nuclear weapons states (United States, Russia, Britain, France, and China) and establishes procedures for the peaceful use of nuclear energy by the nonnuclear weapons states. Four nonmembers of the NPT are known or believed to have nuclear weapons: India, Pakistan, North Korea, and Israel. North Korea, which was initially a member of the NPT, withdrew in 2003 and has aggressively pursued a nuclear weapons program ever since. Efforts to complete a Comprehensive Nuclear Test-Ban Treaty (adopted by the UN in 1996) are also geared toward preventing the spread of nuclear weapons. As of 2023, 177 states have ratified the treaty; another nine have signed, but not ratified, it (the United States, Iran, China, Israel, Egypt, Yemen, Nepal, Papua New Guinea, and Sri Lanka).

ARMS/CONTROL/DISARMAMENT AND CONFLICT, CRISIS, AND WAR

Over time, various policymakers, leaders, IOs, citizen groups and non-governmental organizations, and policy advocacy organizations have embraced arms control and, for some, disarmament (e.g., Adler 1992; Knopf 1998). For example, the Carnegie Endowment for International Peace's James Acton, Thomas MacDonald, and Pranay Vaddi (2021) advocated an arms control agenda for the future designed "to mitigate acute nuclear risks by developing practical, concrete, and innovative ideas for interstate cooperation … [and] to catalyze the restart of U.S.-Russian risk-reduction efforts and to productively engage third parties, especially China". Such advocacy is, of course, premised on the conclusion that arms control is effective and necessary as a means to manage conflict, crisis, and war. Countless pages have been devoted to detailing the nature, practices, histories, and plans for controlling arms. But, have arms control efforts worked?

Empirical analyses of the effectiveness of arms control are rarer than accounts of negotiations, descriptions of types, plans for progress, and critiques of the efforts in general. As Fuhrmann and Lupu (2016) point out, much scholarship addresses the effectiveness of treaties and/or international institutions on such international issues as human rights, the environment, economic relations, and other matters – often with positive and optimistic conclusions. However, specific empirical analyses of the effects of arms control are much less common. Many scholars are pessimistic. For example, Coe and Vaynman (2020: 342) argue that effective arms control agreements themselves are rare and hard to establish because they require monitoring that makes arming "transparent enough to assure its compliance but not so much as to threaten its security". Thee (1978) argues that the more limited agreements that are established actually harm substantive progress in arms control and disarmament. When established and in place, Schofield (2000) argues that there are structural conditions and contexts in which arms control contributes more to war than to peace, including conditions of multipolarity. Most broadly, Downs, Rocke, and Barsoom (1996) cast doubt on the substantive significance of treaty compliance in general, of which arms control is part.

However, in addition to the evidence from studies of the effects of treaties and institutions in other areas (some of which we discuss in more detail in Chapter 12), some empirical analyses are more optimistic. Such analyses highlight the role of arms control in establishing stability in deterrence relationships, reducing uncertainty, and improving cooperation. Some also conclude that the provisions of arms control agreements have had positive effects on the management of conflict, crisis, and war. For example, in contrast to previous studies casting doubt on their efficacy (e.g., Leeds and Mattes 2007; Gibler and Vasquez 1998), Mattes and Vonnahme (2010) examined the effects of nonaggression agreements and concluded that they appear to reduce conflict between signatories, even when controlling for relevant context and selection effects. Fuhrmann and Lupu (2016) examine the effects of the NPT and conclude that the NPT reduces the probability that states will seek nuclear weapons quite significantly and has thus curtailed nuclear proliferation. In combination with other studies of treaty affects, empirical analyses such as these suggest positive contributions for arms control as a means for addressing the conflict and competition inherent in arms acquisition, deterrence, and conflict, crisis, and war more generally.

SUMMING UP AND MOVING FORWARD

As our previous chapters have established, the interests and objectives of states and other players are often different, leading to conflict and, sometimes, to crisis and war. Grounded in the diversity of states and their perspectives on world politics, and anchored in the formally anarchic structure of the international system where the absence of authoritative central institutions means coordination and cooperation are inherently difficult, states are often driven by uncertainty, even fear, that their interests will not be protected unless they take action themselves. For states, this self-help incentive triggers a range of strategies and approaches to managing conflict, crisis, and war.

In this chapter, we have reviewed a set of those actions: diplomacy; economic coercion; defense, deterrence, and alliances; and arms control. Our discussion provides important context and description and summarizes key empirical research on the results that follow when states avail themselves of these approaches to conflict, crisis, and war. A common theme that runs through them is that each of these avenues often proves unsuccessful, especially when states pursue them unilaterally. In Chapter 12, we turn to efforts to address conflict, crisis, and war by working with others – cooperation through international governmental organizations and non-governmental organizations.

> **CONSIDER THIS: THE LAW OF UNINTENDED CONSEQUENCES**
>
> A basic premise of the security dilemma is that sometimes the things that states do to make themselves secure create greater insecurity. Consider our discussion of the state-based approaches to conflict, crisis, and war, and the empirical evidence we have summarized on each.
>
> *In what situations are state-based approaches to conflict, crisis, and war most and least likely to be effective and avoid security dilemma-related consequences?*

12
Working with and through others: IGOs, NGOs, and conflict, crisis, and war

PROLOGUE

In July 2023, United Nations Secretary-General António Guterres presented "A New Agenda for Peace" (United Nations 2023) to UN member states. This proposal focused on building, strengthening, and expanding multilateral efforts to manage conflict, crisis, and war in the rapidly changing world and was the result of a multi-year process of consultation among the Secretary-General's office; member states; organizations and departments of the UN system; and regional and other international organizations (IOs) such as the African Union (AU); European Union; League of Arab States; Organization of American States (OAS); Organization for Security and Co-operation in Europe; North Atlantic Treaty Organization; and civil society organizations, almost four dozen of which submitted formal written proposals (United Nations Political and Peacebuilding Affairs 2023).

The resulting policy brief, "A New Agenda for Peace", included 12 proposals in five areas of priority: (1) prevention at the global level; (2) preventing conflict and violence and sustaining peace; (3) strengthening peace operations and addressing peace enforcement; (4) novel approaches to peace and potential domains of conflict; and (5) strengthening international governance. Among the twelve sets of recommendations, Guterres included:

- Action 8: Strengthen peace operations and partnerships (priority 3)
- Action 9: Address peace enforcement (priority 3)
- Action 11: Prevent the weaponization of emerging domains and promote responsible innovation, including cyberspace, outer space, and autonomous weapons systems (priority 4)
- Action 12: Build a stronger collective security machinery, including empowerment of the UN General Assembly and reform of the UN Security Council and the use of the UNSC veto by its permanent members (priority 5)

In his proposal, Secretary-General Guterres argued:

> The collective security system that the United Nations embodies has recorded remarkable accomplishments. It has succeeded in preventing a new global conflagration. International cooperation – spanning from sustainable development, disarmament, human rights and women's empowerment to counter-terrorism and the protection of the environment – has made humanity safer and more prosperous. Peacemaking and peace-keeping have helped to end wars and prevent numerous crises from escalating into full-blown violence. Where wars broke out, collective action by the United Nations often helped shorten their duration and alleviate their worst effects (United Nations 2023: 3).

However, Guterres also emphasized that:

> Achieving peace and prosperity in a world of interlocking threats demands that Member States find new ways to act collectively and cooperatively. My vision for a robust collective security system rests on Member States moving away from a logic of competition. Cooperation does not require States to forgo their national interest, but to recognize that they have shared goals (United Nations 2023: 11).

The Secretary-General concluded that:

> Member States are central to these solutions. They have the primary responsibility and more capacities than any other actor to enact the changes needed to transform peace and security. But they must not work alone. The scale of threats that we face require all-of-society approaches at the national level, and all-of-humanity approaches at the international level (United Nations 2023: 33).

In sum, it is obvious that the Secretary-General is calling for a significantly more active UN role around the world. How will these words potentially translate into action?

OVERVIEW

Cooperation among states to manage conflict, crisis, and war is often challenging. Involving non-state actors such as international governmental organizations (IGOs) and non-governmental organizations (NGOs) brings further complications owing in part to the anarchic nature of the international system (which works against states surrendering authority to others) and the diversity of states and other players in world politics (which works against shared values and consensus on issues). In spite of this, states and non-state actors cooperate extensively across many issues to achieve common goals and to manage conflicts and disagreements without resorting to violence. And yet, cooperation among these players often fails, with conflict leading to crisis and sometimes war as a consequence. In the previous chapter, we reviewed a variety of approaches used by states themselves to manage conflict, crisis, and war. In this chapter, we consider avenues that involve IGOs and NGOs. By their nature, these avenues involve cooperative efforts and, often, collective action, as the quote from Secretary-General Guterres indicates.

At first glance, the benefits of cooperation to manage the inevitable conflicts over interests and issues that arise in world politics seem obvious and compelling. Indeed, as Fearon (1995) argued, the costs and risks of resorting to war over conflicts are so high that rational states have incentives to cooperate to resolve conflicts and avoid the gamble of war. Yet in world politics, cooperation is often more difficult to attain than we might expect. Cooperation can benefit everyone, but establishing the institutions, norms, and rules for cooperation is difficult, and the lack of authoritative institutions beyond states themselves makes adherence to rules and compliance with institutions uneven.

As we have considered in previous chapters, the anarchic nature of world politics certainly complicates cooperation in multiple ways. At the foundation, the absence of a central enforcer to prevent and punish wrongdoing creates incentives for the major political players – states – to take care of themselves and their own interests instead of cooperating. Along with the anarchic structure of the international system, the diversity of world politics also complicates cooperation. The great diversity in the size, perspectives, experiences, regime type, economic capabilities, culture, interests, leader personalities, and many other factors makes common values and principles hard to come by in world politics. Add in the variety of non-state actors with their own identities, interests, and purposes, and this diversity just gets more difficult to manage. So, turning to non-state actors such as IGOs and NGOs to manage conflict, crisis, and war is bound to face significant limitations.

Chapter 12 unfolds in seven additional major sections. Following the starting points of this introductory section 1, we summarize international law as an approach to manage conflict, crisis, and war in section 2, with empirical studies of compliance a special focus in section 3. Sections 4–5 discuss IGOs, with collective security as a special focus. In sections 6–7, we turn to the role and efforts of NGOs to contribute to the management of conflict, crisis, and war and review the empirical record of their role and impact. We offer summary insights in the final section 8.

INTERNATIONAL LAW: DEFINITION AND CONTEXT

Beginning with the Dutch jurist Hugo Grotius – whose 1625 treatise *On the Law of War and Peace* is widely regarded as the first book on international law – international law was thought to hold great promise for the establishment of peace and justice in world politics. Yet, because international law involves the absence of authoritative institutions to make, enforce, and interpret laws and shared values and principles among members of the international system, it has proven more elusive and limited than Grotius and others like him have hoped. According to Anne-Marie Slaughter (1995: 516), international law "comprises all the law that regulates activity across and between territorial boundaries". To consider its role in managing conflict, crisis, and war, we first discuss important context: its sources and issues related to its enforcement.

Most scholars look to Article 38(1) of the charter for the modern-day World Court, or International Court of Justice, as the starting point on the sources of international law. According to Article 38(1) of this 1946 charter, international law comes from: (1) international conventions (treaties) agreed to by states; (2) international custom; (3) general principles of law recognized by civilized nations; and (4) judicial decisions and the writings of eminent jurists. Of these, the first two are understood as primary sources and the last two as secondary or auxiliary ones. Since 1946, the practices and decisions of IOs such as the United Nations are also considered a fifth source of international law.

As a source of international law, a treaty is a formal, written agreement among states and is regarded as binding on the signatories. Indeed, a key principle of international law is *pacta sunt servanda* – or "the treaty must be served" – which holds that a formal agreement between states establishes legal obligations that should be upheld once made. However, states are not obligated to sign treaties, and the 1969 Vienna Convention on the Law of Treaties makes it clear that states that are forced to sign treaties are not obligated to uphold them. With respect to conflict, crisis, and war, treaties exist across a great many dimensions, from arms control (see Chapter 11) and war and the use of force to conflicts arising from disputes over resources, territory, and many other issues.

Although treaties are probably the most significant source of international law in the contemporary context, historically most law derives from custom, which the World Court defined as "general practice [of states] accepted as law". Custom involves both a general behavior and a sense of obligation to adhere to it (known as *opinio juris*). For example, over time most states sharing a river as their boundary chose to mark their border at the midpoint of the river. This general practice eventually became the expected solution when subsequent disputes over river boundaries arose.

The first auxiliary source of international law rests on the idea that evidence of a general practice among states (i.e., a custom) might be seen by identifying laws and practices that many states have adopted and enacted in their own societies. To the extent that many states have laws that look the same, such generally accepted and adopted laws suggest a custom and may form the basis for a treaty codifying the practices. A second auxiliary source of international law points us to what other courts (both domestic and international) and legal experts (lawyers, judges, etc.) have identified as law in previous decisions and legal writing. Usually, court decisions involve those of international courts like the World Court or the European Court of Justice (ECJ), but in recent decades court decisions relevant to international law sometimes include those at the national or even local level.

Finally, although they are not mentioned in the World Court's statute, increasingly since 1946 the decisions of the most authoritative IOs have also been considered sources of international law. For the most part, those decisions stem from the norms and principles embodied in the charters that establish such organizations, which member states sign when they join. In some ways, then, ensuing decisions – such as when the UN Security Council (UNSC) pronounces a judgment on state behavior or the World Trade Organization (WTO) rules against a member state's trade practices – are more like interpretation and application of "treaty law", with the organization's charter as the treaty. However, such organizations also interpret customary law and help shape what is regarded as custom and the legal obligations on states that stem from it. They also help develop norms and laws with their decisions and recommendations on what should be considered international law. Finally IOs may address unclear or ill-defined areas of international law to issue decisions that are partly applications and interpretations and partly assertions of principles. Together, these sources provide the international community with the emerging and evolving norms and rules of international law.

> **IN FOCUS: THE JUST WAR TRADITION AND INTERNATIONAL LAW**
>
> Clearly tied to Western traditions and thought, including the moral arguments of philosophers and the Catholic Church, the development of international laws of war has long emphasized two questions: (a) *jus ad bellum*, or when the use of force is justified, and (b) *jus in bello*, or how wars should be fought once they have started. A third matter has been increasingly addressed in recent decades: *jus post bellum*, or justice after war, which addresses post-conflict issues such as peace agreements and war crimes tribunals.

It is often said that most states uphold their obligations to most international laws most of the time. Given that so much of international law emerges from custom and treaty, which states enter into voluntarily, this is not surprising. International law can and does contribute to orderly and predictable patterns that help guide behavior. Moreover, the principle of reciprocity leads most states to follow laws and conventions so that others will be more likely to do so as well.

However, and perhaps especially in conflict, crisis, and war, such general compliance is interrupted by significant exceptions. Enforcement becomes an issue in those exceptions, which are often significant and salient issues in world politics. For example, most states do not attack other states most of the time. But what happens when one does, as when Russia invaded Ukraine in February 2022?

The anarchic structure of the international system and the great diversity of its relevant actors pose challenges for the three main avenues for enforcement: national, horizontal, or vertical.

- In national enforcement, states enforce some international law through their own national legal systems. In many such issues of national enforcement, national and local governments consider, and even integrate, international law into their rules and practices. Some states have integrated international law into their own national constitutions, either by revision or when they were initially drafted.
- In horizontal enforcement – the most common approach to enforcing international law – states themselves take measures to punish another state when it violates an international law. In terms of conflict, crisis, and war, states can protest diplomatically, they can threaten and enact a variety of economic sanctions, and they can threaten or use force in a wide range of ways to punish the violator (see our discussion in Chapter 11).
- In vertical enforcement, international institutions enforce international law. Because few international institutions have the authority and/or capability to enforce international law against violators, vertical enforcement is relatively rare.

Some challenges for these enforcement mechanisms are apparent. For example, with horizontal mechanisms states themselves determine when a violation occurs, and what to do in response, which opens the door for a highly selective application of law. Measures such as diplomacy, sanctions, and the use of force are of limited effectiveness, as we discussed in the previous chapter. Finally, to the extent that horizontal enforcement is likely to work, it is most effective when the measures are broadly enacted by a relatively large multilateral coalition. Given the great diversity of interests, linkages, and capabilities, assembling such a coalition is difficult to achieve.

International institutions are often limited to identifying and condemning violations and recommending or authorizing the member states of the organizations to take actions to enforce a rule or punish a violator. For instance, the International Court of Justice, or World Court, the 15-judge panel located in The Hague, Netherlands, hears cases on disputes between states (but only between states, and only states can bring cases). However, the World Court does not have compulsory jurisdiction; both parties to a dispute must voluntarily submit the case to the court before it can act. From its establishment right after World War II until mid-2023, the World Court rendered decisions in a total of about 190 cases, a small number in comparison to the instances of conflict and issues of international law that have arisen in that period (see https://www.icj-cij.org/list-of-all-cases). Most other international courts are limited by the same issues, whether they are courts established by regional organizations, or specialized courts such as the International Criminal Court (ICC), which exists to try individuals (not states) accused of committing aggression, genocide, war crimes, and crimes against humanity, or those established to help interpret and apply specific parts of international law, like the World Trade Organization Dispute Settlement Body; the International Tribunal on the Law of the Sea; and special tribunals established for conflicts in the former Yugoslavia, Rwanda, Cambodia, Lebanon, and Sierra Leone.

FOR EXAMPLE: THE UNITED STATES AND INTERNATIONAL LAW

The US has regularly been a champion of the establishment of international courts and other organizations, but its relationship with them has been complex and highlights several key issues about the role and application of international law to conflict, crisis, and war in world politics. Consider three examples.

1. In 1980, the US brought a case against Iran to the World Court seeking a ruling that Iran's hostage-taking of Americans after the overthrow of the Shah violated international law.
2. In 1984, Nicaragua brought a case against the US to the World Court seeking a ruling that the mining of Nicaraguan harbors inflicts damage on Nicaraguan shipping, which the US undertook as part of its support for the Contra rebels and its campaign against the leftist Nicaraguan government. The United States argued that the World Court did not have jurisdiction and then that the United States was exercising its rights to self-defense. When the World Court found in favor of Nicaragua the United States refused to comply and promptly withdrew its acceptance of the World Court's compulsory jurisdiction. The US also vetoed multiple efforts by Nicaragua to gain UN Security Council resolutions against the US.

3. In 1988, Iran brought the US to the World Court, charging it with violations of international air traffic laws. The US agreed to take part in the proceedings but resisted action by the World Court. The case was settled in 1996 by agreement between Iran and the US, which included more than £61 million in US compensation to the families of the Iranian victims. It did not include any admission or acceptance of legal guilt or responsibility.

What do these examples suggest about the nature and enforcement of international law?

INTERNATIONAL LAW AND COMPLIANCE: THE EMPIRICAL RECORD

As an avenue to manage conflict, crisis, and war, the challenges of international law noted above in the preceding paragraph have combined to produce limited effects. While it is likely accurate, as Henkin (1979: 47) asserted, that "almost all nations observe almost all principles of international law and almost all of their obligations almost all of the time", on matters related directly to conflict, crisis, and war, the empirical record is not so positive. Reciprocity, reputation, regime type, the impact of norms, and other factors affect compliance with international laws and agreements (treaties) related to conflict and war, but also to variation and contingent outcomes (e.g., Mitchell and Hensel 2007; von Stein 2017; see also Luck and Doyle 2004).

On area of great interest is the development of international laws of war, which have principally focused on war's legality (*jus ad bellum*) and its practices (*jus in bello*). Despite much attention, efforts such as the Kellogg–Briand Pact to outlaw war or the UN Charter to restrict it to self-defense only have had limited effects (e.g., Pulkowski 2014; see also Tanaka 2018 on international law and peaceful dispute settlement). In terms of controlling the practices of warfare – especially humanitarian laws of war embodied in the Geneva Conventions and thereafter to limit harm to noncombatants, prisoners, and other such matters – compliance and effectiveness has been greater, but still quite limited (e.g., Evangelista and Tannenwald 2017; Sagan 2017; Clark et al. 2018). As Morrow (2002: S41) has argued, "The laws of war have a mixed record of limiting violence during war.... These laws succeed only when the parties comply on their own or reciprocal sanctions dissuade parties who are willing to violate the agreement." Indeed, in empirical terms, international law faces an ongoing crisis of relevance and effectiveness across most fronts: state challenges include revisionist, rejectionist, and denialist threats (Clark et al. 2018) and the changing nature of war to civil and unconventional violence has further challenged international law.

One form of international law – international agreements – has fared better. As we discussed in Chapter 11, alliance agreements have generally been upheld once made, but their effects on conflict and war are quite mixed and contingent (Senese and Vasquez 2008; Kenwick and McManus 2021; Leeds 2003; Kenwick, Vasquez, and Powers 2015; Kenwick and Vasquez 2017). Moreover, as Simmons (1998) has summarized, the decades since the end of World War II have been characterized by the expansion of international agreements and supranational authority across a great many issue-areas, and compliance with these agreements has been substantial (see also von Stein 2017; Lutmar and Carneiro 2018). Peace agreements have also evolved (e.g., Bell 2008, 2010), with data (e.g., Kreutz 2010) and studies on the manner in which they are involved in and emerge from conflict (e.g., Fortna 2004a, 2004b; Mattes and Savun 2009), as well as their role in the duration of peace after agreement, indicating that the nature of the agreement and related guarantees significantly affects their outcomes (e.g., Badran 2014; Fortna 2004a, 2004b; see also Saul and Sweeney 2016 on post-conflict matters).

Given our emphasis on the centrality of territorial issues to conflict and war, one additional area of interest with respect to the impact of international law on conflict, crisis, and war concerns its application to territorial disputes. As we discussed in previous chapters, much scholarship has addressed the origins, effects, and resolution of territorial conflicts. At the center of international conflict and war, territorial disputes are nevertheless resolved peacefully by most parties most of the time (Powell and Weigand 2010; Prorok and Huth 2015). This area of conflict has relatively frequently involved international legal institutions and processes, with findings suggesting that the resort to and impact of such methods depends greatly on the domestic institutions and politics of the parties (e.g., Allee and Huth 2006; Huth, Croco, and Appel 2011; Powell and Weigand 2010).

INTERNATIONAL GOVERNMENTAL ORGANIZATIONS: DEFINITION AND CONTEXT

A second non-state avenue for managing conflict, crisis, and war involves IGOs. IGOs are international institutions whose primary members are states bound together by formal agreement. IGOs may play a role in war prevention and conflict resolution through a variety of means. As in the case of international law, the anarchic nature of the international system and the great diversity of its key actors create constraints on their role and impact.

According to the *Yearbook of International Organizations* (Union of International Associations 2022), of the more than 40,000 active IOs, about 5,000 or so are IGOs (the remainder are NGOs). These IGOs include institutions like the United Nations and the WTO, regional IGOs such as the OAS and the European Union, and many other more specialized bodies like the International Labor Organization and the World Health Organization. Compare this relatively large number to the (just under) 200 independent states of the international system – potential agendas and resulting actions are vast.

What leads states to create IGOs? One set of arguments about the reasons for IGO creation stresses state interests and power and, in particular, the interests of the most powerful states. Realist, Marxist, postcolonial, and feminist perspectives all argue that powerful states create and sponsor IGOs to support norms and practices that advance their interests and to control and constrain the behavior of others. Even liberal perspectives offer power-based arguments that powerful states establish IGOs to serve very broad interests in order and stability, while sacrificing narrower and more specific outcomes and bearing the costs of providing some "public goods" for the benefit of themselves and others (Bull 1977). Less powerful states may also attempt to establish or steer IGOs toward protecting and asserting their interests, relying on their ability to outnumber powerful states in voting procedures within existing IGOs to redirect and create new IGOs (e.g., Krasner 1985; Ikenberry 2000).

Another perspective on the creation of IGOs focuses on the common problems faced by states and other actors in world politics. These arguments emphasize the need and desire among states and others to cooperate to address problems together to expand benefits and reduce conflict. A good example of this argument comes from theories of functionalism and neo-functionalism (e.g., Haas 1958; Schmitter 1969) and the promotion of transnational cooperation on economic and social problems that grows to link societies together. In this context, IGOs are established to enable specific technical cooperation on economic and social issues that build linkages and shared interests among societies. The benefits from these linkages and the cooperation they promote often expand to more areas, leading to even greater cooperation and institutional connections (Mitrany 1966). A good example of this can be seen in the development of the European Union and the various institutions it now involves, though the exit of the United Kingdom and the disillusionment of other EU countries in the past decade are cautionary notes. Another example of this explanation focuses on the presence of transnational problems that transcend state boundaries and cannot be addressed by the actions of any one state. The need to address such issues – like those of the environment, disease, and others – may lead states to establish IGOs to help coordinate their efforts more effectively and efficiently (e.g., Peinhardt and Sandler 2015). States thus have reasons to cooperate and manage conflicts and, once established, the IGOs that are created to help them do so take on lives of their own and influence and channel state behavior.

Collectively, these arguments suggest a range of roles and functions for IGOs in managing conflict, crisis, and war. IGOs may serve as:

- instruments for some states to advance their interests and influence other states;
- forums for states to communicate, negotiate, and advance their interests;
- participants in bargaining and negotiation in third-party diplomacy;
- participants in the generation and dissemination of information and technical expertise;
- players who regularize interactions and habits of behavior on issues and facilitate national and transnational linkages and networks that contribute to norms of procedure and behavior;
- organizations that coordinate and pool resources to address common problems;
- institutions that generate and institutionalize norms and rules;
- organizations that reduce uncertainty, enhance communication and interactions, and reduce the incentives for cheating in world politics;
- players who constrain state behavior and expand avenues for cooperation and punishment.

With as many as 5,000 IGOs in the world today, we cannot identify and discuss them all. In this section, we offer relatively simple categorizations of their types and provide examples of each.

Type I: Decision Process. One way to distinguish IOs is according to how they make their decisions. This not only highlights some important differences but also lends itself to some insights on the role, influence, and impact of different kinds of IOs. We can distinguish between three core decision processes: majority rule, weighted voting, and unit veto, which has two sub-types. Some IGOs make their decisions by simple or modified majority rule. A good example is the UN General Assembly, in which all member states have equal representation, and each state has one vote. On any given issue, the majority rules (a two-thirds threshold is required for issues related to peace and security, new members, and the peacekeeping budget). Not surprisingly, this decision rule is generally favored by less powerful states such as those of the developing world, for the simple fact that they outnumber the powerful and wealthy. IGOs with majority voting rules are often used to establish new IOs or subsidiaries that reflect the interests of the majority as well (e.g., Krasner 1985).

Other IGOs adopt a weighted voting decision rule, in which member voting power is allocated according to some factor such as size, power, wealth, or the like. This provides greater control and influence to those countries that have a greater role or responsibility, bear greater burdens for providing resources, or just have more power. A good example is the International Monetary Fund (IMF). All members of the IMF are represented but are assigned a share of the vote based on the size of their contribution – or quota – to the IMF's lending capital (which is, in turn, based on the size of the country's economy). France and the United Kingdom, for example, each have about 4.0% of the votes, Japan has about 6.1%, and Germany has about 5.3%. China has about 6.0%, but the United States has about 16.5% of the vote, the largest share. Contrast these percentages with, say, Sierra Leone, which has less than 0.1% of the vote, Chile, which has about 0.4%, India, which has about 2.6%, or Brazil, which has about 2.2%. It is also worth noting that the IMF usually requires a 70% majority for aid and financing decisions and an 85% majority for major decisions, such as those involving IMF decision-making processes, which means the United States can block the latter all on its own.

In IGOs with a unit veto decision rule, some or all members can block decisions with their votes. A pure unit veto decision rule requires unanimity, so every member effectively exercises a veto. This was the case in the League of Nations, the forerunner to the United Nations. A modified unit veto assigns veto power to some members of the IGO. The best example of this decision rule is the UNSC, which is made up of 15 members. Ten of those members are elected by the UN General Assembly (with regional allocations for Africa, Latin America, Asia, Europe, Eastern Europe, and "other areas") for two-year terms, and each of these members has one vote in the UNSC. The other five members – the United States, Russia, China, France, and the United Kingdom – are permanent. These P5 (or Perm-5, as they are often known) are the main founders of the UN and the world's first official nuclear weapons states, and each possesses a veto so that if any one of them votes against a substantive Security Council measure, it is defeated (see Table 12.1 on usage of the veto power by P5 members since 1946). Passage of substantive measures also requires at least nine affirmative votes, which means, in effect, that the ten elected members together have a collective veto to block the P5 in the unlikely event that they are unified.

Type II: Scope and Membership. IGOs may also be categorized by scope (the range of issues they address) and membership (who is eligible to join them). For scope, a simple distinction we can make is between IOs that address multiple issues across the political, economic, and social spheres and those that address just a single issue. In terms of membership, we can simply

Table 12.1   UN Security Council vetoes by P5 members, 1946–2022

Country	1946–1959	1960–1969	1970–1979	1980–1989	1990–2000	2001–22
United States	0	0	21	42	5	15
United Kingdom	2	1	12	14	0	0
France	2	0	7	7	0	0
Russia	66	14	6	4	2	30
China*	0	0	1	0	2	27

Note: *China's seat on the UN Security Council was held by Taiwan from 1949 to 1971 before the UN General Assembly voted to recognize the People's Republic of China (mainland) as the lawful representative of China.
Source: Data compiled from Security Council Veto List, http://research.un.org/en/docs/sc/quick.

Table 12.2   A typology of international organizations

Membership	Scope	
	Single Issue	Multiple Issue
Global	International Monetary Fund World Bank World Trade Organization	United Nations
Regional	Andean Common Market European Environment Agency Inter-American Institute for Cooperation on Agriculture Asia-Pacific Economic Cooperation	European Union Organization of American States African Union Association of Southeast Asian Nations

distinguish between IOs that allow any state to join (global) and those that restrict membership based on geographic region (regional). If we combine these two dimensions, we get the categories shown in Table 12.2. Let's take up each with some examples.

First, there are a wide variety of global, single-issue IOs that include members from all over the world but concentrate on a single issue. Examples of these include:

- The IMF, established following World War II as part of the Bretton Woods system of international financial organizations to improve cooperation and coordination of the world's economy. This 189-member global, single-issue organization has weighted voting and originally served two purposes: (a) as a source of emergency lending for countries with balance-of-payments crises, with loans drawn from the pooled resources of IMF member states, and (b) as an exchange rate regime in which member currencies were pegged within a small range of fluctuation to the fixed value of the US dollar, which ended in 1971 when the US unilaterally suspended the fixed exchange rate of the dollar, starting a floating exchange rate system that continues today. Since its existence, the IMF

has also served as a kind of global economy watchdog, collecting and disseminating economic information about member states and the world economy to facilitate planning and coordination.
- The World Bank, a group of five institutions that are also part of the Bretton Woods system, was created to provide long-term developmental loans to members. Voting power in the World Bank is weighted by member contributions, which are based on member-states' economies. The main emphasis of the World Bank's lending activities is poverty reduction and sustainable development.
- The WTO established in 1995 to replace its predecessor, the General Agreement on Tariffs and Trade (GATT). GATT/WTO promotes trade liberalization through most-favored nation (MFN) status (in the United States, MFN is now referred to as NTR, or normal trade relations). Each member is required to give all other members the lowest tariff rate available – this rate was considered the MFN rate. The key to the WTO is its enforcement powers over free-trade rules and practices. Basically, if one state blocks another state from selling its products, the two states can go to the Dispute Settlement Body – effectively a "trade court" – and the WTO will determine if a rule is being broken. If the trade barrier is illegal under WTO rules, then the plaintiff state is permitted to sanction the other state to regain the revenue lost by not being able to sell its goods and services.

Many other such global, single-issue IGOs exist for issues related to the environment, global health, human rights, nuclear energy, and a great variety of other things.

Second, there are many regional, single-issue IOs. A common issue on which such IGOs focus is economic cooperation. A large number of the regions and subregions of the world have some kind of economic organization to promote trade and economic integration. For example, consider the 21-member Asia-Pacific Economic Cooperation (APEC), established in 1989 to foster economic growth, strengthen the Asia-Pacific community, and reduce tariffs and other trade barriers across the Asia-Pacific region. A subregional example is the Andean Common Market – a customs union for Bolivia, Ecuador, Colombia, and Peru. Just as for global IOs of this type, regional, single-issue IOs exist for the environment, global health, human rights, nuclear energy, and a great variety of other things.

Third, there are regional, multiple-issue organizations who play a meaningful role in many issues and areas of world politics. Regionalism, typically defined by geographic proximity and interdependence among a specific group of states (as well as non-state actors), seeks to foster cooperation among such players for their mutual benefit. In the latter 20th and early 21st centuries, regional organizations became increasingly important in world politics, and IGOs of this type began as regional, single-issue IGOs (economic) and have expanded into other issue-areas.

- In the Middle East, regional organizations are the least developed. The League of Arab States was created in 1945 to promote and foster Arab unity, but its role has been very limited. Its main body is a council formed of the foreign ministers of its member states, which now includes 22 countries (Syria's membership was suspended in 2011 because of its actions in its civil war but reinstated in May 2023). The Gulf Cooperation Council

(GCC) was established in 1981 and includes the six Arab states of the Persian Gulf region: Bahrain, Kuwait, Qatar, Saudi Arabia, Oman, and the United Arab Emirates. The GCC was created to promote economic cooperation among its members but also as a response to the threat posed by Iran after the Shi'a Iranian revolution.

- In Asia, in addition to APEC (discussed earlier), there is the Association of Southeast Asian Nations (ASEAN), which currently has ten member states. Very decentralized and more informal than other regional organizations, ASEAN stresses consultation, coordination, and consensus building, and it also hosts the ASEAN Regional Forum (ARF) to promote cooperative security in Asia, which now includes 28 members (including the EU, the United States, Russia, India, China, Canada, and others).
- In Africa, the AU has 55 current members and has the goal of becoming as unified as the EU at some point. One interesting aspect of the AU is its Pan-African Parliament, mostly as a consultative body, to which each member sends five legislators (one of which must be a woman). The AU also created the Economic, Social and Cultural Council; the African Court of Justice; the African Central Bank; the African Monetary Fund; and the African Investment Bank. Subregional organizations in Africa have also been established, including the Economic Community of West African States (ECOWAS) and the Southern African Development Community (SADC) as well.
- In the Western Hemisphere, the OAS includes all 35 countries from North, Central, and South America and the Caribbean. The OAS includes a General Assembly, a Permanent Council, and an Inter-American Council for Integral Development (all of which are one state–one vote, majority institutions); a secretariat to handle day-to-day activities; an Inter-American Court of Human Rights; and an Inter-American Development Bank. The OAS also has a number of specialized agencies that address health, gender, and cultural matters, among other things. The role of the OAS has expanded since the end of the Cold War, moving from US-dominated efforts to resist communism to a greater variety of roles in conflict resolution, support for democracy and human rights, and other activities. Subregional organizations in the Western Hemisphere include the United States–Mexico–Canada Agreement (the USMCA, formerly the North American Free Trade Agreement, or NAFTA), the Southern Common Market (MERCOSUR), the Andean Common Market (discussed earlier), the Central American Common Market (CACM), and the Caribbean Community (CARICOM).

The largest, most developed, and most authoritative multiple-issue regional organization is the European Union, which unites 27 European countries in an economic, social, and political organization characterized by a common market and currency (for 19 of its members), with central political and economic institutions such as the European Parliament (EP), the Council of the European Union, the European Council, the European Commission (EC), the ECJ, and the European Central Bank.

After centuries of war, culminating in the devastation of World War II that left much of the continent of Europe in ruin, European leaders began to try to build regional institutions that would unite their countries in cooperative structures that would help them work together and avoid such costly wars in the future. These efforts led first to the creation of the European

Coal and Steel Community (ECSC) in 1951, with six original members establishing a common market centered on the trade of French coal and German steel. From this beginning, the European Union of today expanded to the European Economic Community (EEC) in 1958, added new members the United Kingdom, Ireland, and Denmark in the 1970s, and Spain and Portugal in the 1980s. The European Union emerged in 1992 with the conclusion of the Maastricht Treaty, which strengthened European political and legal structures and economic integration. Austria, Finland, and Sweden joined in 1995, bringing membership to 15. Subsequent treaties of Amsterdam (1997), Nice (2003), and Lisbon (2007) all strengthened EU institutions and regional democratic practices, and the EU also continued to expand, this time to the east to include members from Eastern Europe for the first time. In 2004, ten new states – Cyprus, Czech Republic, Estonia, Hungary, Latvia, Lithuania, Malta, Poland, Slovak Republic, and Slovenia – joined the EU. Romania and Bulgaria followed in 2008, and Croatia joined in 2013. The EU now has 27 members spanning Western and Eastern Europe, but lost the United Kingdom in 2020, which completed the process of leaving the EU initiated after a 2016 national referendum.

The EU today has many agencies and sub-agencies that attend to a broad array of matters (see Figures 12.1a and b), the organization's structure revolves around five main institutions with executive, legislative, and judicial functions.

The most powerful institution is the EC, which is basically the executive branch of the EU. It has its own budgetary powers, which gives it substantial independence from member-state pressures, and its purpose is to represent the interests of the European Union as a whole, not any individual member states. The 27-member (one from each member state) Commission is headed by a president (in 2023, Germany's Ursula von der Leyen) and oversees policy development in agriculture, trade, social policy, the environment, and other areas. Each office or portfolio in the Commission is led by an individual from a different EU member country, and the president of the Commission (not the member states themselves) appoints these individuals.

The European Council is made up of the heads of government of the EU member states, who come together collectively at EU Summits twice every six months (more frequently if needed) to represent the interests of their member states within the EU. Highly visible, the European Council has little executive or legislative power over EU policy, mostly serving as an advisory and agenda-setting body.

The legislative institutions of the EU include the Council of Ministers (CoM) and the EP. The CoM, more formally the Council of the European Union, is the more powerful of the two and can be seen as an "upper house", like the US Senate. Council membership varies depending on the issue at hand: when defense and security matters are on the agenda, member states send their defense ministers; when foreign affairs are at hand, foreign ministers attend; if the issue is economic, finance ministers show up. No matter who attends, when the CoM meets, its members represent their member states and are themselves members of their national governments. Any and all EU legislation must be approved by the CoM. Most of the time, the EP must also approve legislation but in some instances the CoM has exclusive legislative authority, and the parliament can serve only in an advisory function.

The EP is the second of the two legislative institutions and is often seen as the "lower house". Since the UK's exit from the EU in 2020, 705 seats are allocated proportionally according to

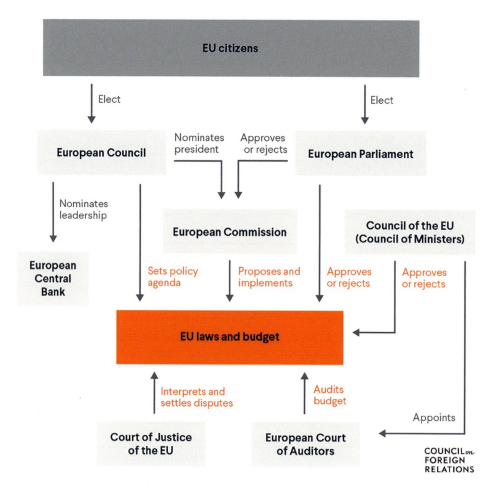

Figure 12.1a The institutions of the European Union

population. Germany has the most seats (96), and Cyprus, Malta, and Luxembourg have the minimum (6). All of these representatives to the EP are directly elected, so the parliament is regarded as the most democratic of the EU institutions. No other IGO, regional or otherwise, has such a body with real authority. Elections are held every five years (since 1979), and citizens in each member state directly elect their representatives, who serve only in the EP (not in their member-state parliaments) and are elected to serve the interests of European citizens and the EU as a whole, not the specific interests of their home states. In the EP, representatives sit with fellow members of their political parties (e.g., Conservative, Social Democrat, Greens) from all over Europe, not with other representatives from their home countries. The parliament amends, approves, or rejects EU laws, together with the CoM, in areas such as consumer protection, the single market, workers' rights, asylum and immigration, agriculture, the environment, and animal welfare, but not in foreign and defense policy. The EP also has shared authority over the EU budget (with the CoM) and oversees the EC.

EXECUTIVE

European Council
The EU's 27 national leaders
Sets policy agenda

European Commission
27 commissioners, nominated by the European Council and approved by Parliament
Proposes and implements legislation

LEGISLATIVE

European Parliament
705 members, directly elected by EU citizens
Approves or rejects legislation

Council of the European Union (Council of Ministers)
27 national ministers, grouped by policy area
Approves or rejects legislation

JUDICIAL

Court of Justice of the European Union
Two courts, with judges appointed jointly by national governments
Interprets EU law and settles disputes

European Court of Auditors
27 members, appointed by the Council of Ministers
Audits budget

FINANCIAL

European Central Bank
President and executive board appointed by the European Council
Maintains the stability of the euro and oversees the European financial system

COUNCIL on FOREIGN RELATIONS

Figure 12.1b The institutions of the European Union

The judicial branch of the EU is the ECJ, widely regarded as the most powerful and successful international court of its kind. It is charged with interpreting EU law and ensuring that it is applied equally across all member states. There is one judge for each member state. The power of the ECJ is illustrated by the fact that when national law is seen to be in violation of EU law, member states must change their national laws to come into compliance with EU law.

Fourth, the most obvious global, multiple-issue IO is the United Nations, which addresses virtually every issue that can be imagined in world politics in one way or another. Established in 1945, its roots extend back to the Concert of Europe (1815–1854) and, especially, the League of Nations (1919–1945), an IGO dedicated to collective security and the resolution of disputes between states. While the central focus of the League of Nations was collective security, it proved ineffective in practice. Its members had difficulty defining aggression and enlisting the support of great powers to counter it when it did not directly involve them. Further, the League Council's requirement for unanimous decisions prevented it from responding to the aggression by Germany, Italy, and Japan that caused World War II.

During World War II, the United States and United Kingdom led work on a new organization to be established after the war. Fifty-one countries joined and drafted the UN Charter in San Francisco in 1945. Although the UN shared its predecessor's emphasis on peace and security, it was designed to be a broader IGO from the start. The UN Charter identifies its main purposes as peace and security, the development of friendly relations and harmony among nations, and cooperation on international problems. It also embraces the sovereign equality of all states and restricts the UN from interfering in the domestic jurisdiction of its members. It is a global IGO, with all states entitled to membership once they sign and ratify the UN Charter. From the original 51 members, the UN grew to its current membership of 193 countries, driven by the decolonization of Africa, Asia, and the Middle East during its first three decades and then the post-Cold War emergence of independent states primarily from the former Soviet Union and Eastern/Central Europe. Once they join, member states participate in an extensive IGO, which has its headquarters in New York City and major offices in Geneva (Switzerland), Vienna (Austria), and Nairobi (Kenya). The UN also has regional commissions and specialized agencies located throughout the world.

IN FOCUS: THE BASIC PURPOSES OF THE UN

According to Chapter 1, Article 1 of the UN Charter, the new IO formed after World War II had four main purposes:

Article I
The purposes of the United Nations are:

1. To maintain international peace and security, and to that end: to take effective collective measures for the prevention and removal of threats to the peace, and for the suppression of acts of aggression or other breaches of the peace, and to bring about by peaceful means, and in conformity with the principles of justice and international law, adjustment or settlement of international disputes or situations which might lead to a breach of the peace.
2. To develop friendly relations among nations based on respect for the principle of equal rights and self-determination of peoples, and to take other appropriate measures to strengthen universal peace.
3. To achieve international co-operation in solving international problems of an eco-

nomic, social, cultural, or humanitarian character, and in promoting and encouraging respect for human rights and for fundamental freedoms for all without distinction as to race, sex, language, or religion.
4. To be a centre for harmonizing the actions of nations in the attainment of these common ends.

Article II
The Organization and its Members, in pursuit of the Purposes stated in Article I, shall act in accordance with the following Principles.

1. The Organization is based on the principle of the sovereign equality of all its Members.
2. All Members, in order to ensure to all of them the rights and benefits resulting from membership, shall fulfill in good faith the obligations assumed by them in accordance with the present Charter.
3. All Members shall settle their international disputes by peaceful means in such a manner that international peace and security, and justice, are not endangered.
4. All Members shall refrain in their international relations from the threat or use of force against the territorial integrity or political independence of any state, or in any other manner inconsistent with the Purposes of the United Nations.
5. All Members shall give the United Nations every assistance in any action it takes in accordance with the present Charter, and shall refrain from giving assistance to any state against which the United Nations is taking preventive or enforcement action.
6. The Organization shall ensure that states which are not Members of the United Nations act in accordance with these Principles so far as may be necessary for the maintenance of international peace and security.
7. Nothing contained in the present Charter shall authorize the United Nations to intervene in matters which are essentially within the domestic jurisdiction of any state or shall require the Members to submit such matters to settlement under the present Charter; but this principle shall not prejudice the application of enforcement measures under Chapter VII.

Figure 12.2 provides a sense of how the purposes of the UN are carried out through its structure and institutions.

The UN General Assembly (UNGA) is the plenary body of the UN, so all UN members have a seat in the assembly. It functions on a one state–one vote, majority-rule principle (with a two-thirds majority required for some issues), and it is the central forum for discussion of global issues. As less-developed countries gained numerical dominance, the UNGA began to reflect the perspectives and priorities of those countries, as it offered the smallest countries in the world their most important diplomatic opportunities. The UNGA may debate any issue that arises under the UN Charter, and its work is achieved mostly through its wide range of committees that operate year-round. The UNGA meets formally each year in September.

The UNSC is a 15-member council that carries the primary UN responsibilities for peace, security, and collective security operations. It can meet at any time it is deemed necessary and holds meetings each year in conjunction with the UNGA meetings as well. Operating via the

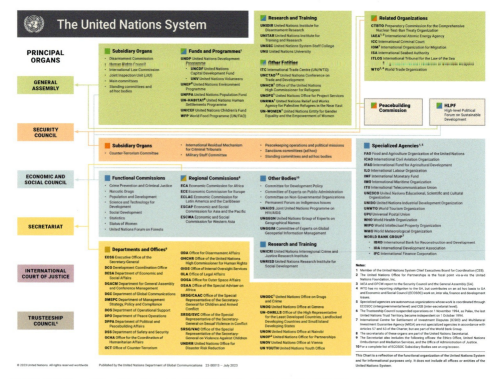

Figure 12.2 The structure and institutions of the United Nations

P5 veto system discussed earlier, the UNSC is entitled to investigate any dispute it considers important for international peace and security, and UN members can bring issues to the UNSC as well. The Cold War largely froze the UNSC, but since its end, it has been more active, and it engages in a range of efforts, including resolutions condemning specific behavior, efforts to mediate conflicts before they erupt, authorizing sanctions against states deemed to violate the peace, dispatching peacekeeping forces and establishing cease-fires to provide opportunities for conflict resolution, and authorizing military action against aggressors.

The UN Secretariat is the UN's major administrative arm. Employing almost 38,000 staff in New York and around the world, the Secretariat manages and administers the activities authorized by the UNGA and the UNSC. As suggested by the entries in Figure 12.2, the Secretariat covers a wide range of functions, from peacekeeping operations and humanitarian issues to public information and facilities safety. The Secretariat is directed by the UN Secretary-General who has some discretion in administering the UN budget and can call special sessions of the UNGA. The occupant of the position – currently António Guterres of Portugal – can also bring issues to the UNSC for consideration.

The UN's goals involving problems of an economic, social, and cultural nature are primarily the responsibility of the UN Economic and Social Council (ECOSOC), and it is the broadest and largest of the UN's organs. The UN website officially describes ECOSOC as the central forum for discussing international economic and social issues, and for formulating policy recommendations addressed to member states and the United Nations system. It has 54 members elected by the UNGA for three-year terms, and it meets one month of each year. ECOSOC at least nominally supervises a wide array of commissions, committees, and specialized agencies, the most well known of which include the WTO and IMF, the Commission on Human Rights, the UN Children's Fund (UNICEF), the World Health Organization, the International Atomic Energy Agency, the UN Educational, Scientific and Cultural Organization (UNESCO), and a whole host of others on such things as the status of women, population, and refugees. Seventy percent of the human and financial resources of the UN fall under ECOSOC's purview.

The Trusteeship Council was originally established to supervise territories emerging from colonial rule after World War II. It contributed to the process of decolonization in the first three decades of the UN. It discharged its last responsibility in 1994 with the independence of Palau and has suspended its operations.

The International Court of Justice (World Court), which we discussed earlier in this chapter, is the principal judicial body of the UN. The UNGA and UNSC elect its 15 judges to nine-year terms, and they must come from different countries. Their decisions are rendered by majority vote.

INTERNATIONAL GOVERNMENTAL ORGANIZATIONS: THE EMPIRICAL RECORD

In the context of the broad roles and functions of IGOs just discussed, two areas of IGO activity related to conflict, crisis, and war are especially important, and the focus on significant empirical research: conflict resolution and collective security/peace operations. We discuss select empirical research on each briefly in the following paragraphs.

Conflict Resolution

In the broad context of diplomacy, which we discussed in the preceding chapter, both regional and international organizations may play a role in conflict resolution as hosts or forums for negotiations (good offices), which is particularly relevant in multilateral diplomacy (e.g., Henriksen 2006; Muldoon and Aviel 2020; Muldoon et al. 2005). As we discussed earlier, they are also engaged in more binding forms such as arbitration and adjudication, often through regional and international courts (Gent and Shannon 2010, 2011; Mitchell and Hensel 2007). Here, we focus on their roles and effectiveness in mediation, which is a central approach to managing conflict, crisis, and war between and within states that is "a type of third-party intervention … is a consent-based process of changing a situation of conflict in the direction toward peace, without resorting to either the use of force or the law" (Svensson 2020; see also Young 1967; Greig and Diehl 2012).

A very large body of scholarship has focused on mediation generally, and on mediation by regional and IOs as a subset of that literature. Empirical findings tend to find positive effects of mediation generally (e.g., Walter 2002; Bercovitch and Gartner 2006; Peck 2001), though state-based mediation may be more effective than UN-based efforts. For example, according to Savun (2009), about half of state mediators secured ceasefires, compared to less than 40% of UN mediations. However, the results of IGO mediation efforts are also quite situation-specific depending in part on how effect/success is measured. According to Svensson (2020: 10), studies based on time to war termination, signing of a settlement, recurrence of war, duration of agreement, or duration of peace find varying levels of impact. Some studies suggest that the timing and conditions under which mediation occurs affect its outcomes (e.g., Greig 2005; see also our discussion of timing of diplomatic efforts and the concept of "ripeness" in Chapter 11). Other studies have found that IGO involvement results in longer negotiation processes and that mediation effects may be more positive in the short term (e.g., reaching a cease-fire) than the long term (preserving peace) (e.g., Simonelli 2011; Beardsley 2008; Greig 2001; see also Terris 2022 and Greig and Diehl 2012). Finally, according to Hansen, Mitchell, and Nemeth (2008), "international organizations are more likely to help disputing parties reach an agreement if [the organization has] more democratic members, [the organization is] highly institutionalized, and when [the organization uses] binding management techniques".

FOR EXAMPLE: ECOWAS AND THE WEST AFRICA/NIGER CONFLICT

In the summer of 2023, the West African country of Niger experienced a coup led by its military leaders, who suspended the constitution and arrested the president and his family. In response, the Economic Community of West African States (ECOWAS) imposed sanctions and sought to build support for a collective military intervention under the authority of the UN Charter, the ECOWAS treaty, and the rules of the African Union. Over time, Niger's defiance stymied ECOWAS and its member states proved increasingly unwilling to back its efforts. Mali and Burkina Faso soon joined Niger, and the three ECOWAS members announced their decisions to withdraw from ECOWAS in early 2024, accusing the IGO of "becoming a threat to its members". In February 2024, under pressure from the three defiant states and from other ECOWAS members, the IGO announced that it was lifting most of the sanctions it had imposed the previous summer in an effort to persuade Niger, Mali, and Burkina Faso to remain in ECOWAS.

Collective Security and Peace Operations

A second key area of IGO engagement in managing conflict, crisis, and war is through collective security and peace operations. The broad context of this avenue is the general effect of IGOs on peace and conflict. Numerous empirical studies conclude that IGOs, and especially shared memberships among states in them, are associated with more peaceful relations and more peaceful settlement of conflicts among their members (e.g., Russett and Oneal 2001; Russett, Oneal, and Davis 1998; Boehmer, Gartzke, and Nordstrom 2004; Lupu and Greenhill 2017; Pevehouse and Russett 2006), although not necessarily for low severity conflicts among certain actors (e.g., Fausett and Volgy 2010). However, IGOs also play a more direct role in the management of conflict, crisis, and war through their role in collective security and peace operations, especially since the end of World War II.

Much scholarly attention has been devoted to the history, purposes, evolution, and practices of such engagement. Claude (1962; 1984) offers foundational studies (see also Cronin 2017 for a good review), and many pages have been devoted to discussion of the 19th Century Concert of Europe, the League of Nations and its weaknesses and failures in the 1920s and 1930s, and the UN and UN Security Council and its role, constraints, and potential after World War II. Suffice it to say that in practice, the historical record of collective security has been one of unrealized promise.

In the context of largely ineffective collective security structures, the post-World War II decades were characterized by the emergence of peace operations, which soon became "the most visible face of the United Nations (UN) and the organization's mechanism for maintaining what the UN Charter refers to as 'international peace and security'" (Williams 2017: 1; see also Durch 1993, 2006). Multifaceted, peace operations is a broad category for a range of efforts to cope with conflict, crisis, and war (e.g., Diehl 2008) that includes such things as preventive diplomacy, peacemaking, peacekeeping, post-conflict peacebuilding, and peace enforcement (e.g., Boutros-Ghali 1992). Such operations are also undertaken by regional and subregional organizations as well (e.g., Diehl and Lepgold 2003; Diehl and Cho 2006).

Understanding the impact and effectiveness of peace operations turns first on accounting for different types. For example, Diehl (2000) differentiates among four categories (monitoring; limiting damage; restoring civil societies; and coercive) while Findlay (2002) and Bellamy, Williams, and Griffin (2009) include some or all of the following: preventive deployment (Bellamy, Williams, and Griffin 2009); traditional peacekeeping (Findlay 2002; Bellamy, Williams, and Griffin 2009); managing transition operations (Bellamy, Williams, and Griffin 2009); expanded peacekeeping (Findlay 2002; Bellamy, Williams, and Griffin 2009); peace enforcement (Findlay 2002; Bellamy, Williams, and Griffin 2009); peace support operations (Bellamy, Williams, and Griffin 2009); and enforcement (Findlay 2002). Such varying missions are used in different kinds of conflict situations, so gauging their effectiveness is highly context-dependent.

So, what does the empirical record tell us about the effectiveness of these operations? As Diehl's (2008: 124) core work argues, peace operations "are neither uniformly desirable nor to be systematically avoided". A key part of understanding the role and effects of peace operations turns on recognition that they are selectively applied, typically to the hardest of situations (Aydin 2010; Binder 2015; Fortna 2008). Factoring that into the assessment generally results in more optimistic results (e.g., Fortna 2003, 2008). In civil conflict, even in that light, a great many factors feed into success or failure, which is also subject to a wide variety of measures (e.g., Walter 2002; Passmore 2020; Blechman and Vaccaro 1995).

In some instances, peace operations may confound peacemaking by complicating contacts between the principals or slowing a hurting stalemate, central to "ripeness" as we discussed in Chapter 11 (e.g., Greig and Diehl 2005). Overall, the variation may depend on some combination of (1) operational factors; (2) contextual factors associated with the conflict; and (3) behavioral factors related to the parties and other states (Diehl 2008: 132–145). Fortna (2008) concludes that peace operations improve the durability of peace in both civil and interstate conflicts. According to a study by Doyle and Sambanis (2006), which examined more than 60 UN peacekeeping missions between 1947 and 2006, peace operations increase the likelihood of success for peacebuilding, although missions are situation-specific and require careful tailoring to the characteristics of each case. However, they also conclude that UN missions are most effective immediately after the end of the war, economic development is key to reducing the resumption of fights over time, and supporting new actors committed to the peace, building governing institutions, and monitoring implementation of peace settlements are critical to success.

NON-GOVERNMENTAL ORGANIZATION: DEFINITION AND CONTEXT

Our final non-state avenue for managing conflict, crisis, and war involves NGOs. With individual members who may come from almost any country, NGOs advocate and act on shared ideas, positions, or goals, and they make choices to protect, defend, and advance those shared notions. They may play a role in war prevention and conflict resolution through a variety of means.

As issue-based organizations, NGOs are usually focused on specific problems such as poverty, injustice, women's rights, the environment, and many others. Quite a few NGOs have been awarded the Nobel Peace Prize for their consequential work, including the American Friends Service Committee and the Friends Service Council, the International Committee of the Red Cross (ICRC) and the League of Red Cross Societies, Amnesty International, International Physicians for the Prevention of Nuclear War, the International Campaign to Abolish Nuclear Weapons, and the Organisation for the Prohibition of Chemical Weapons.

NGOs provide a variety of services in the global community. These include the following types:

- Humanitarian relief programs (such as the France-based *Médecins Sans Frontières/Doctors Without Borders* or UK-based Oxfam)
- Economic development programs (such as the US-based Bill and Melinda Gates Foundation or the Switzerland-based Aga Khan Development Network)
- Educational programs (such as Belgium-based Education International or the Switzerland-based Foundation for Education and Development)
- Civil society development programs (such as US-based groups like the Global Fund for Women or the Civil Society Development Foundation)
- Human rights empowerment and protection programs (like UK-based Amnesty International or US-based Human Rights Watch)
- Environmental protection programs (like Friends of the Earth International or Greenpeace)

In a world of about 200 independent states and perhaps 5,000 or so IGOs, the more than 50,000 international NGOs active in world politics (Worldwide Association of NGOs 2024) quite clearly constitutes an extensive array of players and makes any detailed accounting of so many impossible. We offer a few examples in some key areas related to conflict and security to illustrate the landscape: NGOs focusing on personal, economic, health, and environmental security.

Personal Security-oriented NGOs

These NGOs emphasize the needs of people to be safe from physical harm. At one extreme is the threat of nuclear war. A number of NGOs work to prevent the use of nuclear weapons. One such actor is the US-based Nuclear Threat Initiative. In 2008, it created the World Institute for Nuclear Security in Vienna, Austria, which joins together NGO and national officials from Australia, Finland, Norway, the United Kingdom, and the United States, along with representatives of the International Atomic Energy Agency, in a cooperative effort to strengthen the protection of existing nuclear materials from theft or misuse.

Other examples include the International Campaign to Ban Landmines, the many human rights organizations in the world, including Amnesty International, Human Rights Watch, and the Universal Human Rights Network (Unirights), which emphasizes the resolution of internal conflicts, demobilization of armed groups, reintegration of insurgents into society, civilian peacekeeping, and other human rights issues related to protection from violence. Its partner organizations include NGOs concerned with better peacekeeping; the needs of displaced people; and promoting democracy, civil society, and the rule of law internationally.

Economic Security-oriented NGOs

Perhaps less directly related to conflict, crisis, and war, NGOs seeking to ensure the economic security of others are extensively active in world politics and seek to ameliorate conditions that generate conflict, especially those related to scarcity. For example, the French-based Afrique Verte International (Green Africa International) and the Swiss-based Fondation Assistance Internationale target food issues in West Africa, seeking to reduce deprivation that might lead to civil conflict. Both of these NGOs work extensively with hundreds of others, both international and local, in their efforts.

NGOs addressing energy issues include the International Network for Sustainable Energy (INFORSE), a Danish-based network of 140 NGOs working in 60 different countries in Europe, Africa, North and South America, and Asia. Created at the Earth Summit in Rio de Janeiro in 1992, it has observer status at the UN's ECOSOC and has participated in the environmental conferences that followed the 1992 Earth Summit. Another Denmark-based network is more oriented to problem-solving at the local level. The Global Network on Energy for Sustainable Development seeks to help countries develop energy sources that are cleaner, more efficient, and sustainable over the long term.

Health Security-oriented NGOs

There are many ways to address health security and NGOs active in this arena contribute to the management of conflict, crisis, and war by addressing conditions that lead to conflict and violence, and by mitigating the consequences of violent conflict on health both during and after conflict. The prime example of this is the ICRC, a private international humanitarian organization whose sole mission is to "protect the lives and dignity of victims of armed conflict and other situations of violence and to provide them with assistance". Similarly, the International Rescue Committee, Oxfam International, *Médecins Sans Frontières*/Doctors Without Borders, and many others prioritize efforts to aid people affected by armed conflict.

Others in this category take a more indirect route, focusing on health more generally. For example, many NGOs seek to promote better health for diseases that are difficult to treat. A good example is HIV/AIDS, with much emphasis placed on sub-Saharan Africa in this regard, as there are more cases of HIV/AIDS there than anywhere else. According to UN data (UNAIDS 2023), in 2022, almost 21 million people from East and Southern Africa were living with HIV/AIDS – that's about 7% of the population ages 15–49. Examples of such NGOs and networks of NGOs include the Network of African People Living with HIV/AIDS, the Eastern African National Networks of AIDS Service Organisations, the Canada-Africa Prevention Trials Network, and the African-European HIV Vaccine Development Network. Still other NGOs focus on the health concerns of underserved communities. A good example is the Global Health Council, which brings medical care to women and children and to those facing HIV/AIDS, malaria, and tuberculosis; it also promotes the development of health care systems more broadly. It and its members conduct programs and projects in over 150 countries in North America, the Caribbean, South America, Africa, the Middle East, the Caucasus region of Eurasia, South Asia, and Southeast Asia.

Environmental Security-oriented NGOs

These NGOs are relevant to conflict, crisis, and war because the effects of environmental degradation are increasingly linked to strife (e.g., Homer-Dixon 1999; Nyanaro 2023; Raleigh and Urdal 2007). A good example of an NGO working this category is the Swiss-based International Society of Doctors for the Environment. This NGO links doctors whose focus is on environmentally caused health problems – such as the linkage of pollution to disease and early death. Another, the Transnational Institute, links a number of resource-based networks in Africa, Europe, and the Western Hemisphere to ensure that local people have access to and control over clean water supplies and to protect environmental resources such as water supplies and forests from ownership by corporations. The Climate Action Network Europe (CAN-Europe) focuses on climate change, emissions, and sustainable energy issues in Europe. This network links together 1,500 NGOs across 170 member organizations in 38 European states. The broader global Climate Action Network has similar regional networks in North America, Latin America, Asia, and Africa.

As the preceding examples that help to illustrate the very broad NGO landscape suggest, many of these NGOs play consequential roles across a variety of issues in world politics. As they engage in the issues of their choice, NGOs play at least three important roles in international politics: (a) they popularize ideas; (b) they influence states' IGOs on agendas and actions, and (c) they take direct action on problems; and they encourage and enable cooperation.

Ideas

NGOS are regularly involved in the process of creating or changing norms in world politics. Norms, or unwritten standards of acceptable and unacceptable behavior, help reduce the consequences of anarchy in the international system and establish shared purposes and areas of cooperation. As in all norm development in world politics, which may arise from multiple sources and players, NGO efforts tend to follow a norms life cycle. As Finnemore and Sikkink (1998) have summarized, the first phase of the cycle involves creating new norms, which means getting others to share the vision and commitment. NGOs engaging in this function seek to define or frame issues in ways designed to persuade others to accept that the values or goals they are pressing are legitimate ones for the public arena. For example, these goals could include the idea that it is unacceptable to ignore the victims of conflicts or that access to adequate nutrition or health care is a human right and essential to human security. The second phase is a norms cascade, in which the range of actors supporting the norm increases until it reaches the agendas of governments. Finally, the third phase is norm internalization, in which so many international actors share the norm that following it becomes virtually automatic. In such instances, when the norm is not honored, conflict follows.

> **IN FOCUS: NGOS AND THE CONSEQUENCES OF VIOLENT CONFLICT**
>
> As more and more wars are internal in the modern era (or intrastate), the fighting increasingly takes place in the midst of civilian populations. What do many civilians do in such a situation? As the war in Ukraine illustrates, they flee, which creates enormous human security issues for the refugees and the surrounding countries. NGOs such as those mobilized by WANGO, the World Association of Non-Governmental Organizations, play an active role in such situations. In the case of Ukraine, for example, WANGO worked to get needed relief goods – like food, water, clothing, and blankets – to refugees inside Ukraine. To get needed medical care to those in Ukraine, WANGO coordinated with Christian Disaster Response, *Médecins Sans Frontières*/Doctors Without Borders, Razom, Revived Soldiers Ukraine, and Samaritan's Purse while UNICEF USA focused on the needs of children there. As Ukrainian refugees entered the surrounding countries, they were aided by such NGOs as the Ocalenie Foundation, International Rescue Committee, Norwegian Refugee Council, Polish Humanitarian Action, Razom, Recipe for Independence Foundation, AidRom, *Médecins Sans Frontières*/Doctors Without Borders, NGO Charity Centre for Refugees in Moldova, and World Vision.

NGOS IN ACTION

Influencing Other Actors and Taking Direct Action

Most NGOs aim their efforts at getting other actors such as states and IGOs to act or acting directly to solve problems of their own choosing themselves, or both. As Keck and Sikkink (1998) have argued, one way this may happen is through what they describe as the boomerang model, as shown in Figure 12.3. If NGOs within a state are unsuccessful in changing the state's actions that they oppose (which is quite often the case in authoritarian states), they can reach out to international NGOs, which can then pressure other states, IGOs, and the target state from outside. These NGOs can also take direct action, mobilizing their resources to mitigate the problem on the ground, working with local citizens and groups in the process (which may or may not "shame" other states and IGOs to do more as well). States that might be unwilling to change as a result of domestic pressures from their own citizens might change their behavior when it becomes clear that their behavior has hurt them internationally.

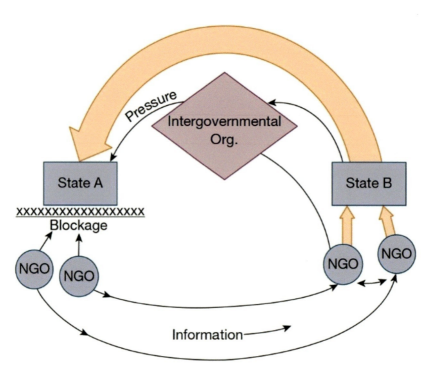

Figure 12.3   The Boomerang Model of NGO activity

Encouraging and Enabling Cooperation

NGOs routinely foster cooperation across borders, mobilizing information, resources, and people to work together to solve problems. They may advocate for, prompt, and also endorse international treaties and agreements to facilitate international cooperation, in part by lending support and credibility to the agreement and helping to persuade state policymakers to embrace it. NGOs monitor the actions of states to ensure effective cooperation with established norms. For example, many human rights NGOs such as Amnesty International, Freedom House, and Human Rights Watch regularly report on the human rights records of states.

Non-governmental Organizations and the Problem of War: the Empirical Record

The discussion above and many of the examples we have discussed in the preceding paragraphs offer good evidence of role and impact, even if in an anecdotal fashion. In particular, the last several pages and their discussion of four types of NGOs addressing security and conflict-related issues, broadly defined suggest much about the expanding role of NGOs in world politics in general over the past several decades, and in conflict, crisis, and war in particular. Here, we finish our discussion with three final observations about the empirical record as it concerns the role and impact of NGOs.

First, over the past three to four decades, NGOs have been increasingly active in the diplomatic arena (e.g., Boyer and Butler 2017; Butler and Boyer 2017; Muldoon and Aviel 2020; Muldoon et al. 2005). In particular, they have been engaged in multilateral and conference diplomacy and in "track-two" diplomacy on a variety of matters that concern conflict, crisis, and war. In so doing, they help to define problems and the agenda, prompt and support action by other players, including states and IGOs, and shape ideas and options.

With respect to conflict and war in particular, NGOs have had growing roles and impact over the last four decades as well. These have tended to involve four key effects: (1) early warning functions, where NGOs alert other players to conflict-and violence-generating problems and affect efforts to prevent them; (2) human rights monitoring, where NGOs provide information about performance and problems and help to shape international reactions; (3) relief and rehabilitation, where NGOs assist the victims of violent conflict, as we have described in several examples in the preceding pages of this chapter; and (4) conflict resolution activities, where NGOs participate in diplomacy, conflict management activities and services, and planning and implementation of peacebuilding activities, especially those that link local groups to national and international efforts (e.g., Aall 1996; Anderson 1996; Barnes et al. 1996; Branco 2011; Keck and Sikkink 1998).

A few examples help to illustrate the empirical evidence of NGO role and impact. First, Murdie and Peksen (2014) show how NGOs focused on human rights are central to the decisions of states and IGOs to intervene militarily in humanitarian crises and conflicts. Their analysis shows information, advocacy, and "shaming" by human rights NGOs make military intervention by states and/or IGOs more likely. We study this example further in the systemist example (See Figure 12.4) that follows. Second, substantial evidence shows that NGOs "constitute an efficient supplement for states and international organizations in the management of civil conflicts and proxy wars" (e.g., Irrera 2021: 6). Finally, Wilson, Davis, and Murdie (2016) provide evidence that networks of international NGOs focused on conflict and conflict resolution (which they call CROs) not only engage in innovative programs to promote peace, but these NGO networks are associated with more peaceful outcomes for states. As they conclude (Wilson, Davis, and Murdie 2016: 442), "When a state is more embedded within the CRO, international bellicosity from that state is diminished …. At the dyadic level … the greater the number of possible CRO informational channels between the states in the dyad, the less bellicosity within the dyad." Thus, the empirical evidence suggests growing roles and impact of NGOs on conflict, crisis, and war.

> **FOR EXAMPLE: THE IMPACT OF HUMAN RIGHTS INGO SHAMING ON HUMANITARIAN INTERVENTIONS**
>
> Figure 12.4 conveys the analytical arguments from Murdie and Peksen (2014), which focuses on shaming efforts from human rights organizations (HROs) in connection with humanitarian intervention (HI). While some have credited media with mobilizing public opinion in favor of HI, the article puts forward HROs as more likely to have impact. The reason is that HROs command more public trust than television or, for that matter, government. Data analysis for 129 states from 1990 to 2005 produces highly favorable results: HIs are much more likely in response to HRO shaming efforts assessed in terms of both quantity and intensity. Moreover, these substantively important results hold up in the presence of any number of confounding factors included in the research design. In sum, the statistical findings from this study have important implications for HI in both academic and policy-related terms.

SUMMING UP AND MOVING FORWARD

In this chapter, we viewed avenues to manage conflict, crisis, and war that involve IGOs and NGOs and, by nature, cooperative and collective action. While the benefits of states working with and through IGOs, and alongside NGOs, seem significant, doing so faces barriers and complications that make it problematic in many situations. Some of these difficulties are easily traced to the anarchic nature of world politics and the diversity of actors in world politics, not just among states and nations, but with all the non-state actors with their own identities, interests, and purposes, as well.

Our review in this chapter addresses international law and the problem of compliance, IGOs and the issues of conflict resolution and collective security, and NGOs and their roles and impact in diplomacy and conflict processes before, during, and after violence. As we have seen, while these non-state players are varied and extensive, their roles and impact are constrained by the nature of the gameboard on which they play, and by the influence of states.

IGOS AND NGOS

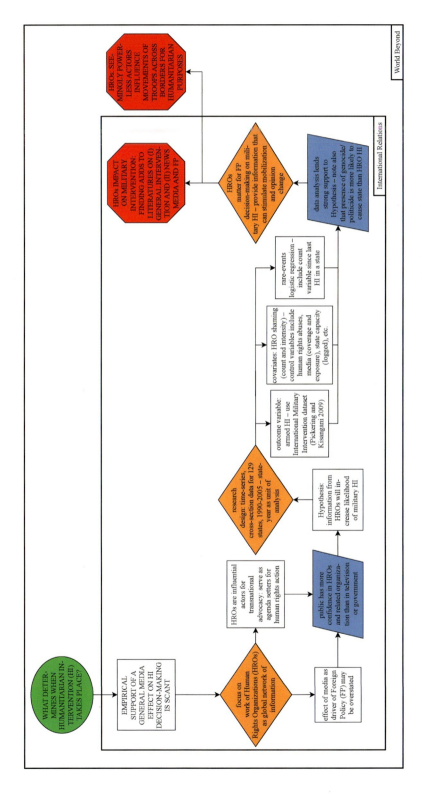

Figure 12.4 The impact of human rights international non-governmental organizations (INGO) shaming on humanitarian intervention

CONSIDER THIS: THE STRUGGLE TO COOPERATE

As we noted at the outset of this chapter, states and non-state actors cooperate extensively to manage conflicts and disagreements without resorting to violence. And yet, cooperation among these players often fails, with conflict leading to crisis and sometimes war as a consequence, across both material and ideational issue-areas. Thinking about this chapter, and back to our discussion of issues in Chapter 4:

When (e.g., on what issues and in what situations and roles) do non-state actors have the greatest success in contributing to the management of conflict, crisis, and war?

13
What do we know about conflict, crisis, and war?

PROLOGUE

Conflict, crisis, and war have evolved throughout history in response to technological advancements and other changes. Inventiveness can work to the advantage of offense or defense at any given time, with implications for how international relations will take place. Change in technology can be either qualitative or quantitative in nature. For example, cannons began to appear on European battlefields in the 12th century – a major qualitative change in the use of force (McNeill 1982). Over the course of time, these devices became increasingly easy to use, accurate, and devastating in their fire – an example of quantitative change since their invention. At this point, it is easy to look back and chart the major developments of the cannon as the ancestor of modern field artillery. For any new technology, the story is as yet untold and perhaps hard to foresee.

What, for instance, can be said right now about the Artificial Intelligence (AI) revolution? How will this invention play out in the arenas of conflict, crisis, and war in the future? In the language we have used in this book, AI may revolutionize both material and ideational aspects of international relations – action and thought, respectively. Even at this early stage of development for AI, signals are in place that point toward potentially drastic change in world politics. Consider the world of chess, a time-honored game of strategy. Even the best human players are no longer able to challenge the top AI programs such as AlphaZero and Stockfish. Moreover, the machine learning of AI programs means that the gap between them and human beings can be expected to widen further with time. This type of change, moreover, is unlikely to be restricted to games like chess.

While the preceding example refers to a board game, it has significant implications for the degree to which humanity will be able to control its technologies in the future. The AI revolution serves as a reminder that whatever is known about conflict, crisis, and war at any given time will never be the final story – technological advancement alone is enough to guarantee the academic and policy-related value of continuing research in this subject area.

OVERVIEW

Conflict, crisis, and war is a multifaceted subject area. A single book, at best, can provide a comprehensive introduction in order to provide a foundation for further study of conflict, crisis, and war. Given the subject matter, we have also sought to present the academic material in a way that maintains clarity and therefore a viable connection with policy-related concerns.

This chapter unfolds in three additional sections. Section two conveys a systemist graphic review of the work carried out in this volume. The third section reflects upon the central argument of the study, which focuses on the value of an integrated approach. The fourth and final section offers ideas about future research, along with a few final thoughts.

A SYSTEMIST GRAPHIC REVIEW

Figure 13.1 conveys the analysis that has unfolded within the pages of this book. The system is the discipline of International Relations, with the World Beyond as its environment. Within International Relations, the macro and micro levels correspond, respectively, to the discipline as a whole and individual scholars within it. Subfigures present the series of arguments from preceding chapters in the most accessible way.

Figure 13.1a gets underway with movement from the World Beyond into the macro level of International Relations: "CONFLICT CRISIS, AND WAR (CCW) AT CENTER OF ATTENTION FOR POLICYMAKERS – POTENTIAL CONSEQUENCES FOR SURVIVAL OF STATES" → "SUSTAINED EFFORTS TO UNDERSTAND AND EXPLAIN CCW". As an initial point, the component before the arrow appears as a green oval. After the grim experience of the Great War, later known as World War I, leaders understood the dangers of war when fought with increasingly sophisticated and devastating weapons. The founding of the modern discipline of International Relations ensued in response to the need for applied knowledge about the resolution, management, and prevention of conflict, crisis, and war.

Figure 13.1a shows the pathway shifting from the macro to micro level with "SUSTAINED EFFORTS TO UNDERSTAND AND EXPLAIN CCW" → "central argument: explanation of, and coping with, CCW: requires *integrated approach*: address multiple Levels of Analysis (LA) and connect them to each other". The sum of experience in studies of conflict, crisis, and war points away from accounts that emphasize a single cause or step in a given process. Instead, a more promising approach brings together insights from across the standard levels of analysis – system, state, and individual.

Movement continues at the micro level in Figure 13.1a: "central argument: explanation of, and coping with, CCW: requires *integrated approach*: address multiple Levels of Analysis (LA) and connect them to each other" → "foundations of book: scientific realism, analytic eclecticism, and multilevel graphic approach of systemism". The combination of the items after the arrow carries out an integrated approach. Scientific realism serves as a reminder that not all processes are material – ideational factors come into at least some, and probably many, explanations. Analytic eclecticism encourages a panoramic search for explanation, as opposed to a narrowing of the scope via commitment to a particular paradigm. Systemist graphics can

WHAT DO WE KNOW ABOUT CONFLICT, CRISIS, AND WAR?

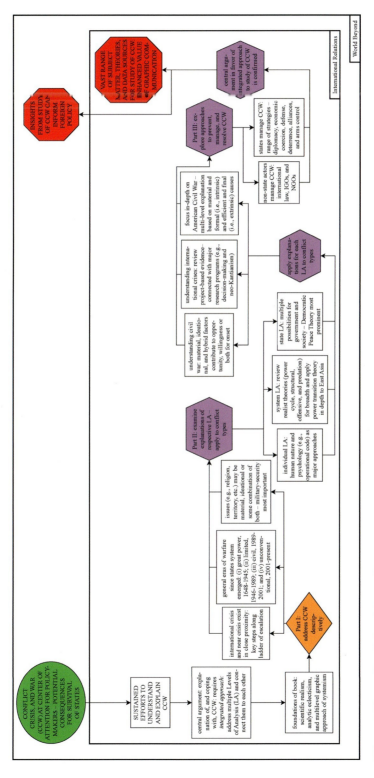

Figure 13.1 Conflict, crisis, and war

CONFLICT, CRISIS, AND WAR IN WORLD POLITICS

Figure 13.1a

WHAT DO WE KNOW ABOUT CONFLICT, CRISIS, AND WAR?

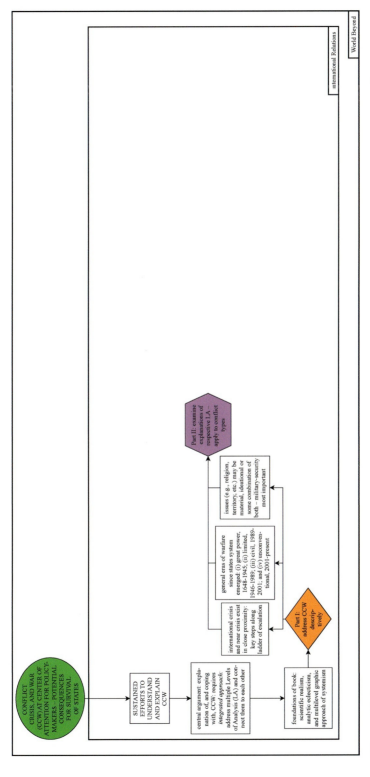

Figure 13.1b

CONFLICT, CRISIS, AND WAR IN WORLD POLITICS

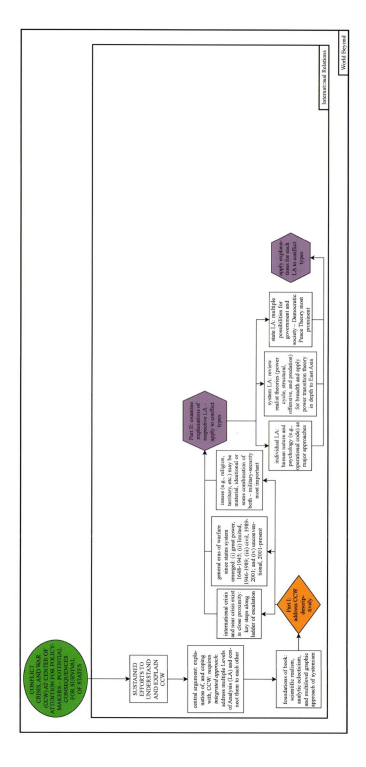

Figure 13.1c

WHAT DO WE KNOW ABOUT CONFLICT, CRISIS, AND WAR?

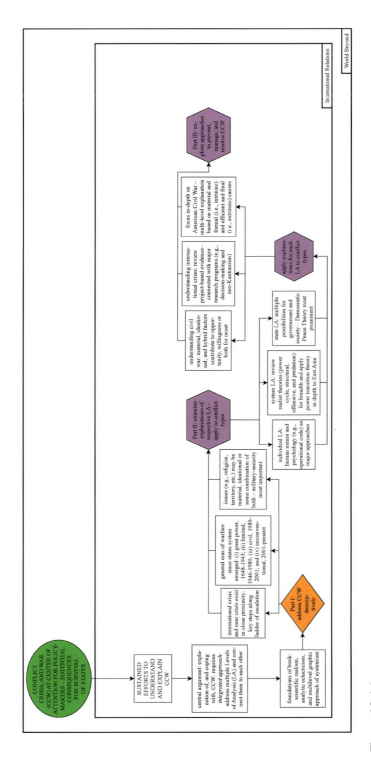

Figure 13.1d

CONFLICT, CRISIS, AND WAR IN WORLD POLITICS

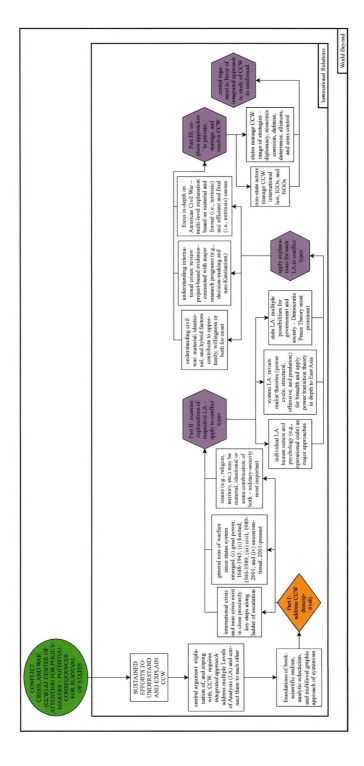

Figure 13.1e

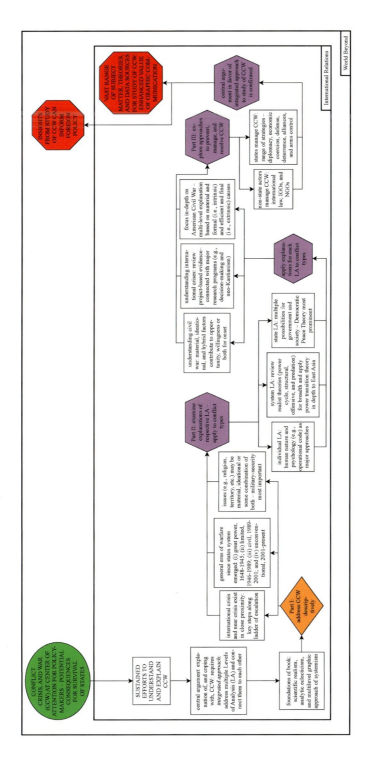

Figure 13.1f

serve as a check on theoretical completeness, as well as logical consistency, for any would-be explanation of conflict, crisis, and war.

Figure 13.1a sees the micro route advance with "foundations of book: scientific realism, analytic eclecticism, and multilevel graphic approach of systemism" → 'Part I: address CCW descriptively". As a point of divergence, an orange diamond depicts the component after the arrow. Description is a natural first step in the study of conflict, crisis, and war – or any phenomenon that is being investigated in a way consistent with science. Indeed, once something has been described adequately, it becomes much more amenable to explanation, at least in principle.

Figure 13.1b shows multiple pathways moving ahead at the micro level: "Part I: address CCW descriptively" → "international crisis and near crisis exist in close proximity: key steps along ladder of escalation"; "general eras of warfare since states system emerged: (i) great power, 1648–1945; (ii) limited, 1946–1989; (iii) civil, 1989–2001; and (iv) unconventional, 2001-present"; "issues (e.g., religion, territory, etc.) may be material, ideational or some combination of both – military-security most important". Near crisis and crisis, adjacent to each other in conceptual terms, emerge as potentially crucial steps along the road to war. Greater attention to near crises may help to identify factors that cause escalation to crisis and, in turn, to highly destructive wars such as the one currently being carried out by Russia against Ukraine. Along those lines, knowledge about the evolution of conflict, crisis, and war should prove valuable. While interstate and intrastate war are becoming less and more frequent respectively, realizing their interconnectedness and reverberating effects in the current era of unconventional war is important. With regard to issues, military-security remains preeminent. However, aspects such as territory and religion can impact upon each other and affect the ways conflict, crisis, and war play out in significant ways.

Pathways come together in Figure 13.1b with "international crisis and near crisis exist in close proximity: key steps along ladder of escalation"; "general eras of warfare since states system emerged: (i) great power, 1648–1945; (ii) limited, 1946–1989; (iii) civil, 1989–2001; and (iv) unconventional, 2001-present"; "issues (e.g., religion, territory, etc.) may be material, ideational or some combination of both – military-security most important" → "Part II: examine explanations of respective LA – apply to conflict types". As a node, the component after the arrow takes the form of a purple hexagon. A review of event types, frequencies, and trends, along with the range of issues involved, prepares the way for movement from description to explanation.

Figure 13.1c launches multiple pathways with "Part II: examine explanations of respective LA – apply to conflict types" → "system LA: review realist theories (power cycle, structural, offensive, and predation) for breadth and apply power transition theory in depth to East Asia"; "state LA: multiple possibilities for government and society – Democratic Peace Theory most prominent"; "individual LA: human nature and psychology (e.g., operational code) as major approaches". As expected from the outset of this volume, theories from all levels of analysis show significant ability to account for conflict, crisis, and war.

Figure 13.1c finishes up with "system LA: review realist theories (power cycle, structural, offensive, and predation) for breadth and apply power transition theory in depth to East Asia"; "state LA: multiple possibilities for government and society – Democratic Peace Theory most prominent"; 'individual LA: human nature and psychology (e.g., operational code) as major approaches" → "apply explanations for each LA to conflict types". The nodal component after the arrow appears as a purple hexagon. After a general review of theories across levels of analysis, it becomes feasible to apply them in accounting for conflict, crisis, and war.

Figure 13.1d shows multiple pathways emerging at the micro level with "apply explanations for each LA to conflict types" → "understanding international crises: review project-based evidence – connected with major research programs (e.g., decision-making and neo-Kantianism)"; "understanding civil war: material, ideational, and hybrid factors contribute to opportunity, willingness or both for onset"; "focus in-depth on American Civil War – multilevel explanation based on material and formal (i.e., intrinsic) and efficient and final (i.e., extrinsic) causes". First, research from the International Crisis Behavior Project has contributed significantly to what is known about the onset, processes, and outcomes and legacies of such events. Second, aggregate data analysis has produced a wealth of findings that establish the importance of any number of disciplines – history and psychology are just two among them – in accounting for civil wars. Third, and finally, the American Civil War case (Chapter 10) provides depth to complement the breadth of the two chapters on international crises and civil wars that preceded it. Material, ideational, and hybrid factors come together to produce a complex but still manageable account of the events leading up to the American Civil War.

Figure 13.1d shows pathways coming together: → "understanding international crises: review project-based evidence – connected with major research programs (e.g., decision-making and neo-Kantianism)"; "understanding civil war: material, ideational, and hybrid factors contribute to opportunity, willingness or both for onset"; "focus in-depth on American Civil War – multilevel explanation based on material and formal (i.e., intrinsic) and efficient and final (i.e., extrinsic) causes" → "Part III: explore approaches to prevent, manage, and resolve CCW". With description and explanation in place, our attention turns to what is known about policies to resolve, manage, and even prevent conflict, crisis, and war.

Multiple routes emerge from the purple hexagon in Figure 13.1e with "Part III: explore approaches to prevent, manage, and resolve CCW" → "states manage CCW: range of strategies – diplomacy, economic coercion, defense, deterrence, alliances, and arms control"; "non-state actors manage CCW: international law, IGOs, and NGOs". Efforts from states and non-state actors such as IGOs and NGOs combine to bring out the importance of looking at all levels of analysis in the quest to resolve, manage, and prevent instances of conflict, crisis, and war.

Pathways come together in Figure 13.1e with "states manage CCW: range of strategies – diplomacy, economic coercion, defense, deterrence, alliances, and arms control"; "non-state actors manage CCW: international law, IGOs, and NGOs" → "central argument in favor of integrated approach to study of CCW is confirmed". As a node, the component after the arrow takes the form of a purple hexagon. Taken together, the actors and activities listed confirm the value of an integrated and multilevel approach with regard to conflict resolution, management, and prevention – the same conclusion that would be reached about description and explanation when looking back into the earlier pathways.

Figure 13.1f shows each route reaching a point of completion: "central argument in favor of integrated approach to study of CCW is confirmed" → "VAST RANGE OF SUBJECT

MATTER, THEORIES, AND DATA SOURCES FOR STUDY OF CCW: ENHANCED VALUE OF GRAPHIC COMMUNICATION"; "INSIGHTS FROM STUDY OF CCW CAN INFORM FOREIGN POLICY". As points of termination, the components after the arrow appear as red octagons. The first conclusion reflects the value added at many points in the volume from systemist graphics that facilitate understanding of the diverse material covered in the text. The second conclusion serves as an affirmation of the practical utility of what scholarship on conflict, crisis, and war has to offer.

> **IN FOCUS**
>
> Apply the systemist graphic approach to the analysis that appears in a chapter from this book – or, if preferred, an academic article or chapter from another book. (We recommend avoiding an attempt on a full-length book without a great deal of experience beforehand.) Begin the process by identifying a system and its environment. With Figure 13.1 as an example to follow, trace out the analytical argument of the chapter or article.

REVISITING THE CENTRAL ARGUMENT

Across the pages of this volume, we have attempted to navigate the enormous and complex landscape of conflict, crisis, and war. Conflicts arise between the players of world politics (states and non-state actors). Some instances of strife are resolved peacefully; some escalate to crisis or near crisis; some erupt in violence and war. Making sense of these outcomes – their nature and origins, their dynamics and causes, and the ways that the players on the stage of world politics attempt to manage and resolve them – has long been a central aim of the study of international relations.

Our central argument, throughout the pages of this book, is that *explanation and understanding of conflict, crisis and, war and avenues for coping with and managing their challenges requires an integrated approach.* As we discussed in our first chapter, analytic eclecticism focuses on a comprehensive search for causal factors across paradigms and theoretical perspectives rather than a quest that is restricted to a particular approach. Organizing by levels of analysis – as we have done – facilitates analytic eclecticism by keeping the focus on causal variables rather than theories and arguments (e.g., Levy and Thompson 2010: 14, 207). In doing so, we stress that studying conflict, crisis, and war requires attention to multiple levels of analysis and making efforts to connect them to each other for more thorough and nuanced understanding. Embracing analytic eclecticism and multiple levels of analysis thus offers opportunity to find connections and interactions among different types of causal mechanisms normally taken in isolation from each other within separate research traditions.

We began our introduction by laying out the conceptual and empirical foundations of our study. In Chapter 2, we established the meaning of conflict, crisis (and near crisis), and war and their connections to each other. The following chapter (3) explored historical and empirical patterns in the development and occurrence of each step on the ladder of escalation, highlighting elements of both continuity and change. Of special significance, we focused on the changing nature, location, types, and participants in conflict, crisis, and war. As we described through discussion of the empirical data, interstate conflict, crisis, and war have become less centered on "great powers" and more limited, especially since World War II. Increasingly, the locations and participants are in the developing world, and the nature of war since the end of the Cold War at the least, and perhaps since the end of World War II, has been increasingly intrastate. Civil war, non-state war, and internationalized civil war make up the face of modern war. Considering these patterns, we reflected on potential reasons for those developments.

In Chapter 4, we directed our attention to issues and their centrality for conflict, crisis, and war. In doing so we drew on multiple paradigms, both material and ideational categories, and crossing and connecting the levels of analysis. All of that is consistent with our argument on the necessity of multilevel linkages in the search for understanding and explanation. Our discussion focused on the centrality of territory and the role of ideational factors such as religion.

Our attention turned to review and exploration of the key arguments and empirical evidence about conflict, crisis, and war at the system (Chapter 5), state (Chapter 6), and individual (Chapter 7) levels. In each chapter, we provided a sample of core arguments central to each level of analysis and reviewed empirical findings for each as well. Notably, no single level or explanation proved sufficient for the complex topics at hand. Chapters 8 and 9 provided a similar review of crisis and civil war respectively, with even more emphasis on multilevel connections and explanations. Chapter 10 then reflected on the nature of causation and drew on Kurki's (2002, 2008) framework to examine the American Civil War as a case study in multilevel explanation, with applications to and implications for the study of other conflicts, crises, and wars.

Our final two substantive chapters focused on the exploration of the actions states themselves take to manage conflict, crisis, and war (Chapter 11), and the engagement and roles of non-state actors in efforts to cooperate to do the same (Chapter 12). Both, we argued, are complicated by the nature of the international system, the diversity of the actors, both state and non-state, and characteristics of individual leaders. In each instance, empirical evidence demonstrates the challenges presented by, and the mixed results of, these efforts toward conflict management.

Throughout the preceding pages, we have both implicitly and explicitly presented and emphasized the importance of an integrated approach that focuses on variables, not paradigms, and that crosses and connects insights and arguments from multiple levels of analysis to explain and understand conflict, crisis, and war and avenues for coping with and managing their challenges. It should be clear by now that no single theory, explanation, or level of analysis is sufficient for those tasks. Rather – and consistent with analytic eclecticism – islands of explanation from a range of paradigms and levels of analysis shed light on different elements and aspects. These islands also offer opportunity for connection – bridging, if you will – among them.

Drawing on the material from the preceding chapters, let us reflect on some of the multilevel connections that might be made to provide explanation of conflict, crisis, and war. One possibility, to which we have alluded frequently, is that offered by Cashman (2013). Stressing the diversity of types of war, and the related diversity of causes, Cashman (2013) suggests, and our preceding chapters support, that multilevel connections might be made by organizing explanations into a set of *pathways* to war.

Five such pathways, Cashman (2013: 486–487) suggests, might offer fruitful opportunity for these integrated explanations.

- Path 1: a "steps to war" path that draws heavily on Senese and Vasquez (2008), Vasquez (1993, 2011), and others. Centered on the importance of territory, this path weaves material and ideational elements, and causal factors at multiple levels, to shed significant light on major wars among great powers especially.
- Path 2: a "domestic instability" path that centers first on state-level factors and connects them to both individual and system-level elements. As Cashman (2013: 486) suggests, this path includes diversionary war dynamics (see our discussion in Chapter 6) and "kick them while they are down" dynamics that might drive states of all kinds.
- Path 3: a "hegemonic struggle" path that draws on historical and cyclical arguments such as power transition theory (see our discussion in Chapter 5) and blends system, dyadic, state, and even individual-level explanations to understand past and, potentially, future, patterns of great power warfare.
- Path 4: a "wars of inequality" path centered on domestic/state-level and individual-level factors that also draw in key system-level explanations such as predation. This path might help to shed light on interstate wars of strong versus weak and weak versus strong, but also applies to intrastate wars (i.e., "greed and grievance" conflicts) as well.
- Path 5: a "nation-state imbalance" path centered first on ideational factors and secondarily on material factors. As Cashman (2013: 487) argues, "the root causes of these wars stem from issues of identity, the fear of others, and the social construction of 'us' and 'them'". This path is applicable to both intrastate and interstate conflict and war.

Of course, other pathways beyond these may exist, given the complexity and diversity of conflict, crisis, and war. Note also that thinking in terms of pathways draws attention, once again, to the potential value of the systemist graphic approach in the quest for logical consistency and theoretical completeness.

A second approach to multilevel connections that might be made to provide explanation of conflict, crisis, and war emerges from Levy and Thompson (2010). Their survey of the causes of war leads them to conclude that discussion of "which level is important" is less helpful than efforts to "draw on variables from multiple levels of analysis" (Levy and Thompson 2010: 212). Consistent with our perspective, they too stress the "different types of war have different causes, and that different causal variables have a different impact on different types of war" (Levy and Thompson 2010: 209). Their effort to make multilevel connections leads them to a number of observations, including:

- State-level variables are more central to intrastate war than interstate wars;
- System- and individual-level variables have greater impact on interstate wars than intrastate wars;
- Regime-type and individual-level variables work together, so that individual leaders and their characteristics matter more in less democratic regimes (state-level variable)

and vice versa, in personalist regimes more than oligarchic regimes, and in presidential democracies more than parliamentary democracies;
- Rivalries leading to conflict between two states are shaped by system-level factors such as the distribution of power, but also by state-level factors such as instability;
- Leader attributes and calculations – including their propensity for risk-taking – work in tandem with state-level and system-level factors to shed light on when power shifts lead to conflict and war and when they do not.
- Organizing by proximate and distant (underlying) causes offers opportunity to integrate casual variables at different levels of analysis, and:
- Multiple pathways to war exist and involve factors at different levels of analysis.

Such observations only highlight further the need for analytic eclecticism and integration of theory and explanation across levels of analysis. And the preceding set of assertions also combine to serve as a reminder of the potential utility of a systemist diagrammatic approach in pulling respective ideas together into a coherent whole.

To these helpful insights, we offer one additional approach. We suggest that theories and explanations at different levels of analysis in part reflect attention to different questions about war. Differentiating along these lines offers additional opportunities to link explanations to connect across the levels. While explanation at each level is complex and varied, and overlap certainly exists, consider the following:

- System-level explanations and theories are most relevant for understanding patterns in the frequency and occurrence of conflict and war, and secondarily for understanding patterns in the participants of conflict and war;
- State-level explanations and theories are especially helpful for understanding patterns in the participants of conflict and war, and secondarily for specific choices and decisions to engage in conflict and war;
- Individual-level explanations and theories are especially helpful for understanding specific choices and decisions to engage in conflict and war, and secondarily for understanding patterns in the participants of conflict and war.

Much of our preceding discussion offers insights and support for these differentiations, but also suggests that these questions work together to offer meaningful opportunity for multilevel integration. Consider the example in For Example: Connecting the Levels and reflect on other multilevel linkages you might make as well.

FOR EXAMPLE: CONNECTING THE LEVELS

In light of the preceding analysis, consider just one possibility among many: connecting the insights of power transition theory to regime-type and leader risk propensity to provide insights on when war is most likely, between what participants, with particular kinds of leaders making decisions. Apply this line of reasoning to any combination of states that are not currently at war. Put differently, when brought into engagement with each other, where do the preceding theories suggest to look for danger?

FUTURE RESEARCH AND FINAL THOUGHTS

Given the complexity of problems and the urgency of multiple conflicts and ongoing military actions in the contemporary global system, the central argument of this volume – calling attention to the essential nature of a multilevel and integrated approach toward explanation and understanding – seems more appropriate than ever. The contents of this book suggest that an integrated multilevel approach – with scientific realism, analytic eclecticism, and systemist combined to form a foundation – is well suited to explain and understand both present and future challenges around the globe. Future research therefore should attempt to apply the framework from this volume to rising issues on the world agenda, for example, AI as outlined at the outset of this chapter.

To be sure, as we have seen in our preceding chapters, the complexity of the problem and issues, and the challenges for integration across the levels, is daunting, to say the least. Part of the challenge is that the paths from conflict to crisis to war are so varied from case to case. Another is that quite often system-level, state-level, and individual-level explanations each offer a convincing account of a given instance. Indeed, the answer to "can the theory at [fill in the level of analysis] explain [fill in the name of the conflict, crisis, or war]" is often "yes". But, perhaps asking "Does it do so sufficiently" opens the door to other insights, arguments, and explanations that account for another part of the story of that particular case. And yet, each of them may appear equally plausible and helpful. This then, in our view, is a powerful argument for making the effort to link explanations across levels and provides even further support for the merits of analytical eclecticism.

Finally, this study has attempted to convey conflict, crisis, and war in primarily academic terms while maintaining relevance to policy. Many accomplishments have been detailed along the way with regard to theory and evidence about conflict, crisis, and war. At the same time, the insights of this volume are not restricted to the classroom. While we have not emphasized the practical, policy implications, we trust you have found those connections as well. In the broadest sense, we think an accurate, nuanced understanding of why a conflict, crisis, and/or war occurred, or how one was resolved or ended while another was not, is essential and highly relevant to policy choices going forward. Moreover, the complex array of paths and causes, and their attendant explanations and theories, along with the very mixed outcomes of *every* one of the avenues and approaches to managing conflict, crisis, and war we reviewed in chapters 11 and 12, argue strongly for resisting simply formulas or "one size fits all" solutions as conflict occurs, crises develop, and wars erupt. We hope that what you have learned through reading this book will help you to grapple with the rapid and sometimes even overwhelming changes that are the hallmark of the new millennium.

> **CONSIDER THIS: UNDERSTANDING CONFLICT, CRISIS, AND WAR**
>
> *How has your worldview – especially as it relates to the challenges of conflict, crisis, and war in world politics – changed, if at all, through your encounter with this book? In what way(s) do you see international relations the same versus differently?*

14
References

Aall, Pamela. 1996. *NGOs and Conflict Management*. Washington, DC: United States Institution of Peace.
Abdelaza, Khalid. 2021. Sudan Formally Requests Four-Party Mediation over Ethiopian Dam. *Reuters*, March 16, 2021. https://www.reuters.com/article/uk-sudan-ethiopia-dam-idUSKBN2B80QK
Abebe, Daniel. 2014. Egypt, Ethiopia, and the Nile: The Economics of International Water Law. *Chicago Journal of International Law*, 15(1), 27–46.
Acton, James, Thomas MacDonald, and Pranay Vaddi. 2021. *Reimagining Nuclear Arms Control: A Comprehensive Approach*. Washington, DC: Carnegie Endowment for International Peace.
Adler, Emmanuel. 1992. The Emergence of Cooperation: National Epistemic Communities and the International Evolution of the Idea of Nuclear Arms Control. *International Organization*, 46(1), 101–145.
Akbaba, Yasemin, and Zeynep Taydas. 2011. Does Religious Discrimination Promote Dissent? A Quantitative Analysis. *Ethnopolitics*, 10(3–4): 271–295.
Albertini, Luigi. 1952. *The Origins of the War of 1914*. Oxford: Oxford University Press.
Alden, Edward. 2022. Canada's Trucker Protests: What to Know About the "Freedom Convoy" [Online]. Council on Foreign Relations, February 11. https://www.cfr.org/in-brief/canadas-trucker-protests-what-know-about-freedom-convoy
Allee, Todd L., and Paul K. Huth. 2006. The Pursuit of Legal Settlements to Territorial Disputes. *Conflict Management and Peace Science*, 23(4), 285–307.
Allen, Susan H. 2005. The Determinants of Economic Sanctions Success and Failure. *International Interactions*, 31(2), 117– 138.
Allen, Susan H. 2008. Political Institutions and Constrained Response to Economic Sanctions. *Foreign Policy Analysis*, 4(3), 255–274.
Allison, Graham T. 1971. *Essence of Decision: Explaining the Cuban Missile Crisis*. Boston, MA: Little Brown.
Allison, Graham T. 2017a. *Destined for War: Can America and China Escape Thucydides Trap?* New York: Houghton Mifflin Harcourt.
Allison, Graham T. 2017b. *Destined for War: Can America and China Escape Thucydides' Trap?* London: Scribe UK.
Almond, Gabriel A., R. Scott Appleby, and Emmanuel Sivan. 2003. *Strong Religion: The Rise of Fundamentalisms Around the World*. Chicago, IL: University of Chicago Press.
Anderson, Mary. 1996. Humanitarian NGOs in Conflict Intervention. In Chester A. Crocker, Fen Hampson, and Pamela Aall (eds.), *Managing Global Chaos*. Washington, DC: United States Institute of Peace Press, pp. 343–354.
Angell, Norman. 1911. *The Great Illusion: A Study of the Relation of Military Power in Nations to Their Economic and Social Advantage* (3rd ed.). New York and London: G.P. Putnam's and Sons.
Archer, Clive. 2003. Introduction. In Clive Archer and Pertti Joenniemi (eds.), *The Nordic Peace*. London: Routledge, pp. 1–23.
Ardrey, Robert. 1966. *The Territorial Imperative: A Personal Inquiry into the Animal Origins of Property and Nations*. New York: Atheneum.
Art, Robert J. 1980. To What Ends Military Power? *International Security*, 4(4), 3–35.
Art, Robert J., and Patrick Cronin (eds.). 2003. *The United States and Coercive Diplomacy*. Washington, DC: US Institute of Peace.
Asal, Victor, and Kyle Beardsley. 2007. Proliferation and International Crisis Behavior. *Journal of Peace Research*, 44(2), 139–155.

Aydin, Aysegul. 2010. Where Do States Go? Strategy in Civil War Intervention. *Conflict Management and Peace Science*, 27(1), 47–66.

Ayferam, Gashaw. 2023. The Nile Dispute: Beyond Water Security. Middle East Analysis (Carnegie Endowment for International Peace), January 19, 2023. https://carnegieendowment.org/sada/88842

Azar, Edward. 1990. *The Management of Protracted Social Conflict: Theory and Cases*. Aldershot: Dartmouth.

Babbie, Earl. 2001. *The Practice of Social Research* (9th ed.). Belmont, CA: Wadsworth Publishing Company.

Babst, Dean V. 1964. Elective Governments – A Force for Peace. *The Wisconsin Sociologist*, 3, 9–14.

Babst, Dean V. 1972. A Force for Peace. *Industrial Research*, 14, 55–58.

Badie, Dina. 2010. Groupthink, Iraq, and the War on Terror: Explaining US Policy Shift Toward Iraq. *Foreign Policy Analysis*, 6(4), 277–296.

Badran, Ramzi. 2014. Intrastate Peace Agreements and the Durability of Peace. *Conflict Management and Peace Science*, 31(2), 193–217.

Bakke, Kristin M., and Erik Wibbels. 2006. Diversity, Disparity, and Civil Conflict in Federal States. *World Politics*, 59(1), 1–50.

Baldwin, David A. 1985. *Economic Statecraft*. Princeton, NJ: Princeton University Press.

Baldwin, David A. 1999/2000. The Sanctions Debate and the Logic of Choice. *International Security*, 26(3), 80–107.

Baldwin, David A., and Robert A. Pape. 1998. Evaluating Economic Sanctions. *International Security*, 23(2), 189–98.

Balz, Dan, and Bob Woodward. 2002. Ten Days in September. *Washington Post*, January 27– February 3, 2002, A1.

Barbieri, Katherine. 1996. Economic Interdependence: A Path to Peace or a Source of Interstate Conflict? *Journal of Peace Research*, 33(1), 29–49.

Barbieri, Katherine. 2002. *The Liberal Illusion: Does Trade Promote Peace?* Ann Arbor, MI: University of Michigan Press.

Barceló, Joan. 2020. Are Western-Educated Leaders Less Prone to Initiate Militarized Disputes? *British Journal of Political Science*, 50(2), 535–566.

Barnes, Harry, Joyce Neu, Sue Palmer, Sara Tindall, Kirk Wolcott, and DiAnn Watson. 1996. *The International Guide to NGO Activities in Conflict Resolution and Prevention*. Carter Center (http://www.cartercenter.org/documents/

Basedau, Matthias, Jonathan Fox, and Ariel Zellman. 2023. *Religious Minorities at Risk*. Oxford: Oxford University Press.

Baum, Matthew A., and Philip B. K. Potter. 2015. *War and Democratic Constraint: How the Public Influences Foreign Policy*. Princeton, NJ: Princeton University Press.

Beardsley, Kyle. 2008. Agreement without Peace? International Mediation and Time Inconsistency Problems. *American Journal of Political Science*, 52(4), 723–740.

Beardsley, Kyle. 2011. *The Mediation Dilemma*. Ithaca, NY: Cornell University Press.

Beardsley, Kyle, and Victor Asal. 2009a. Nuclear Weapons and Shields. *Conflict Management and Peace Science*, 26(3), 235–255.

Beardsley, Kyle, and Victor Asal. 2009b. Winning with the Bomb. *Journal of Conflict Resolution*, 53(2), 278–301.

Beardsley, Kyle, Patrick James, and Jonathan Wilkenfeld. 2025. *A Century of International Crises, 1918–2017*. Ann Arbor, MI: University of Michigan Press.

Beardsley, Kyle, Patrick James, Jonathan Wilkenfeld, and Michael Brecher. 2020. The International Crisis Behavior Project. In John Preston (ed.), *Encyclopedia of Crisis Analysis*. Oxford: Oxford University Press.

Beardsley, Kyle, Patrick James, Jonathan Wilkenfeld, and Michael Brecher. 2023. http://www.icb.umd.edu/dataviewer/, accessed 25 November, 2023.

Beardsley, Kyle, David Quinn, Bidisha Biswas, and Jonathan Wilkenfeld. 2006. Mediation Style and Crisis Outcomes. *Journal of Conflict Resolution*, 50(1), 58–86.

Beer, Francis A. 1974. *How Much War in History: Definitions, Estimates, Extrapolations and Trends*. Beverly Hills, CA: Sage.

Bell, Christine. 2008. *On the Law of Peace: Peace Agreements and the Lex Pacificatoria*. Oxford: Oxford University.

REFERENCES

Bell, Christine. 2010. Contemporary peace agreements and accords. In Nigel J. Young (ed.), The *Oxford International Encyclopedia of Peace*. Oxford: Oxford University Press. Retrieved from: http://www.oxfordreference.com/view/10.1093/acref/9780195334685.001.0001/acref-9780195334685-e-142

Bellamy, Alex J., Paul D. Williams, and Stuart Griffin. 2009. *Understanding Peacekeeping* (2nd ed.). Cambridge: Polity.

Bennett, D. Scott, and Allan C. Stam. 1998. The Declining Advantages of Democracy: A Combined Model of War Outcomes and Duration. *Journal of Conflict Resolution*, 42(3), 344–66.

Bercovitch, Jacob. 1996. Understanding Mediation's Role in Preventative Diplomacy. *Negotiation Journal*, 12(3), 241–58.

Bercovitch, Jacob., and Scott S. Gartner. 2006. Is There Method in the Madness of Mediation: Some Lessons for Mediators from Quantitative Studies of Mediation. *International Interactions*, 32(4), 329–54.

Bern, Daryl J. 1970. *Beliefs, Attitudes, and Human Affairs*. Belmont CA: Brooks/Cole.

Berridge, Geoff R. 2015. *Diplomacy: Theory and Practice*. London: Palgrave Macmillan.

Bidder, Benjamin, and Markus Becker. (2022). Russia Is Becoming Poorer and More Backward. *Der Spiegel*, September 16, 2022. https://www.spiegel.de/international/world/the-ukraine-war-russia-is-becoming-poorer-and-more-backward-a-8ba48998-bd7b-4167-a892-4b00b09e7743 [11/04/2022]

Biddle, Stephen, and Stephen Long. 2004. Democracy and Military Effectiveness: A Deeper Look. *Journal of Conflict Resolution*, 48(4), 525–46.

Biersteker, Thomas J., Sue E. Eckert, and Marcos Tourinho. 2016. *Targeted Sanctions: The Impacts and Effectiveness of United Nations Action*. Cambridge: Cambridge University Press.

Binder, Martin. 2015. Paths to Intervention: What Explains the UN's Selective Response to Humanitarian Crises? *Journal of Peace Research*, 52(6), 712–726.

Birt, Raymond. 1993. Personality and Foreign Policy: The Case of Stalin. *Political Psychology*, 14(4), 607–625.

Blechman, Barry M., and Stephen S. Kaplan. 1978. *Force Without War: U.S. Armed Forces as a Political Instrument*. Washington, DC: Brookings Institution.

Blechman, Barry M., and Tamara Coffman Wittes. 1998. Defining Moment: The Threat and Use of Force in American Foreign Policy Since 1989. Occasional Paper No. 6, May 1998. Stanford, CA. Henry L. Stimson Center.

Blechman, Barry M., and J. Matthew Vaccaro (eds.). 1995. *Towards an Operational Strategy of Peace Enforcement: Lessons from Interventions and Peace Operations*. Washington, DC: DFI International.

Boehmer, Charles, Erik Gartzke, and Timothy Nordstrom. 2004. Do Intergovernmental Organizations Promote Peace? *World Politics*, 57(1), 1–38.

Boettcher, William A. 1995. Context, Methods, Numbers, and Words: Prospect Theory in International Relations. *Journal of Conflict Resolution*, 39(3), 561–83.

Boettcher, William A. 2004. Military Intervention Decisions Regarding Humanitarian Crises: Framing Induced Risk Behavior. *Journal of Conflict Resolution*, 48(3), 331–55.

Boutros-Ghali, Boutros. 1992. *An Agenda for Peace*. New York, NY: UN.

Boyer, Mark A., and Michael Butler. 2017. Diplomacy and Negotiation by the Numbers: More Than an Art Form? *Oxford Research Encyclopedia on Politics*. https://doi.org/10.1093/acrefore/9780190228637.013.336

Branco, Carlos. 2011. Nongovernmental Organizations in the Mediation of Violent Intra-State Conflict: The Confrontation between Theory and Practice in the Mozambican Peace Process. *JANUS. NET*, 2(2), 77–79.

Braumoeller, Bear. 2019. *Only the Dead: The Persistence of War in the Modern Age*. Oxford: Oxford University Press.

Brecher, Michael. 1999. International Studies in the Twentieth Century and Beyond: Flawed Dichotomies, Synthesis, Cumulation. *International Studies Quarterly*, 43(2), 231–264.

Brecher, Michael. 2018. *The World of Protracted Conflicts*. Lanham, MD: Lexington Press.

Brecher, Michael, Patrick James, and Jonathan Wilkenfeld. 2000. Escalation and War in the Twentieth Century: Findings from the International Crisis Behavior Project. In John A. Vasquez (ed.), *What Do We Know About War?* Lanham, MD: Rowman & Littlefield Publishers, pp. 37–53.

Brecher, Michael, and Jonathan Wilkenfeld. 1997. *A Study of Crisis*. Ann Arbor, MI: University of Michigan Press.

Brecher, Michael, and Jonathan Wilkenfeld. 2000. *A Study of Crisis*. Ann Arbor, MI: University of Michigan Press.

Brecher, Michael, Jonathan Wilkenfeld, Kyle Beardsley, Patrick James, and David Quinn. 2023. International Crisis Behavior Data Codebook, Version 15. [Dataset: ICB2 (Actor Level)]. *ICB Project*. https://sites.duke.edu/icbdata/data-collections/

Bremer, Stuart A. 1980. National Capabilities and War Proneness. In J. David Singer (ed.), *Correlates of War II: Testing Some Realpolitik Models*. New York: Free Press, pp. 57–82.

Bremer, Stuart A. 1993 Democracy and Militarized Interstate Conflict, 1816–1965. *International Interactions*, 18(3), 231–49.

Bremer, Stuart A. 2000. Who Fights Whom, When, Where, and Why? In John A. Vasquez (ed.), *What Do We Know About War?* Lanham, MD: Rowman & Littlefield, pp. 23–36.

Britannica. 2024a. What is the Syrian Civil War? https://www.britannica.com/question/What-is-the-Syrian-Civil-War, accessed August 10, 2024.

Britannica. 2024b. Chinese Civil War, 1945–1949. https://www.britannica.com/event/Chinese-Civil-War, accessed August 10, 2024.

Brock, Kathy L., and Geoffrey Hale (eds.). 2023. *Managing Federalism Through Pandemic*. Toronto: University of Toronto Press.

Brodie, Bernard. (ed.). 1946. *The Absolute Weapon*. New York, NY: Harcourt, Brace.

Brodie, Bernard. 1959. *Strategy in the Missile Age*. Princeton, NJ: Princeton University Press.

Brodie, Bernard. 1978. The Development of Nuclear Strategy. *International Security*, 2(4), 65–83.

Brown, Davis. 2020. *War and Religion in the Secular Age: Faith and Interstate Armed Conflict Onset*. New York, NY: Routledge.

Brown, Davis, and Patrick James. 2018a. The Religious Characteristics of States: Classic Themes and New Evidence for International Relations and Comparative Politics. *Journal of Conflict Resolution*, 62(6), 1340–1376.

Brown, Davis, and Patrick James. 2018b. Religious Characteristics of States Dataset Project- Demographics v. 2.0. *The ARDA*, https://www.thearda.com/data-archive?fid=RCSDEM2&tab=1

Bruce Bueno de Mesquita and William H. Riker. 1982. An Assessment of the Merits of Selective Nuclear Proliferation. *Journal of Conflict Resolution*, 26(2), 283–306.

Buhaug, Halvard, Scott Gates, and Päivi Lujala. 2009. Geography, Rebel Capability, and the Duration of Civil Conflict. *Journal of Conflict Resolution*, 53(4), 544–569.

Bunge, Mario. 1996. *Finding Philosophy in Social Science*. New Haven, CT: Yale University Press.

Bull, Hedley. 1977. *The Anarchical Society*. New York: Columbia University Press.

Butcher, Charity. 2023. Diversionary Theories of Conflict: The Promises and Challenges of an Opportunities Approach. *Oxford Research Encyclopedia on International Studies*. https://doi.org/10.1093/acrefore/9780190846626.013.606

Butcher, Charity, and Makda Maru. (2018). Diversionary Tactics and the Ethiopia–Eritrea War (1998–2000). *Small Wars & Insurgencies*, 29(1), 68–90.

Butler, Michael, and Mark A. Boyer. 2017. International Negotiation in a Foreign Policy Context. *Oxford Research Encyclopedia of International Studies*, 1–31.

Butterfield, Herbert. 1951. *History and Human Relations*. London: Collins.

Callahan, William A. 2010. *China: The Pessoptimist Nation*. Oxford: Oxford University Press.

Carden, Allen. 1986. Religious Schism as a Prelude to the American Civil War: Methodists, Baptists, and Slavery. *Andrews University Seminary Studies* 24(1), 13–29.

Cashman, Greg. 2013. *What Causes War? An Introduction to Theories of International Conflict*. New York, NY: Rowman & Littlefield.

Cashman, Greg, and Leonard C. Robinson. 2007. *An Introduction to the Causes of War: Patterns of Interstate Conflict from World War I to Iraq*. Lanham, MD: Rowman & Littlefield.

CBS News. 2023. https://www.cbsnews.com/live-updates/chinas-spy-balloon-unidentified-objects-shot-down-what-we-know-so-far/

Chakravartty, Anjan. 2007. *A Metaphysics for Scientific Realism: Knowing the Unobservable*. Cambridge: Cambridge University Press.

Chakravartty, Anjan. 2011. Scientific Realism. *Stanford Encyclopedia of Philosophy*. http://plato.stanford.edu/entries/scientific-realism/

Chan, Steve. 2010. Progress in the Democratic Peace Research Agenda. *Oxford Research Encyclopedia on International Studies*. https://doi.org/10.1093/acrefore/9780190846626.013.280

Chernow, Ron. 2017. *Grant*. New York, NY: Penguin Press.

Chiozza, Giacomo, and Hans E. Goemans. 2004. Avoiding Diversionary Targets. *Journal of Peace Research*, 41(4), 423–443.

Chiu, Daniel Y. 2003. International Alliances in the Power Cycle Theory of State Behavior. *International Political Science Review,* 24(1), 123–136.

Choi, Seung-Whan, and Patrick James. 2007. Media Openness, Democracy and Militarized Interstate Disputes. *British Journal of Political Science*, 37(1), 23–46.

Choucri, Nazli., and Robert C. North. 1975. *Nations in Conflict: National Growth and International Violence*. New York, NY: Freeman.

Cilizoglu, Menevis, and Navin A. Bapat. 2020. Economic Coercion and the Problem of Sanctions-Proofing. *Conflict Management and Peace Science*, 37(4), 385–408.

Cilizoglu, Menevis, and Bryan R. Early. 2021. Researching Modern Economic Sanctions. *Oxford Research Encyclopedia on International Studies*. https://doi.org/10.1093/acrefore/9780190846626.013.599

Citrin, Jack, Morris S. Levy, and Matthew Wright. 2023. *Immigration in the Court of Public Opinion*. New York, NY: Polity.

Clark, Ian, Sebastian Kaempf, Christian Reus-Smit, and Emily Tannock. 2018. Crisis in the Laws of War: Beyond Compliance and Effectiveness. *European Journal of International Relations*, 24(2), 319–343.

Claude, Inis L. 1962. *Power and International Relations*. New York: Random House.

Claude, Inis L. 1984. Swords into Plowshares. New York: Random House.

Clay, K. Chad. 2018. Threat by Example: Economic Sanctions and Global Respect for Human Rights. *Journal of Global Security Studies,* 3(2), 133–149.

Coe, Andrew, and Jane Vaynman. 2020. Why Arms Control Is So Rare. *American Political Science Review*, 114(2), 342–355.

Collier, Paul, and Anke Hoeffler. 2004. Greed and Grievance in Civil War. *Oxford Economic Papers*, 56(4), 563–595.

Collingwood, Robin George. 1946. *The Idea of History*. Oxford: Oxford University Press.

Coppedge, Michael, John Gerring, Carl H. Knutsen, Staffan I. Lindberg, Jan Teorell, David Altman, Michael Bernhard, M. Steven Fish, Adam Glynn, Allen Hicken, Anna Luhrmann, Kyle L. Marquardt, Kelly McMann, Pamela Paxton, Daniel Pemstein, Brigitte Seim, Rachel Sigman, Svend-Erik Skaaning, Jeffrey Staton, Agnes Cornell, Lisa Gastaldi, Haakon Gjerløw, Valeriya Mechkova, Johannes von Römer, Aksel Sundtröm, Eitan Tzelgov, Luca Uberti, Yi-ting Wang, Tore Wig, and Daniel Ziblatt. 2020. *V-Dem Codebook v10*. Varieties of Democracy (V-Dem) Project.

Cornut, Jérémie. 2015. Analytic Eclecticism in Practice: A Method for Combining International Relations Theories. *International Studies Perspectives*, 16(1), 50–66.

Correlates of War Project. 2017. http://www.correlatesofwar.org/data-sets

Cortright, David, and George A. Lopez (eds.). 1995. *Economic Sanctions: Panacea or Peacebuilding in a Post-Cold War World?* Boulder, CO: Westview.

Cortright, David, and George A. Lopez. 2002. *Smart Sanctions: Targeting Economic Statecraft*. New York, NY: Rowman & Littlefield.

Cottam, Martha. 1994. *Images and Intervention: US Policies in Latin America*. Pittsburgh, PA: University of Pittsburgh Press.

Council on Foreign Relations. 2024. *Conflict in Syria*. https://www.cfr.org/global-conflict-tracker/conflict/conflict-syria, accessed 25 February, 2024.

Cronin, Bruce. 2017. Security Regimes: Collective Security and Security Communities. *Oxford Research Encyclopedia on International Studies*. https://doi.org/10.1093/acrefore/9780190846626.013.296

Croon, Janet Elizabeth (ed.). 2018. *The War Outside My Window: The Civil War Diary of LeRoy Wiley Gresham, 1860–1865*. El Dorado Hills, CA: Savas Beatie.

Cunningham, David E., Kristian Skrede Gleditsch, and Idean Salehyan. 2009. It Takes Two: A Dyadic Analysis of Civil War Duration and Outcome. *Journal of Conflict Resolution*, 53(4), 570–597.

Dahlerup, Drude. 1988. From a Small to a Large Minority: Women in Scandinavian Politics. *Scandinavian Political Studies,* 11(4), 275–299.

Danilovic, Vesna, and Joe Clare. 2017. Deterrence and Crisis Bargaining. *Oxford Research Encyclopedia on International Studies*, 1–28.

Daut, Marlene L. 2023. *Awakening the Ashes: An Intellectual History of the Haitian Revolution*. Chapel Hill, NC: University of North Carolina Press.

Davis Jr., James W. 2000. *Threats and Promises: The Pursuit of International Influence*. Baltimore, MD: Johns Hopkins University Press.
DeRouen, Karl R. 1995. The Indirect Link: Politics, the Economy, and the Use of Force. *Journal of Conflict Resolution*, 39(4), 671–695.
Diehl, Paul F. 1983. Arms Races and Escalation: A Closer Look. *Journal of Peace Research*, 20(5), 349–259.
Diehl, Paul F. 1985. Arms Races to War: Testing Some Empirical Linkages. *The Sociological Quarterly*, 26(3), 331–349.
Diehl, Paul. F. 2000. Forks in the Road: Theoretical and Policy Concerns for 21st Century Peacekeeping. *Global Society*, 14(3), 337–360.
Diehl, Paul F. 2008. *Peace Operations*. Cambridge: Polity.
Diehl, Paul F., and Young-Im Cho. 2006. Passing the Buck in Conflict Management: The Role of Regional Organizations in the Post-Cold War Era. *The Brown Journal of World Affairs*, 12(2), 191–202.
Diehl, Paul F., and Gary G. Goertz. 2012. The Rivalry Process: How Rivalries are Sustained and Terminated. In John A. Vasquez (ed.), *What Do We Know About War?* (2nd ed.). Lanham, MD: Rowman & Littlefield, pp. 83–109.
Diehl, Paul F., and Joseph Lepgold (eds.). 2003. *Regional Conflict Management*. Lanham, MD: Rowman & Littlefield.
Dixon, Jeffrey. 2009a. What Causes Civil Wars? Integrating Quantitative Research Findings. *International Studies Review*, 11(4), 707–735.
Dixon, Jeffrey. 2009b. Emerging Consensus: Results from the Second Wave of Statistical Studies on Civil War Termination. *Civil Wars*, 11(2), 121–136.
Dixon, William J. 1994. Democracy and the Peaceful Settlement of International Conflict. *American Political Science Review*, 88(1), 14–32.
Doran, Charles F. 1971. *The Politics of Assimilation: Hegemony and Its Aftermath*. Baltimore, MD: Johns Hopkins University Press.
Doran, Charles F. 1989. Systemic Disequilibrium, Foreign Policy Role, and the Power Cycle: Challenges for Research Design. *Journal of Conflict Resolution*, 33(3), 371–401.
Doran, Charles F. 1991. *Systems in Crisis: New Imperatives of High Politics at Century's End*. Cambridge: Cambridge University Press.
Doran, Charles F. 2012. Power Cycle Theory and the Ascendance of China: Peaceful or Stormy? *SAIS Review*.
Doran, Charles F., and Wes Parsons. 1980. War and the Cycle of Relative Power. *American Political Science Review*, 74(4), 947–965.
Downs, George W., David M. Rocke, and Peter N. Barsoom. 1996. Is the Good News About Compliance Good News About Cooperation? *International Organization*, 50(3), 379–406
Doyle, Michael W. 1986. Liberalism and World Politics. *American Political Science Review*, 80(4), 1151–1169.
Doyle, Michael W., and Nicholas Sambanis. 2006. *Making War and Building Peace: United Nations Peace Operations*. Princeton, NJ: Princeton University Press.
Drezner, Daniel. 1999. *The Sanctions Paradox: Economic Statecraft and International Relations*. Cambridge: Cambridge University Press.
Dror, Yehezkel. 1971. *Crazy States: A Counterconventional Strategic Problem*. Lexington, MA: Heath Lexington Books.
Drury, A. Cooper. 2001. Sanctions as Coercive Diplomacy: The U.S. President's Decision to Initiate Economic Sanctions. *Political Research Quarterly*, 54(3), 485–508.
Drury, A. Cooper., and Dursun Peksen. 2014. Women and Economic Statecraft: The Negative Impact International Economic Sanctions Visit on Women. *European Journal of International Relations*, 20(2), 463–490.
Duelfer, Charles A., and Stephen Benedict Dyson. 2011. Chronic Misperception and International Conflict: The U.S.-Iraq Experience. *International Security*, 36(1), 73–100.
Durch, William J. (ed.). 1993. *The Evolution of UN Peacekeeping*. London: Macmillan.
Durch, William J. (ed.). 2006. *Twenty-First Century Peace Operations*. Washington, DC: US Institute of Peace.
Dyer, Gwynne. 2005. *War*. Toronto: Vintage Canada.
Early, Bryan R. 2015. *Busted Sanctions: Explaining Why Economic Sanctions Fail*. Stanford, CA: Stanford University Press.

Early, Bryan R. 2016. Confronting the Implementation and Enforcement Challenges Involved in Imposing Economic Sanctions. In N. Ronzitti (ed.), *Coercive Diplomacy, Sanctions and International Law*. Leiden: Brill Nijhoff, pp. 43–69.

Early, Bryan R., and Menevis Cilizoglu. 2020. Economic Sanctions in Flux: Enduring Challenges, New Policies, and Defining the Future Research Agenda. *International Studies Perspectives*, 21(4), 438–77.

Early, Bryan R. and Dursun Peksen. 2019. Searching in the Shadows: The Impact of Economic Sanctions on Informal Economies. *Political Research Quarterly*, 72(4), 821–34.

Early, Bryan R., and Keith A. Preble. 2020. Going Fishing Versus Hunting Whales: Explaining Variation in the United States' Enforcement of Economic Sanctions. *Security Studies*, 29(2), 231–67.

Eckhardt, William. 1991. War-Related Deaths Since 3000 BC. *Bulletin of Peace Proposals*, 22(4), 437–43.

Elasfar, Dara. 2023. "No Other Alternative": Egypt Worries as Climate Change, Dam Project Threaten Nile Water Supply. *ABC News*. April 19, 2023. https://abcnews.go.com/US/alternative-egypt-worries-climate-change-dam-project-threaten/story?id=98481819

Elliott, Kimberly Ann. 2009. Assessing UN Sanctions After the Cold War: New and Evolving Standards of Measurement. *International Journal*, 65(1), 85–97.

Enterline, Andrew J., and Kristian Skrede Gleditsch. 2000. Threats, Opportunity, and Force: Leaders' Externalization of Domestic Pressure. *International Interactions*, 26(1), 21–53.

Eriksson, Mikael and Peter Wallensteen. 2004. Armed Conflict, 1989-2003. *Journal of Peace Research*, 41, 625–636.

Etheredge, Lloyd. 1978. *A World of Men: The Private Sources of American Foreign Policy*. Cambridge, MA: MIT Press.

Evangelista, Matthew, and Nina Tannenwald (eds.). 2017. *Do the Geneva Conventions Matter?* New York, NY: Oxford Academic.

Fabbro, David. 1978. Peaceful Societies: An Introduction. *Journal of Peace Research*, 15(1), 67–83.

Farber, Henry S. and Joanne Gowa. 1995. Politics and Peace. *International Security*, 20(2), 123–146.

Farnham, Barbara (ed.). 1994. *Avoiding Losses/Taking Risks: Prospect Theory and International Conflict*. Ann Arbor, MI: University of Michigan Press.

Farnham, Barbara. 1997. *Roosevelt and the Munich Crisis: A Study of Political Decision-Making*. Princeton. NJ: Princeton University Press.

Fausett, Elizabeth, and Thomas J. Volgy. 2010. Intergovernmental Organizations (IGOs) and Interstate Conflict: Parsing Out IGO Effects for Alternative Dimensions of Conflict in Postcommunist Space. *International Studies Quarterly*, 54(1), 79–101.

Favretto, Katja. 2009. Should Peacemakers Take Sides? Major Power Mediation, Coercion, and Bias. *American Political Science Review*, 103(2), 248–263.

Fearon, James D. 1994a. Domestic Political Audiences and the Escalation of International Disputes. *American Political Science Review*, 88(3), 577–592.

Fearon, James D. 1994b. Signaling vs the Balance of Power and Interests: An Empirical Test of a Crisis Bargaining Model. *Journal of Conflict Resolution*, 38(2), 236–269.

Fearon, James D. 1995. Rationalist Explanations for War. *International Organization*, 49(3), 379–414.

Fehrenbacher, Don E. 1978. *The Dred Scott Case: Its Significance in American Law and Politics*. Oxford: Oxford University Press.

Feng, Yi, Zhijun Gao, and Zining Yang. 2020. East Asia: China's Campaign to Become a New World Leader. In Jacek Kugler, and Ronald L. Tammen (eds.), *The Rise of Regions: Conflict and Cooperation*. New York, NY: Rowman & Littlefield, pp. 37–54.

Filson, Darren, and Suzanne Werner. 2004. Bargaining and Fighting: The Impact of Regime Type on War Onset, Duration, and Outcomes. *American Journal of Political Science*, 48(2), 296–313.

Findlay, Trevor. 2002. *The Use of Force in United Nations Peace Operations*. Oxford: Oxford University Press for SIPRI.

Finnemore, Martha, and Kathryn Sikkink. 1998. International Norm Dynamics and Political Change. *International Organization*, 52(4), 887–917.

Fisher, Roger, and William Ury. 1983. *Getting to Yes: Negotiating Agreement Without Giving In*. New York, NY: Penguin.

Fordham, Benjamin O. 2017. More Than Mixed Results: What We Have Learned from Quantitative Research on the Diversionary Hypothesis. *Oxford Research Encyclopedia on Politics*. https://doi.org/10.1093/acrefore/9780190228637.013.280

Fortna, Virginia Page. 2003. Inside and Out: Peacekeeping and the Duration of Peace after Civil and Interstate Wars. *International Studies Review*, 5(4), 97–114.

Fortna, Virginia Page. 2004a. *Peace Time: Cease-Fire Agreements and the Durability of Peace*. Princeton, NJ: Princeton University Press.

Fortna, Virginia Page. 2004b. Does Peacekeeping Keep Peace? International Intervention and the Duration of Peace After Civil War. *International Studies Quarterly*, 48(2), 269–292.

Fortna, Victoria Page. 2008. *Does Peacekeeping Work?: Shaping the Belligerents' Choices after Civil War*. Princeton, NJ: Princeton University Press.

Fortna, Virginia Page. 2015. Do Terrorists Win? Rebels' Use of Terrorism and Civil War Outcomes. *International Organization*, 69(3), 519–556.

Foster, Dennis M. 2006. State Power, Linkage Mechanisms, and Diversion Against Nonrivals. *Conflict Management and Peace Science*, 23(1), 1–21.

Fox, Jonathan. 2002. *Ethnoreligious Conflict in the Late Twentieth Century: A General Theory*. Lanham, MD: Lexington Books.

Fox, Jonathan. 2018. *An Introduction to Religion and Politics: Theory and Practice* (2nd ed.). New York, NY: Routledge.

Fox, Jonathan, Patrick James, and Yitan Li. 2009. Religious Affinities and International Intervention in Ethnic Conflicts in the Middle East and Beyond. *Canadian Journal of Political Science* 42(1), 161–186.

Fox, Jonathan, and Nukhet Sandal. 2011. State Religious Exclusivity and International Crises, 1990–2002. In Patrick James (ed.), *Religion, Identity, and Global Governance: Ideas, Evidence, and Practice*. Toronto: University of Toronto Press, pp. 81–107.

Fox, Jonathan, and Shmuel Sandler. 2004. *Bringing Religion into International Relations*. New York, NY: Palgrave Macmillan.

Freehling, William W. 1990. *The Road to Disunion: Secessionists at Bay, 1776–1854: Volume I*. Oxford: Oxford University Press.

Freehling, William W. 1992. *Prelude to Civil War: The Nullification Controversy in South Carolina, 1816–1836*. Oxford: Oxford University Press.

Freehling, William W. 2008. *The Road to Disunion: Secessionists Triumphant, 1854–1861: Volume II*. Oxford: Oxford University Press.

Freehling, William W., and Craig M. Simpson (eds.). 1992. *Secession Debated: Georgia's Showdown in 1860*. Oxford: Oxford University Press.

Friedberg, Aaron L. 2000. *In the Shadow of the Garrison State: America's Anti-Statism and Its Cold War Grand Strategy*. Princeton, NJ: Princeton University Press.

Frisch, Hillel. 2011. *Israel's Security and Its Arab Citizens*. Cambridge: Cambridge University Press.

Fry Douglas P. 2012. Life Without War. *Science*, 336(6083), 879–884.

Fuhrmann, Matthew. 2021. Nuclear Weapons. In Sara McLaughlin Mitchell and John A. Vasquez (eds.), *What Do We Know About War?* (3rd ed.). Lanham, MD: Rowman & Littlefield, pp. 103–119.

Fuhrmann, Matthew, and Yonatan Lupu. 2016. Do Arms Control Treaties Work? Assessing the Effectiveness of the Nuclear Nonproliferation Treaty. *International Studies Quarterly*, 60(3), 530–539.

Fukuyama, Francis. 1992. *The End of History and the Last Man*. New York, NY: Free Press.

Fusco, Giuseppe, and Alessandro Minelli. 2010. Phenotypic Plasticity in Development and Evolution: Facts and Concepts. *Philosophical Transactions of the Royal Society B: Biological Sciences*, 365(1540), 547–556.

Gaddis, John Lewis. 1986. The Long Peace: Elements of Stability in the Postwar International System. *International Security*, 10(4), 99–142.

Gallagher, Maryann, and Susan H. Allen. 2013. Presidential Personality: Not Just a Nuisance. *Foreign Policy Analysis*, 10(1), 1–21.

Gan, Nectar. 2023. Xi Jinping Tells China's National Security Chiefs to Prepare for "Worst Case" Scenarios. *CNN*. June 1, 2023. https://www.cnn.com/2023/05/31/china/china-xi-national-security-meeting-intl-hnk/index.html#:~:text=Chinese%20leader%20Xi%20Jinping%20has,perceived%20internal%20and%20external%20threats

Gansen, Sarah, and Patrick James. 2022. The Russo-Ukrainian War: Insights from Systemism in a Pedagogical Setting. *New Area Studies*, 3(1), 1–35.

Gartner, Scott S., Chin-Hao Huang, Yitan Li, and Patrick James. 2021. *Identity in the Shadow of a Giant: How the Rise of China Is Changing Taiwan*. Bristol: Bristol University Press.

Gartzke, Erik. 2007. The Capitalist Peace. *American Journal of Political Science*, 51(1), 166–91.

Gartzke, Erik, and J. Joseph Hewitt. 2010. International Crises and the Capitalist Peace. *International Interactions*, 36(2), 115–145.

Gartzke, Erik, Quan Li, and Charles Boehmer. 2001. Investing in the Peace: Economic Interdependence and International Conflict. *International Organization*, 55(2), 391–438.

Gates, Scott, Torbjørn L. Knutsen, and Jonathon W. Moses. 1996. Democracy and Peace: A More Skeptical View, *Journal of Peace Research*, 33(1), 1–10.

Geller, Daniel. 1990. Nuclear Weapons, Deterrence, and Crisis Escalation. *Journal of Conflict Resolution*, 34(2), 291–310.

Gelpi, Christopher. (1997). Democratic Diversions: Governmental Structure and the Externalization of Domestic Conflict. *Journal of Conflict Resolution*, 41(2), 255–282.

Gelpi, Christopher, and Michael Griesdorf. 2001. Winners or Losers? Democracies in International Crisis, 1918–94. *American Political Science Review*, 95(03), 633–647.

Genovese, Eugene D. 1969. *The World the Slaveholders Made*. New York, NY: Vintage.

Gent, Stephen E. 2009. Scapegoating Strategically: Reselection, Strategic Interaction, and the Diversionary Theory of War. *International Interactions*, 35(1), 1–29.

Gent, Stephen E., and Megan Shannon. 2010. The Effectiveness of International Arbitration and Adjudication: Getting into a Bind. *The Journal of Politics*, 72(2), 366–380.

Gent, Stephen E., and Megan Shannon. 2011. Decision Control and the Pursuit of Binding Conflict Management: Choosing the Ties that Bind. *Journal of Conflict Resolution*, 55(5), 710–734.

George, Alexander L. 1969. The "Operational Code": A Neglected Approach to the Study of Political Leaders and Decision Making. *International Studies Quarterly*, 13(2), 190–222.

George, Alexander L. 1991. *Forceful Persuasion: Coercive Diplomacy as an Alternative to War*. Washington, DC: United States Institute of Peace.

George, Alexander L., David K. Hall, and William E. Simons. 1971. *The Limits of Coercive Diplomacy: Laos, Cuba, Vietnam*. Boston, MA: Little Brown.

George, Alexander L., and Richard Smoke. 1974. *Deterrence and American Foreign Policy: Theory and Practice*. New York, NY: Columbia University.

Ghose, Gaurav, and Patrick James. 2006. Third-Party Intervention in Ethno-Religious Conflict: Role Theory, Pakistan, and War in Kashmir, 1965. In Jonathan Fox and Shmuel Sandler (eds.), *Religion in World Conflict*. New York, NY: Routledge, pp. 133–50.

Gibler, Douglas M., and Meredith Reid Sarkees. 2004. Measuring Alliances: The Correlates of War Formal Interstate Alliance Dataset, 1816–2000. *Journal of Peace Research*, 41(2), 211–22.

Gibler, Douglas M., and John A. Vasquez. 1998. Uncovering the Dangerous Alliances, 1495–1980. *International Studies Quarterly*, 42(4), 785–807.

Gilovich, Thomas, Dale Griffin, and Daniel Kahneman (eds.). 2002. *Heuristics and Biases: The Psychology of Intuitive Judgment*. Cambridge: Cambridge University Press.

Glad, Betty. 1983. Black-and-White Thinking: Ronald Reagan's Approach to Foreign Policy. *Political Psychology*, 4(1), 33–76.

Gleditsch, Nils Petter, Peter Wallensteen, Mikael Eriksson, Margareta Sollenberg, and Håvard Strand. (2002). Armed Conflict 1946–2001: A New Dataset. *Journal of Peace Research*, 39(5), 615–637.

Goldstein, Joshua S. 1992. A Conflict-Cooperation Scale for WEIS data. *Journal of Conflict Resolution*, 36(2), 369–385.

Goodwin, Doris Kearns. 1991. *Lyndon Johnson and the American Dream*. New York, NY: St. Martin's Press.

Gourevitch, Peter. 1978. The Second Image Reversed: The International Sources of Domestic Politics. *International Organization*, 32(4), 881–912.

Gowa, Joanne. 1999. *Ballots and Bullets: The Elusive Democratic Peace*. Princeton, NJ: Princeton University Press.

Gowa, Joanne, and Tyler Pratt. 2019. The Democratic Peace Debate. In Asle Toje and Bard Nikolas Vik Steen (eds.), *The Causes of Peace: What We Know Now*. Nobel Symposium Proceedings. Norwegian Nobel Institute, pp. 221–248.

Graff, Corinne, Janet Lewis, and Susan E. Rice. 2006. *Poverty and Civil War: What Policymakers Need to Know*. https://www.cfr.org/global-conflict-tracker/conflict/war-yemen, accessed 28 February, 2024.

Green, Jane, and Raluca L. Pahontu. 2021. Mind the Gap: Why Wealthy Voters Support Brexit. Available at SSRN: https://ssrn.com/abstract=3764889 or http://dx.doi.org/10.2139/ssrn.3764889

Green, Michael. 2009. *Politics and America in Crisis: The Coming of the Civil War*. New York, NY: Praeger.
Greig, J. Michael. 2001. Moments of Opportunity: Recognizing Conditions of Ripeness for International Mediation Between Enduring Rivals. *Journal of Conflict Resolution*, 45(6), 691–718.
Greig, J. Michael. 2005. Stepping into the Fray: When Do Mediators Mediate? *American Journal of Political Science*, 49(2), 249–266. https://doi.org/10.2307/3647675
Greig, J. Michael, and Paul F. Diehl. 2005. The Peacekeeping–Peacemaking Dilemma. *International Studies Quarterly*, 49(4), 621–646.
Greig, J. Michael, and Paul F. Diehl. 2012. *International Mediation*. Cambridge: Polity Press.
Grotius, Hugo. 1625. *On the Law of War and Peace*, edited and annotated by Stephen C. Neff. Cambridge: Cambridge University Press, 2012.
Grzymala-Busse, Anna. 2011. Time Will Tell? Temporality and the Analysis of Causal Mechanisms and Processes. *Comparative Political Studies*, 44(9), 1267–1297.
Gudmestad, Robert H. 2011. *Steamboats and the Rise of the Cotton Kingdom*. Baton Rouge, LA: LSU Press.
Haas, Ernst B. 1958. *The Uniting of Europe: Political, Social and Economic Forces, 1950–1957*. Stanford, CA: Stanford University Press.
Haas, Michael. 1980. Societal Approaches to the Study of War. In Richard. A. Falk and Samuel S. Kim (eds.), *The War System: An Interdisciplinary Approach*. Boulder, CO: Westview.
Haass, Richard N. 1990. *Conflicts Unending: The United States and Regional Disputes*. New Haven, CT: Yale University Press.
Hagan, Joe D. 1994. Domestic Political Systems and War Proneness. *Mershon International Studies Review*, 38(Supplement 2), 183–207.
Hagan, Joe D. 2010. Regime Type, Foreign Policy, and International Relations. In Nukhet Sandal (ed.), *Oxford Research Encyclopedia of International Studies*. Oxford: Oxford University Press.
Hagan, Joe D. 2017. Diversionary Theory of War in Foreign Policy Analysis. In David R. Dreyer (ed.), *Oxford Research Encyclopedia of Politics*. Oxford: Oxford University Press, pp. 1–32.
Hague, William. 2008. *William Wilberforce: The Life of the Great Anti-Slave Trade Campaigner*. New York, NY: Houghton Mifflin Harcourt.
Hamilton, Keith, and Richard Langhorne. 2011. *The Practice of Diplomacy: Its Evolution, Theory and Administration* (2nd ed.). London: Routledge.
Hancock, Landon E. 2001. To Act or Wait: A Two-Stage View of Ripeness. *International Studies Perspectives*, 2(2), 195–205.
Hansen, Holley E., Sara McLaughlin Mitchell, and Stephen C. Nemeth. 2008. IO Mediation of Interstate Conflicts: Moving Beyond the Global Versus Regional Dichotomy. *Journal of Conflict Resolution*, 52(2), 295–325. https://doi.org/10.1177/0022002707313693
Hasenclever, Andreas, and Volker Rittberger. 2003. Does Religion Make a Difference? Theoretical Approaches to the Impact of Faith on Political Conflict. In Pavlos Hatzopoulos and Fabio Petito (eds.), *Religion in International Relations: The Return from Exile*. New York, NY: Palgrave Macmillan, pp. 107–145.
Hassner, Ron E. 2009. *War on Sacred Grounds*. Ithaca, NY: Cornell University Press.
Hassner, Ron E. 2016. *Religion on the Battlefield*. Ithaca, NY: Cornell University Press.
Haynes, Jeffrey. 2013. *An Introduction to International Relations and Religion* (2nd ed.). New York, NY: Pearson.
Haynes, Kyle. 2016. Diversity and Diversion: How Ethnic Composition Affects Diversionary Conflict. *International Studies Quarterly*, 60(2), 258–271.
Hebron, Lui, Patrick James, and Michael Rudy. 2007. Testing Dynamic Theories of Conflict: Power Cycles, Power Transitions, Foreign Policy Crises and Militarized Interstate Disputes. *International Interactions*, 33(1), 1–29.
Hebron, Lui, and John F. Stack Jr. 2016. *Globalization: Debunking the Myths*. New York, NY: Rowman & Littlefield.
Hedges, Chris. 2003. *War is a Force That Gives Us Meaning*. New York, NY: Anchor Books.
Hegre, Håvard, John R. Oneal, and Bruce M. Russett. 2010. Trade Does Promote Peace: New Simultaneous Estimates of the Reciprocal Effects of Trade and Conflict. *Journal of Peace Research*, 47(6), 763–774.
Henkin, Louis. 1979. *How Nations Behave*. New York, NY: Columbia University Press.

REFERENCES

Henrikson, Alan K. (ed.). 1986. *Negotiating World Order: The Artisanship and Architecture of Global Diplomacy*. Wilmington, DE: Scholarly Resources.

Henrikson, Alan K. (2006). Diplomacy's Possible Futures. *The Hague Journal of Diplomacy*, 1(1), 3–27.

Hensel, Paul R. 1999. An Evolutionary Approach to the Study of Interstate Rivalry. *Conflict Management and Peace Science*, 17(2), 175–206.

Hensel, Paul R. 2001. Contentious Issues and World Politics: The Management of Territorial Claims in the Americas, 1816–1992. *International Studies Quarterly*, 45(1), 81–109.

Hensel, Paul R. 2012. Territory: Geography, Contentious Issues, and World Politics. In John A. Vasquez (ed.), *What Do We Know About War?* Lanham, MD: Rowman & Littlefield, pp. 3–26.

Hensel, Paul R., and Sara McLaughlin Mitchell. 2016. From Territorial Claims to Identity Claims: The Issue Correlates of War (ICOW) Project. *Conflict Management and Peace Science*, 34(2), 126–140.

Hermann, Charles F. (ed.). 1972. *International Crises: Insights from Behavioral Research*. New York, NY: The Free Press.

Hermann, Margaret. 1980. Explaining Foreign Policy Behavior Using the Personal Characteristics of Political Leaders. *International Studies Quarterly*, 24(1), 7–46.

Hermann, Margaret. 2005. Saddam Hussein's Leadership Style. In Jerrold M. Post (ed.), *The Psychological Assessment of Political Leaders*. Ann Arbor, MI: University of Michigan Press, pp. 375–386.

Herz, John. 1951. *Political Realism and Political Idealism: A Study in Theories and Realities*. Chicago, IL: University of Chicago Press.

Hobson, John. 1965. *Imperialism: A Study*. Ann Arbor, MI: University of Michigan Press.

Hollis, Martin, and Steve Smith. 1992. *Explaining and Understanding International Relations*. Oxford: Oxford University Press.

Holmes, Marcus, and Karen Yarhi-Milo. 2017. The Psychological Logic of Peace Summits: How Empathy Shapes Outcomes of Diplomatic Negotiations. *International Studies Quarterly*, 61(1), 107–122.

Holsti, Kalevi J. 1991. *Peace and War: Armed Conflicts and International Order 1964–1989*. Cambridge: Cambridge University Press.

Holsti, Ole R. 1967. Cognitive Dynamics and Images of the Enemy: Dulles and Russia. In John C. Farrell and Asa P. Smith (eds.), *Image and Reality in World Politics*. New York, NY: Columbia University Press, pp. 16–39.

Holsti, Ole R. 1970. The Operational Code Approach to the Study of Political Leaders: John Foster Dulles' Philosophical and Instrumental Beliefs. *Canadian Journal of Political Science*, 3(1), 123–57.

Holsti, Ole R. 1972. *Crisis, Escalation, War*. Montreal: McGill-Queen's University Press.

Holsti, Ole R. 1977. *The Operational Code as an Approach to the Analysis of Beliefs Systems: Final Report to the National Science Foundation*. Grant SOC 75-15368. Durham, NC: Duke University.

Holsti, Ole R., P. Terrence Hopmann, and John D. Sullivan. 1973. *Unity and Disintegration in International Alliances: Comparative Studies*. New York, NY: Wiley.

Homer-Dixon, Thomas F. (1999). *Environment, Scarcity, and Violence*. Princeton, NJ and Oxford: Princeton University Press.

Horowitz, Michael C., Rose McDermott, and Allan C. Stam. 2005. Leader Age, Regime Type, and Violent International Relations. *Journal of Conflict Resolution*. 49(5), 661–685.

Horowitz, Michael C., Philip Potter, Todd S. Sechser, and Allan C. Stam. 2018. Sizing Up the Adversary. *Journal of Conflict Resolution*, 62(10), 2180–2204.

Horowitz, Michael C., and Allan C. Stam. 2014. How Prior Military Experience Influences the Future Militarized Behavior of Leaders. *International Organization* 68(3), 527–559.

Horowitz, Michael C., Allan C. Stam, and Cali Ellis. 2015. *Why Leaders Fight*. Cambridge: Cambridge University Press.

Hudson, Valerie M., Bonnie Ballif-Spanvill, Mary Caprioli, and Chad F. Emmett. 2017. The Heart of the Matter: The Security of Women, the Security of States. *Military Review*, 97(3). http://www.armyupress.army.mil/Journals/Military-Review/English-Edition-Archives/May-June-2017/Hudson-Heart-of-the-Matter

Hufbauer, Gary Clyde, Jeffrey J. Schott, Kimberly Ann Elliott, and Barbara Oegg. 2009. *Economic Sanctions Reconsidered* (3rd ed.). New York, NY: Columbia University Press.

Huth, Paul K. 1988. *Extended Deterrence and the Prevention of War*. New Haven, CT: Yale University Press.

Huth, Paul K. 1990. The Extended Deterrent Value of Nuclear Weapons. *Journal of Conflict Resolution*, 34(2), 270–290.

Huth, Paul K., D. Scott Bennett, and Christopher Gelpi. 1992. System Uncertainty, Risk Propensity, and International Conflict among the Great Powers. *Journal of Conflict Resolution,* 36(3), 478–517.

Huth, Paul K., Sarah E. Croco, and Benjamin J. Appel. 2011. Does International Law Promote the Peaceful Settlement of International Disputes? Evidence from the Study of Territorial Conflicts Since 1945. *American Political Science Review,* 105(2), 415–436.

Huth, Paul K., and Bruce M. Russett. 1984. What Makes Deterrence Work? Cases from 1900 to 1980. *World Politics,* 36(4), 496–526.

Iakhnis, Evgeniia, and Patrick James. 2021. Near Crises in World Politics: A New Dataset. *Conflict Management and Peace Science,* 38(2), 224–243.

Iakhnis, Evgeniia, Stefanie Neumeier, Anne van Wijk, and Patrick James. 2020. International Crises Interrogated: Modeling the Escalation Process with Quantitative Methods. In John Preston (ed.), *Encyclopedia of Crisis Analysis.* Oxford: Oxford University Press.

Idika-Kalu, Cecilia. 2023. Women, Education, and Violence: How Women Displaced into Camps in North-East Nigeria Take Up Education. *Development Policy Review* 41(6), 1–13.

Ikenberry, G. John. 2000. *After Victory: Institutions, Strategic Restraint, and the Rebuilding of Order After Major Wars.* Princeton, NJ: Princeton University Press.

Immelman, Aubrey. 2017. The Leadership Style of U.S. President Donald J. Trump. Working Paper No. 1.2. Collegeville and St. Joseph, MN: St. John's University and the College of St. Benedict, Unit for the Study of Personality in Politics. http://digitalcommons.csbsju.edu/psychology_pubs/107/

Inoguchi, Takashi. 2003. Conclusion: Generating Equilibrium, Generating Power Cycles. *International Political Science Review,* 24(1), 167–72.

Irrera, Daniel. 2021. Non-State Actors and Conflict Management in Proxy Wars. *Oxford Research Encyclopedia on International Studies.* https://doi.org/10.1093/acrefore/9780190846626.013.641

Jadoon, Amira, and Bryan R. Early. 2024. Conditional Effects of Arms Embargoes on Civilian Targeting. *Foreign Policy Analysis,* 20(2), April 2024, orae008, https://doi.org/10.1093/fpa/orae008

Jakobsen, Peter Viggo. 2020. Coercive Diplomacy as Crisis Management. *Oxford Research Encyclopedia on Politics.* https://doi.org/10.1093/acrefore/9780190228637.013.1624

James, Carolyn C. 2021. Canada's Arctic Boundaries and the United States: Binational vs. Bilateral Policy Making in North America. In Geoffrey Hale and Greg Anderson (eds.), *Navigating a Changing World: Canada's International Policies in an Age of Uncertainties.* Toronto: University of Toronto Press, pp. 355–377.

James, Patrick. 1988. *Crisis and War.* Montreal and Kingston: McGill-Queen's University Press.

James, Patrick. 2002. *International Relations and Scientific Progress: Structural Realism Reconsidered.* Columbus, OH: Ohio State University Press.

James, Patrick. 2004. Systemism, Social Mechanisms, and Scientific Progress: A Case Study of the International Crisis Behavior Project. *Philosophy of the Social Sciences* 34(3), 352–370.

James, Patrick. 2019. What Do We Know About Crisis, Escalation and War? A Visual Assessment of the International Crisis Behavior Project. *Conflict Management and Peace Science,* 36(1), 3–19.

James, Patrick. 2022. *Realism and International Relations: A Graphic Turn Toward Scientific Progress.* Oxford: Oxford University Press.

James, Patrick. 2023. *Systemist International Relations.* San Diego, CA: Cognella.

James, Patrick, and Frank Harvey. 1992. The Most Dangerous Game: Superpower Rivalry in International Crises, 1948–1985. *The Journal of Politics,* 54(1), 25–53.

James, Patrick, and Athanasios Hristoulas. 2020. North America. In Jacek Kugler and Ronald L. Tammen (eds.), *The Rise of Regions: Conflict and Cooperation.* New York, NY: Rowman & Littlefield.

James, Patrick, and John R. Oneal. (1991). The Influence of Domestic and International Politics on the President's Use of Force. *Journal of Conflict Resolution,* 35(2), 307–332.

Janis, Irving L. 1972. *Victims of Groupthink.* Boston, MA: Houghton Mifflin.

Janis, Irving L. 1982. *Groupthink.* Boston, MA: Houghton Mifflin.

Janis, Irving L., and Leon Mann. 1977. *Decision Making: A Psychological Analysis of Conflict, Choice, and Commitment.* New York, NY: Free Press.

Jenne, Erin K. 2015. *Nested Security: Lessons in Conflict Management from the League of Nations and the European Union.* Ithaca, NY: Cornell University Press.

Jenne, Erin K., and Milos Popovic. 2017. Managing Internationalized Civil Wars. *Oxford Research Encyclopedia on International Studies.* https://doi.org/10.1093/acrefore/9780190228637.013.573

Jentleson, Bruce W. 1991. The Reagan Administration and Coercive Diplomacy: Restraining More Than Remaking Governments. *Political Science Quarterly*, 106(1), 57–82.

Jervis, Robert. 1970. *The Logic of Images in International Relations*. New York, NY: Columbia University Press.

Jervis, Robert. 1976. *Perception and Misperception in International Politics*. Princeton, NJ: Princeton University Press.

Jervis, Robert. 1978. Cooperation Under the Security Dilemma. *World Politics,* 30(2), 167–214.

Jervis, Robert. 1988. War and Misperception. *The Journal of Interdisciplinary History*, 18(4), 675–700.

Jervis, Robert. 1989. Rational Deterrence: Theory and Evidence. *World Politics,* 41(2), 183–207.

Jervis, Robert. 1993. Arms Control, Stability, and Causes of War. *Political Science Quarterly,* 108(2), 239–253.

Jervis, Robert, Richard Ned Lebow, and Janice Gross Stein. 1984. *Psychology and Deterrence*. Baltimore, MD: Johns Hopkins University Press.

Johnson, Dominic D. P. 2004. *Overconfidence and War: The Havoc and Glory of Positive Illusions*. Cambridge, MA: Harvard University Press.

Johnson, Dominic D. P., and Dominic Tierney. 2011. The Rubicon Theory of War: How the Path to Conflict Reaches the Point of No Return. *International Security*, 36(1), 7–40.

Johnson, Jesse C., and Brett Ashley Leeds. 2011. Defense Pacts: A Prescription for Peace? *Foreign Policy Analysis,* 7(1), 45–65.

Jones, Adam. 2017. *Genocide: A Comprehensive Introduction* (3rd ed.). New York, NY: Routledge.

Kaarbo, Juliet, and Ryan K. Beasley. 2008. Taking It to the Extreme: The Effect of Coalition Cabinets on Foreign Policy. *Foreign Policy Analysis*. 4(1), 67–81.

Kahn, Herman. 1960. *On Thermonuclear War*. Princeton, NJ: Princeton University Press.

Kahneman, Daniel. 1973. *Attention and Effort*. New York, NY: Prentice-Hall.

Kahneman, Daniel. 2011. *Thinking, Fast and Slow*. New York, NY: Farrar, Straus and Giroux.

Kahneman, Daniel, and Amos Tversky. 1979. Prospect Theory: An Analysis of Decision under Risk. *Econometrica*, 47(2), 263–91.

Kahneman, Daniel, and Amos Tversky (2004). Conflict Resolution: A Cognitive Perspective. In Eldar Shafir (Ed.), *Preference, Belief, and Similarity: Selected Writings by Amos Tversky*. Boston, MA: Boston Review, pp. 729–746.

Kahneman, Daniel, Paul Slovic, and Amos Tversky (eds.). 1982. *Judgment Under Uncertainty: Heuristics and Biases*. Cambridge: Cambridge University Press.

Kalb, Marvin, and Deborah Kalb. 2011. *Haunting Legacy: Vietnam and the American Presidency from Ford to Obama*. Washington, DC: Brookings Institution.

Kallio, Enni. 2015. Land Degradation in War and Conflict Regions. https://environment-review.yale.edu/land-degradation-war-and-conflict-regions-0, accessed 28 February 2024.

Kanter, Rosabeth Moss. 1977. Some Effects of Proportions on Group Life: Skewed Sex Ratios and Responses to Token Women. *American Journal of Sociology*, 82(1), 965–990.

Kaplan, Morton A. 1957. *System and Process in International Politics*. New York, NY: Wiley.

Katzenstein, Peter J., and Rudra Sil. 2008. Eclectic Theorizing in the Study and Practice of International Relations. In Christian Reus-Smit, and Duncan Snidal (eds.), *The Oxford Handbook of International Relations*. Oxford: Oxford University Press, pp. 109–130.

Kaufman, Stuart J. 2001. *Modern Hatreds: The Symbolic Politics of Ethnic War*. Ithaca, NY: Cornell University Press.

Keck, Margaret E., and Kathryn Sikkink. 1998. *Activists Beyond Borders: Advocacy Networks in International Politics*. Ithaca, NY: Cornell University Press.

Keegan, John. 2011. *A History of Warfare*. NY: Random House.

Kelly, Raymond C. 2000. *Warless Societies and the Origin of War*. Ann Arbor, MI: University of Michigan Press.

Kenwick, Michael, and Roseanne W. McManus. 2021. Deterrence Theory and Alliance Politics. In John A. Vasquez and Sara McLaughlin Mitchell (eds.), *What Do We Know About War*? (3rd ed.). New York, NY: Routledge, pp. 41–62.

Kenwick, Michael, and John A. Vasquez. 2017. Defense Pacts and Deterrence: Caveat Emptor. *The Journal of Politics,* 79(1), 329–334.

Kenwick, Michael, John A. Vasquez, and Matthew Powers. 2015. Do Alliances Really Deter? *The Journal of Politics,* 77(4), 943–954.

Keohane, Robert O. 2013. Big Questions in the Study of World Politics. In Robert Goodin (ed.), *The Oxford Handbook of Political Science*. Oxford: Oxford University Press, pp. 769–775.

Keohane, Robert O., and Joseph S. Nye. 1977. *Power and Interdependence: World Politics in Transition*. Boston, MA: Little Brown.

Keshk, Omar M. G., Brian M. Pollins, and Rafael Reuveny. 2004. Trade Still Follows the Flag: The Primacy of Politics in a Simultaneous Model of Interdependence and Armed Conflict. *The Journal of Politics*, 66(1), 1155–1179.

Kessler, Glenn. 2003. U.S. Decision on Iraq Has Puzzling Past. *Washington Post*, January 12, 2003, A1.

Khong, Yuen Foong. 1992. *Analogies at War: Korea, Munich, Dien Bien Phu, and the Vietnam Decisions of 1965*. Princeton, NJ: Princeton University Press.

Kim, Hyung Min, and David L. Rousseau. 2005. The Classical Liberals Were Half Right (or Half Wrong): New Tests of the "Liberal Peace", 1960–88. *Journal of Peace Research*, 42(5), 523–543.

King, Gary, and Langche Zeng. 2001. Explaining Rare Events in International Relations. *International Organization*, 55(3), 693–715.

Kisangani, Emizet F., and Jeffrey Pickering. 2007. Diverting with Benevolent Military Force: Reducing Risks and Rising Above Strategic Behavior. *International Studies Quarterly*, 51(2), 277–299.

Kisangani, Emizet F., and Jeffrey Pickering. 2011. Democratic Accountability and Diversionary Force Regime Types and the Use of Benevolent and Hostile Military Force. *Journal of Conflict Resolution*, 55(6), 1021–1046.

Kisangani, Emizet F., and Jeffrey Pickering. 2021. *African Interventions: State Militaries, Foreign Powers, and Rebel Forces*. Cambridge: Cambridge University Press.

Klein, James P., Gary G. Goertz, and Paul F. Diehl. 2006. The New Rivalry Data Set: Procedures and Patterns. *Journal of Peace Research*, 43(3), 331–348.

Knopf, Jeffrey. 1998. *Domestic Society and International Cooperation: The Impact of Protest on US Arms Control Policy*. Cambridge: Cambridge University Press.

Kowert, Paul A., and Margaret Hermann. 1997. Who Takes Risk? Daring and Caution in Foreign Policy Making. *Journal of Conflict Resolution*, 41(5), 611–637.

Krasner, Stephen D. 1985. *Structural Conflict: The Third World Against Global Liberalism*. Berkeley, California: University of California Press

Kremenyuk, Victor A. (ed.). 2002. *International Negotiation: Analysis, Approaches, Issues* (2nd ed.). San Francisco, CA: Jossey-Bass.

Kreutz, Joakim. 2010. How and When Armed Conflicts End: Introducing the UCDP Conflict Termination Dataset. *Journal of Peace Research*, 47(2), 243–250.

Kuperman, Alan J. 2008. The Moral Hazard of Humanitarian Intervention: Lessons from the Balkans. *International Studies Quarterly*, 52(1), 49–80.

Kurki, Milja. 2002. Causes of a Divided Discipline: A Critical Examination of the Concept of Cause in International Relations Theory. *Global Politics Network* www.globalpolitics.net, accessed April 15, 2022.

Kurki, Milja. 2008. *Causation in International Relations: Reclaiming Causal Analysis*. Cambridge: Cambridge University Press.

Kydd, Andrew H. 2003. Which Side Are You On? Bias, Credibility, and Mediation. *American Journal of Political Science*, 47(4), 597–611.

Kydd, Andrew H. 2006. When Can Mediators Build Trust? *American Political Science Review*, 100(3), 449–462.

Kydd, Andrew H. 2010. Rationalist Approaches to Conflict Prevention and Resolution. *Annual Review of Political Science*, 13(1), 101–121.

Kydd, Andrew H., and Scott Straus. 2013. The Road to Hell? Third-Party Intervention to Prevent Atrocities. *American Journal of Political Science*, 57(3), 673–684.

Lake, David A. 1992. Powerful Pacifists: Democratic States and War. *American Political Science Review*, 86(1), 24–37.

Lakwete, Angela. 2005. *Inventing the Cotton Gin: Machine and Myth in Antebellum America*. Baltimore, MD: Johns Hopkins University Press.

Lamb, Christopher. 1988. *How to Think About Arms Control, Disarmament, and Defense*. Englewood Cliffs, NJ: Prentice Hall.

Lasswell, Harold D. 1941. The Garrison State. *American Journal of Sociology*, 46(4), 455–468.

Laub, Zachary. 2023. Syria's Civil War: The Descent into Horror. Council on Foreign Relations.

Lauren, Paul Gordon, Gordon A. Craig, and Alexander L. George. 2007. *Force and Statecraft: Diplomatic Challenges of Our Time* (4th ed.). New York, NY: Oxford University Press.

Layne, Christopher. 1994. Kant or Cant: The Myth of the Democratic Peace. *International Security*, 19(2), 5–49.

Lebow, Richard Ned. 1981. *Between Peace and War: The Nature of International Crisis*. Baltimore, MD: John Hopkins University Press.

Lebow, Richard Ned. 2003. *The Tragic Vision of Politics: Ethics, Interest, Orders*. Cambridge: Cambridge University Press.

Lebow, Richard Ned and Janice Gross Stein. 1989. Rational Deterrence: I Think, Therefore I Deter. *World Politics*, 41(2), 208–224.

Lebow, Richard Ned, and Benjamin Valentino. 2009. Lost in Transition: A Critique of Power Transition Theories. *International Relations*, 23(3), 389–410.

Leeds, Brett Ashley. 2003. Do Alliances Deter Aggression? The Influence of Military Alliances on the Initiation of Militarized Interstate Disputes. *American Journal of Political Science*, 47(3), 427–439.

Leeds, Brett Ashley, and David R. Davis. 1997. Domestic Political Vulnerability and International Disputes. *Journal of Conflict Resolution*, 41(6), 814–834.

Leeds, Brett Ashley, and Michaela Mattes. 2007. Alliance Politics During the Cold War: Aberration, New World Order, or Continuation of History? *Conflict Management and Peace Science*, 24(3), 183–199.

Leeds, Brett Ashley, and T. Clifton Morgan. 2018. The Quest for Security: Alliances and Arms. *Oxford Research Encyclopedia of International Studies*, 1–21.

Leeds, Brett Ashley, Jeffrey M. Ritter, Sara Mitchell, and Andrew Long. 2002. Alliance Treaty Obligations and Provisions, 1815–1944. *International Interactions*, 28(3), 237–60.

Leites, N. 1951. *The Operational Code of the Politburo*. New York: McGraw-Hill.

Lektzian, David, and Patrick M. Regan. 2016. Economic Sanctions, Military Interventions, and Civil War Outcomes. *Journal of Peace Research*, 53(4), 554–568.

Lemke, Douglas. 2002. *Regions of War and Peace*. Cambridge: Cambridge University Press.

Lemke, Douglas. 2003. Development and War. *International Studies Review*, 5(4), 55–63.

Leng, Russell J. 1983. When Will They Ever Learn? Coercive Bargaining in Recurrent Crises. *Journal of Conflict Resolution*, 27(3), 379–419.

Lenin, Vladimir I. 1939. *Imperialism: The Highest Stage of Capitalism*. New York: International Publishers.

Levi, Ariel S., and Glen Whyte. 1997. A Cross-Cultural Exploration of the Reference Dependence of Crucial Group Decisions under Risk: Japan's 1941 Decision for War. *Journal of Conflict Resolution*, 41(6), 792–813.

Levy, Jack S. 1981. Alliance Formation and War Behavior. *Journal of Conflict Resolution*, 25(4), 581–613.

Levy, Jack S. 1983a. *War in the Great Power System, 1495–1975*. Lexington, KY: University of Kentucky Press.

Levy, Jack S. 1983b. Misperception and the Causes of War: Theoretical Linkages and Analytical Problems. *World Politics*, 36(1), 76–99.

Levy, Jack S. 1989a. The Diversionary Theory of War: A Critique. In Manus I. Midlarsky (ed.), *Handbook of War Studies*. New York, NY: Unwin Hyman, pp. 259–288.

Levy, Jack S. 1989b. The Causes of War: A Review of Theories and Evidence. In Philip E. Tetlock, Jo L. Husbands, Robert Jervis, Paul C. Stern, and Charles Tilly (eds.), *Behavior, Society, and Nuclear War*. New York: Oxford University Press, pp. 209–333.

Levy, Jack. 1989c. The Origin and Prevention of Major Wars. *Journal of Interdisciplinary History*, 18(4), 653–673.

Levy, Jack S. 1990–1991. Preferences, Constraints, and Choices in July 1914. *International Security*, 15(3), 151–186.

Levy, Jack S., and T. Clifton Morgan. 1984. The Frequency and Seriousness of War: An Inverse Relationship? *Journal of Conflict Resolution*, 28(4), 731–749.

Levy, Jack S., and T. Clifton Morgan. 1986. The War-Weariness Hypothesis: An Empirical Test. *American Journal of Political Science*, 30(1), 26–49.

Levy, Jack S., and William R. Thompson. 2010. *Causes of War*. Malden, MA: Wiley-Blackwell.

Lewis, Michael. 2016. *The Undoing Project: A Friendship that Changed Our Minds*. New York, NY: WW Norton.

Lipson, Charles. 2003. *Reliable Partners: How Democracies Have Made a Separate Peace.* Princeton, NJ: Princeton University Press.

Lloyd, Robert B., Melissa Haussman, and Patrick James. 2019. *Religion and Health Care in East Africa: Lessons from Uganda, Mozambique and Ethiopia.* Bristol: Policy Press of Bristol University Press.

Lobell, Steven E. 2006. The International Realm, Framing Effects, and Security Strategies: Britain in Peace and War. *International Interactions,* 32(1), 27–48.

Lobell, Steven E., and Philip Mauceri. 2004. Diffusion and Escalation of Ethnic Conflict. In Steven E. Lobell and Philip Mauceri (eds.), *Ethnic Conflict and International Politics: Explaining Diffusion and Escalation.* New York, NY: Palgrave Macmillan, pp. 1–34.

Lorenz, Konrad. 1966. *On Aggression.* New York, NY: Bantam.

Lounsbery, Marie Olson. 2016. Foreign Military Intervention, Power Dynamics, and Rebel Group Cohesion. *Journal of Global Security Studies,* 1(2), 127–141.

Lounsbery, Marie Olson, and Alethia H. Cook. 2011. Rebellion, Mediation, and Group Change: An Empirical Investigation of Competing Hypotheses. *Journal of Peace Research,* 48(1), 73–84.

Luck, Edward C., and Michael W. Doyle. 2004. *International Law and Organization: Closing the Compliance Gap.* Lanham, MD: Rowman & Littlefield.

Lupu, Yonatan, and Brian Greenhill. 2017. The Networked Peace: Intergovernmental Organizations and International Conflict. *Journal of Peace Research,* 54(6), 833–848.

Lutmar, Carmela, and Cristiane Carneiro. 2018. *Compliance in International Relations.* Oxford Research Encyclopedia on Politics. https://doi.org/10.1093/acrefore/9780190228637.013.576

Madden, Payce. 2019. Africa in the News: Disagreement Over the Great Ethiopian Renaissance Dam, Rwanda-Uganda Dispute Talks. *Brookings* (blog). September 21, 2019. https://www.brookings.edu/blog/africa-in-focus/2019/09/21/africa-in-the-news-disagreement-over-the-great-ethiopian-renaissance-dam-rwanda-uganda-dispute-talks/

Magalhães, Jose Calvet de. 1988. *The Pure Concept of Diplomacy.* New York, NY: Greenwood Press.

Malik, Julia, Anna Marie Obermeier, and Siri Aas Rustad. 2022. Conflict Trends: A Global Over-view 1946–2021. PRIO Paper 2022. Peace Research Institute Oslo, pp. 21–26.

Mansbach, Richard W., and John A. Vasquez. 1981. *In Search of Theory: A New Paradigm for Global Politics.* New York, NY: Columbia University Press.

Mansfield, Edward D., and Brian M. Pollins. 2001. The Study of Interdependence and Conflict: Recent Advances, Open Questions, and Directions for Future Research. *Journal of Conflict Resolution,* 45(6), 834–859.

Mansfield, Edward D., and Brian M. Pollins (eds.). 2003. *Economic Interdependence and International Conflict: New Perspectives on an Enduring Debate.* Ann Arbor, MI: University of Michigan Press.

Mansfield, Edward D., and Jack Snyder. 1995. Democratization and the Danger of War. *International Security,* 20(1), 5–38.

Mansfield, Edward D., and Jack Snyder. 2005. *Electing to Fight: Why Emerging Democracies Go To War.* Cambridge, MA: MIT Press.

Maoz, Zeev. 1983. Resolve, Capabilities, and the Outcomes of Interstate Disputes. *Journal of Conflict Resolution,* 27(2), 195–229.

Maoz, Zeev. 1996. *Domestic Sources of Global Change.* Ann Arbor, MI: University of Michigan Press.

Maoz, Zeev, Palul L. Johnson, Jasper Kaplan, Fiona Ogunkoya, and Aaron P. Shreve. 2019. The Dyadic Militarized Interstate Disputes (MIDs) Dataset Version 3.0: Logic, Characteristics, and Comparisons to Alternative Datasets. *Journal of Conflict Resolution,* 63(3), 811–835.

Maoz, Zeev, and Bruce M. Russett. 1992. Alliance, Contiguity, Wealth, and Political Stability: Is the Lack of Conflict Among Democracies a Statistical Artifact? *International Interactions,* 17(3), 245–267.

Maoz, Zeev, and Bruce Russett. 1993. Normative and Structural Causes of Democratic Peace, 1946–1986. *American Political Science Review,* 87(3), 624–638.

Mattes, Michaela, and Burcu Savun. (2009). Fostering Peace After Civil War: Commitment Problems and Agreement Design. *International Studies Quarterly,* 53(3), 737–759.

Mattes, Michaela, and Greg Vonnahme. 2010. Contracting for Peace: Do Nonaggression Pacts Reduce Conflict? *The Journal of Politics,* 72(4), 925–938.

McAdams, Dan. 2016. The Mind of Donald Trump. *The Atlantic,* June 2016. https://www.theatlantic.com/magazine/archive/2016/06/the-mind-of-donald-trump/480771/

McCourt, David M. 2022. Knowledge Communities in US Foreign Policy Making: The American China Field and the End of Engagement with the PRC. *Security Studies,* 31(4), 593–633.

McDermott, Rose. 1998. *Risk-Taking In International Politics: Prospect Theory in American Foreign Policy*. Ann Arbor, MI: University of Michigan Press.

McDermott, Rose. 2004. Prospect Theory in Political Science: Gains and Losses from the First Decade. *Political Psychology*, 25(2), 289–312.

McDonald, Patrick J. 2007. The Purse Strings of Peace. *American Journal of Political Science*, 51(3), 569–582.

McDonald, Patrick J. 2009. *The Invisible Hand of Peace: Capitalism, the War Machine, and International Relations Theory*. Cambridge: Cambridge University Press.

McDoom, Omar S. 2020. *The Path to Genocide in Rwanda: Security, Opportunity, and Authority in an Ethnocratic State*. Cambridge: Cambridge University Press.

McGlen, Nancy E., and Meredith Reid Sarkees. 1993. *Women in Foreign Policy: The Insiders*. New York, NY: Routledge.

McGlen, Nancy E., and Meredith Reid Sarkees. 1995. *The Status of Women in Foreign Policy*. New York, NY: Foreign Policy Association.

McGlen, Nancy E., and Meredith Reid Sarkees. 2006. Foreign Policy Decision-Makers: The Impact of Albright and Rice. Paper presented at the annual meeting of the International Studies Association, San Diego, March 22.

McMillan, Susan M. 1997. Interdependence and Conflict. *Mershon International Studies Review*, 41(1), 33–58.

McNeill, William H. 1982. *The Pursuit of Power: Technology, Armed Force, and Society Since A.D. 1000*. Chicago, IL: University of Chicago Press.

Mearsheimer, John J. 1990. Why We Will Soon Miss the Cold War. *The Atlantic*, August 1990. https://www.theatlantic.com/past/docs/politics/foreign/mearsh.htm

Mearsheimer, John J. 2014 [2001]. *The Tragedy of Great Power Politics*. New York, NY: WW Norton.

Mearsheimer, John J. 2018. *The Great Delusion: Liberal Dreams and International Relations*. New Haven, CT: Yale University Press.

Meernik, James. 2000. Modeling International Crises and the Political Use of Military Force by the USA. *Journal of Peace Research*, 37(5), 547–562.

Middle East Monitor. 2023. Renaissance Dam: Ethiopia Announces 90% Completion, While Egypt Minister Says It Will Harm Economic Stability. https://www.middleeastmonitor.com/20230325-renaissance-dam-ethiopia-announces-90-completion-while-egypt-minister-says-it-will-harm-economic-stability/

Miller, William J., and Brian C. Pohanka. 2000. *An Illustrated History of the Civil War: Images of an American Tragedy*. Alexandria, VA: Time-Life Books.

Mitchell, Sara McLaughlin. 2002. A Kantian System? Democracy and Third-Party Conflict Resolution. *American Journal of Political Science*, 46(4), 749–759.

Mitchell, Sara McLaughlin, and Paul R. Hensel. 2007. International Institutions and Compliance with Agreements. *American Journal of Political Science*, 51(4), 721–737.

Mitchell, Sara McLaughlin, and Brandon C. Prins. 2004. Rivalry and Diversionary Uses of Force. *Journal of Conflict Resolution*, 48(6), 937–961.

Mitchell, Sara McLaughlin, and Clayton L. Thyne. 2010. Contentious Issues as Opportunities for Diversionary Behavior. *Conflict Management and Peace Science*, 27(5), 461–485.

Mitrany, David. 1966. *A Working Peace System*. San Antonio, TX: Quadrangle Press.

Morgan, Patrick. 1983 [1977]. Deterrence: A Conceptual Analysis (2nd ed.). Beverly Hills, CA: Sage.

Morgan, Patrick. 2003. *Deterrence Now*. Cambridge: Cambridge University Press.

Morgan, Patrick. 2018a. Nuclear Strategy. *Oxford Research Encyclopedia on International Studies*, 1–31.

Morgan, Patrick. 2018b. The Concept of Deterrence and Deterrence Theory. In William R. Thompson (ed.), *The Oxford Encyclopedia of Empirical International Relations*. New York, NY: Oxford University Press, pp. 293–317.

Morgan, T. Clifton. and Navin A. Bapat. 2003. Imposing Sanctions: States, Firms, and Economic Coercion. *International Studies Review*, 5(4), 65–79.

Morgan, T. Clifton, Navin A. Bapat, and Yoshiharu Kobayashi. 2014. Threat and Imposition of Economic Sanctions 1945–2005: Updating the TIES Data Set. *Conflict Management Peace Science*, 31(5), 541–558.

Morgenthau, Hans J. 1946. *Scientific Man Versus Power Politics*. Chicago, IL: University of Chicago Press.

Morrow, James D. 2002. The Laws of War, Common Conjectures, and Legal Systems in International Politics. *The Journal of Legal Studies*, 31: S41–S60.
Most, Benjamin A., and Harvey Starr. 1989. *Inquiry, Logic and International Politics*. Columbia, SC: University of South Carolina Press.
Mousseau, Michael. 2009. The Social Market Roots of Democratic Peace. *International Security*, 33(4), 52–86.
Mousseau, Michael. 2010. Coming to Terms with the Capitalist Peace. *International Interactions*, 36(2), 185–192.
Mousseau, Michael. 2013. The Democratic Peace Unraveled: It's the Economy. *International Studies Quarterly*, 57(1), 186–197.
Mousseau, Michael. 2018. Grasping the Scientific Evidence: The Contractualist Peace Supersedes the Democratic Peace. *Conflict Management and Peace Science*, 35(2), 175–192.
Mousseau, M., Hegre, H., and Oneal, John R. 2003. How the Wealth of Nations Conditions the Liberal Peace. *European Journal of International Relations*, 9(2), 277–314.
Moyo, Inocent, and Christopher C. Nshimbi. 2019. *African Borders, Conflict, Regional and Continental Integration*. New York, NY: Routledge.
Mueller, John. 1990. *Retreat from Doomsday: The Obsolescence of Major War*. New York, NY: Basic Books.
Mueller, John. 2005. The Iraq Syndrome. *Foreign Affairs*, 84(6), 44–54.
Muldoon, Jr., James P., and Joann Fagot Aviel. 2020. Multilateral Diplomacy. *Oxford Research Encyclopedia on International Studies*, 1–17.
Muldoon, Jr., James P., Joann Fagot Aviel, Richard Reitano, and Earl Sullivan (eds.). 2005. *Multilateral Diplomacy and the United Nations Today* (2nd ed.). Boulder, CO: Westview Press.
Murauskaite, Egle E., and Allison Astorino-Courtois. 2023. Conceptual Framework for Managing International Crises, 1990–2020. In Jonathan Wilkenfeld and Egle E. Murauskaite (eds.), *Escalation Management in International Crises: The United States and Its Adversaries*. Cheltenham, UK and Northampton, MA: Edward Elgar, pp. 52–77.
Murdie, Amanda, and Dursun Peksen. 2014. The Impact of Human Rights INGO Shaming on Humanitarian Interventions. *The Journal of Politics*, 76(1), 215–228.
Nai, Allesandro, Ferran Martinez i Coma, and Jürgen Maier. 2019. Donald Trump, Populism, and the Age of Extremes: Comparing the Personality Traits and Campaigning Styles of Trump and Other Leaders Worldwide. *Presidential Studies Quarterly*, 49(3): 609–643.
Neumann, Iver B. 2005. To Be a Diplomat. *International Studies Perspectives*, 6(1), 72–93.
Neumann, Iver B. 2012. *At Home with the Diplomats: Inside a European Foreign Ministry*. Ithaca, NY: Cornell University Press.
Neumann, Iver B. 2013. *Diplomatic Sites: A Critical Enquiry*. London: Oxford University Press.
Neumann, Iver B. 2020. Diplomatic Tenses: A Social Evolutionary Perspective on Diplomacy. *Diplomatica*, 5(1), 156–157.
Neumann, Iver B., and Halvard Leira (eds.). 2013. *International Diplomacy* (volumes 1–4). Thousand Oaks, CA: Sage.
Nyanaro, George. 2023. Amplifying the Impact: Climate Change and Environmental Degradation in the Context of Armed Conflict Globally. Available at SSRN: https://ssrn.com/abstract=4680711
Odell, John, and Dustin Tingley. 2013. Negotiating Agreements in International Relations. In Jane Mansbridge and Cathie Jo Martin (eds.), *Negotiating Agreement in Politics*. Washington, DC: American Political Science Association, pp. 144–182.
Oktay, Sibel. 2022. *Governing Abroad: Coalitions Politics and Foreign Policy in Europe*. Ann Arbor, MI: University of Michigan Press.
Oneal, John R., and Bruce M. Russett. 1997. The Classical Liberals Were Right: Democracy, Interdependence, and Conflict, 1950–1985. *International Studies Quarterly*, 41(2), 267–293.
Oneal, John R., Bruce M. Russett, and Michael L. Berbaum. 2003. Causes of Peace: Democracy, Interdependence, and International Organizations, 1885–1992. *International Studies Quarterly*, 47(3), 371–393.
Organski, A. F. K. 1958. *World Politics*. New York, NY: Alfred A. Knopf.
Organski, A. F. K., and Jacek Kugler. 1980. *The War Ledger*. Chicago, IL: University of Chicago Press.

Østby, Gudrun, and Henrik Urdal. 2010. *Education and Civil Conflict: A Review of the Quantitative, Empirical Literature*. Background paper for the Education for All Global Monitoring Report 2011, The Hidden Crisis: Armed Conflict and Education. Oslo, Norway: UNESCO.

Ostrom, Charles W., and Brian L. Job. 1986. The President and the Political Use of Force. *American Political Science Review*, 80(2), 541–566.

Owen, John M. 1994. How Liberalism Produces Democratic Peace. *International Security*, 19(2), 87–125.

Owen, John M. 1997. *Liberal Peace, Liberal War: American Politics and International Security*. Ithaca, NY: Cornell University Press.

Owen, John. M. 2012. Economic Interdependence and Regional Peace. In T. V. Paul (ed.), *International Relations Theory and Regional Transformation*. Cambridge: Cambridge University Press, pp. 107–132.

Özdamar, Özgur, and Yasemin Akbaba. 2014. Religious Discrimination and International Crises: International Effects of Domestic Inequality. *Foreign Policy Analysis* 10(4), 413–430.

Pape, Robert A. 1997. Why Economic Sanctions Do Not Work. *International Security* 22(2), 90–136.

Pape, Robert A. 1998. Why Economic Sanctions Still Do Not Work. *International Security* 23(1), 66–77.

Parasiliti, Andrew T. 2003. The Causes and Timing of Iraq's Wars: A Power Cycle Assessment. *International Political Science Review,* 24(1), 151–165.

Parker, Claire. 2022. U.S. Imposes Sanctions on Putin's Reported Girlfriend. *Washington Post*. August 2, 2022. https://www.washingtonpost.com/world/2022/08/02/alina-kabaeva-putin-partner-treasury-sanctions/

Passmore, Tim J. A. 2020. United Nations Peacekeeping and Civil Conflict. *Oxford Research Encyclopedia on International Studies*. https://doi.org/10.1093/acrefore/9780190846626.013.551

Pearce, Susanna. 2006. Religious Rage: A Quantitative Analysis of the Intensity of Religious Conflicts. In Jonathan Fox and Shmuel Sandler (eds.), *Religion in World Conflict*. New York, NY: Routledge, pp. 39–58.

Peceny, Mark, Caroline C. Beer, and Shannon Sanchez-Terry. 2002. Dictatorial Peace? *American Political Science Review*, 96(1), 15–26.

Peck, Connie. 2001. The Role of Regional Organizations in Preventing and Resolving Conflict. In Chester A. Crocker, Fen Osler Hampson, and Pamela Aall (eds.), *Turbulent Peace: The Challenges of Managing International Conflict*. Washington, DC: United States Institute of Peace Press, pp. 561–84.

Peinhardt, Clint, and Todd Sandler. 2015. *Transnational Cooperation: An Issue-Based Approach*. New York: Oxford Academic.

Peksen, Dursun. 2009. Better or Worse? The Effect of Economic Sanctions on Human Rights. *Journal of Peace Research*, 46(1), 59–77.

Peksen, Dursun. 2011. Economic Sanctions and Human Security: The Public Health Effect of Economic Sanctions. *Foreign Policy Analysis*, 7(3), 237–251.

Peksen, Dursun, and A. Cooper Drury. 2009. Economic Sanctions and Political Repression: Assessing the Impact of Coercive Diplomacy on Political Freedoms. *Human Rights Review,* 10(3), 393–411.

Peksen, Dursun, and A. Cooper Drury. 2010. Coercive or Corrosive: The Negative Impact of Economic Sanctions on Democracy. *International Interactions*, 36(3), 240–264.

Perry, Kate. 2022. Better For Whom? Sanction Type and the Gendered Consequences for Women. *International Relations,* 36(2), 151–175.

Pevehouse, Jon and Bruce M. Russett. 2006. Democratic International Governmental Organizations Promote Peace. *International Organization,* 60(4), 969–1000.

Phillips, Anne. 1995. *The Politics of Presence*. Oxford: Clarendon Press.

Phillips, Jason. 2018. *Looming Civil War: How Nineteenth Century Americans Imagined the Future*. Oxford: Oxford University Press.

Pickering, Jeffrey, and Emizet F. Kisangani. 2005. Democracy and Diversionary Military Intervention: Reassessing Regime Type and the Diversionary Hypothesis. *International Studies Quarterly*, 49(1), 23–43.

Pickering, Jeffrey, and Emizet F. Kisangani. 2010. Diversionary Despots? Comparing Autocracies' Propensities to Use and to Benefit From Military Force. *American Journal of Political Science*, 54(2), 477–493.

Plantey, Alain. 2007. *International Negotiation in the Twenty-First Century*. New York, NY: Routledge.

Poast, Paul. 2023. War is Persistent, but Not Prevalent. Twitter thread, April 8, 2023 at https://twitter.com/ProfPaulPoast/status/1644670125797253120

Polachek, Soloman William. 1980. Conflict and Trade. *Journal of Conflict Resolution*, 24(1), 55–78.

Posen, Barry R. 1993. The Security Dilemma and Ethnic Conflict. *Survival*, 35(1), 27–47.
Post, Jerrold M. 1993. Current Concepts of the Narcissistic Personality: Implications for Political Psychology. *Political Psychology*, 14(1), 99–121.
Post, Jerrold M. 2005. *The Psychological Assessment of Political Leaders*. Ann Arbor: University of Michigan Press.
Potter, David M. 1976. *The Impending Crisis 1848–1861*. New York, NY: Harper & Row.
Powell, Emilia Justyna and Krista E. Weigand. 2010. Legal Systems and Peaceful Attempts to Resolve Territorial Disputes. *Conflict Management and Peace Science*, 27(2), 129–151.
Powell, Jim. 2021. *Losing the Thread: Cotton, Liverpool and the American Civil War*. Liverpool: Liverpool University Press.
Powell, Robert. 1988. Nuclear Brinkmanship with Two-Sided Incomplete Information. *American Political Science Review*, 82(1), 155–178.
Powell, Robert. 2002. Bargaining Theory and International Conflict. *Annual Review of Political Science*, 5(1), 1–30.
Prins, Brandon C. 2005. Interstate Rivalry and the Recurrence of Crises. *Armed Forces and Society*, 31(3), 323–51.
Prorok, Alyssa K., and Paul K. Huth. 2015. International Law and the Consolidation of Peace Following Territorial Disputes. *The Journal of Politics*, 77(1), 161–74.
Pulkowski, Dirk. 2014. *The Law and Politics of International Regime Conflict*. New York, NY: Oxford University Press.
Putnam, Robert D. 1988. Diplomacy and Domestic Politics: The Logic of Two-Level Games. *International Organization*, 42(3), 427–460.
Quackenbush, Stephen L. 2015. *International Conflict: Logic and Evidence*. Los Angeles, CA: Sage.
Quattrone, George A., and Amos Tversky. 1988. Contrasting Rational and Psychological Analysis of Political Choice. *American Political Science Review*, 82(3), 719–736.
Raleigh, Clionadh. Political Marginalization, Climate Change, and Conflict in African Sahel States. *International Studies Review*, 12(1) 69–86. https://doi.org/10.1111/j.1468-2486.2009.00913.x
Raleigh, Clionadh, and Henrik Urdal. 2007. Climate Change, Environmental Degradations, and Armed Conflict. *Political Geography*, 26(6), 674–694.
Rathbun, Brian C. 2014. *Diplomacy's Value: Creating Security in 1920s Europe and the Contemporary Middle East*. Ithaca, NY: Cornell University Press.
Rathbun, Brian C. 2019. *Reasoning of State: Realists, Romantics and Rationality in International Relations*. Princeton, NJ: Princeton University Press.
Rauchhaus, Robert. 2009. Evaluating the Nuclear Peace Hypothesis: A Quantitative Approach. *Journal of Conflict Resolution*, 53(2), 258–277.
Ray, James Lee. 1995. *Democracy and International Politics: An Evaluation of the Democratic Peace Proposition*. Columbia, SC: University of South Carolina Press.
Reed, William, and David H. Clark. 2000. War Initiators and War Winners: The Consequences of Linking Theories of Democratic War Success. *Journal of Conflict Resolution*, 44(3), 378–395.
Regan, Patrick M. 2002. Third-Party Interventions and the Duration of Intrastate Conflicts. *Understanding Civil War*, 46(1), 55–73.
Regan, Patrick M. 2009. *Sixteen Million One: Understanding Civil War*. Boulder, CO: Paradigm Publishers.
Regan, Patrick M., and Sam R. Bell. 2010. Changing Lanes or Stuck in the Middle: Why Are Anocracies More Prone to Civil Wars? *Political Research Quarterly* 63(4), 747–759.
Reiter, Dani. 2017. Is Democracy a Cause of Peace? *Oxford Research Encyclopedia on Politics*. https://doi.org/10.1093/acrefore/9780190228637.013.287
Reiter, Dani. and Allan C. Stam. 1998. Democracy, War Initiation, and Victory. *American Political Science Review*, 92(2), 377–389.
Renshon, Jonathan. 2008. Stability and Change in Belief Systems. *Journal of Conflict Resolution*, 52(6), 820–849.
Renshon, Jonathan, and Arthur Spirling. 2015. Modeling "Effectiveness" in International Relations. *Journal of Conflict Resolution*, 59(2), 207–238.
Rhamey, Jr., J. Patrick, and Tadeusz Kugler. 2020. *Power, Space, and Time: An Empirical Introduction to International Relations*. New York, NY: Rowman & Littlefield.
Richardson, Lewis F. 1960. *Arms and Insecurity*. Pittsburgh, PA: Boxwood Press.

Rider, Toby J., and Andrew P. Owsiak. 2021. *On Dangerous Ground: A Theory of Bargaining, Border Settlement, and Rivalry*. Cambridge: Cambridge University Press.

Rokeach, Milton. 1960. *The Open and Closed Mind*. New York, NY: Basic Books.

Rosati, Jerel. 2000. The Power of Human Cognition in the Study of World Politics. *International Studies Review*, 43, 45–75.

Rosati, Jerel. 2010. Political Psychology, Cognition and Foreign Policy Analysis. In Bob Denmark (ed.), *Compendium of International Studies*, (volume IX). Charleston, SC: ISA and Blackwell, pp. 5732–5755.

Rosati, Jerel, and Colleen Miller. 2018. Political Psychology, Cognition, and Foreign Policy Analysis. *Oxford Research Encyclopedia on International Studies*. https://doi.org/10.1093/acrefore/9780190846626.013.466

Rosato, Sebastian. 2003. The Flawed Logic of Democratic Peace Theory. *American Political Science Review*, 97(4), 585–602.

Rosecrance, Richard, and Arthur Stein (eds.). 1993. *The Domestic Bases of Grand Strategy*. New York, NY: Cornell University Press.

Rosenberg, Elizabeth, Daniel Drezner, Julia Solomon-Strauss, and Zachary K. Goldman. 2016. *The New Tools of Economic Warfare*. Center for New American Security. https://www.cnas.org/publications/reports/the-new-tools-of-economic-warfare-effects-and-effectiveness-of-contemporary-u-s-financial-sanctions

Roser, Max, Joe Hasell, Bastian Herre, and Bobbie Macdonald. 2016. War and Peace. Published online at OurWorldInData.org. Retrieved from: https://ourworldindata.org/war-and-peace [Online Resource].

Rowe, David M. 2018. Economic Sanctions and International Security. *Oxford Research Encyclopedia of International Studies*, 1–20.

Ruane, Abigail E., and Patrick James. 2012. *The International Relations of Middle-Earth: Learning from the Lord of the Rings*. Ann Arbor, MI: University of Michigan Press.

Rubin, Lawrence. 2014. *Islam in the Balance: Ideational Threats in Arab Politics*. Stanford, CA: Stanford University Press.

Rummel, Rudolph J. 1981. *Understanding Conflict and War: The Just Peace* (volume 5). Beverly Hills, CA: Sage.

Russett, Bruce M. 1963. The Calculus of Deterrence. *Journal of Conflict Resolution*, 7(2) 97–109.

Russett, Bruce M. 1969. The Calculus of Deterrence. In James Rosenau (ed.), *International Politics and Foreign Policy*. New York, NY: Free Press, pp. 359–369.

Russett, Bruce M. 1993. *Grasping the Democratic Peace*. Princeton, NJ: Princeton University Press.

Russett, Bruce. M., and Oneal, John R. 2001. *Triangulating Peace: Democracy, Interdependence and International Organizations*. New York, NY: WW Norton.

Russett, Bruce M., John R. Oneal, and David R. Davis. 1998. The Third Leg of the Kantian Tripod for Peace: International Organizations and Militarized Disputes, 1950–1985. *International Organization*, 52(3), 441–467.

Sagan, Scott D. (ed.). 2017. The Changing Rules of War. *Daedalus*, 146(1), 6–10.

Sagan, Scott D., and Kenneth N. Waltz. 2002. *The Spread of Nuclear Weapons: A Debate Renewed* (2nd ed.). New York, NY: WW Norton.

Sample, Susan. 1997. Arms Races and Dispute Escalation: Resolving the Debate. *Journal of Peace Research*, 45(3), 315–326.

Sample, Susan. 1998. Military Buildups, War, and Realpolitik: A Multivariate Model. *Journal of Conflict Resolution*, 42(2), 156–175.

Sample, Susan. 2002. The Outcomes of Military Buildups: Minor States and vs Major Powers. *Journal of Peace Research*, 39(6), 669–691.

Sample, Susan. 2014. From Territorial Claim to War: Timing, Causation, and the Steps to War. *International Interactions*, 40(2), 270–285.

Sample, Susan. 2018. Anticipating War: War Preparations and the Steps to War Thesis. *British Journal of Political Science*, 48(2), 489–511.

Sample, Susan. 2021. Arms Races. In John A. Vasquez and Sara McLaughlin Mitchell (eds.), *What Do We Know About War?* (3rd ed.). New York, NY: Routledge, pp. 63–80.

Samuelson, William, and Richard Zeckhauser. 1988. Status Quo Bias in Decision-Making. *Journal of Risk and Uncertainty* 1(1) 7–59.

Sandal, Nukhet, and Jonathan Fox. 2013. *Religion in International Relations Theory: Interactions and Possibilities*. New York, NY: Routledge.

Sarkees, Meredith Reid, and Frank Whelon Wayman. 2010. *Resort to War: 1816–2007*. Washington, DC: CQ Press.
Sartori, Anne E. 2002. The Might of the Pen: A Reputational Theory of Communication in International Disputes. *International Organization*, 56(1), 121–149.
Saul, Matthew, and James A. Sweeney (eds.). 2016. *International Law and Post-Conflict Reconstruction Policy*. London: Routledge
Savun, Burcu. 2009. Mediator Types and the Effectiveness of Information-Provision Strategies in the Resolution of International Conflict. In Jacob Bercovitch and Scott S. Gartner (eds.), *International Conflict Mediation: New Approaches and Findings*. London: Routledge, pp. 96–114.
Schelling, Thomas C. 1960. *The Strategy of Conflict*. Cambridge, MA: Harvard University Press.
Schelling, Thomas C. 1966. *Arms and Influence*. New Haven, CT: Yale University Press.
Schenoni, Luis Leandro. 2018. The Argentina–Brazil Regional Power Transition. *Foreign Policy Analysis*, 14(4), 469–489.
Schmitter, Philippe C. 1969. Three Neo-Functional Hypotheses About European Integration. *International Organization*, 23(1), 161–166.
Schneider, Gerald. 2022. Capitalist Peace Theory: A Critical Appraisal. *Oxford Research Encyclopedia on Politics*. https://doi.org/10.1093/acrefore/9780190228637.013.314
Schneider, Gerald, and Nils Petter Gleditsch. 2013. *Assessing the Capitalist Peace*. New York, NY: Routledge.
Schofield, Julian. 2000. Arms Control Failure and the Balance of Power. *Canadian Journal of Political Science*, 33(4), 747–777.
Scott, James M., Yasemin Akbaba, Ralph Carter, and A. Cooper Drury. 2024. *IR: Seeking Security, Prosperity, and Quality of Life in a Changing World* (5th ed.). Washington, DC: CQ Press.
Sechser, Todd S. 2004. Are Soldiers Less War-Prone than Statesman? *Journal of Conflict Resolution*, 48(5), 746–774.
Sechser, Todd S., and Matthew Fuhrmann. 2017. *Nuclear Weapons and Coercive Diplomacy*. Cambridge: Cambridge University Press.
Sen, Amartya. 1985. *Commodities and Capabilities*. New York, NY: Elsevier Science.
Sending, Ole Jacob, Vincent Pouliot, and Iver B. Neumann (eds.). 2015. *On Diplomacy and the Making of World Politics*. London: Cambridge University Press.
Senese, Paul D., and John A. Vasquez. 2008. *The Steps to War: An Empirical Study*. Princeton, NJ: Princeton University Press.
Sharp, Paul. 1999. For Diplomacy: Representation and the Study of International Relations. *International Studies Review*, 1(1): 33–57.
Sherman, Ryne. 2015. The Personality of Donald Trump. *Psychology Today*, September 17, 2015. https://www.psychologytoday.com/us/blog/the-situation-lab/201509/the-personality-donald-trump
Shifrinson, Joshua R. Itkzkowitz. 2018. The Rise of China, Balance of Power Theory and US National Security: Reasons for Optimism. *Journal of Strategic Studies*, 43(2), 175–216.
Shifrinson, Joshua R. Itkzkowitz. 2019. *Rising Titans, Falling Giants: How Great Powers Exploit Power Shifts*. Ithaca, NY: Cornell University Press.
Shifrinson, Joshua R. Itkzkowitz. 2020. Parternship or Predation? How Rising States Contend with Declining Great Powers. *International Security*, 45(1), 90–126.
Shinkman, Paul D. 2019. Study: US No Longer Dominant Power in the Pacific. US News and World Report. August 20 (https://usnews.com/news/world-report/articles/2019-08-20/us-no-longer-dominant-power-in-the-pacific-study).
Shirk, Susan L. 2007. *China: Fragile Superpower*. Oxford: Oxford University Press.
Sil, Rudra. 2000. The Foundations of Eclecticism: The Epistemological Status of Agency, Culture, and Structure in Social Theory. *Journal of Theoretical Politics*, 12(3), 353–387.
Sil, Rudra. 2009. Simplifying Pragmatism: From Social Theory to Problem-Driven Eclecticism. *International Studies Review*, 11(3), 648–652.
Sil, Rudra, and Peter J. Katzenstein. 2010. *Beyond Paradigms: Analytic Eclecticism in the Study of World Politics*. New York, NY: Palgrave Macmillan.
Simmons, Beth A. 1998. Compliance with International Agreements. *Annual Review of Political Science*, 1(1), 75–93.
Simonelli, Nicole M. 2011. Bargaining over International Multilateral Agreements: The Duration of Negotiations. *International Interactions*, 37(2), 147–169.

Singer, J. David. 1961. The Level-of-Analysis Problem in International Relations. *World Politics,* 14(1), 77–92.

Singer, J. David, and Thomas R. Cusack. 1981. Periodicity, Inexorability, and Steersmanship in International War. In Richard Merritt and Bruce M. Russett (eds.), *From National Development to Global Community: Essays in Honor of Karl W. Deutsch.* Herts, England: Allen and Unwin, pp. 404–425.

Singer, J. David, and Melvin Small. 1966. Formal Alliances, 1815–1939: A Quantitative Description. *Journal of Peace Research,* 3(1), 1–32.

Singer, J. David, and Melvin Small. 1968. Alliance Aggregation and the Onset of War, 1815–1945. In J. David. Singer (ed.), *Quantitative International Politics: Insights and Evidence.* New York, NY: Free Press, pp. 247–86.

Singer, J. David, and Melvin Small. 1972. *The Wages of War, 1816. 1965: A Statistical Handbook.* New York: John Wiley and Sons.

Sisson, Melanie W., James A. Siebens, and Barry M. Blechman (eds.). 2020. *Military Coercion and US Foreign Policy: The Use of Force Short of War.* London: Routledge.

Siverson, Randolph M., and Joel King. 1979. Alliances and the Expansion of War. In J. David Singer and Michael D. Wallace (eds.), *To Augur Well: Early Warning Indicators in World Politics.* Beverly Hills, CA: Sage, pp. 37–49.

Siverson, Randolph M., and Harvey Starr. 1991. *The Diffusion of War: A Study of Opportunity and Willingness.* Ann Arbor, MI: University of Michigan Press.

Slantchev, Branislav L. 2004. How Initiators End Their Wars: The Duration of Warfare and the Terms of Peace. *American Journal of Political Science.* 48(4), 813–829.

Slaughter, Anne-Marie. 1995. International Law in a World of Liberal States. *European Journal of International Law,* 6(3), 503–538.

Small, Melvin, and J. David Singer. 1970. Patterns in International Warfare, 1816–1965. The ANNALS of the American Academy of Political and Social Science, 391(1), 145–155.

Small, Melvin, and J. David Singer. 1982. *Resort to Arms: International and Civil Wars, 1816–1980.* Beverly Hills, CA: SAGE Publications.

Smith, Alastair. 1996. Diversionary Foreign Policy in Democratic Systems. *International Studies Quarterly,* 40(1), 133–153.

Smith, Alastair, and Allan C. Stam. 2003. Mediation and Peacekeeping in a Random Walk Model of Civil and Interstate War. *International Studies Review,* 5(4), 115–135.

Snyder, Glenn H. 1984. The Security Dilemma in Alliance Politics. *World Politics,* 36(4), 461–495.

Snyder, Glenn H., and Paul Diesing. 1977. *Conflict Among Nations: Bargaining, Decision Making, and System Structure in International Crises.* Princeton, NJ: Princeton University Press.

Snyder, Jack. 1991. *Myths of Empire.* Ithaca, NY: Cornell University Press.

Sobek, David. 2007. Rallying Around the Podesta: Testing Diversionary Theory Across Time. *Journal of Peace Research,* 44(1), 29–45.

Sperandei, Maria. 2006. Bridging Deterrence and Compellence: An Alternative Approach to the Study of Coercive Diplomacy. *International Studies Review,* 8(2), 253–280.

Spiro, David E. 1994. The Insignificance of the Liberal Peace. *International Security,* 19(2), 50–86.

Starkey, Brigid, Mark A. Boyer, and Jonathan Wilkenfeld. 2005. *Negotiating a Complex World: An Introduction to International Negotiation.* Lanham, MD: Rowman & Littlefield.

Starr, Harvey, and G. Dale Thomas. 2005. The Nature of Borders and International Conflict: Revisiting Hypotheses on Territory. *International Studies Quarterly,* 49(1), 123–139.

Stedman, Stephen John. 1991. *Peacemaking in Civil War: International Mediation in Zimbabwe, 1974–1980.* Boulder, CO: Lynne Rienner.

Stein, Janice Gross. 1987. Extended Deterrence in the Middle East: American Strategy Reconsidered. *World Politics,* 39(3), 326–352.

Stein, Janice Gross. 1991. Reassurance in International Conflict Management. *Political Science Quarterly,* 106(3), 431–451.

Stein, Janice Gross. 1992. Deterrence and Compellence in the Gulf, 1990–91: A Failed or Impossible Task? *International Security,* 17(2),147–179.

Stein, Janice Gross. 2016. Foreign Policy Decision Making: Rational, Psychological, and Neurological. In Steve Smith, Amelia Hadfield, and Tim Dunne (eds.), *Foreign Policy: Theories, Actors, Cases.* London: Oxford University Press, pp. 101–116

Stein, Janice Gross, and Louis W. Pauly. 1993. *Choosing to Co-Operate: How States Avoid Loss*. Baltimore, MD: Johns Hopkins University Press.
Steinbruner, John D. 1974. *The Cybernetic Theory of Decision*. Princeton, NJ: Princeton University Press.
Stern, Jessica. 2003. *Terror in the Name of God: Why Religious Militants Kill*. New York NY: HarperCollins.
Svensson, Isak. 2020. Mediation of Interstate Conflict and Civil Wars. *Oxford Research Encyclopedia on International Studies*. https://doi.org/10.1093/acrefore/9780190846626.013.528
Taliaferro, Jeffrey W. 2004a. *Balancing Risks: Great Power Intervention in the Periphery*. Ithaca, NY: Cornell University Press.
Taliaferro, Jeffrey W. 2004b. Power Politics and the Balance of Risk: Hypotheses on Great Power Intervention in the Periphery. *Political Psychology*, 25(2), 177–211.
Taliaferro, Jeffrey W. 2017. Prospect Theory and Foreign Policy Analysis. *Oxford Research Encyclopedia on International Studies*. https://doi.org/10.1093/acrefore/9780190846626.013.281
Tammen, Ronald L., Jacek Kugler, and Douglas Lemke. 2017a. Power Transition Theory. *Oxford Bibliographies in International Relations*. DOI: 10.1093/obo/9780199743292-0038
Tammen, Ronald L., Jacek Kugler, and Douglas Lemke. 2017b. Foundations of Power Transition Theory. *Oxford Research Encyclopedia*. DOI: 10/1093/acrefore/9870190228637.013.296
Tammen, Ronald L., Jacek Kugler, Douglas Lemke, Allen C. Stam III, Mark Abdollahian, Carole Alsharabati, Brian Efird and A. F. K. Organski. 2000. *Power Transitions: Strategies for the 21st Century*. Washington, DC: CQ Press.
Tammen, Ronald L., and Ayesha Wahedi. 2020. East Asia: China on the Move. In Jacek Kugler and Ronald L. Tammen (eds.), *The Rise of Regions: Conflict and Cooperation*. New York, NY: Rowman & Littlefield, pp. 19–35.
Tanaka, Yoshifumi. 2018. *The Peaceful Settlement of International Disputes*. Cambridge: Cambridge University Press, 2018.
Taydas, Zeynep, Jason Enia, and Patrick James. 2011. Why Do Civil Wars Occur? Another Look at the Theoretical Dichotomy of Opportunity Versus Grievance. *Review of International Studies*, 37(5), 2627–2650.
Taydas, Zeynep, Dursun Peksen, and Patrick James. 2010. Why Do Civil Wars Occur? Understanding the Importance of Institutional Quality. *Civil Wars*, 12(3), 195–217.
Taylor, Michael. 1976. *Anarchy and Cooperation*. London: John Wiley and Sons.
Terpstra, Robert. 2019. President Al-Sisi Outlines Importance of Mutual Understanding on Renaissance Dam. *Daily News Egypt*. September 25, 2019. https://dailynewsegypt.com/2019/09/25/president-al-sisi-outlines-importance-of-mutual-understanding-on-renaissance-dam/
Terriff, Terry, Aaron Karp, and Regina Karp (eds.). 2008. *Global Insurgency and the Future of Armed Conflict: Debating Fourth-Generation Warfare*. New York, NY: Routledge.
Terris, L. 2022. Unintended Consequences of International Mediation. *Oxford Research Encyclopedia on Politics*. https://doi.org/10.1093/acrefore/9780190228637.013.1916
Tetlock, Philip E. 1998. Social Psychology and World Politics. In Daniel Todd Gilbert, Susan T. Fiske, and Gardner Lindzey (eds.), *The Handbook of Social Psychology*. Boston, MA: McGraw-Hill, pp. 868–912.
Tetlock, Philip, E. 2006. *Expert Political Judgment – How Good Is It? How Can We Know?* Princeton, NJ: Princeton University Press.
Thee, Marek. 1978. Failure of Arms Control, and Strategies for Disarmament. *Bulletin of Peace Proposals*, 9(4), 375–377.
Thies, Cameron G. 2004. State Building, Interstate and Intrastate Rivalry: A Study of Post-Colonial Developing Country Extractive Efforts, 1975–2000. *International Studies Quarterly*, 48(1), 53–72.
Thomas, Evan. 2002. Chemistry in the War Cabinet. *Newsweek*, January 28, 2002, 26–31.
Thompson, William R. 2016. Trends in the Analysis of Interstate Rivalries. Unpublished manuscript.
Thompson, William R. 2020. Humpty Dumpty Had a Great Fall? Making Sense of Longer-Term Ups and Downs in Middle Eastern Rivalries. In Imad Mansour and William R. Thompson (eds.), *Shocks and Rivalry in the Middle East and North Africa*. Washington, DC: Georgetown University Press, pp. 39–58.
Thompson, William R., and David R. Dreyer. 2011. *Handbook of International Rivalries*. Washington, DC: CQ Press.
Tian, Nan, Diego Lopes da Silva, Xiao Liang, Lorenzo Scarazzato, Lucie Béraud-Sudreau, and Ana Carolina de Oliviera Assis. 2022. Trends in World Military Expenditure. *SIPRI Fact Sheet*. April 2023.

Tir, Jaroslav. 2010. Territorial Diversion: Diversionary Theory of War and Territorial Conflict. *The Journal of Politics*, 72(2), 413–425.

Toft, Monica Duffy. 2021. Getting Religion Right in Civil Wars. *Journal of Conflict Resolution,* 65(9), 1607–1634.

Tomz, Michael. 2007. Domestic Audience Costs in International Relations: An Experimental Approach. *International Organization*, 61(4), 821–840.

Trager, Robert. 2016. The Diplomacy of War and Peace. *Annual Review of Political Science* 19(1), 205–228.

Transparency International. 2024. *Corruption Perceptions Index.* https://www.transparency.org/en/cpi/2014, accessed February 28, 2024.

Treverton, Gregory F. 2000. *Framing Compellent Strategies.* Rand Document MR-1240-OS. http://www.rand.org/public

UCDP/PRIO. 2023. Armed Conflict Dataset. https://legacy.prio.org/Data/Armed-Conflict/UCDP-PRIO/, accessed March 9, 2023.

UNAIDS 2023. Factsheet 2023: Global HIV Statistics. https://www.unaids.org/en/resources/fact-sheet#:~:text=39.9%20million%20%5B36.1%20million%E2%80%9344.6,AIDS%2Drelated%20illnesses%20in%202023.

Union of International Associations. 2022. *Yearbook of International Organizations.*

United Nations. 2012. Guidance for Effective Mediation. United Nations. https://peacemaker.un.org/sites/peacemaker.un.org/files/GuidanceEffectiveMediation_UNDPA2012%28english%29_0.pdf

United Nations. 2023. *A New Agenda for Peace. Our Common Agenda.* Policy Brief 9. United Nations Office of the Secretary-General. https://www.un.org/sites/un2.un.org/files/our-common-agenda-policy-brief-new-agenda-for-peace-en.pdf

United Nations Political and Peacebuilding Affairs. 2023. *A New Agenda for Peace.* https://dppa.un.org/en/a-new-agenda-for-peace

US Department of Defense. 2011. *Dictionary of Military and Associated Terms* (As amended through April 10). Collingdale, PA: Diane Publishing.

Valeriano, Brandon. 2012. Becoming Rivals: The Process of Rivalry Development. In John A. Vasquez (ed.), *What Do We Know about War?* (2nd ed.). Lanham, MD: Rowman & Littlefield, pp. 63–82.

Valeriano, Brandon, Benjamin Jensen, and Ryan C. Maness. 2018. *Cyber Strategy: The Evolving Character of Power and Coercion.* New York, NY: Oxford University Press.

Van Evera, Stephen. 1999. *Causes of War: Power and the Roots of Conflict.* Ithaca, NY: Cornell University Press.

Vasquez, John A. 1993. *The War Puzzle.* Cambridge: Cambridge University Press.

Vasquez, John A. 1995. Why Do Neighbors Fight? Proximity, Interaction, or Territoriality. *Journal of Peace Research* 32(3), 277–293.

Vasquez, John A. 2001. Mapping the Probability of War and Analyzing the Possibility of Peace: The Role of Territorial Issues. *Conflict Management and Peace Science*, 18(2), 145–174.

Vasquez, John A. 2011. Territorial Paths to War: Their Probability of Escalation, 1816–2001. In John A. Vasquez and Marie Henehan (eds.), *Territory, War, and Peace.* London: Routledge, pp. 133–147.

Vasquez, John A., and Marie T. Henhan (eds.). 2010. *Territory, War and Peace.* London: Routledge.

Vertzberger, Yaacov Y. I. (1995). Rethinking and Reconceptualizing Risk in Foreign Policy Decision-Making: A Sociocognitive Approach. *Political Psychology* 16(2), 347–380.

Vis, Barbara, and Dieuwertje Kuijpers. 2018. Prospect Theory and Foreign Policy Decision-Making: Underexposed Issues, Advancements, and Ways Forward. *Contemporary Security Policy*, 39(4), 575–589.

von Clausewitz, Carl. 1997. *On War.* Translated by J. J. K. Graham. Wordsworth Classics of World Literature. Ware, England: Wordsworth Editions.

von Stein, Jana. 2017. Compliance with International Law. *Oxford Research Encyclopedia on International Studies.* https://doi.org/10.1093/acrefore/9780190846626.013.55

Waal, Alex De. 2015. Opinion | Sisi Goes to Addis Ababa. *The New York Times*, January 26, 2015, sec. Opinion. https://www.nytimes.com/2015/01/27/opinion/sisi-goes-to-addis-ababa.html

Walker, Stephen G. 1977. The Interface between Beliefs and Behavior: Henry Kissinger's Operational Code and the Vietnam War. *Journal of Conflict Resolution* 21(1), 129–168.

Walker, Stephen G., and Mark Schafer. 2018. Operational Code Theory: Beliefs and Foreign Policy Decisions. *Oxford Research Encyclopedia on International Studies*. https://doi.org/10.1093/acrefore/9780190846626.013.411

Walker, Stephen G., Mark Schafer, and Gary Smith. 2018. The Operational Codes of Donald Trump and Hillary Clinton. *The Oxford Handbook of Behavioral Political Science*. DOI:10.1093/OXFORDHB/9780190634131.013.4

Walker, Stephen G., Mark Schafer, and Michael D. Young. 1999. Presidential Operational Codes and Foreign Policy Conflicts in the Post-Cold War World. *Journal of Conflict Resolution*, 43(5), 610–625.

Walker, Stephen G., Mark Schafer, and Michael D. Young. 2005. Profiling the Operational Codes of Political Leaders. In Jerrold M. Post (ed.), *The Psychological Assessment of Political Leaders*. Ann Arbor, MI: University of Michigan Press, pp. 215–245.

Wallace, Michael D. 1979. Arms Races and Escalation: Some New Evidence. *Journal of Conflict Resolution*, 23(1), 3–16.

Walt, Stephen M. 1987. *Origins of Alliances*. Ithaca, NY: Cornell University Press.

Walt, Stephen M. 1996. *Revolution and War*. Ithaca, NY: Cornell University Press.

Walter, Barbara F. 2002. *Committing to Peace: The Successful Settlement of Civil Wars*. Princeton, NJ: Princeton University Press.

Walter, Barbara F. 2022. *How Civil Wars Start and How to Stop Them*. New York, NY: Crown.

Waltz, Kenneth N. 1959. *Man, the State, and War: A Theoretical Analysis*. New York, NY: Columbia University Press.

Waltz, Kenneth N. 1979. *Theory of International Politics*. Reading, MA: Addison Wesley.

Waltz, Kenneth N. 1990. Nuclear Myths and Political Realities. *American Political Science Review*, 84(3), 731–745.

Wang, Kevin, and James Lee Ray. 1994. Beginners and Winners: The Fate of Initiators of Interstate Wars Involving Great Powers Since 1495. *International Studies Quarterly*, 38(1), 139–154.

Wayman, Frank Whelon. 1990. Alliances and War: A Time-Series Analysis. In Charles S. Gochman and Alan Ned Sabrosky (eds.), *Prisoners of War? Nation-States in the Modern Era*. Lexington, MA: Lexington Books, pp. 93–113.

Weart, Spencer R. 1998. *Never at War: Why Democracies Will Not Fight One Another*. New Haven, CT: Yale University Press.

Weede, Eric. 1980. Arms Races and Escalation: Some Persisting Doubts. *Journal of Conflict Resolution*, 24(2), 285–287.

Weede, Eric. 1995. Economic Policy and International Security: Rent-Seeking, Free Trade and Democratic Peace. *European Journal of International Relations*, 1(4), 519–537.

Weiner, Robert, and Paul Sharp. 2017. Diplomacy and War. *Oxford Research Encyclopedia on International Studies*, 1–7.

Weitsman, Patricia. 2017. Alliances and War. *Oxford Research Encyclopedia on International Studies*, https://doi.org/10.1093/acrefore/9780190846626.013.118

White, Ralph K. 1970. *Nobody Wanted War: Misperception in Vietnam and Other Wars*. New York, NY: Doubleday.

White, Ralph K. 2004. Misperception and War, Peace and Conflict: *Journal of Peace Psychology*, 10(4), 399–409.

Whiting, Allen S. 1960. *China Crosses the Yalu: The Decision to Enter the Korean War*. Stanford, CA: Stanford University Press.

Wight, Colin. 2007. A Manifesto for Scientific Realism in IR: Assuming the Can-Opener Won't Work. *Millennium: Journal of International Studies*, 35(2), 379–398.

Wight, Colin. 2016. Maps, Models, and Theories: A Scientific Realist Approach Toward Validity. In Annette Freyberg-Inan, Ewan Harrison, and Patrick James (eds.), *Evaluating Progress in International Relations: How Do You Know?* New York, NY: Routledge, pp. 31–50.

Wilkenfeld, Jonathan, and David Quinn. 2023. One Hundred Years of International Crises, 1918–2018. In Jonathan Wilkenfeld and Egle E. Murauskaite (eds.), *Escalation Management in International Crises: The United States and Its Adversaries*. Cheltenham, UK and Northampton, MA: Edward Elgar, pp. 78–109.

Wilkenfeld, Jonathan, Kathleen Young, David Quinn, and Victor Asal. 2005. *Mediating International Crises*. London: Routledge.

Williams, Michael C. 1998. Identity and the Politics of Security. *European Journal of International Relations,* 4(2), 204–225.

Williams, Michael C., and Iver B. Neumann. 2000. From Alliance to Security Community: NATO, Russia, and the Power of Identity. *Millennium: Journal of International Studies,* 29(2), 357–387.

Williams, Paul. 2017. Peace Operations. *Oxford Research Encyclopedia on International Studies.* https://doi.org/10.1093/acrefore/9780190846626.013.37

Wilkenfeld, Jonathan. 1968. Domestic and Foreign Conflict Behavior of Nations. *Journal of Peace Research,* 5, 56–69.

Wilson, Edward O. 1975. *Sociobiology: The New Synthesis.* Cambridge, MA: Harvard University Press.

Wilson, Maya, David R. Davis, and Amanda Murdie. 2016. The View from the Bottom: Networks of Conflict Resolution Organizations and International Peace. *Journal of Peace Research,* 53(3), 442–458.

Winchester, Simon. 2005. *Krakatoa: The Day the World Exploded: August 27, 1883.* New York, NY: Harper Perennial.

Winter, David G. 2005. Saddam Hussein: Motivations and Mediation of Self-Other Relationships. In Jerrold M. Post (ed.), *The Psychological Assessment of Political Leaders.* Ann Arbor, MI: University of Michigan Press. pp. 370–374.

Wolford, Scott. 2021. What Do We Know About Leaders and War? In Sara McLaughlin Mitchell and John A. Vasquez (eds.), *What Do We Know about War?* (3rd ed.). Lanham, MD: Rowman & Littlefield, pp. 244–259.

Wood, Reed M. 2008. "A Hand Upon the Throat of the Nation": Economic Sanctions and State Repression, 1976–2001. *International Studies Quarterly,* 52(3), 489–513.

Woodward, C. Vann (ed.) 1981. *Mary Chesnut's Civil War.* New Haven, CT: Yale University Press.

Worldwide Association of NGOs. 2024 *Worldwide NGO Directory.* https://www.wango.org/resources.aspx?section=ngodir#:~:text=The%20Worldwide%20NGO%20Directory%20is,in%20more%20than%20190%20countries

Wright, Quincy. 1942. *A Study of War.* Chicago, IL: University of Chicago Press.

Wright, Quincy. 1965. *A Study of War, Revised Edition.* Chicago, IL: University of Chicago Press.

Yacoubian, Mona. 2023. Syria's Stalemate Has Only Benefitted Assad and His Backers. United States Institute of Peace.

Yarhi-Milo, Keren. 2018. *Who Fights for Reputation: The Psychology of Leaders in International Conflict.* Princeton, NJ: Princeton University Press.

Yoon, Young-Kwan. 2003. Introduction: Power Cycle Theory and the Practice of International Relations. *International Political Science Review,* 24(1), 5–12.

Young, Oran R. 1967. *Intermediaries: Third-Parties in International Crises.* Princeton, NJ: Princeton University Press.

Young, Oran R. 1968. *The Politics of Force.* Princeton, NJ: Princeton University Press.

Yuan, Jingdong. 2015. The Rise of China and the Emerging Order in Asia. In Mingjiang Li and Kaylan M. Kemburi (eds.), *China's Power and Asian Security.* New York, NY: Routledge, pp. 25–37.

Zagare, Frank C. 1990. Rationality and Deterrence. *World Politics,* 42(2), 238–260.

Zagare, Frank C., and D. Marc Kilgour. 2000. *Perfect Deterrence.* Cambridge: Cambridge University Press.

Zakaria, Fareed. 1998. *From Wealth to Power: The Unusual Origins of America's World Role.* Princeton, NJ: Princeton University Press.

Zaloga, Steven J. 2008. *Panther vs. Sherman.* Oxford: Osprey Publishing.

Zartman, I. William. 1995. Dynamics and Constraints in Negotiations in Internal Conflicts. In I. William Zartman (ed.), *Elusive Peace: Negotiating an End to Civil Wars.* Washington, DC: Brookings Institution, pp. 3–29.

Zartman, I. William. 2000. Ripeness: The Hurting Stalemate and Beyond. In Paul C. Stern and Daniel Druckman (eds.), *International Conflict Resolution After the Cold War.* Washington, DC: National Academy Press, pp. 225–50.

Zartman, I. William, and Saadia Touval. 2007. International Mediation. In Chester A. Crocker, Fen Osler Hampson, and Pamela Aall (eds.), *Leashing the Dogs of War: Conflict Management in a Divided World.* Washington, DC: United States Institute of Peace Press, pp. 437–454.

Zellman, Ariel, and Jonathan Fox. 2020. Defending the Faith? Assessing the Impact of State Religious Exclusivity on Territorial MID Initiation. *Politics and Religion,* 13, 465–491.

Zenko, Micah. 2010. *Between Threats and War: U.S. Discrete Military Operations in the Post–Cold War World*. Stanford, CA: Stanford University Press.

Zetter, Kim. (2014). *Countdown to Zero Day: Stuxnet and the Launch of the World's First Digital Weapon*. New York, NY: Crown.

Zhang, Enyu, and Patrick James. 2022. All Roads Lead to Beijing: *Systemism*, Power Transition Theory and the Belt and Road Initiative. *Chinese Political Science Review*, 8(1), 18–41.

Zinnes, Dina A. 1976. *Contemporary Research in International Relations: A Perspective and a Critical Appraisal*. New York, NY: Free Press.

INDEX

9/11 attacks 45, 145–7

Abe, Shinzo 24
action-reaction cycles 237–8, 250, 252
active causes *see* extrinsic causes
Adams, John Quincy 213
adjudication 240t11.1
adjustment bias 146
administration 265
Afghanistan War 45
Afghanistan–Pakistan conflict 56
African Sahel states 61–2, 63f3.12
African Union (AU) 284
aggregate data analysis 231–3, 232t10.2, 313
aggressor theory 264–5
AI *see* Artificial Intelligence
aid sanctions 244
Al-Sisi, Abdel Fattah 20
Albertini, Luigi 12
alliances 95, 237, 247, 256–60
Allison, Graham 100–1
Almond, Gabriel A. 75
American border conflict 19
American Civil War 201, 205–7, 206m10.1, 210–30, 234, 313
    aggregate data analysis 231–3, 232t10.2
    blockades 243
    events leading to 218–19t10.1, 220, 221–7f10.1
analysis, levels of 6, 77, 188n6, 304–5, 313–14, 316–18
analytic eclecticism 3, 8–10, 47, 80, 87, 118, 304, 314
anarchy 42, 94, 139, 237, 273
anchoring bias 146
Angell, Norman 119
anocracy 191, 231
apartheid regimes 244–5
APEC *see* Asia-Pacific Economic Cooperation
Arab Spring 40
arbitration 240t11.1
Aristotelian philosophy 207–8, 210
armed conflict
    by region, 1946–2021 55f3.6
    interstate 61, 77
    patterns of 54
arms control 263–70, 266–7t11.3
arms races 249–50, 261

Artificial Intelligence (AI) 303
ASEAN *see* Association of Southeast Asian Nations
Asia-Pacific Economic Cooperation (APEC) 283
Assad regime 40–1, 183
Association of Southeast Asian Nations (ASEAN) 284
Astorino-Courtois, Allison 157
asymmetric war 39, 62
attitudinal rivalry 52
AU *see* African Union
authoritarian regimes 122, 126, 133–4
autocracy 122
autocratic peace 126
availability bias 146
Ayferam, Gashaw 20
Ayodhya mosque destruction 51–2

BACE *see* belief in ability to control events
Badie, Dina 153
balance of power 94, 96
balancing dynamics, alliances 257
Balz, Dan 146
bandwagoning 256–7
Barceló, Joan 142
bargaining 238, 241
Beardsley, Kyle 157
Beecher Stowe, Harriet, *Uncle Tom's Cabin* 214, 217, 229, 233
behavioral dimensions 50, 120
belief 144–5, 147–9
belief in ability to control events (BACE) 166
Bell, Sam R. 191
Bellamy, Alex J. 293
Belt and Road Initiative (BRI) 102, 111–12
Bercovitch, Jacob 243
Berlin Wall 68–70, 156
bilateral agreements 265
bilateral diplomacy 239
bipolarity 96, 97t5.1, 113
Blechman, Barry M. 262
Boettcher, William A. 151
Boomerang Model, NGO activity 298f12.3
border conflicts 19, 118
Boyer, Mark A. 241
Brecher, Michael 209
Brexit 66
BRI *see* Belt and Road Initiative

Brodie, Bernard 253
Brooks, Preston S. 214, 229
Brown, Davis 74, 77
Brown, John 214–15, 217, 229
Bunge, Mario 10
Bush, George H. W. 148
Bush, George W. 145–6, 150, 153
Butcher, Charity 122
Butler, Michael 241
Butterfield, Herbert 237

cannons 303
capability approach 189–90
capitalism 119
capitalist peace 120
Cashman, Greg 96, 117, 136, 142, 150, 153, 315–16
Castro, Fidel 23, 187
causal effects 5
causal inferences 144, 146
causal mechanisms 126n7
causal processes 5
causal theory 4
causation 207
cause-and-effect, theory 5, 207–11
causes, types 207–8, 217
CCW *see* conflict, crisis and war
Chamberlain, Neville 137
Chechnyan civil war 189
China
    decolonization 102, 110
    deglobalization 112
    development model 111
    military spending 248–9
    predation theory 99
    Taiwan conflict 123–4
    US relations 100–1
Chinese civil war 189
Chiu, Daniel Y. 95
Christianity 76, 77
Churchill, Winston 137, 138, 192, 238
Cilizoglu, Menevis 246
civil society development 294
civil war 40–1, 45, 61, 183–204, 255
    causes 207–11, 217, 231
    definitions 185, 186t9.1
    era of 65
    internationalized 40, 45, 53, 61
    likelihood 192
    multilevel analysis 205–34

    onset analysis 186–7n3-4, 187–8n5, 188t9.2, 192–200, 193–8f9.1
    outcomes/legacies 203–4t9.A2
    previous conflict connection 233
    processes 202t9.A1
    see also American Civil War
classical realism 67, 139–40
classified information 6–7
Claude, Inis L. 293
Clay, K. Chad 246–7
climate change 61–2, 63f3.12, 296
Clinton, Bill 148
Clinton, Hillary 149, 155f7.A1
coalitions 9, 121
Cod Wars 68–9
coding 159
Coe, Andrew 270
coercive diplomacy 157, 261, 262
coercive policies 243–7
cognition 125
    Type I 137, 138, 143, 149, 231
    Type II 137, 144, 149, 231
cognitive consistency 145, 149
cognitive heuristics 145
cognitive psychology 145–7, 150
cognitive stability 144–5
cognitive structures 144–5
Cold War 44, 46–7, 68–9, 97, 102, 110–11, 156–7, 251–2, 255, 257, 290
collective security 292–4
Collingwood, Robin George 210
CoM *see* Council of the European Union
commercial liberalism 119
communication, importance of 265
compellence 261, 262
compliance, international law 278–9
component, use of term 10n3
concrete stakes 68
Confederate States of America (CSA) 205, 216, 217, 230, 233
confidence-building agreements 267–8
confirmation bias 146
conflict
    definition 47
    patterns 47–55, 62, 114
    visualizing 133–5
conflict behavior 144, 151
conflict, crisis and war (CCW)
    central argument 314–17
    pathways to 312–13, 316
conflict management 88–9, 148, 236–71

conflict resolution 291–2
constitutive causes *see* intrinsic causes
constructivism 74–5
contiguity variable 118
contingency 101–2
conventional war 39, 62
cooperation 42, 120, 273–4, 280, 299, 302
cooperation–conflict dimension 47, 49
Correlates of War (COW) Project 27, 47, 117–18, 259
correlation 207
corruption 190
Council of the European Union 285–6
covariance 4
COW Project *see* Correlates of War Project
crisis
 as global phenomenon 57
 initiator role 162
 issues connected with 70, 71t4.1
 ladder of escalation 42
 likelihood 160, 169
 onset analysis 160, 161t8.1
 origins of 160–2
 outcomes/legacies 166–70, 167–8t8.3
 patterns of 114
 project-based research 157–60
 state-centered view 160
 use of term 22
crisis actors 22–3, 25
crisis behavior 120
crisis management 166, 181
CSA *see* Confederate States of America
Cuban Missile Crisis 23, 251
Cuban Revolution 187
cultural environment 139, 241
cultural-status issues 70, 71t4.1
custom 275
customary law 275–6
cyberwarfare 62, 64

Davis, David R. 122
Davis, Jr., James W. 151
De Bow's Review 213, 215, 217, 228, 233
deaths
 conflicts
  1400–2013 48f3.1
  1989–2021 49f3.2
 non-state conflict 60
 state-based conflict, 1946–2021 58f3.8
 technology impact 46
decision processes, IOs 280–1

decision-making
 prospect theory view 151
 research program 166, 169
decolonialization 102, 110
deductive reasoning 7
defence 247–50, 260
deglobalization 112
democracy 4–5, 8, 111, 122
Democratic Party, US 214–15
Democratic Peace Theory 126–35, 312–13
demographic factors 189–90
description 4–5, 312
deterrence 247, 250–6
Diehl, Paul F. 50–1, 293
difference feminists 140
diplomacy 238–43, 263, 291–2, 299–300
direct deterrence 251
disarmament 263–70
discrimination 190, 233
disruptive crises 22
diversionary theory 121–2
Dixon, Jeffrey 184, 186, 188, 192
domestic conflict 185
 see also civil war
domestic instability 316
domestic political conditions 121–2
"domino" theory 110
Doran, Charles F. 96
Douglas, Stephen A. 214, 215–16, 230
Douglass, Frederick 212
Downs, George W. 270
Doyle, Michael W. 126, 293
Dr. Strangelove 252
Dror, Yehezkel 116
duration dimension, rivalry 50
dyadic-level analysis 6, 77, 126, 161–2, 168, 188n6
dynamic realist theories 94–5

Early, Bryan R. 246
East Asian system 92, 94, 102–13, 103–9f5.1
East China Sea crisis 23–5, 99
EC *see* European Commission
ECJ *see* European Court of Justice
economic coercion 243–7
economic-developmental issues 70, 71t4.1, 294
economic exchange 119–20, 210
economic factors 73, 119–21
economic sanctions 243–6
economic security-oriented IOs 295
ECOSOC *see* UN Economic and Social Council
ECOWAS treaty 292

educational factors 191, 233
educational programs 294
efficient cause 209, 220
endowment effect 151, 231
enemy images 145–6
enforcement, international law 276–8
environment–system linkages 11, 14, 28
environmental protection programs 294
environmental security-oriented IOs 296
EP *see* European Parliament
escalation 5, 135
    ladder of 18, 26, 41–2, 42f2.2, 238
ethnic conflict 76, 166
ethnic diversity 190
ethnic dominance 190
ethnic strife 75
ethnonational identification 123
ethology 139
EU *see* European Union
Euromaidan revolution 25–6
European Commission (EC) 284, 285
European Court of Justice (ECJ) 284, 287–8
European Parliament (EP) 284, 285–6
European Union (EU) 280, 284–8, 286–7f12.1
event-centered rivalry 50, 52
explanatory theory 5
export sanctions 244
extended deterrence 251, 253
extra-state wars 27
extrinsic causes 208–10, 217–18

faith-based conflict *see* religion
Farnham, Barbara 150
Fearon, James D. 274
feminist approaches 140
film depictions 57, 59, 121
final cause 209–10, 217, 220
financial sanctions 244
Findlay, Trevor 293
Finnemore, Martha 297
Fisher, Roger 87, 216, 238
fishing rights 68–9
Fitzhugh, George, *Cannibals All!* 215, 217, 233
force
    displays of 260
    limited use 262
    uses of 260–2
foreign policy 39, 127–32f6.1, 133–5, 152f7.1
foreign policy crises 22–5, 77, 158
formal causes 208–9
Fort Sumter 205, 206m10.1, 220

Fortna, Virginia Page 293
fourth-generation war 62
Fox, Jonathan 74–6, 80
Franco-Prussian War 71–2
Fry, Douglas P. 139
Fugitive Slave Law 211, 220, 233
Fuhrmann, Matthew 251, 253, 269–70
functional form 11
functional relations 11f1.1

Gaddafi, Muammar 40
Gansen, Sarah 123
Garrison, William Lloyd 212, 217, 233
Gartzke, Erik 120
GATT *see* General Agreement on Tariffs and Trade
Gaza War 14, 45
GCC *see* Gulf Cooperation Council
gender differences 140–1
gender equality 142
General Agreement on Tariffs and Trade (GATT) 283
genetic factors 139
Geneva Conventions 265
genocidal warfare 4–5
geographic agreements 268
geographic factors 189
George, Alexander L. 147, 255, 262
GERD *see* Grand Ethiopian Renaissance Dam
global IOs 282–3, 288
globalization 49
Goertz, Gary G. 50–1
Goldstein, Joshua S. 49
good offices 240t11.1
Gourevitch, Peter 191
government declassification 6–7
Grand Ethiopian Renaissance Dam (GERD) 20
graphic techniques 2, 14, 133, 171–82, 192–200, 220, 304–14
gray zone activities 158, 180
great power war 59f3.9, 60, 65, 95, 97–8
Great War *see* World War I
greed 184, 191–2
grievances 184, 192
Grotius, Hugo 274
groupthink 153
Gulf Cooperation Council (GCC) 283–4
Gulf War 249
Guterres, António 272–4

Haass, Ernst B. 243

Hagan, Joe D. 121, 133
Hague conferences 263
Hague Conventions 265
Hainan Island 92, 93m5.1
Hamdok, Abdalla 20
Hasenclever, Andreas 74
Hassner, Ron E. 117, 169
    War on Sacred Grounds 67, 74, 80, 89–90
health security-oriented IOs 295–6
hegemonic struggle 316
Henehan, Marie T. 73
Henkin, Louis 278
Hensel, Paul R. 70, 72, 262
Herz, John 237
Hewitt, J. Joseph 120
HI *see* humanitarian intervention
hierarchy 94, 99
hindsight bias 146
Hiroshima 250
historical analogies 146
Hitler, Adolf 4, 137
Holocaust 4
Holsti, K. J. 69–70, 73, 90, 145, 147
horizontal law enforcement 276, 277
horizontal proliferation control 269
Horn of Africa 21m2.1
Horowitz, Michael C. 142
hostility levels, rankings 49
Houthi rebellion 181–2
HROs *see* human rights organizations
hub-and-spokes system 110
human experiences, psychology 142–7
human nature 67, 138–42
human rights 247, 294, 295
human rights organizations (HROs) 299–300, 301f12.4
humanitarian intervention (HI) 300, 301f12.4
humanitarian organizations 294, 296
humiliation 4, 125
Hussein, Saddam 95, 143, 147, 150
Huth, Paul K. 253
hybrid characteristics 190

ICB Project 158–9, 313
ICJ *see* International Court of Justice
ICOW Project *see* Issue Correlates of War Project
idealists 67n1
ideational aspects 52, 117, 123–5, 160–1, 165–6, 169, 190–1
ideational realities 210–11
identity
    societal-level 190
    state-level 123
ideological issues 73
IGOs *see* international governmental organizations
image formation 145–6
IMF *see* International Monetary Fund
immigration, US 213
import sanctions 244
India, nuclear weapons 245, 252
India–Pakistan conflict 51–2, 162, 165–6, 169, 210
individual-level analysis 137–55, 169, 220n8, 316–17
indivisibility 87–8
inductive reasoning 7
inequality, wars of 316
informally organized groups 53
informally organized identity groups 53–4
Inoguchi, Takashi 96
institutional patterns, regime type 126
institutionalization, sacred spaces 87
instrumental beliefs 149–50
instrumental violence 76
instrumentalism 74, 80
insurgency 189, 191
intangible elements, territory 71
integrated approach 304, 318
interdependence 120–1
international agreements 278
international conflict 19–22
International Court of Justice (ICJ) 275, 277
international crisis 22–6
    1918–2017 56f3.7
    behavioral dimension 120
    definition 22, 55, 158
    near crisis as 57
    outcomes/legacies 166–70, 167.8t8.3
    processes 162–6, 163–4t8.2
    project-based research 157–60
    recent examples 56–7
    religious involvement 76
international governmental organizations (IGOs) 279–88, 291–4
international law 274–8
International Monetary Fund (IMF) 281, 282–3
international organizations (IOs) 170, 238, 272–302
    typology 282t12.2, 283–4
international relations (IR)
    foundation of 26
    prospect theory 151

regime type 127–32f6.1, 133
scientific realism 7
international system
    anarchic nature of 273
    anarchy versus hierarchy 94
    features 98
    macro level connections 38, 102
    structure 22, 28, 117
    theory 5
international war 26–41
internationalized civil war 40, 45, 53, 61
interstate conflict 19, 52, 61, 77
interstate pairs 8
interstate war 26–39, 260
intrastate armed conflict 61
intrastate wars 27, 40–1, 45, 255
intrinsic causes 208, 217
IOs *see* international organizations
IR *see* international relations
Iran 170, 171, 179–82, 245, 277–8
Iranian Revolution 170
Iraq Wars 45, 95, 146–7, 153, 249
irredentism 123
Islamic State organizations 40, 41, 75–6
Israel 9, 88, 255
Israel–Palestine conflict 239
Issue Correlates of War (ICOW) Project 70
issues 69–70, 315
    of power 67
    stake proposals 68, 241

Jackson, Andrew 213
James, Patrick 2, 19, 77, 102, 111–12, 123
Japan 209, 245, 250, 264
Jenne, Erin K. 53, 187, 200
Jentleson, Bruce W. 262
Jervis, Robert 146, 237, 242, 264
Jones, Adam 4
judicial branch, EU 287–8
judicial decisions 275
just war tradition 276

Kahneman, Daniel 149–50
Kansas–Nebraska Act 214, 229
Kant, Immanuel 119, 126
Kaplan, Stephen S. 262
Kashmir 165–6
Katzenstein, Peter J. 9
Keck, Margaret E. 298
Keegan, John 47
Kennedy, John F. 23, 145

Keohane, Robert O., *Power and Interdependence* 67
Kisangani, Emizet F. 54, 122
Klein, James P. 50
Korean War 157
Kurds 41, 122
Kurki, Milja 207–11, 233

LA *see* Levels of Analysis
ladder of escalation 18, 26, 41–2, 42f2.2, 238
latent conflict 169
law enforcement 276–8
leader attributes 140–2, 187, 317
learning function 119
Lebow, Richard Ned 255
Lee, Robert E. 215
Leeds, Brett Ashley 122, 259
legislative institutions, EU 285–6
Leites, N. 147
Lemke, Douglas 102
Leng, Russell J. 262
Levels of Analysis (LA) 6, 77, 188n6, 304–5, 313–14, 316–18
Levy, Jack S. 46, 135, 138, 140, 154, 259
liberalism 119, 258f11.3
The Liberator newspaper 212, 217, 233
limited conflict 99
limited war 65, 315
Lincoln, Abraham 215–16, 230, 243
Lloyd, Robert B. 74
Lobell, Steven E. 151, 184
long cycle theory 94
Louisiana Purchase 212, 213
Lupu, Yonatan 269–70

McDermott, Rose 150
MacDonald, Thomas 269
macro-macro linkages 11, 28
macro-micro linkages 11, 28
MAD *see* mutually assured destruction
Malik, Julia 46, 53–4, 60
Mansbach, Richard W. 67–8, 72, 87
Mansfield, Edward D. 122
material aspects 117, 118–23, 160–1, 165, 169, 189
material causes 208, 217, 220
material realities 210–11
matter concept 208
Mattes, Michaela 270
Mauceri, Philip 184
Mearsheimer, John J. 98, 257
mediated crisis 55

mediation 240t11.1, 243, 291–2
MFN status *see* most-favored nation status
micro-macro linkages 11
micro-micro linkages 11
MID dataset *see* Militarized Interstate Dispute dataset
Middle East 9, 283–4
MIDs *see* militarized interstate disputes
militarization 50
Militarized Interstate Dispute (MID) dataset 49, 50f3.3, 77
militarized interstate disputes (MIDs) 50, 70, 72, 80, 126
military capability 253
military hostilities 22
military power 237, 250–1, 256
military-security issues 70, 71t4.1
military spending 247, 248t11.2
Miller, Colleen 144
miscalculation 149–50
misperception 149–50
Missouri Compromise 212, 228–9
Mitchell, Sara McLaughlin 70
Morgan, Patrick 255
Morgenthau, Hans J. 139
Morrow, James D. 278
Most, Benjamin A. 184
most-favored nation (MFN) status 283
Mueller, John 44–5, 60, 119
multilateral agreements 265
multilateral diplomacy 239, 291
multilateral sanctions 244
multilevel analysis 205–34, 316, 318
multipolarity 96, 97t5.1
Murauskaite, Egle E. 157
Murdie, Amanda 299
mutually assured destruction (MAD) 251–2

Nagasaki 250
Nai, Allesandro 143
nation-state creation 73
nation-state imbalance 316
national attributes 118–19
national identity 20, 241
national law enforcement 276
NATO alliances 256–7, 259
near crisis 18–19, 22–3, 25–6, 42, 57, 70, 312
negotiation 216, 238–40, 239f11.1, 241–2
neo-Kantian research 162, 168, 169
nested security 200
NGOs *see* non-governmental organizations

Nicaragua 277
Niger conflict 292
Nile River conflict 20
nominal description 4
non-governmental organizations (NGOs) 294–7, 298–300
non-state actors 19, 27, 57, 255, 274
non-state conflict 27, 53–4, 54f3.5, 60, 61f3.11
nonproliferation 253
nonspuriousness 4, 207
norm internalization 297
normative patterns, regime type 126
norms life cycle 297
North Korea 57, 116, 143, 252–3, 255
Northern Ireland, the "Troubles" 75–6, 190
NPT agreement 269–70
nuclear deterrence 157, 251–3, 255
nuclear disarmament 263–4
nuclear weapons 147, 179, 210
 development 250–3
 sanctions 245
 security-oriented IOs 295
 START agreement 269
 states with 254m11.1, 255, 269
Nye, Joseph S., *Power and Interdependence* 67

OAS *see* Organization of American States
obsolescence of war 119
Occam's Razor 93
offensive realism 97–8, 112
oil resources 184
operational codes 147–9, 155f7.A1
operational description 4
opportunity 184, 189–91
Organization of American States (OAS) 284
Organski, A. F. K. 99
organized groups 53

P5 members, IOs 282t12.1, 290
Pakistan, nuclear weapons 245, 252
Pakistan–India conflict 51–2, 162, 165–6, 169, 210
Palestine–Israel conflict 239
paradigm wars 9
Parasiliti, Andrew T. 95
parsimony 5
Pauly, Louis W. 150
peace 119–20, 126–35, 259
 regions of 102, 115f5A.1
peace agreements 279
peace operations 272–3, 292–4
Peace Research Institute of Oslo (PRIO) 52–3, 76

peaceful societies 139–40
Pearce, Susanna 75, 76
Pearl Harbor attack 209
Peceny, Mark 126
Peksen, Dursun 299
perception processes 149
personal security–oriented NGOs 295
personality traits 142–3
philosophical beliefs 149–50
Pickering, Jeffrey 54, 122
Pinckney Resolutions 212–13
Poast, Paul 47
polarity theory 96, 113
political-diplomatic issues 70, 71t4.1
political instability 121
political marginalization 61–2, 63f3.12
polycentrism 160, 168
Popovic, Milos 53
population pressures 118, 232
populism 49
Pottawatomie Massacre 214, 217
poverty 191, 233
power, of issues 67
power-based arguments 279–80
power cycle theory 95–6, 112
power endowments 72
power-oriented realism 9
power politics 54, 67, 69, 70
power transition 99–100
Power Transition Theory (PTT) 54–5, 94, 99–102, 103–9f5.1
predation theory 98–9, 112
predictive theory 5
preemption 260–1
prescriptive theory 5
preventive use of force 260–1
primordialism 74–5
Prins, Brandon C. 262
PRIO see Peace Research Institute of Oslo
processes
    civil war 202t9.A1
    international crisis 162–6, 163–4t8.2
    negotiation 241–2
    scientific realism 7
prospect theory 150–1, 152f7.1, 242
prosperity 162n4
protection dynamic, alliances 256
protracted conflict 57, 161, 166, 169, 209
proximity/contiguity variable 118
psychological factors 147–51
psychological needs 142–3

psychology 142–7
PTT see Power Transition Theory
Putin, Vladimir 1, 8, 123, 236
Putnam, Robert D. 88

Quackenbush, Stephen L. 27
qualitative limitations, weapons 269
Quinn, David 159

Raleigh, Clionadh 61
Rann of Kutch crisis 162
Rathbun, Brian C. 137
rational choice 147, 151
Reagan, Ronald 140, 268
realism 67, 70, 100
realist paradigm 9
realist theories 94–9, 312
Regan, Patrick M. 191
regime change 125
regime instability 191, 231
regime type 8, 126, 127–32f6.1, 133–5, 209
    analysis 316–17
    foreign policy link 127–32f6.1, 133–5
    use of force 262
regional IOs 283–5
regional systems 10
regionalism 283
regression to the mean 146
religion 74–89
religious exclusivity 161
religious fundamentalism 75
representation bias 146
Republican Party, US 214–15
resistance point 239
retaliatory threats 251
revolutionary change 125, 134
Richardson, Lewis F. 250
risk acceptance 151
risk aversion 150–1
Rittberger, Volker 74
rivalry 50–1, 55
    analysis 317
    definition 50–1
    as final cause 210
    operational codes 149
    stimulants for 51
    without settled border 165–6
Robinson, Leonard C. 150
rogue states 116
Roosevelt, Theodore 239–40
Rosati, Jerel 144

Rosecrance, Richard 121
Roser, Max 46, 60
Rowe, David M. 245
Rubin, Lawrence 125
rules of war 265
Russett, Bruce M. 253
Russia, nuclear weapons 255
Russia–Ukraine War 1, 8, 28, 29–37f2.1, 38–9, 45, 123, 156, 236
Rwandan genocide 5

sacred grounds, war on 78–9f4.1, 81–6f4.1
sacred spaces 77, 80, 87, 88
Saiki, Akitaka 24
Sambanis, Nicholas 293
Sample, Susan 249
sanctions 243–7
"sanctions paradox" 246
Sandler, Nukhet 76
Sandler, Shmuel 76
Schafer, 147–8
Schelling, Thomas 242, 253, 261–2
schema theory 145
Schofield, Julian 270
scientific realism 3, 6–8, 45, 117, 304
Scott, Dred 215, 230
secessionism 123, 158
"Secessionitis" 205, 217–18
security 98
security dilemma 237, 246, 249–50, 256, 259, 264, 271
security-oriented IOs 272–3, 292–4, 295–6
selective attention/perception 144
selective memory 144
Senese, Paul D. 72
sensitivity, sanctions 247
settlement gaps 239
Shifrinson, Joshua R. Itkzkowitz 98–9
Shirk, Susan L. 123
Sierra Leone 191
Sikkink, Kathryn 297, 298
Sil, Rudra 9
Simmons, Beth A. 278
Singer, J. David 259
Sisson, Melanie W. 262
Slaughter, Anne-Marie 274
slavery 211–17, 220, 228–33
Small, Melvin 259
Smoke, Richard 255
Snyder, Glenn H. 121
Snyder, Jack 122

social symbols 88
social systems 11f1.1
societal-level factors 169, 190
Soleimani assassination 170–82, 172–8f8.1, 173t8.4
Somalia 191
spatial consistency 50
spiral theory 264–5
stake proposals 67–8, 241
Star of the West steamer attack 216n6
Starr, Harvey 184
START *see* Strategic Arms Reduction Talks
state-based conflict
    death rates, 1946–2021 58f3.8
    decrease in frequency 60
    locations, 2021 60f3.10
    management of 236–71
    trends, 1946–2021 53f3.4
state-level analysis 153, 316
state-level theories 116–36
state system, emergence of 61–2
static realist theories 95
Stedman, Stephen John 243
Stein, Arthur 121
Stein, Janice Gross 150, 255
Steinbruner, John 144
steps-to-war model 72, 250, 316
stimulus-response process 249–50
Strategic Arms Reduction Talks (START) 268–9
strategic rivalry 52, 72
strategic territory 71
structural realism 96, 97t5.1
Suga, Yoshihide 24
Sumner, Charles 214, 229
symbolic issues 68–9, 74, 88
sympathy 73
Syrian civil war 40–1, 183
system-level analysis 6, 316
system-level theories 92–115
system linkages 11, 13t1.1, 14, 28, 199
system structure 96, 117
systemism 3, 10–15, 151
systemist causal analysis 217–30
systemist graphics 2, 14, 133, 171–82, 192–200, 220, 304–14, 305–11f13.1
systemist notation 15t1.2

Taiwan conflict 123–4
Taliaferro, Jeffrey W. 150–1
Tammen, Ronald L. 101
tangible elements, territory 71

tariffs 213
Taylor, Michael 42
technological advancement 46, 303
temporal order 4, 207
territorial claims 70, 250
territorial disputes 118n1, 279
territory 71–3, 76, 77–09, 110, 169
terrorism 62, 253
Thatcher, Margaret 140–1
theory 3–6, 16
    components of 4–5
"thick" religion 89
Thies, Cameron G. 52
third-party diplomacy 239–40, 240t11.1, 242
third-party sanctions 244
Thompson, William R. 52, 135, 138, 140, 154
threat
    of force 260
    gravity of 165
    imminent 261
    inevitable 261
    signaling 242
Thucydides trap 100–1
trade relations 283
trade sanctions 244
Trager, Robert 242
transcendent issues 68–9, 74, 87
transnational cooperation 280
transnational ideologies 125
treaties 265, 266–7t11.3, 269–70, 275, 278, 292
trigger violence 162, 169
Trump, Donald 143, 149, 155f7.A1, 170–1, 180–1
Tversky, Amos 149–50

UCDP *see* Uppsala Conflict Data Program
Ukrainian War 1, 8, 28, 29–37f2.1, 38–9, 45, 123, 156, 236
ultranationalists 123
UN *see* United Nations
UN Economic and Social Council (ECOSOC) 290–1
UN General Assembly (UNGA) 289–90
UN Secretariat 290
UN Security Council 282t12.1
Uncle Tom's Cabin (Beecher Stowe) 214, 217, 229, 233
unconventional war 39, 40, 62, 65, 255, 312
UNGA *see* UN General Assembly
unilateral sanctions 244
United Nations Security Council (UNSC) 289–90
United Nations (UN) 272, 288–91, 290f12.2, 293

United States (US)
    China relations 100–1
    Civil War 205–7, 210–30, 234, 243
    international law 277–8
    Iran relations 170, 171, 179–82
    nuclear weapons 255, 264
UNSC *see* United Nations Security Council
Uppsala Conflict Data Program (UCDP) 27–8, 53
Ury, William 87, 216, 238
US *see* United States
USSR
    Cold War crisis 68–9, 156
    collapse of 8, 28, 44, 184
    foreign policy crisis 23

V-Dem Project *see* Varieties of Democracy Project
Vaddi, Pranay 269
Valeriano, Brandon 51, 64
variable, use of term 10n3
Varieties of Democracy (V-Dem) Project 4–5
Vasquez, John A. 67–8, 72, 73, 87, 250
Vaynman, Jane 270
vertical law enforcement 276–7
veto players 53, 281, 290
victory, likelihood 168
Vietnam War 118, 146, 150
violence
    centrality 165–6
    decision-making 169
    humiliation and 125
    religion and 75–6
    severity 165–6, 181
    stress connection 166
violent conflict 162, 295–6, 299
VIRP *see* Visual International Relations Project
Visual International Relations Project (VIRP) 2
von Clausewitz, Carl 62
Vonnahme, Greg 270
vulnerability, sanctions 247

Waal, Alex De 20
Walker, Stephen G. 147–8
Wallace, Michael D. 250
Waltz, Kenneth N. 6, 96, 117, 137
war
    empirical definitions 27–8
    evolution of 46–7, 57–64, 90
    film depictions 57, 59
    as highest level of escalation 135
    international laws of 278

likelihood 168–9
location changes 61
obsolescence of 119
pathways to 312–13, 316
patterns of 114
regions of 102, 115f5A.1
shifting face of 39
war weariness argument 118–19
Washington Consensus 111
water, politics of 20, 21m2.1
"weakest link" assumption 77n8
weapons 208, 263–4, 269
Weitsman, Patricia 259
West African/Niger conflict 292
White, Ralph 150
Wilberforce, William 211
Wilkenfeld, Jonathan 8, 159
willingness 189–91
Wilson, Edward O. 139
Wilson, Maya 300
win-set 88

Wittes, Tamara Coffman 262
women leaders 140–2
Woodward, Bob 146
World Bank 283
World Court *see* International Court of Justice
World War I 26, 57, 99, 265, 266–7t11.3, 304
World War II, effects of 209, 284, 288, 293, 315

Yanukovych, President 25
Yarhi-Milo, Keren 144
Yemen civil war 190
Yoon, Young-Kwan 96
Yugoslavia, break up of 190

Zelenskyy, Volodymyr 1
Zellman, Ariel 80
Zenko, Micah 262
"zero-day" vulnerabilities 64
zero-sum games 22
Zhang, Enyu 102, 111–12